RIEVAULX ABBEY AND ITS SOCIAL CONTEXT, 1132–1300

MEDIEVAL CHURCH STUDIES

8

RIEVAULX ABBEY AND ITS SOCIAL CONTEXT, 1132–1300

Memory, Locality, and Networks

Emilia Jamroziak

BREPOLS

A catalogue-in-publication record
for this book is available from the
British Library

D/2005/0095/1
ISBN: 2-503-52177-0

Printed in the E.U. on acid-free paper

Contents

Acknowledgements

During the course of writing this book I have accumulated many debts of gratitude both professional and personal. The original research on Rievaulx Abbey was undertaken in connection with a PhD thesis at the University of Leeds (sponsored by the ORS, Tetley, and Lupton scholarship and the School of History University of Leeds), and I benefited greatly from the encouragement and guidance of my supervisor, Dr Wendy Childs. Since then, my further work on this fascinating Cistercian monastery has profited from advice, criticisms, and suggestions from many academic friends and colleagues: Professor David Bates, Professor Arnoud-Jan A. Bijsterveld, Professor David Crouch, Professor Marsha Dutton, Professor Peter Fergusson, Dr Brian Golding, Professor Diana Greenway, Dr Julian Haseldine, Professor Paul Hyams, Professor Nancy Partner, Dr David Postles, and Professor Steven White.

The anonymous reader offered very insightful and helpful critique. Dr Janet Burton offered exceptionally generous assistance; her criticisms and suggestions have improved this work immeasurably. Chapters 1, 4, and 6 benefited from the comments of these who heard parts of their earlier versions at the International Medieval Congress in Leeds, the International Congress on Medieval Studies in Kalamazoo, conferences in Leicester, Birmingham, and Canterbury, as well as seminars at the University of Durham, University of Southampton, University of Sheffield, University of York, and University of Leeds. The commissioning editor, Dr Simon Forde, has been very helpful and encouraging in getting this project completed. Deborah A. Oosterhouse provided diligent copy-editing. Needless to say, any remaining errors and shortcomings remain entirely my own responsibility.

I would like to thank the librarians and archivists in the Bodleian Library (Oxford), the British Library, the Brotherton Library (Leeds), the Institute of Historical Research, the National Library of Scotland, and the North Yorkshire County Record Office in Northallerton for assisting me in tracking down sources and elusive references. The staff of University Library in Edinburgh had been particularly helpful in fast-tracking my last-minute book orders.

Parts of chapter 3 are reproduced with the kind permission of the editorial board of *Cîteaux* from my article 'Rievaulx Abbey and its Patrons: Between Cooperation and Conflict', *Cîteaux: Commentarii Cistercienses*, 53 (2002), 51–71. Parts of chapter 4 are reproduced with the kind permission of the editor of the *Yorkshire Archaeological Journal* from my article 'Considerate Brothers or Predatory Neighbours? Rievaulx Abbey and Other Monastic Houses in the Twelfth and Thirteenth Centuries', *Yorkshire Archaeological Journal*, 73 (2001), 29–40.

Helen Brown, Dr Karen Hurtnup, and Dr Jenny McLeod very generously helped me with difficulties of English grammar and read through the entire manuscript, and Dr Bernd Kaskas kindly helped with proofreading.

On a more personal level, I would like to thank my former colleagues at the University of Leeds, the University of Southampton, and the Institute of Historical Research, University of London, and my current colleagues at the University of Edinburgh for providing friendly and stimulating work environments. I would like to express my gratitude to Axel Müller of the International Medieval Institute in Leeds for his continuing encouragement and support with all things medieval. Finally, my greatest debt is to my parents, who always encouraged my passion for history and supported my professional choices.

Maps and Tables

Abbreviations

Bodl. Dodsw.	Oxford, Bodleian Library, Dodsworth MSS
Cartulary	*Cartularium de Abbatie de Rievalle*, ed. by James C. Atkinson, Surtees Society, 83 (Durham: Andrews, 1889)
CChR	*Calendar of Charter Rolls*, 6 vols (London: H.M.S.O., 1903–27)
Charters of Mowbray	*Charters of the Honour of Mowbray 1107–1191*, ed. by Diane E. Greenway, British Academy Records of Social and Economic History, n.s., 1 (London: Oxford University Press, 1972)
CPL	*Calendar of Entries in the Papal Registers Relating to Great Britain and Ireland*, vol. I, *Papal Letters (1198–1304)*, ed. by W. H. Bliss (London, 1893)
CPR	*Calendar of Patent Rolls* (London: H.M.S.O., 1901–)
CR	*Calendar of Close Rolls* (London: H.M.S.O., 1892–)
CRR	*Curia Regis Rolls* (London: H.M.S.O., 1922–)
DNB	*Dictionary of National Biography*, ed. by L. Stephen and S. Lee, 63 vols (London, 1885–1900)
EEA	*English Episcopal Acta*, vol. V, *York 1070–1154*, ed. by Janet Burton (Oxford: British Academy, 1988); vol. XX, *York 1154–1181*, ed. by Marie Lovatt (Oxford: British Academy, 2000)
EYC	*Early Yorkshire Charters*, ed. by William Farrer, vols I–III (Edinburgh: Ballantyne, Hanson, 1914–16) and Charles

	Clay, vols IV–XII, Yorkshire Archaeological Society Record Series, extra series (Wakefield: Yorkshire Archaeological Society, 1935–65)
Life of Ailred	Walter Daniel, *The Life of Ailred of Rievaulx*, trans. and introd. by F. M. Powicke (London: Nelson, 1950)
Peerage	*Complete Peerage, or a History of the Houses of Lords and all its Members from the Earliest Times*, by G. E. C[okayne], rev. by V. Gibbs, H. A. Doubleday, and G. H. White, 13 vols (London: St Catherine Press, 1910–59)
PL	*Patrologiae Latina Cursus Completus*, ed. by J.-P. Migne, 221 vols (Paris, 1844–64)
PR	*Patent Rolls of the Reign of Henry III*, 6 vols (London: H.M.S.O., 1901–13)
PU	*Papsturkunden in England*, ed. by Walter Holtzmann, vols I and II (Berlin: Weidmann, 1931–36); vol. III (Göttingen: Vandenhoeck & Ruprecht, 1952)
Statuta	Joseph Canivez, *Statuta Capitulorum Ordinis Cisterciensis ab anno 1116 ad annum 1786*, 8 vols (Louvain-la-Neuve: Revue d'histoire ecclèsiastique, 1933–41)
VCH	*Victoria County History: Yorkshire*, 3 vols (London: Constable, 1907–13)
YD	*Yorkshire Deeds*, vols I and II, ed. by W. Brown, Yorkshire Archaeological Society Record Series, 39 and 50 (Leeds: Yorkshire Archaeological Society, 1909 and 1914)
ZDO1/	Northallerton, North Yorkshire County Record Office, Orde-Powlett papers, ZDO1/0208–0256

Introduction[*]

The ruins of Rievaulx Abbey, located in the steep valley of the river Rye on the North Yorkshire moors, are one of the most picturesque sights in that region of England. Before the advent of modern tourism, the remote location and melancholic atmosphere of the ruined monastery appealed strongly to the romantic sensibilities of the nineteenth century. Thus, the early interest in Rievaulx Abbey and its ruins had a mainly antiquarian character. Pre-1860s works are illustrated with etchings or early photographs which reveal the strong aesthetic, rather than historical, interest of the authors.[1] The first more systematic study of the abbey's architecture was initiated when the site of Rievaulx Abbey came into the possession of the Office of Works in 1918, and this was followed by extensive archaeological excavations under the direction of Charles Peers in 1919–21. In recent years, under the guardianship of English Heritage, the ruins of the monastery have become a model of how a historical monument can be turned into a tourist attraction without transforming it into a theme park. Rievaulx Abbey was drawing one hundred thousand visitors per year by the mid-1990s. English Heritage also published a very

[*] A number of charters from the cartulary of Rievaulx Abbey have been republished in the volumes of *Early Yorkshire Charters*. The dating of the individual charters by the editors of *EYC* has been followed here if convincing; otherwise I have suggested alternative dates. The references to the entries in the cartulary which were published only in the volume edited by J. Atkinson direct the reader to the printed version, for the sake of convenience, but I have consulted and quoted directly from the manuscript as the published version contains numerous omissions and some errors in transcription. All the translations from Latin are mine unless stated otherwise.

[1] T. D. Whitaker, *A Series of Views of the Abbeys and Castles in Yorkshire* (London, 1820); W. Richardson, *The Monastic Ruins of Yorkshire*, 2 vols (York, 1844); W. Monkhouse, *Brief Historical and Descriptive Account of Rievaulx Abbey with Lithographic Views and Ground-plan of the Abbey* (York, 1845); P. H. Delamotte and J. Cundall, *A Photographic Tour among the Abbeys of Yorkshire* (London, 1856).

informative and well-designed guidebook of the site, which can serve as an example of how to bring medieval history to a wider audience.[2] Although the ruins are extensive, they cannot fully convey the scale of this religious house and its impact on the surrounding area in the Middle Ages.

Rievaulx Abbey was one of the most important and largest of the Cistercian abbeys in England. It was a second Cistercian foundation in this country, established in 1132 by a prominent nobleman, Walter Espec, one of the so-called new men of King Henry I. The foundation of Rievaulx Abbey is often seen as a prime example of the popularity and rapid growth of the Cistercian order in the first half of the twelfth century. The accumulation of estates by Rievaulx, first and foremost due to the generosity of its neighbours of various social ranks, from the lesser knights to barons, brought this monastic house into direct contact with an ever-increasing number of people and institutions. By the early thirteenth century the area of Rievaulx's granges stretched as far as Worsborough to the south of Yorkshire and to the north-east as far as the coast in present day Middlesbrough. A high proportion of the abbey's land consisted of pastures, and by the mid-thirteenth century Rievaulx was an important producer of high quality wool. The wool was first sold to Flemish and then to Italian merchants. The trade was highly successful until the devastating epidemic of the sheep-scab in the late 1270s and the early 1280s, when the combination of advance-payment contracts and the sudden loss of the flocks caused a bankruptcy of Rievaulx Abbey in 1279 and 1288.[3] Although wool production recovered, the Scottish wars caused substantial damage to the abbey's estates, and the monastic precinct itself was ransacked by the Scots after the battle of Byland in 1322. The already low numbers of lay brothers had been further reduced by the Black Death which devastated the monastic community in 1348–49 whilst the majority of the granges were leased to laypeople.[4] Although the architectural development on the abbey's precinct in the fourteenth and fifteenth centuries shows considerable wealth, the schism in the Church deeply affected the Cistercian order, and Rievaulx, along with all the houses in Britain belonging to that order, was virtually cut off from the Cistercian centre in France. The financial pressure of royal taxation in the fourteenth and fifteenth centuries was also very damaging to the economic well-being of the abbey. When the house was dissolved in 1538 the community of Rievaulx Abbey consisted of twenty-one monks and the abbot. The monastic precinct and the home granges were acquired by Thomas, Earl of Rutland, a descendant of the Ros family who were patrons of the house.

Despite the considerable interest given to the material remains of the abbey, its development as a social institution has not been sufficiently explored. The focus of the

---

[2] Glyn Coppack and Peter Fergusson, *Rievaulx Abbey* (London: English Heritage, 1994).

[3] For an analysis of the economic condition of Rievaulx Abbey in that period, see Emilia Jamroziak, 'Rievaulx Abbey as a Wool Producer in the Late Thirteenth Century: Cistercians, Sheep and Big Debts', *Northern History*, 40 (2003), 197–218.

[4] Janet E. Burton, 'The Estates and Economy of Rievaulx Abbey in Yorkshire', *Cîteaux: Commentarii Cistercienses*, 49 (1998), 29–94 (pp. 89–90).

literature remains primarily on the architectural aspects of Rievaulx Abbey and to a lesser degree on its economy and estates. Although it features in many studies on the history of the Cistercian order in Britain and ecclesiastical institutions in the North, there is not a single monograph devoted to the history of Rievaulx Abbey.[5] The reason for this neglect, which is highlighted by the attention which the other important Cistercian house in the area — Fountains Abbey — has received, is mainly due to the meagre preservation of the written sources related to the history of Rievaulx Abbey. Only recently have architectural historians started to investigate the material remains in their social context. The book by Peter Fergusson, Stuart Harrison, and Glyn Coppack, *Rievaulx Abbey: Community, Architecture, Memory*, fulfils the promise of the title.[6] The history of the monastic architecture is firmly placed in the context of its usage, how the buildings were altered to accommodate the changing expectations and needs of the monastic community. Janet Burton has reconstructed the process of land accumulation and grange formation by the abbey and the major economic developments in the history of this institution.[7] Rievaulx Abbey has been known to the academic audience as the monastic community governed by Ailred of Rievaulx, its third and most prominent abbot. Although Ailred's theological writings have been studied extensively by literary scholars and theologians, they have been analysed largely in isolation from the social realities of the monastic community he led.[8] Marsha Dutton and Douglass Roby have challenged the image of the other-wordly Ailred and examined his active public persona in the political and ecclesiastical arena.[9]

---

[5] David Knowles, *The Monastic Order in England: A History of its Development from the Times of St Dunstan to the Fourth Lateran Council 940–1216* (Cambridge: Cambridge University Press, 1963), pp. 227–45; Glyn Coppack, *Book of Abbeys and Priories* (London: English Heritage, 1990), pp. 26–27, 134, 136; Janet E. Burton, *Monastic and Religious Orders in Britain 1000–1300* (Cambridge: Cambridge University Press, 1994), pp. 69–74; Burton, *The Monastic Order in Yorkshire, 1069–1215* (Cambridge: Cambridge University Press, 1999), pp. 99–104.

[6] Peter Fergusson, Stuart Harrison, and Glyn Coppack, *Rievaulx Abbey: Community, Architecture, Memory* (New Haven: Yale University Press, 2000).

[7] Burton, 'Estates and Economy'.

[8] There is a very substantial body of works devoted to the spiritual writings of Ailred, concentrating particularly strongly on the themes of love and friendship as well as pastoral work and preaching. Most recently: A. Masoliver, '"De spirituali amicitia" by Saint Aelred of Rievaulx: From "Particular Friendship" to Holy "Philia" and "Agape"', *Studia Monastica*, 44 (2002), 373–90; R. M. Karras, 'Friendship and Love in the Lives of Two Twelfth-Century English Saints', *Journal of Medieval History*, 14 (1988), 305–20; Augustin Belisle, 'Pastoral Spirituality of Aelred of Rievaulx', *Studia Monastica*, 25 (1983), 93–113; Philippe Nouzille, *Expérience de Dieu et théologie monastique au XIIe siècle: Étude sur les sermons d'Aelred de Rievaulx* (Paris: Editions du Cerf, 1999); Aelred Squire, 'The Literary Evidence for the Preaching of Aelred of Rievaulx', *Cîteaux: Commentarii Cistercienses*, 11 (1960), 245–51.

[9] Douglass Roby 'Chimera of the North: The Active Life of Ailred of Rievaulx', in *Cistercian Ideals and Reality*, ed. by John R. Sommerfeldt, Cistercian Studies Series, 60 (Kalamazoo: Cistercian Publications, 1978), pp. 152–69; Marsha L. Dutton, 'The Conversion and Vocation

My book is not simply a narrative of the history of Rievaulx Abbey between 1132 and 1300. It focuses on the interaction between Rievaulx Abbey and its social environment which was formed by the various groups of neighbours, including patrons and their families, lay benefactors, and people who lived near the estates of the abbey, as well as other monasteries in the area. Higher ecclesiastical officials, Archbishops of York, Bishops of Durham, and their respective chapters and deans and priors, played an important and often complex role for the abbey. The themes of contact, cooperation, and conflict between Rievaulx Abbey and its neighbours are explored against the broader background of lay-monastic interaction. My book addresses problems that were characteristic of the contacts between lay society and monks in the High Middle Ages, such as reciprocity and the means of building and sustaining interaction between the laity and religious houses. The case of Rievaulx Abbey is used to test these claims and to explore the extent to which the Cistercians were innovative or traditional in their relationship with neighbours, who consisted of not only the laity but also other religious institutions and the secular Church. The time span of this book allows me to examine changes in the patterns of interaction over the four to five generations who lived through the twelfth and thirteenth centuries.

Chronologically, my investigation starts in 1132 with the foundation of the abbey and continues to 1300. The upper time limit has been chosen to reflect a change in both the economic and social practice of the abbey. The twelfth century was undoubtedly the era of the greatest expansion of monasticism, particularly Cistercian, in the North of England, while the thirteenth century saw a slow drop in the number of grants to religious houses, but also a continuation of the relationships with many families of benefactors, and a consolidation of monastic granges. The number of grants from benefactors, particularly in the form of land, significantly decreased after 1300, and monastic granges were leased to laypeople instead of employing the direct labour of lay brothers and paid workers. The first half of the fourteenth century also brought very destructive Scottish raids and increased financial pressure from the Crown as well as the disastrous famine that struck between 1315 and 1322. In 1322 Rievaulx and another Cistercian abbey, Byland, were ransacked by the Scots and their lands repeatedly ruined by these attacks.[10] The financial pressure of royal taxation during the Anglo-French wars in the thirteenth century, and even more so in the fourteenth, was a constant financial drain on the abbey's income. Although Rievaulx Abbey continued to enjoy a fairly stable and even prosperous existence in the later Middle Ages and remained one of the focal points of devotional practices in the locality, the early fourteenth century opened a distinctively new chapter of Rievaulx's history.[11]

---

of Aelred of Rievaulx: A Historical Hypothesis', in *England in the Twelfth Century: Proceedings of the 1989 Harlaxton Symposium*, ed. by Daniel Williams (Woodbridge: Boydell, 1990), pp. 31–50.

[10] *Chronica Monasterii de Melsa: A fundatione usque annum 1396 auctore Thoma de Burton, abbate*, vol. III, ed. by E. A. Bond, Rolls Series, 43 (London: Longman, 1868), p. 346.

[11] The evidence from late medieval wills shows that Rievaulx was still an object of pious donation. In 1510 John Clervaux requested to be buried at the choir door in the abbey church

The structure of this book reflects the main areas of contact between the abbey and the outside world. This division is based partly on the structure of the main source — the cartulary itself — which reflects the world of social interactions of Rievaulx. Each chapter concentrates on a separate social group with which Rievaulx Abbey interacted. They are organized in descending order, that is, from the closest neighbours to the most distant ones. The first chapter examines the cartulary of the abbey which is the key source for understanding the early relationship between Walter Espec and his favourite house and the formation of the early 'support group' among his tenants. It provides also the most important evidence for the monastic community's perception of its neighbours and benefactors. It then moves on to explore the mechanisms of the uneasy and distant contacts between Rievaulx and its patrons, members of the Ros family. The second chapter explores what it meant to be a good neighbour of the abbey and how gifts shaped relationships between the abbey and its benefactors. The third chapter examines the breakdown of these relationships, conflicts between Rievaulx and its neighbours, and their resolutions. The fourth chapter concentrates on the abbey's relations with other monastic houses and demonstrates the high level of sophistication of local politics. The reality of being a neighbour among the religious houses in Yorkshire is discussed in relation to the Cistercian ideal of friendship and brotherhood and its practical application. The fifth chapter is a study of the abbey's contacts with the representatives of the secular Church, namely Archbishops of York, Bishops of Durham, archdeacons, deans, priors, and their respective chapters. They played a distinct role in securing Rievaulx's possessions, rights, and tithe exemptions, yet their interactions were not free from tensions and conflicting expectations. Investigation of their mutual contacts also reveals how the position and role of the Cistercian abbey within the Church changed over the course of the twelfth and thirteenth centuries. The final chapter explores the expectations of the laypeople of the abbey and vice versa, including friendship, countergifts, and commemoration. These important elements of building and sustaining relationships with the lay world are discussed against the background of changing Cistercian practice and the tension between isolationism on the one hand and important local considerations on the other.

The aim of this book is not only to explore the specific case of Rievaulx Abbey and its social environment in North Yorkshire, but also to address broader issues of the interactions between medieval monasteries and laypeople, the mechanism of the formation of relationships between monastic communities and laypeople, and the

---

and left a monetary bequest for the establishment of a chantry there (the Abbot of Rievaulx was also appointed as the chief executor of his will); in 1515 Sir Ralph Scrope requested to be buried in the abbey church and promised £20 in gold for the prayers on the day of his burial; and in 1524 a close neighbour of the abbey, John Rogerson of Rievaulx, left a bequest of twenty shillings for masses and absolution in addition to a gift of a pair of beads to the shrine of St Ailred. *Testamenta Eboracensia: A Selection of Wills from the Registry at York*, vol. v, Surtees Society, 79 (London: J. B. Nichols, 1884), pp. 20–21, 63, 194.

dynamics of these relationships. Cistercian monasteries are often seen as a special case since their ideology of separation from the outside world eliminated many of the close ties which existed between Benedictine houses and their benefactors. The question of how Rievaulx adopted the Cistercian format to its own local conditions and needs is addressed throughout this book.

The scarcity of sources has been mentioned earlier as a chief reason for the neglect of Rievaulx Abbey by historians. The following section provides a brief overview of what documents are at our disposal and how they illuminate the twelfth- and thirteenth-century history of Rievaulx Abbey and its social context.

Sources

Violent destruction was the recurring feature of Rievaulx's post-Dissolution history and a cause of the almost complete disappearance of the once extensive archives of Rievaulx.[12] The major surviving source from Rievaulx Abbey is the cartulary of the house, created in the late twelfth century, some time after 1179, probably in the late 1180s or early 1190s. It is the earliest surviving English Cistercian cartulary, and its form and structure are highly unusual. The cartulary therefore deserves particular attention, not just on account of the information contained in it, but also because it is a very rare example of a cartulary created in the early phases of institutional growth. The majority of Cistercian cartularies were compiled in the second half of the thirteenth century, often containing layers of earlier groupings of charters. Many other types of inventories were constructed at that time as a response to the growth of monastic archives and concerns over their preservation.[13] The Burgundian Cistercian cartularies analysed by Constance Bouchard were created in the thirteenth century. In fact, she argues that cartularies were produced only a century or so after the foundation when a sufficient amount of material had been accumulated to justify the making of a volume.[14] The case of the Rievaulx cartulary suggests that concern over the preservation of information was only one of many reasons for its creation.

Although there were other cartularies or inventories of charters originating from Rievaulx Abbey that were probably assembled in the thirteenth century, none of them has survived. A second cartulary was recorded in 1640 as being in the possession of the Earl of Rutland at Belvoir Castle, and parts of it were copied by Roger Dodsworth in the seventeenth century (Bodl. Dodsw. lxxxv, fols 53–57, 71^{v}–72), but

---

[12] For an excellent analysis of the post-Dissolution history of Rievaulx Abbey, see Fergusson, Harrison, and Coppack, *Rievaulx Abbey*, pp. 187–213.

[13] For an example of a multilayered cartulary created in stages between the late twelfth and thirteenth centuries on the bases of early compilations, see David Postles, 'The Garendon Cartularies in BL, Lansdowne 415', *British Library Journal*, 22 (1996), 161–71.

[14] Constance B. Bouchard, *Holy Entrepreneurs: Cistercians, Knights, and Economic Exchange in Twelfth-Century Burgundy* (Ithaca, NY: Cornell University Press, 1991), p. 17.

when the Belvoir Castle collection was catalogued by the Historical Manuscripts Commission in the early twentieth century, the cartulary was not found there.[15] Roger Dodsworth's copy of the index of this cartulary suggests that the material in the volume was organized topographically, according to the places to which it referred. A third cartulary or register was known to be in the possession of William Lite of Wilburgham in Cambridgeshire in the seventeenth century but is no longer extant.[16]

The surviving cartulary of Rievaulx Abbey was published in 1889 by the Surtees Society which printed many other Yorkshire monastic cartularies, including Guisborough and Whitby. This edition, by the Rev. James Atkinson, exemplifies many traditional editorial practices.[17] Almost half of the published edition of the Rievaulx cartulary consists of documents which are not its original components. Some are clearly distinguished — for example, extracts from archbishops' registers, and rolls of Feet of Fines — but some documents are inserted into the body of the cartulary, potentially misleading the reader. For example, there is a cluster of twenty-four charters inserted by the editor after charter 145 (as 145a, 145b, and so on) which are related to Rievaulx holdings in East (Low) Bolton in Wensleydale (they will be discussed in more detail in chapter 2). Although the editor explained their provenance in a footnote, it is not clear why they should be inserted in the body of the cartulary. In several places the editor changed the order of the entries. The Appendix (pp. 359–427) contains a selection of some, but not all, of the thirteenth-century additions to the cartulary, which have been taken out of their original contexts. The list of the abbey's accessions on fols 15–16 [new fols 19–20] and the incomplete calculation of the abbey's lands (expressed in carucates) on fol. 16^{v} [new fol. 20^{v}], which in the manuscript precede the entries, were moved to the back of the volume and printed on pp. 260–63. The editor also rather arbitrarily and without explanation cut out formal parts of the entries, such as the *pro anima* phrases and the corroboration formulae, which were thought to be formulaic. This was a common editorial practice of that time which reflected the interests of these historians in charters as a source of information for the estates, their location and character, and names of benefactors, but not in the form of the charters. Such an approach contradicts the intentions of the compiler of the cartulary who did not leave out these conventional phrases when copying charters into the cartulary because they constituted an important part of the document.[18] In addition, halfway through the published edition, on pp. 205–50, Atkinson

---

15 G. R. C. Davis, *Medieval Cartularies of Great Britain: A Short Catalogue* (London: Longman, 1958), p. 92. A new edition is in preparation by Prof. David Smith of the Borthwick Institute, University of York.

16 William Dugdale, *Monasticon Anglicanum*, rev. by J. Caley, H. Ellis, and B. Bandinel, vol. V (London, 1846), p. 277.

17 *Cartularium de Abbatie de Rievalle*, ed. by John C. Atkinson, Surtees Society, 83 (Durham: Andrews, 1889).

18 Ludo J. R. Milis, *Angelic Monks and Earthly Men: Monasticism and its Meaning to Medieval Society* (Woodbridge: Boydell, 1992), p. 88.

inserted a large number of additional documents from the Dodsworth manuscripts from the Bodleian Library. Although these charters are related to Rievaulx Abbey, they were not a part of the original cartulary. The editor incorporated them with consecutive numbering, with a footnote stating that the following charters were part of the Dodsworth manuscripts. Nevertheless, superficially they appear to be part of the original cartulary. The original structure of the cartulary manuscript and its implications are discussed in the first chapter.

Other important sources which give information about the history of Rievaulx Abbey were created outside the walls of the monastery. Curia Regis Rolls, Assize Rolls, and Feet of Fines are the most important sources of information about contacts between Rievaulx Abbey and its lay neighbours. These documents were produced by courts of law, for reasons different from those which led to the creation of the cartulary. The court case documentation was made externally, by a third party — the courts — and provides information for only one stage of the process, usually the final period of a conflict between the abbey and specific individuals. The entries tend to be standardized, using formulaic legal language of the court proceedings. Sometimes these documents give fairly lengthy descriptions; in particular, they lay out how the litigant and defendant presented their cases, the way in which they described their rights to particular properties, and even which documents were displayed to prove their claims. The character of these legal documents emphasizes conflict rather than any type of co-operation. It creates an impression that the most common form of contact between the abbey and its neighbours was disagreement. This rather biased perspective is due to the fact that peaceful, everyday coexistence between Rievaulx Abbey and its neighbours left very little direct trace in the sources. There was simply no reason to record it.

Other externally produced documents provide rather patchy information. Archiepiscopal rolls and charters of the Archbishops of York and Bishops of Durham shed some light on the relationship between the secular Church hierarchy and the abbey of Rievaulx.[19] This documentation is, however, rather biased towards the mid-twelfth century when the contacts between these institutions were most dynamic. The statutes of the Cistercian Chapter General provide concise but valuable information on Rievaulx's involvement in the politics of the Cistercian order.[20] They also illuminate

---

[19] *Durham Episcopal Charters 1071–1152*, ed. by H. S. Offler, Surtees Society, 179 (Gateshead: Northumberland Press, 1968); *EEA*, vol. v; *EEA*, vol. xx; *The Register of Rolls of Walter Gray Lord Archbishop of York 1215–1255*, ed. by J. Raine, Surtees Society, 56 (Durham: Andrews, 1872); *The Register of Walter Giffard Lord Archbishop of York 1266–1279*, ed. by W. Brown, Surtees Society, 109 (Durham: Andrews, 1904); *The Register of William Wickwane Lord Archbishop of York 1279–1285*, ed. by W. Brown, Surtees Society, 114 (Durham: Andrews, 1907); *The Register of John Le Romeyn Lord Archbishop of York 1286–1296*, part 1, ed. by W. Brown, Surtees Society, 123 (Durham: Andrews; London: B. Quaritch, 1913).

[20] *Statuta*; *Twelfth-Century Statutes from the Cistercian General Chapter*, ed. by Chrysogonus Waddell, Studia et Documenta, 12 (Brecht: Cîteaux-Commentarii Cistercienses, 2002); *Narrative and Legislative Texts from Early Cîteaux*, ed. and trans. by Chrysogonus Waddell, Studia et Documenta, 9 (Pontigny: Cîteaux-Commentarii Cistercienses, 1999).

the mechanisms of conflict resolution between monasteries belonging to this order. Similarly, collections of papal letters and bulls give indications of the involvement of the highest Church authorities in the protection of the rights of Rievaulx Abbey.[21] Selected narrative sources have also been discussed in this book, primarily those directly connected with Rievaulx Abbey: Abbot Ailred's *Relatio de Standardo* and *De sanctimoniali de Wattun*, and Walter Daniel's *Vita Aelredi*, as well as William of Newburgh's *Historia Rerum Anglicarum* which provides important information on the ecclesiastical politics of twelfth-century Yorkshire.[22]

The relative scarcity of the sources is to some extent compensated for by the abundance of secondary literature devoted to many aspects of the history of the Cistercian order. No work on the interactions between religious communities and laypeople can ignore the wealth of scholarship devoted to various aspects of this phenomenon. Furthermore, a book about one Cistercian house and its locality must respond to some of the key questions which historians have been asking and engage in the current debates on the relationship of the Cistercian houses with their surroundings.

Key Debates, Questions, and Approaches

The foundation of Rievaulx Abbey and its early development is a good test case of the approaches and interpretation of Cistercian practice, in particular the ideal/reality model which was for a long time seen as a paradigm of Cistercian history. The study of this institution provides a strong argument for seeing the development of individual monasteries and the Cistercian order itself in the light of the pragmatic changes and evolution occurring in the course of the twelfth and thirteenth centuries. Above all, local practice did vary even on the level of regions; thus the history of Fountains Abbey differs significantly from that of Rievaulx. Although both houses belonged to the same order, they had to respond to different challenges coming from their neighbours and benefactors, and their responses were dependent primarily on their knowledge of local conditions and their ties to the neighbourhood. Thus, inevitably, the analyses of Rievaulx Abbey bring me to the debates over the development of the Cistercian order. The core of this discussion, which continued for most of the last century, has been the issue of the attitudes and responses of the Cistercian order to

---

21 *CPL*; *Original Papal Documents in England and Wales from the Accession of Pope Innocent III to the Death of Pope Benedict XI (1198–1304)*, ed. by Jane E. Sayers (Oxford: Oxford University Press, 1999); *PU*.

22 Ailred of Rievaulx, 'Relatio de Standardo', in *Chronicles of the Reigns of Stephen, Henry II and Richard I*, vol. III, ed. by Richard Howlett, Rolls Series, 82 (London: Longman, 1886), pp. 181–99; Ailred of Rievaulx, 'De sanctimoniali de Wattun', *PL*, 195, cols 789–96; *Life of Ailred*; William of Newburgh, 'Historia Rerum Anglicarum', in *Chronicles of the Reigns of Stephen, Henry II and Richard I*, vol. I, ed. by Richard Howlett, Rolls Series, 82 (London: Longman, 1884), pp. 20–503; for other works, see Bibliography.

social and economic developments of the time, which usually have been analysed on the level of the whole order, rarely on the basis of microstudies of individual houses. The starting point of these investigations for many ecclesiastical and economic historians has been the early records of the Chapter General (dated by Canivez to 1134 and now by Chrysogonus Waddell to 1147 and Constance Berman to the 1150s), which banned Cistercian possession of rents, dependant peasants, mills, and marketplaces. The only acceptable way of earning a living for the monks was direct labour. The economic separation from the social environment also implied a detachment from the lay world and the remote location of the monasteries, away from settlements.[23] In the past, these regulations have been interpreted by historians as the 'ideal' of Cistercian life, practised in the early stage of the order's development. Any indication of an adverse practice has been perceived as a symptom of declining standards. For example, James E. Madden explained what he called the failure of the Cistercian order on the grounds that their growing involvement in trade and banking led to the loss of their original ideals. In their attempts to save their exemption privileges, to which they were, in his understanding, no longer entitled having entered market exchange, the Cistercians had to pay large sums, which contributed to the moral and financial 'bankruptcy of the order'.[24]

Moral judgments have been particularly strong in the works of monastic historians who developed a notion of the 'golden age' of Cistercian practice before the death of St Bernard, a 'golden age' characterized by austere conditions and self-sufficiency. The subsequent economic success of the order was interpreted by these scholars as an accidental by-product of the self-sufficiency model combined with the advantages of papal privileges. The scholars belonging to that school assumed that material success was not an original aim of the white monks and that the wealth accumulated by the order was in contradiction to the ideology of the 'golden age'.[25] Only more detailed studies of Cistercian houses across Europe have revealed a growing body of evidence that the Cistercian order, even before 1153, did not follow consistently the strict observance of St Benedict's rule. Clear evidence that practices that differed from the prescribed Cistercian ideal were present from the beginning of the order's growth, such as the ownership of tithes and mills and the abandonment of secluded sites for more economically viable areas, led to the development by Louis Lekai of a theory of 'ideal' versus 'reality' in his history of the Cistercian order.[26]

---

[23] *Narrative and Legislative Texts*, ed. by Waddell, p. 460; Constance H. Berman, *The Cistercian Evolution: The Invention of a Religious Order in Twelfth-Century Europe* (Philadelphia: University of Pennsylvania Press, 2000), pp. 48–51.

[24] James E. Madden, 'Business, Monks, Banker Monks, Bankrupt Monks: The English Cistercians in the Thirteenth Century', *Catholic Historical Review*, 49 (1963), 341–64 (p. 364).

[25] Knowles, *Monastic Order*, pp. 217–45; Lester K. Little, *Religious Poverty and the Profit Economy in Medieval Europe* (London: Paul Elek, 1978), pp. 90–96.

[26] Louis J. Lekai, *The Cistercians: Ideal and Reality* (Kent, OH: Kent State University, 1977), pp. 282–333. The elaboration of this hypothesis: Louis J. Lekai, 'Ideals and Reality in

Although the ideal of self-sufficiency never existed as a written and coherent law and the directives of the Chapter General could not have been enforced across the order, Lekai interpreted the 'ideal' as a guiding principle for Cistercian houses. In Lekai's interpretation, the numerous cases of broken rules or regulations did not indicate, as they had in earlier works, symptoms of decline. The speed of the growth and geographical spread of the order required a flexible approach, and without it the order would never have succeeded in achieving what it did in the course of the twelfth century. The true symptoms of decline, according to Lekai, can be identified only after 1300 and were characterized by the sharp decline in the number of new foundations as well as the chronic financial problems of many houses.[27] A stream of publications based on Lekai's thesis followed this influential book. These studies proved, however, that more than anything else local practices were far from the 'ideal versus reality' model even at the early stages.[28]

Economic historians have analysed Cistercian practices from a different perspective. Many early works stressed the innovative approach of the Cistercian order, the widespread reclamation of wasteland and forest clearance which brought significant increases in crop production via directly cultivated granges. The white monks came to be perceived as pioneers with technical skills, as exemplified by the opinion expressed by Coburn Graves: 'If any one attribute is laid to the Cistercians, it is that they were unrivalled reclaimers of waste.'[29] A particular variation on this theme, with strong political overtones, was the 'frontier thesis', which was developed by German scholars in the nineteenth century. It claimed that the establishment of the Cistercian houses in the Slavic territories in the late twelfth century aided the expansion of the German population and, by implication, Western — meaning superior — civilization eastwards.[30]

From this perspective, the order was often seen as being at the forefront of the economic and technological changes in the twelfth century.[31] In contrast to the

---

Early Cistercian Life and Legislation', in *Cistercian Ideals and Reality*, ed. by Sommerfeldt, pp. 4–29.

[27] Lekai, 'Ideals and Reality', pp. 23–26.

[28] Berman, *Cistercian Evolution*, pp. 55–56.

[29] Coburn V. Graves, 'The Economic Activities of the Cistercians in Medieval England (1128–1307)', *Analecta Sacri Ordinis Cisterciensis*, 13 (1957), 3–60 (p. 16).

[30] Paul Wehrmann, *Kloster Kolbatz und die Germanisierung Pommerns*, Königliches Bismarck-Gymnasium zu Pyritz (Pyritz: [n. pub.], 1905); G. D. Wellstein, 'Die grauen Mönche als Träger deutscher Kultur im Osten', *Ostdeutsche Monatshefte*, 6 (1926), 117–31; for a modern criticism of the frontier thesis, see for example Siegfried Epperlein, 'Gründungsmythos deutscher Zisterzienserklöster westlich und östlich der Elbe im hohen Mittelalter und der Bericht des Leubuser Mönches im 14. Jahrhundert', *Jahrbuch für Wirtschaftsgeschichte*, 3 (1967), 303–35.

[31] George Duby, *Rural Economy and Country Life in the Medieval West* (1962), trans. by Cynthia Postan (Columbia: University of South Carolina Press, 1990), pp. 70–71, 199; M. M.

monastic historians who developed notions of the 'ideal' and 'reality' in the history of the Cistercian order, some economic historians interpreted early Cistercian legislation (particularly the *Exordium Parvum* and the early statutes of the Chapter General) as a conscious economic plan. In Richard Roehl's interpretation the Cistercian order had a clearly defined economic plan on the level of individual abbeys, and the Chapter General enforced a certain amount of uniformity for that purpose.[32] This system was very efficient until, as Coburn Graves explains, the crisis of the Cistercian economy which was caused by high consumption in the monastic communities. The widespread introduction of wool production caused a decline in direct labour.[33] Roehl went even further in asserting that the economic plan of the Cistercian order failed because of the success and popularity of the order. This presumed plan linked both the religious aim of austerity and seclusion and economic self-sufficiency. The high profitability of the latter and further economic expansion led to a change in the lifestyle and quality of religious practice of the monks because '[a] program of religious reform had been associated with a normative economic program: deviation from the ideal in one respect implied deviation in the other'.[34]

More recently these two bipolar interpretations by both monastic and economic historians have been challenged by historians of the order. Bouchard questioned the use of Cistercian legislative sources, particularly the early records of the Chapter General, as a reflection of the 'ideal' practices as opposed to the later practices of the corrupted 'reality'. She demonstrated that the Cistercian monasteries from the very beginning accepted 'forbidden' types of gifts such as mills, rents, and serfs and did not try to hide it. The later crisis of Cistercian monasticism was not the result of simple diversion from the 'ideal' path by the monks, but the outcome of much more complex social and economic changes of the later Middle Ages.[35] Bouchard's findings have been confirmed by Isabel Alfonso's critical study of Portuguese Cistercian abbeys. Alfonso points to the variety of connections between the granges belonging to these houses and the surrounding areas, which were not confined to the stereotypical organization of the Cistercian monastery.[36] The debate of the 'ideal-reality' issue has been summarized by Berman, who has deconstructed the assumption of Cistercian economic practices. She asserts that

---

Postan, *The Medieval Economy and Society* (1972; repr. Harmondsworth: Penguin, 1976), p. 102; Edward Miller and John Hatcher, *Medieval England: Rural Society and Economic Change 1086–1348* (London: Longman, 1978; repr. 1990), p. 33.

[32] Richard Roehl, 'Plan and Reality in a Medieval Monastic Economy: The Cistercians', *Studies in Medieval and Renaissance History*, 9 (1972), 83–113 (pp. 84–94).

[33] Graves, 'Economic Activities', p. 54.

[34] Roehl, 'Plan and Reality', p. 112.

[35] Constance B. Bouchard, 'Cistercian Ideals versus Reality: 1134 Reconsidered', *Cîteaux: Commentarii Cistercienses*, 39 (1988), 217–31.

[36] Isabel Alfonso, 'Cistercians and Feudalism', *Past and Present*, no. 133 (1991), 3–30.

> there was never a total divorce between ideal and reality in the early Cistercian history. For, in a variety of ways, even though ideology did not mirror the actual practice of the order, there was still a connection between its ideology and its economic practices. Moreover, ideology tended to sustain or justify practice, although often in indirect, even convoluted ways.[37]

In her latest book, she goes even further in deconstructing the process of order formation. She argues that the Cistercian order emerged from a variety of reform movements as a coherent organization only in the second half of the twelfth century. Part of her hypothesis of the late development of the Cistercians as an organized and structured order is based on her redating of key Cistercian documents. In particular, Berman pushed the dating of *Exordium Cistercii* and *Summa Cartae Caritatis* from *c.* 1123 and *c.* 1130 to 1165.[38] Although Berman's dating has been much criticized, it provides a further argument for seeing the early history of the order and its individual abbeys as a prolonged process.[39] But I would like to concentrate in my study of Rievaulx Abbey on another issue raised by Berman's book. Part of the problem in the debate over the development of the Cistercian order is the level of generalization which ignores the vastly different geographical and social conditions of the Cistercian order in France, England, Germany, Eastern Europe, and Scandinavia. Many studies, including Berman's work, tend to use evidence from France as the basis of their general statement about the practice and evolution of the whole order. By the time the Cistercian order spread to Northern, Central, and Eastern Europe in the second half of the twelfth century, the Cistercian strategy of expansion had to adapt to the very different social, political, economic, and even geographical conditions that existed across Europe. This included not only routine acceptance of churches, tithes, rents, or even serfs, but often a close reliance on the local bishops, regular reliance on the support of the founders, and the presence of many lay burials in the monastic churches. This, however, should not be considered as evidence of a lack of discipline or a departure from the order's ideology. On the contrary, this ability to adjust to different and changing conditions was the reason for the success of the Cistercian order in various conditions.

The close analysis of the development of Rievaulx Abbey provides a further argument in the debate among the historians of the order, who stress the predominance of the local practice above any centrally coordinated plan allegedly followed by the

[37] Constance H. Berman, 'The Development of Cistercian Economic Practice during the Lifetime of Bernard of Clairvaux: The Historical Perspective on Innocent II's 1132 Privilege', in *Bernard Magister*, ed. by John R. Sommerfeldt, Cistercian Studies Series, 135 (Spencer, MA: Cistercian Publications, 1992), pp. 303–13 (p. 308).

[38] Berman, *Cistercian Evolution*, pp. 46–92, 237–41.

[39] For the most comprehensive review of Berman's book, see Chrysogonus Waddell, 'The Myth of Cistercian Origins: C. H. Berman and the Manuscript Sources', *Cîteaux: Commentarii Cistercienses*, 51 (2000), 299–386.

Cistercian houses. Terms such as 'ideal' or 'decline' seem more and more out of place in the context of religious houses which successfully redefined their attitudes to the lay benefactors and bishops and even to their own landholdings. The change, which was a constant element of Rievaulx Abbey's development, came in response to the evolving conditions of its social environment.

Although my book investigates Yorkshire society from the perspective of the abbey, we must remember that the laypeople approached Rievaulx with their own set of ideas and expectations. One of the crucial problems addressed in the course of this book is the motivation of laypeople for founding religious houses and donating land to them and their expectations of the religious communities. Without properly addressing this issue we cannot examine the complexities of lay-monastic interactions, which were, after all, based on these underlining motivations. Although the role of lay nobility in the successful spread of the Cistercian order throughout Europe has been emphasized in the literature, the motivation of these people remains a debatable issue. In the last thirty years there has been an enormous growth in scholarship devoted to religious foundations, the intentions of donors, and the issue of gift exchange in a monastic context. The great obstacle for many historians analysing the motivations which lay behind grants to monasteries is, as David Crouch rightly pointed out, that 'historians tend to be cynical both by nature and training and treat patrons' motivation very suspiciously'.[40]

Generally, there seem to be three main lines of approach to the issue of the motivations behind monastic foundations and donations. The first one interprets the spiritual intentions expressed by the founders and donors in the charters as concealed secular interest, sometimes even as evidence of sales.[41] These historians suspect that spiritual motivations were a kind of cover-up for more mundane motivations and that the real reasons for the donation to the religious houses were predominantly material. Bennett Hill asserts that many of the gifts were in reality concealed sales, but the payments were not recorded in the charters in order to disguise the true nature of these transactions.[42] Christopher Harper-Bill maintains that 'many grants were in reality commercial transactions'.[43] Emma Mason emphasizes the ambivalence of relationships between monastic houses and their patrons more cautiously, without discarding spiritual motivation. In her interpretation donations were often made 'with an eye to

[40] David Crouch, *The Image of Aristocracy in Britain, 1000–1300* (London: Routledge, 1992), p. 311.

[41] See, for example, Bennett D. Hill, *English Cistercian Monasteries and their Patrons in the Twelfth Century* (Urbana: University of Illinois Press, 1968), pp. 62–79; Victoria Chandler, 'Politics and Piety: Influences on Charitable Donations during the Anglo-Norman Period', *Revue Bénédictine*, 90 (1980), 63–71 (p. 65).

[42] Hill, *English Cistercian Monasteries*, p. 57.

[43] C. Harper-Bill, 'The Piety of the Anglo-Norman Knightly Class', in *Proceedings of the Battle Conference on Anglo-Norman Studies II 1979*, ed. by Allen R. Brown (Woodbridge: Boydell, 1980), pp. 62–77 (p. 67).

the material wellbeing of the donor rather than to that of the recipient'.[44] This ambivalence was, in her understanding, inherent to this relationship which was designed to promote not only the spiritual but also the temporal interests of the lay patron.

The second line of interpretation takes at face value the intentions of the founders and benefactors expressed in charters in order to uncover the basis of the lay-monastic interactions. Ludo Milis points out that the formulae of religious motivations in the charters should not be overlooked as clichés, but treated as meaningful expressions of the benefactors' intentions.[45] In a similar vein, Christopher Holdsworth asserts that the charters themselves hold the main clue to patrons' motivations. He points out that prayers were the main concern of the donors: 'it comes first in their charters and has to be taken seriously.'[46] More recently, Janet Burton has stressed that the religious motivations of Yorkshire benefactors should not be considered as secondary to the political and social considerations.[47]

Finally, the third approach to contacts between religious institutions and lay-people derives from interdisciplinary investigations of social phenomena heavily inspired by ethnology, anthropology, and sociology. Historians belonging to this school argue that the religious foundations and grants are manifestations of deeper, often transcultural, patterns of social behaviour, such as gift giving, exchange, and reciprocity. They look to other cultural milieux for explanations for the mechanisms of medieval religious practices. This approach offers very exciting possibilities, but also poses several interpretational difficulties. Firstly, many of these works use anthropological studies of non-European societies, which are distinctly different from medieval societies although they are both essentially pre-industrial. Historians tend to use anthropological or sociological studies rather selectively, concentrating on the usefulness of their conclusions, disregarding differences in methodology between history and these social sciences. Anthropologists study societies in a direct way, but historians have no access to past societies. The archives and written sources are not comparable with the interviews which anthropologists conduct with the members of the societies under consideration. Secondly, constructs such as 'gift economy' developed by Bronisław Malinowski and Marcel Mauss in the early twentieth century cannot be directly applied to the medieval material. In Mauss's theory based on the gift giving among Maori people, every gift needs its countergift, which also needs to be reciprocated, resulting in a circular process of exchange. The desire for reciprocity was motivated by the belief in 'hau', a kind of spirit of the gift-object, which had power over the recipient and wanted to be returned to the original donor. Therefore

[44] Emma Mason, 'Timeo Barones et Dona Ferentes', in *Religious Motivation: Biographical and Sociological Problems for the Church Historian*, ed. by Derek Baker, Studies in Church History, 15 (Oxford: Blackwell, 1978), pp. 61–75 (p. 70).

[45] Milis, *Angelic Monks*, p. 88.

[46] Christopher Holdsworth, *The Piper and the Tune: Medieval Patrons and Monks*, The Stenton Lecture 1990 (Reading: University of Reading, 1991), p. 17.

[47] Burton, *Monastic Order in Yorkshire*, pp. 182–94.

gift and countergift created a permanent bond between the donor and recipient, while the object remained highly significant. In the Mauss theory this system of exchange was crucial for the functioning of the whole society, maintaining social bonds, diffusing aggression and conflicts.[48] In historical scholarship this model has been applied to early medieval societies in which the volume of monetary exchange was not significant and barter trade very common. George Duby used this theory to explain land donations to the early medieval Church and countergifts in the form of prayers and alms to the poor.[49] Although the notion of reciprocity was crucial for early medieval societies, the 'hau' factor, so important in the Maori context, never existed in the European setting. Since the early 1960s, the important debate in anthropology about the applicability of Western economic and social concepts to non-Western societies has become relevant to historians because it posed the wider issue of cross-cultural interpretations and the usefulness of models developed in an entirely different context.[50] As much as the application of anthropological notions to historical material is often based on superficial similarities between cultural practices, these innovations should not be disregarded. One of the eminent British anthropologists, Edward Evans-Pritchard, acknowledged differences in the methodology between history and anthropology, but recognized a fundamental similarity between both disciplines — both history and anthropology 'translate' other cultural realities into our modern understanding.[51]

In this sense the only way forward in the application of such models as the 'gift economy' to historical investigation is in the form of an archetype which can be used to explain past reality without the necessity of comparing historical and anthropological material to establish direct similarity between two unrelated social realities. In particular, works by Barbara H. Rosenwein provide good examples of inspiration on the analytical level, not using anthropology simply as comparative or illustrative material. In her study of the monastery of Cluny and its patrons she uncovers many layers of interactions and meanings which narrowly focused historical research would not access. She analyses the complexity of landholding between the abbey and the benefactors which was based on the notion of reciprocity.[52] Although the model of

---

[48] Marcel Mauss, *The Gift: Forms and Functions of Exchange in Archaic Societies*, trans. by Ian Cunnison (London: Cohen and West, 1954).

[49] George Duby, *The Early Growth of the European Economy: Warriors and Peasants from the Seventh to the Twelfth Century*, trans. by Howard B. Clarke (Ithaca, NY: Cornell University Press, 1974), p. 56.

[50] See, for example, John Weeks, 'Fundamental Economic Concepts and their Application to Social Phenomena', in *The New Economic Anthropology*, ed. by John Clammer (New York: St Martins Press, 1978), pp. 21–30.

[51] Edward Evans-Pritchard, *Anthropology and History: A Lecture Delivered in the University of Manchester* (Manchester: Manchester University Press, 1961), p. 14.

[52] Barbara H. Rosenwein, *To Be the Neighbor of Saint Peter: The Social Meaning of Cluny's Property, 903–1049* (Ithaca, NY: Cornell University Press, 1989).

gift exchange developed by Rosenwein is applicable to the early medieval context, it cannot, however, be applied to the practices of the Cistercian order, as Berman explains in relation to Constance Bouchard's study of the Burgundian Cistercians and their benefactors.[53] In Berman's interpretation, the countergifts from the Cistercian abbeys to the benefactors were not expressions of the anthropologically understood 'gift economy', but rather a way of preventing claims from members of the donor's family to the land given to the monastery. Although these Cistercian countergifts were motivated by practical and legal considerations, the religious component was always present, which caused an ambiguity of language; for example the terms *donare*, *laudare*, and *vendere* could appear in the context of one donation, that is a particular grant could be given, confirmed, and sold at the same time.[54] This ambiguity of language has caused many historians to interpret Cistercian countergifts in the context of commercial transactions. Joan Wardrop asserts that the countergifts at Fountains Abbey were in reality a type of hidden sale.[55] Her opinion is not an isolated one and is the result of the application of modern concepts to the terminology of the charters. The complex transactions between the Cistercian monks and their benefactors, often involving elements of reciprocity, were actions on many levels at once. The donor could benefit from his or her donation on both a material and a spiritual level at the same time. The presence of material benefit to the donor did not diminish the eschatological value of the grants. There was also no reason to treat these actions as shameful; in fact many charters note proudly the monetary compensations which the monks gave to their benefactors. The last chapter of my book explores, amongst other things, the role of countergifts in relations between Rievaulx Abbey and its benefactors as a part of the mechanism of creating and sustaining bonds.

Although most of the anthropologically inspired works on medieval monastic and lay contacts have come from historians, a successful example of the interdisciplinary model was published in 1995 by a social scientist, Illana Silber. She approaches the problem of gift giving in the medieval Church from the sociological standpoint.[56] Her book is a comparative study of medieval monasticism and Theravada Buddhism with eclectic theoretical inspirations ranging from Marcel Mauss to Anthony Giddens; a large part of her study is also a dialogue with and polemic against the Weberian

---

[53] Bouchard, *Holy Entrepreneurs*.

[54] Constance H. Berman, 'The Debate on Cistercian Contracts: Regarding a Recent Book', *Cîteaux: Commentarii Cistercienses*, 43 (1992), 432–40 (pp. 438–39).

[55] Joan Wardrop, *Fountains Abbey and its Benefactors 1132–1300* (Kalamazoo: Cistercian Publications, 1987), pp. 85–86, 233.

[56] Illana F. Silber, *Virtuosity, Charisma and Social Order: A Comparative Sociological Study of Monasticism in Theravada Buddhism and Medieval Catholicism* (Cambridge: Cambridge University Press, 1995); see also reviews of this book by Lutz Kaelber in *Sociology of Religion*, 5 (1996), 214–15 and by David Smilde in *American Journal of Sociology*, 10 (1996), 1776–78.

idea of the role of religion in the development of the Western world.[57] Despite the large-scale comparative framework of Silber's study, she avoids too broad a generalization. Her interpretation of the reasons for the enduring relationship between monks and lay donors in medieval society is an important voice in the debate:

> Lay donations, in short, are not just a payment for monastic, secular or religious services. Neither are they, however, equivalent to a straightforward commitment to the virtuoso [monastic perfection – EJ] ideals. A more adequate interpretation of donations, rather, is that they contribute to mediating between two otherwise polarized and even antagonistic sectors, between a religious elite exemplifying certain ideals, and lay believers willing to acknowledge the same ideals but unable or unwilling to commit themselves to their fullest enactment. The gift, in this case at least, is perhaps 'total' (in Mauss's sense of being simultaneously economic, religious, political, etc.), but it is also ideologically, a highly pliant and multivocal phenomenon.[58]

Silber's explanation of lay-monastic interaction points to the fundamental reason for the existence of religious communities and their role in medieval society. Despite being intentionally general, this statement can be used as a starting point for many specific historical investigations, which would confirm this model in many particular instances of the multiplicity of social meanings exemplified by the acts of benefactors. The benefactors of Rievaulx Abbey donated land to it for a variety of reasons, eschatological, social, or even political, which were not mutually exclusive, but rather complementary. A grant was given not just because somebody wanted to increase his or her chances of salvation, but also to express the continuity of attachment to the abbey in the later generations of the family of the donor or to express affinity to a lord from whom the benefactor held some land. Although being a monk or nun was highly regarded in medieval society, only a small proportion of noblemen and -women entered the monastery. Giving a donation to the monastery was a way of coming closer to the spiritual benefits of this profession, which they could not or did not want to enter themselves.

The social network of Rievaulx Abbey was based, to a large extent, on reciprocity and building mutual connections, covering a broad range of lay families, religious institutions, and the Church hierarchy. From the perspective of the abbey these links were converging on Rievaulx, and this impression is strongly presented by the central source surviving from the archive of the monastery. Thus, it is best to start the exploration of the social world of the abbey with the cartulary.

---

[57] Silber, *Virtuosity*, p. 6.

[58] Silber, *Virtuosity*, p. 214.

CHAPTER 1

The Rievaulx Cartulary: The Patron, Locality, and Collective Memory

The early history of Rievaulx Abbey cannot be understood without a careful analysis of its cartulary. This source is useful not only for the reconstruction of the process of accumulation of the estates, but more importantly for the examination of the formation and development of the abbey's relationships with its founder, patrons, benefactors, and neighbours. The cartulary shows how the community of Rievaulx perceived the lay world around, the role of key individuals from the Church hierarchy, and its own place within the locality.

The Rievaulx Abbey cartulary represents a genre which is still not fully appreciated by historians. The changing approaches to cartularies by scholars in the last hundred and fifty years or so illustrates well how medieval studies re-evaluates its approaches, methods, and objectives. Initially, cartularies were among the most frequently used types of source for positivist historians who edited them in the second half of the nineteenth century, producing many monumental collections of sources continuously used by generations of medievalists. For those scholars, cartularies were just collections of copied charters — some of them lost in their original form — which needed to be scrutinized to detect any possible forgeries or interpolations. This perception of cartularies as a simple reflection of the archive of a given monastery at the time of the creation of the cartulary led to the common practice of 'improving' the cartularies in the process of editing. It was not uncommon, until recently, for editors to change the order of the entries to place them in what they considered to be the chronological order of issue.[1] Cartularies were primarily valued therefore for the

---

[1] Patrick Geary, 'Entre Gestion et Gesta', in *Les Cartularies: Actes de la Table ronde organisée par l'École nationale des chartes et le G.D.R. 121 de C.N.R.S. (Paris, 5–7 décembre 1991)*, ed. by O. Guyotjeannin, L. Morelle, and M. Parisse, Mémoires et Documents de L'École des Chartes, 39 (Paris: École des Chartes, 1993), pp. 13–26 (p. 13).

amount of information which they transmitted from the original charters which may have been subsequently lost. Their form and structure was not considered to have any particular meaning or significance for the historians analysing them. As Trevor Foulds expressed it, cartularies were and still often are 'considered as a vehicle from which to extract evidence or information'.[2] It is not my intention to add any more condemning comments to the rather dated discussion on the value of the positivist approach to these sources, but it is important to place the cartulary of Rievaulx Abbey in the context of traditional research on this type of source.

An important change in the way in which cartularies have been analysed was brought about by the work of such scholars as Patrick Geary, who re-evaluated the significance of cartulary collections. It has become increasingly clear to the editors of cartularies that they are not simply random collections of copies, and therefore the integrity of their form and the order of the entries should be respected. Only in this way can we ask the traditional questions: who, when, and what? In his excellent study on tenth-century Bavarian cartularies Geary did not concentrate on the content of individual entries, but analysed the structures of the whole collections and the editing methods used by the creators of these cartularies.[3] This approach allowed him to investigate such issues as the collective memory of aristocratic kin of their own past and deliberate manipulations to preserve a desirable version of past events. This line of inquiry has been pursued most recently by Brigitte Resl in relation to the early Italian cartularies and later southern German and Austrian examples.[4] What unites these works on this genre of monastic writing is a strong sense that cartularies had very complex meanings to their creators and users.

The cartulary remained a useful genre for monastic communities beyond the Middle Ages, with new volumes still being produced in the late eighteenth century.[5] There is, however, a substantial difference between cartularies created at various stages of institutional development, between those made in the early years and those written in the established communities, sometimes several hundred years after the foundation. The volume from Rievaulx Abbey is a rare example of a cartulary produced in the formative years of one of these houses, having been created less than a

---

[2] T. Foulds, 'Medieval Cartularies', *Archives*, 18 (1988), 3–35 (p. 4).

[3] P. J. Geary, *Phantoms of Remembrance: Memory and Oblivion at the End of the First Millennium* (Princeton: Princeton University Press, 1994).

[4] Brigitte Resl, 'Von Nutzen des Abschreibens: Überlegungen zu mittelalterlichen Chartularen', in *Vom Nutzen des Schreibens: Soziales Gedächtnis, Herrschaft und Besitz im Mittelalters*, ed. by Walter Pohl and Paul Herold (Vienna: Österreichische Akademie der Wissenschaften, 2002), pp. 205–22.

[5] Cistercian houses in southern Poland, particularly in Mogiła and Jedrzejów, continued to create new cartularies until their suppression in the nineteenth century. *Monasticon Cisterciense Poloniae*, vol. I, ed. by Andrzej Wyrwa, Jerzy Strzelczyk, and Krzysztof Kaczmarek (Poznań: Wydawnictwo Poznańskie, 1999), p. 146.

century after its foundation. It is also one of the oldest Cistercian cartularies in Europe and as such deserves particular attention.

The manuscript, London, British Library, Cotton Julius D. i, is a small volume, 17 x 13 cm, containing 193 parchment folios written in sections with rubrics and initials in red ink. The majority of entries have titles identifying the content of each charter.[6] The original twelfth-century parts are written in very clear book script. Later thirteenth-century insertions show a great variety of hands of much smaller, cursive, documentary script. The small dimensions of the volume as well as the scarce and very simple decoration indicate that the cartulary was intended as a practical tool, rather than a showpiece object. Despite obvious signs of frequent use, such as lacerations of the parchment and its soiling due to frequent leafing, there are very few marginal notes in the volume. Some of the notes have been lost through partial cutting across the top margin when the volume acquired its postmedieval cover; the bottom edges of these notes are still visible.

The first four folios of the volume are blank with the addition of a seventeenth-century genealogy of the Ros family inserted on a folded piece of parchment. Its folios were numbered twice in the nineteenth century, creating two different sets of references. Folios 1–2^{v} [new fols 5–6^{v}] are occupied by several thirteenth-century entries, among them, on fol. 2 [fol. 6], an important mid-thirteenth-century agreement between William de Ros, the patron, and Rievaulx Abbey. Then on fols 3–14^{v} [fols 7–18^{v}] are copied the decrees of the Third Lateran Council of 1179. The significance of this section will be discussed in chapter 4. The decrees are followed by a list of the abbey's accessions titled 'Iste sunt possessiones Rievallenses perhennes quod sic collate sunt nobis' on fols 15–16 [fols 19–20]. This list, which is in chronological order, gives some dates and names of the donors and provides a record of the early grants to Rievaulx. It is based on the contents of the cartulary and supplements it with some dates, but it does not reflect the total content of the volume and concentrates only on a selection of the early grants. It is possible that either the list was not completed or it was not meant as a comprehensive catalogue but rather as a selection of the most important donors and their grants in order to draw particular attention to them. The dates given there were probably supplied by the monastic community itself, since they refer to the events of the last fifty years. 'Iste sunt possessiones' is followed by another list. It is an incomplete calculation of the abbey's lands on fol. 16^{v} [fol. 20^{v}] with names of the donors in the left hand column and the numbers of carucates given to Rievaulx by these individuals in the right hand column. The next section of the cartulary, the index of the volume, with the number of each entry on the left hand side (in red ink) and titles of the charters on the right, is on fols 17–22 [fols 21–26]. It is an integral part of the twelfth-century cartulary but was never fully completed. Two sections of the index, from number 155 to 172 and again from 203

[6] G. R. C. Davis, *Medieval Cartularies of Great Britain: A Short Catalogue* (London: Longman, 1958), p. 92.

to 213, contain only numbers without the titles of the charters to which they refer. In the thirteenth century more entries were added following the logic of the original organization. For example, the title of one of the charters of Bernard de Balliol (no. 154 in the manuscript, no. 115 in the printed edition) was inserted later, both in the index and as a full-text entry in its designated place, in a thirteenth-century hand.

The original twelfth-century body of the cartulary only starts on fol. 24 [fol. 28] with the foundation charter of Walter Espec, which is in fact a composite charter, containing information about two separate donation acts. After the section occupied by charters of the patrons follow copies of other early and important benefactors of the abbey, Bishops William St Barbe (1143–52) and Hugh du Puiset (1153–95) of Durham. In logical order after the ecclesiastical charters come the records of the most important grants of the lay benefactors, beginning with the charters of Roger de Mowbray and his relatives. He was the most prolific lay donor of Rievaulx Abbey, a prominent baron in the North, and a very generous benefactor of many religious institutions. The copies of Roger's charters and those of his mother and son Nigel are followed by a cluster of documents issued by their knights and tenants. The rest of the original twelfth-century cartulary is organized in a similar way, that is, charters are grouped according to the connections between the donors. These connections were created by belonging to the same family either by birth or marriage, or by tenurial ties both vertical and horizontal, that is, between lords and their tenants or between different persons holding land from the same lord.

In many cartularies the documents which were considered as having special importance, such as papal bulls or final concords, were often pulled out of the their topographical context and placed in a more prominent location within the volume.[7] Many such confirmations were also very general in content and scope and therefore not necessarily related to one property or area. In the Rievaulx cartulary a separate section is occupied by copies of royal and papal charters and letters. On fols 125^{v}–140^{v} [fols 129^{v}–144^{v}] there are charters of protection, specific privileges, and one grant of King Henry I (1100–35) and several of King Henry II (1154–89). The documents issued by the Archbishops of York, Thurstan (1114–40), Henry Murdac (1147–53), and Roger du Pont L'Évêque (1154–81), and the Archdeacons and Deans of York, Ralph Baro (1139/40–*c.* 1158/9), Robert de Gant (after 1147–*c.* 1158), and Robert Butevilain (1158–86), appear on fols 147–153^{v} [fols 151–157^{v}]. Finally a large section, on fols 157–173 [fols 161–177], is devoted to the charters, letters, and bulls of popes, predominantly of Pope Alexander III (1159–81) and some of Honorius III (1216–27). Most of them deal with specific issues such as payment of tithes or the monks' complaints about neighbours encroaching on their property. By the late twelfth century Rievaulx Abbey experienced growing pressure on its lands from its neighbours and benefactors, many of whom were of considerable social standing.

[7] David Walker, 'The Organization of Material in Medieval Cartularies', in *The Study of Medieval Records: Essays in Honour of Kathleen Major*, ed. by D. A. Bullough and R. L. Storey (Oxford: Clarendon Press, 1971), pp. 132–50 (pp. 135–36).

The severity of some of these disputes required the authority of the papal legates and the threat of excommunication to bring them to a resolution. Table 1 shows a simplified structure of the cartulary and the implicit division into sections devoted to various groups of benefactors.

Table 1. The Structure of the Rievaulx Cartulary

Folios: old [new]	**Content**
fols 1–2^{v} [fols 5–6^{v}]	A collection of various thirteenth-century entries
fols 3–14^{v} [fols 7–18^{v}]	The Decrees of the Third Lateran Council of 1179
fols 15–16 [fols 19–20]	'Iste sunt possessiones Rievallenses perhennes quod sic collate sunt nobis'
fol. 16^{v} [fol. 20^{v}]	Incomplete calculation of abbey's lands
fols 17–22 [fols 21–26]	Index of the volume
fol. 24 [fol. 28]	The 'foundation charter' (composite)
fols 25^{v}–31 [fols 29^{v}–35]	Ros family charters
fols 31^{v}–34 [fols 35^{v}–38]	Ecclesiastical charters of Bishops of Durham (William of St Barbe, Hugh de Puiset)
fols 34–44 [fols 38–48]	Charters of the Mowbray family and their tenants
fols 46^{v}–48 [fols 50^{v}–54]	Charters of the Gant family and their tenants
fols 54–59^{v} [fols 58–63^{v}]	Birkin family charters
fols 66–70 [fols 70–74]	Balliol family charters
fols 70^{v}–74^{v} [fols 74^{v}–78^{v}]	Normanby family charters
fols 74^{v}–78^{v} [fols 78^{v}–82^{v}]	Ingram family charters
fols 80–83 [fols 84–87]	Sproxton family charters
fols 88^{v}–94^{v} [fols 92^{v}–98^{v}]	Charters of the Tunstall family and their tenants
fols 99–102 [fols 103–106]	Mowbray family charters
fols 110^{v}–115 [fols 114^{v}–119]	Royal charters of Richard I
fol. 116 [fol. 120]	Three late thirteenth-century memoranda
fols 117–125^{v} [fols 121–129^{v}]	Charters related to the dispute over the Waste of Pickering
fols 125^{v}–140^{v} [fols 129^{v}–144^{v}]	Royal charters of Henry I and Henry II
fols 147–153^{v} [fols 151–157^{v}]	Ecclesiastical charters of Archbishops of York (Thurstan, Henry Murdac, Roger de Pont L'Évêque); Archdeacons and Deans of York (Ralph Baro, Robert de Gant, Robert Butevilain)
fols 157–173 [fols 161–177]	Papal bulls and letters of Alexander III and Honorius III

It is not an accident that this cartulary was created in the late twelfth century, which was in many ways a turning point for Rievaulx. By that time the abbey had accumulated substantial estates, but had also begun to have serious problems with its disgruntled benefactors and neighbours. In general, periods of difficulties and uncertainty often generated texts by which a community wanted to reassure itself and to create a sense of a shared past and identity. Although the cartulary is not a narrative, it tells the story of Rievaulx's past through the grants in a coherent and structured form. As Jean-Philippe Genet demonstrated, the creators of the medieval cartularies were not passive copyists, but rather interpreters, who intentionally organized charters in the form of cartularies.[8] The cartulary of Rievaulx Abbey, created some eighty years after its foundation, is a very rare case of a collection which shows the making of an institution which had to pay great attention to neighbourhood politics in order to establish and succeed in this world of close personal links. The charters were grouped predominantly according to the relative importance of the donors and connections between them, not the geographical location of the properties. This latter editorial technique was commonly used in late medieval cartularies, for example in the fifteenth-century cartulary from Byland Abbey discussed by Janet Burton.[9] The late medieval volumes reflect the stability of the monastic holdings and provide a detailed account of the estates accumulated in the previous centuries. Often these later cartularies provide only summaries of the charters, and their witness lists were routinely abbreviated and sometimes omitted.[10] The people listed there were long gone, many of the families were extinct, and the social landscape around the abbeys altered altogether, so knowledge about these people was no longer an important issue.

In contrast to these later cartularies, Rievaulx's cartulary shows the monastic institution during the process of accumulation of lands and preserves the image of the dynamics of its interactions with neighbours. The cartulary's structure allows us to identify not only the abbey's early benefactors, but also connections between them and their relative importance for the abbey. Indeed, the charters were copied in full, including complete witness lists because people named there and their relatives were still important for the abbey as potential donors or at least as passive supporters who expressed their affinity to Rievaulx by witnessing donation ceremonies.

Many Cistercian houses had foundation histories written to assert their identity and the collective understanding of their own past at a similarly early stage. Elizabeth Freeman argues that in the *Fundacione abbathie de Kyrkestall*, created at Kirkstall Abbey, the daughter house of Fountains, the issue of land acquisition is at the forefront of the story. A monastery could not exist and succeed without sufficient landholdings; thus the emotional value attached to the land was expressed in Kirkstall's foundation history as a key element in the formation of the community's self identity. The history of Kirkstall was, to use Freeman's expression, 'mapped through space' in the

---

[8] Jean-Philippe Genet, 'Cartulaires, registres et histoire: L'example anglais', in *Le Métier d'historien au moyen âge: Études sur l'historiographie médiévale*, ed. by Bernard Guenée (Paris: Université de Paris I Panthéon-Sorbonne, Centre de recherches sur l'histoire de l'Occident médiéval, 1977), pp. 95–138 (pp. 95–96, 109).

[9] *The Cartulary of Byland Abbey*, ed. by Janet Burton (Boydell and Brewer for the Surtees Society, forthcoming).

[10] Constance B. Bouchard, 'Monastic Cartularies: Organizing Eternity', in *Charters, Cartularies, and Archive: The Preservation and Transmission of Documents in the Medieval West*, ed. by Adam J. Kosto and Anders Winroth, Papers in Medieval Studies, 17 (Toronto: Pontifical Institute of Mediaeval Studies, 2002), pp. 22–32 (p. 29).

monastic estates and the stories of their acquisition and often difficult retention.[11] In many ways the structure of the Rievaulx cartulary serves the same purpose.

The late twelfth-century cartulary of Rievaulx Abbey remains the central source for an understanding of the abbey's relationship with the outside world. The complex structure of the cartulary indicates its interconnected practical functions and expresses a message about the collective memory of the institution which produced it. By placing charters in a specific order the compiler indicated which grants were more important than others. Also, the simple but effective editorial practice of grouping together charters issued by members of one family or tenants of one lord placed these donations in the context of the local community. Understanding the neighbourhood and family politics was crucial for the abbey, which was still actively expanding its estates and wanted to develop them in a particular direction. Furthermore, the cartulary of Rievaulx Abbey, due to its remarkable structure, was a tool of remembering and commemorating benefactors and patrons. Although the volume was unlikely to be used in a liturgical context, its form, highlighting people over property, made it easy to remember or even commemorate benefactors by preserving their names.

The main body of the cartulary is organized according to some inferable rules which helped to place charters in their context and helped the future users of the volume to find specific documents. The first rule of organization for the entries appears to be according to the connections between people known to the monks. According to this implicit rule, the compiler placed charters issued by the members of one family together, and the charters of the tenants almost always accompany those of their lords. In the occasional cases when one individual held lands from more than one lord, the placement of the tenant's charter indicates which of the connections was considered more important by the abbey. Sometimes horizontal connections, that is, those between the members of one family or tenants of a particular lord, were more important than hierarchical relations. This will be further discussed in the second chapter.

A great majority of the charters in the cartulary are related to grants of land from various laypeople to the abbey. The grant of property, regardless of its size, was not an action confined, in time, to the actual transmission of property from the hands of one owner to another. A grant created, in a great majority of cases, a continuum, that is, a relationship which lasted for more than one generation. These original acts of giving set up connections between the abbey and its benefactors and formed a part of the wider network of relationships not only between the abbey and laypeople, but between the people themselves. It was therefore important for the abbey to recognize these connections and be part of it, preferably on its own terms. The most distinct statement of the role and place of the monastery in the lay society is expressed by the phraseology of the charters. The opening lines of the majority of Rievaulx's charters read, 'Let it be known to these present that I/we have given, and by this charter, have confirmed to God and the church of St Mary of Rievaulx and the monks serving God

[11] Elizabeth Freeman, *Narratives of a New Order: Cistercian Historical Writing in England, 1150–1220*, Medieval Church Studies, 2 (Turnhout: Brepols, 2002), p. 138.

there, for salvation of my soul', not only giving the reason for the existence of the monastery but also providing a clear explanation of its role in the lay society.[12] These formulaic expressions were not meaningless, and there was a reason for copying them in their entirety from the charters into the cartulary. Donation to a monastery was a gift to God entrusted in the hands of the monks. The role of monks as intercessors between the Sacrum and the people gave them a unique place in society. Although donations to religious institutions expressed not just spiritual meanings, the grants could only play their social role in an environment which valued highly the eschatological dimension of the grant. Without that belief the gifts recorded in the charters would have been meaningless. This is a manifestation of the phenomenon described by Silber, when the gifts to the monasteries expressed laypeople's commitment to the religious ideal represented by the monks. Whilst they could not or did not want to join the order, the donations built a bridge 'between two otherwise polarized and even antagonistic sectors'.[13]

The cartulary and its composite elements also give important messages about the social status of the individuals named there. Brigitte Bedos-Rezak pointed out that 'the charters articulated and gave meaning to a specific social structure' by means of the vocabulary which distinguished particular individuals by naming them *miles* or *nobilis*. The participation of members of the donor's kin and neighbours as recorded in the witness lists and rituals noted in the cartulary, such as placing objects on the high altar or giving an additional oath, provided a further symbolic dimension to the legal acts written down in the charters.[14] Cartularies go one step further than charters. By creating a new entity from a great number of charters, they provide an interpretation for these expressions of religious convictions and social aspiration. By their methods of editing and organizing charter material the monks not only preserved the memory of their benefactors and their gifts, but composed this knowledge in the way they wanted it to be remembered. This was not static. As Constance Berman asserts, the placement of charters indicated the relative importance of benefactors and their families not necessarily at the time of the donation, but rather at the time when the cartulary was created.[15] By the late twelfth century some of the earlier connections might have entered a different phase or ceased to exist altogether.

---

[12] 'Sciatis me dedisse, et hac presenti carta mea confirmasse Deo et Ecclesie Sancte Marie Rievallis et monachis ibidem Deo servientibus, pro salute anime.'

[13] Illana F. Silber, *Virtuosity, Charisma and Social Order: A Comparative Sociological Study of Monasticism in Theravada Buddhism and Medieval Catholicism* (Cambridge: Cambridge University Press, 1995), p. 214.

[14] Brigitte Bedos-Rezak, 'Diplomatic Sources and Medieval Documentary Practices', in *The Past and Future of Medieval Studies*, ed. by John Van Engen, Notre Dame Conference in Medieval Studies, 4 (Notre Dame: University of Notre Dame Press, 1994), pp. 313–43 (pp. 320–36).

[15] Constance H. Berman, *The Cistercian Evolution: The Invention of a Religious Order in Twelfth-Century Europe* (Philadelphia: University of Pennsylvania Press, 2000), p. 169.

In a most general sense, then, the cartulary was a way of mapping the world — how elements such as people and places were related to each other, how the social and political environment was understood by the abbey, and how this institution made sense of what was happening to it in terms of its land acquisitions, grants, conflicts, and lawsuits. It also illustrates how the abbey wanted to see its own place in the network of social connections. This perception therefore determined the hierarchy of importance of information and documented the abbey's responses to many external factors. Berman asserts that in many cartularies created after at least a century of a religious house's existence, the past was not a chain but a collection of events, all the acts of donation at different stages in the past had the same timeless and continuous value.[16] The volume from Rievaulx Abbey shows similar fusion of the past, present, and future relationships with the donors, yet this volume also shows a remarkable attention given to preservation of information about the locality and the laypeople. This I attribute primarily to the early creation of the cartulary and the impact of many of the donors and witnesses still being alive at the time of the cartulary's creation. It is also connected to the Cistercian sensitivity to involvement in the lay world, setting the boundaries, both physical (manifested by, among other things, the selectiveness of the lay burials on the monastic precinct and church) but also symbolic (the intentionally permanent separation of the monastic land from that of the laypeople in the carefully copied charters). The second and fifth chapters explore this theme further.

I would be overstretching the point to claim that the Rievaulx cartulary, or any other cartulary of this type, was a narrative form, but it strongly appears that the Rievaulx cartulary tells a story of how the abbey interacted with its benefactors. Apart from being a useful reference book of the copies of the precious and fragile charters, the cartulary was designed to preserve the memory of the institution, its property, and the people who were its benefactors. The structure of the cartulary gives the impression that the abbey was the central point of a complex social network encompassing a large number of laypeople of varying social status and members of other religious institutions in Yorkshire. Almost every charter in this volume proclaims that lands given to Rievaulx were given to God, and thus removed from the realm of this world. Martha Newman compared this process to the theological innovations of the Cistercians: 'Just as Cistercian authors describe the process of converting human love into divine love, so the Cistercians' cartularies demonstrate the steps by which they untangled the layers of rights and obligations attached to secular property and made their land into a religious domain.'[17] It might seem, then, that the abbey was above the worldly concerns of its neighbours, and that the monks only served as guardians of lands given, in fact, to God directly. However, as we compare this picture with information from other sources, particularly legal records, it appears that the abbey was much more a part of a network, rather than its centre, and indeed was

[16] Bouchard, 'Monastic Cartularies', pp. 28–31.

[17] Martha G. Newman, *The Boundaries of Charity: Cistercian Culture and Ecclesiastical Reform 1099–1150* (Stanford: Stanford University Press, 1996), p. 69.

entangled in various conflicts with its neighbours and benefactors to a greater degree than it wanted to acknowledge in the cartulary.

Rievaulx Abbey and its Patron: Foundation and its Memory

Remembering, commemorating, and celebrating the memory of the founder was an important element of the collective memory of the monastic community. This was done not just by emphasizing his or her charters in the cartulary, but in other written or even literary forms. The Cistercian order was striving consciously to establish a new type of practical and symbolic relationship with its patrons and benefactors, one that was more distant and less allowing of lay interference. How was this practically interpreted by the monks of Rievaulx Abbey?

Among the contacts with the outside world of any religious house, regardless of the order, the founder was the most important layperson associated with it and his or her actions often had a strong and direct impact on the formation of the new monastery. In the history of any monastic house the patron's family played an important role as protector, benefactor, and defender. Usually, such a relationship was developed in the early years of the house's existence and then sustained for several generations. In turn patrons enjoyed special spiritual services, such as perpetual prayers, commemorations, and the high status attached to this function. In addition, patrons of the Benedictine houses also enjoyed considerable practical influence over their houses, including custody during vacancies, varying control over abbots' elections, and hospitality.[18]

The tradition and practice of lay patronage over religious houses was several centuries old when the Cistercian order emerged at the beginning of the twelfth century. It also had different expressions in different European regions. The white monks rejected many elements of this tradition by trying to minimize any formal ties between the monasteries and their lay patrons, but this does not mean that they did not need patrons and benefactors. Cistercian houses in England accepted land predominantly in free alms to avoid the necessity of supplying knightly service, but this did not prevent the development of informal and sometimes even close relations with patrons. Since relations with the patrons were personal and thus difficult to regulate, there was a great variety in their practical expression according to the local conditions and expectations. The dynamics of the relationship between a monastery and its various benefactors were usually shaped by the physical proximity of their properties, areas of economic interest, and local politics, but in the case of the relationship between a patron and a monastery, there were certain additional expectations by the latter from the former. The responsibilities of patrons to protect and support their monasteries were fulfilled with various degrees of involvement, and this level of commitment tended to change over the generations under the influence of changing conditions.

[18] Susan Wood, *English Monasteries and their Patrons in the Thirteenth Century* (London: Oxford University Press, 1955), pp. 40–101.

Not only did monasteries need their patrons to give them land and offer protection, but the existence of religious houses also fulfilled many needs of their lay protectors. The foundation of Rievaulx Abbey and the people associated with it provides a good example of several social phenomena occurring among the Anglo-Norman nobility in the first half of the twelfth century. Walter Espec, the founder of the abbey, was advancing his career in the royal service, and his pious foundations were, apart from religious considerations, linked to his attempts to assert his newly acquired social standing.

The reign of King Henry I was a time of profound changes in the administration and governing of the country, which greatly influenced relationships between the King and the magnates. The royal court was still mobile, travelling constantly between Normandy and England, and the King needed advisors around him at all times.[19] The fluctuating membership of the court and the patterns of royal patronage can be traced through the lists of witnesses to the royal charters. Walter Espec's name appeared frequently as a witness, indicating his presence at the court. He was also an addressee of several writs and mandates by Henry I concerning the rights of various monastic institutions in Yorkshire, and he witnessed many royal confirmations of their property rights.[20] Walter Espec came from a Norman family who settled in Bedfordshire. He was a son or nephew of William de Spech who was already tenant-in-chief in Domesday Book, but Walter was the first member of this family to achieve significant social and economic status. During his career Walter acquired three lordships: Old Warden in Bedfordshire, which he inherited from his uncle, and Wark in Northumberland and Helmsley in Yorkshire, which were granted to him by King Henry I.[21] The latter became Espec's main residence. Walter Espec became one of two justices of forests and the itinerant justices of the North, the other being Eustace FitzJohn.[22] The area of their judicial responsibilities was correlated, not accidentally, with the location of their own estates.[23]

---

[19] C. Warren Hollister, *Henry I*, ed. by Amanda Clark Frost (Yale: Yale University Press, 2001), pp. 327–69; C. Warren Hollister and John W. Baldwin, 'The Rise of Administrative Kingship: Henry I and Philip Augustus', *American Historical Review*, 83 (1978), 867–905 (pp. 867–77).

[20] Paul Dalton, *Conquest, Anarchy and Lordship: Yorkshire 1066–1154* (Cambridge: Cambridge University Press, 1994), pp. 306–07.

[21] The honour of Helmsley was part of Count Robert of Mortain's estates in the Domesday Book. Judith A. Green, *The Aristocracy of Norman England* (Cambridge: Cambridge University Press, 1997), pp. 136, 380; I. J. Sanders, *English Baronies: A Study of their Origin and Descent 1086–1327* (Oxford: Clarendon Press, 1960), p. 133.

[22] *DNB*, XVIII, 4; *Magnum Rotulum Scaccarii de anno tricesimo-primo regni Henrici Primi*, ed. by Joseph Hunter (London, 1833), p. 24, 27, 32, 33, 35, 104, 128, 129, 131, 138, 142, 143.

[23] Judith Green, *The Government of England under Henry I* (Cambridge: Cambridge University Press, 1986), p. 81, 109.

Contrary to the old historiographical ideas of King Henry's reign as a period of terror, C. Warren Hollister voices a completely different opinion, pointing towards the politics of patronage and the manipulation of favours which could keep barons more grateful for past favours and hoping for future ones, rather than terrorizing them. Such a policy created a number of prominent individuals who benefited from it and, in turn, supported the King.[24] Walter Espec certainly belonged to the group described as the 'new men' of Henry I and was rewarded by four estates in Yorkshire.[25] The fact that these men were considered 'new' does not mean that they were of a low social standing altogether. Their lineage was in most cases considerably high if not eminent.[26] Importantly, they were a second generation of settlers in England still having interests in Normandy, but increasingly building their main bases in England and these included the foundation of religious houses in England. New monasteries as much as castles became the visible signs of the Norman presence there. By means of religious foundations incoming families 'put down their roots' in the northern frontiers.[27]

The success, both in scale and number, of the Cistercian monasteries in the North was a complex phenomenon on both religious and social levels.[28] The foundation of Rievaulx Abbey was the first in the series of Cistercian houses which became important elements of the social and economic landscape of the region. Although the patrons of Cistercian houses had much less legal power over their monasteries than those of other orders, they could still significantly influence the internal matters of the house as the history of Rievaulx Abbey shows.[29]

The coming of the white monks to Yorkshire was orchestrated by St Bernard himself and supported by King Henry I and Archbishop Thurstan of York. The group of Cistercian monks from Clairvaux led by William, an Englishman, brought a

---

[24] C. Warren Hollister, 'Henry I and the Anglo-Norman Magnates', in his *Monarchy, Magnates and Institutions in the Anglo-Norman World* (London: Hambledon Press, 1986), part 10, pp. 93–107 (p. 99–107).

[25] Green, *Government of England*, pp. 180–81.

[26] Green, *Aristocracy*, p. 9.

[27] David Bates, 'Normandy and England after 1066', *English Historical Review*, 104 (1989), 851–80; Judith Green, 'Aristocratic Loyalty on the Northern Frontiers of England, c. 1100–1174', in *England in the Twelfth Century: Proceedings of the 1988 Harlaxton Symposium*, ed. by Daniel Williams (Woodbridge: Boydell, 1990), pp. 83–100 (p. 94).

[28] Janet E. Burton, *The Monastic Order in Yorkshire, 1069–1215* (Cambridge: Cambridge University Press, 1999), pp. 98–124.

[29] On the influence of patrons on the northern houses, see Derek Baker, 'The Surest Road to Heaven', in *Sanctity and Secularity: The Church and the World*, ed. by Derek Baker, Studies in Church History, 10 (Oxford: Blackwell, 1973), pp. 45–58 (p. 47); Baker, 'Legend and Reality: The Case of Waldef of Melrose', in *Church, Society and Politics*, ed. by Derek Baker, Studies in Church History, 12 (Oxford: Blackwell, 1975), pp. 59–82 (pp. 81–82).

letter from St Bernard to King Henry in 1131. This letter lacks any details or names, but is generally considered to initiate the negotiations to establish Rievaulx Abbey.[30] The choice of the northern location might have been a result of the influence of Yorkshire monks in the circle of St Bernard, but the involvement of Archbishop Thurstan of York is unquestionable. He was known as a patron of monks, correspondent of St Bernard, and supporter of the Cistercian reform.[31] Moreover, his assistance was crucial as the foundation of Rievaulx Abbey took place in his diocese. Later, between May 1133 and January 1140, Archbishop Thurstan issued a confirmation charter of the abbey's initial endowment.[32]

It is not clear at which stage of negotiations and how Walter Espec became involved in the enterprise leading to the foundation of Rievaulx Abbey. Burton points out that Espec was a frequent visitor to the royal court and may well have met the Cistercian delegation sent there by St Bernard. In any case, it is highly unlikely that the Cistercian monks would be sent ahead of any invitation from the prospective founder. Walter had already founded another monastic house, Kirkham Priory, so the idea of being a patron and everything attached to it was not a novelty to him.[33] The royal court, as a meeting place of high Church officials and lay nobility, helped to spread ideas of the new order and popularized the fashion for monastic foundations. The founders of the first four Cistercian monasteries in England were recurrent visitors at the court. Furthermore, the early Cistercian foundations took place in a short time span from each other, which provides a further argument for the strong influence of fashion on the prospective patrons.[34]

---

[30] *Sancti Bernardi Opera*, vol. VII, *Epistolae*, ed. by J. Leclercq and H. Rochais (Rome: Editiones Cistercienses, 1974), no. 92. For an extensive commentary on the letter, see Burton, *Monastic Order in Yorkshire*, pp. 99–100.

[31] David Knowles, *The Monastic Order in England: A History of its Development from the Times of St Dunstan to the Fourth Lateran Council 940–1216* (Cambridge: Cambridge University Press, 1963), p. 230; Donald Nicholl, *Thurstan Archbishop of York: 1114–1140* (York: Stonegate Press, 1964), pp. 151–54; more recently discussed in Burton, *Monastic Order in Yorkshire*, pp. 99–101.

[32] *Cartulary*, no. 218; dated by Burton in *EEA*, V, 51. For more information about his involvement, see pp. 170–71 below.

[33] Burton, *Monastic Order in Yorkshire*, pp. 99–101; William of Newburgh stated in his chronicle that Walter Espec sent an invitation to Bernard of Clairvaux and promised a site for the new monastery: 'Historia Rerum Anglicarum', in *Chronicles of the Reigns of Stephen, Henry II and Richard I*, vol. I, ed. by Richard Howlett, Rolls Series, 82 (London: Longman, 1884), pp. 20–503 (p. 50). Kirkham was founded *c.* 1122: David Knowles and R. Neville Hadcock, *Medieval Religious Houses, England and Wales* (London: Longman, 1971), p. 124.

[34] Janet E. Burton, 'The Foundation of the British Cistercian Houses', in *Cistercian Art and Architecture in the British Isles*, ed. by Christopher Norton and David Park (Cambridge: Cambridge University Press, 1986), pp. 24–39 (p. 27).

According to the information in the 'Iste sunt possessiones' list in the cartulary, Walter Espec granted the abbey's site in 1131. The foundation of Rievaulx Abbey was finalized on 5 March 1132, but the actual foundation process, erecting temporary lodgings for the monks and a provisional church, very likely took longer than a year.[35] Gatherings at the foundation ceremonies were an important event for both the monastic institution and the founder. The ceremony was attended by many noble neighbours, local aristocracy, knights, tenants, family, bishops, and other officials. Such an event was a manifestation of the piety, power, importance, and connections of the founder. As for the monastic institution, the consecration of the monastic church, usually in the form of a provisional, wooden structure, marked the beginning of the formal functioning of a monastic house.

The location of the monastery, just two miles from Espec's castle in Helmsley, offered protection for the new foundation, and the patron could express his piety and status by this close association.[36] Although it is not known who erected the first buildings at Rievaulx Abbey, it is highly possible that the material and the labour were provided by Espec. This was a common practice across Europe, and another Yorkshire foundation, that of Henry de Lacy in Kirkstall, provides an example of active involvement by the founder in the erecting of the monastic buildings.[37] However, the initial grant was not extensive, in fact smaller than that of Kirkham established a few years earlier. It was comprised mainly of moorland.[38] From its location, so close to the founder's residence, it is possible to infer that Rievaulx was particularly important to Walter Espec.

The written sources associated with the foundation are scarce. Rievaulx's foundation charter copied in the cartulary is a composite of two documents related to two different occasions and was created by the compiler of cartulary in order to portray the foundation process in a more coherent manner, putting emphasis on the foundation ceremony rather than on a rather protracted process of land acquisition from the

---

[35] London, British Library, Cotton Julius D. i, fol. 15^{v} [fol. 19^{v}]; P. Leopoldus Janauschek, *Originum Cisterciensium*, vol. I (Vienna, 1877), p. 22; the year 1132 is given by Abbot Ailred himself in his 'Relatio de Standardo', in *Chronicles of the Reigns of Stephen, Henry II and Richard I*, vol. III, ed. by Richard Howlett, Rolls Series, 82 (London: Longman, 1886), pp. 181–99 (p. 184).

[36] Peter Fergusson, Stuart Harrison, and Glyn Coppack, *Rievaulx Abbey: Community, Architecture, Memory* (New Haven: Yale University Press, 2000), p. 37. This location so close to the patron's residence was not unusual. Other Yorkshire monasteries were also located in the vicinity of their founders' seats, in particular Nostell (Pontefract) and Easby (Richmond castle) priories and Roche (Tickhill) and Jervaulx (Richmond castle) abbeys. Burton, *Monastic Order in Yorkshire*, p. 199.

[37] 'The Foundation of Kirkstall Abbey', trans. E. K. Clark, in *Miscellanea*, Thoresby Society, 4 (Leeds: Thoresby, 1893), pp. 179–80.

[38] Janet E. Burton, 'The Estates and Economy of Rievaulx Abbey in Yorkshire', *Cîteaux: Commentarii Cistercienses*, 49 (1998), 29–94 (p. 30).

patron. Composite foundation charters were often created in the Cistercian houses to present a string of donations as a single event.[39] This operation allowed the creation of a myth for the monastic community of its unambiguous origins and a substantial initial endowment. The composite charter does not specify that the new monastery belonged to the Cistercian order, but the entry in the 'Iste sunt possessiones' adds that it was given to the Blessed Abbot Bernard of Clairvaux, emphasizing his role in the foundation process. The list differentiates between two principal grants of Walter Espec in 1132 and 1145.[40] The wording of the entry suggests that it was written after the death of Bernard in 1153 but before his canonization in 1174 (he is described as *beatus* not *sanctus*).[41] The discrepancy between the story narrated by the charter and information given by the 'Iste sunt possessiones' suggests that the compiler of the cartulary wanted to preserve both versions — the formal description in the 'foundation' charter and the frank but brief summary in the other document. Both had their uses for the monastic community. The text of the charter was intended to preserve the story of Rievaulx's origins in the aura of the high royal connections of the founder and the abbey itself, whilst the 'Iste sunt possessiones' was a document primarily for internal consumption.

Burton established that one part of the composite foundation charter relates to the initial endowment in 1132 and the second to an additional grant at the time of the probable retirement of Walter Espec between 1145 and 1153.[42] The first grant consisted of the actual site for the monastic precinct and nine carucates of land. On the second occasion Walter Espec granted Bilsdale, located to the north of the abbey. Some of the witnesses may have been present in 1132 and others, namely Walter's tenants, only between 1145 and 1153.[43]

The opening sentences of the so-called foundation charter outline, in a conventional way, the founder's aims and intentions and list people involved in the foundation in various ways:

> In the name of Holy and Inseparable Trinity, [I] Walter Espec greet all faithful sons of the Holy Catholic Church. Let it be known to you all that I have given in agreement with Henry King of the English and with the assent of Aelina my wife to God and the church of Saint Mary in Rievaulx, in the hand of Abbot William and the brothers serving God there, for the love of God and salvation of the soul of William King of the English, and for the salvation of the soul of Henry King of the English and the salvation of the souls of all their ancestors, and for the souls of my father and my mother and for the soul of

---

[39] BL, Cotton Julius D. i, fols 24–25 [fols 28–29]; *Cartulary*, no. 42. Berman, *Cistercian Evolution*, p. 175.

[40] *Cartulary*, p. 260.

[41] Bernard of Clairvaux was canonized by Pope Alexander III in 1174; however, before 1198 the process of canonization was not yet formalized.

[42] Burton, 'Estates and Economy', p. 30.

[43] *EYC*, x, 147.

> Hugh de Wildecher and for the souls of the father and mother of my wife and [for] all our relatives and ancestors [. . .] to hold in perpetuity.[44]

This short text presents several problems but also provides several possible interpretations as to why Walter Espec and so many other lay noblemen of his time founded religious institutions. For Walter Espec, becoming a founder of Kirkham Priory and later Rievaulx Abbey was part of the advancement of his career since it emphasized his personal connection with King Henry I. However, this does not imply that his foundations were undertaken for cynical, political reasons, but rather that being a founder was part of the new role assumed by Walter. The desire to be a founder was essentially a personal and religious issue, but the choice of order had a broader significance. Here we might see the influence of the court in the choice of the order, and even the probable direct influence of King Henry I emphasized in the charter.

The foundation charter does not specify that Walter Espec expected any prayers, but the very fact that the grant was given directly to God in the hands of the abbot and monks serving Him ensured spiritual advantages. The gift to the Church was in itself a 'good work' and would bring spiritual rewards; prayers of the monks were a kind of 'added value' to the original act of giving. Unlike Benedictine or Cluniac monks, Cistercians

> deserved to be supported for their own sake, and [their] benefactors were therefore relying on the first redemptive mechanism — that they themselves were giving alms directly to the deserving poor — as much as on vicarious good works.[45]

In the foundation grant of Rievaulx Abbey, royal permission was essential for the alienation of the land, which Walter was holding in-chief. Similarly important was *laudatio*, that is, the consent of Walter's wife for the foundation. This was a standard part in the monastic foundation charters. The aim of this clause was to prevent future claims from the individuals related to the founder and who might claim rights to the property. Those individuals giving *laudatio* were clearly distinguished from the witnesses who also may have been related to the founder but had no claims to the land.[46]

---

[44] 'In nomine Sancte et Individue Trinitatis, Walterus Espec universis Sancte Catholice Matris Ecclesie filiis, salutem. Notum sit omnibus vobis me dedisse et concessisse, concessu Henrici Regis Anglorum, et concilio Aeline uxoris mee, Deo et Ecclesie Sancte Marie de Rievalle, in manu Willelmi Abbatis, et fratribus ibidem Deo servientibus, pro Dei amore et salute anime Regis Willelmi Anglorum, et pro salute Henrici Regis Anglorum, et omnium parentum suorum, et pro salute anime patris mei et matris mee, et pro anima Hugonis de Wildecher, et pro animabus patris et matris uxoris mee, et omnium parentum et antecessorum nostorum, [. . .] in perpetuum tenere': *Cartulary*, no. 42.

[45] Benjamin Thompson, 'From "Alms" to "Spiritual Services": The Foundation and Status of Monastic Property in Medieval England', in *Monastic Studies: The Continuity of Tradition II*, vol. II, ed. by Judith Loades (Bangor: Headstart History, 1991), pp. 227–61 (p. 235).

[46] Constance B. Bouchard, *Holy Entrepreneurs: Cistercians, Knights and Economic Exchange in Twelfth Century Burgundy* (Ithaca, NY: Cornell University Press, 1991), pp. 79–87.

King Henry I, who helped to introduce the Cistercians to England, and his father or brother William, with all their ancestors, are listed as recipients of the spiritual benefits of the foundation of Rievaulx Abbey. Similarly, it is not only Walter's and his wife's souls that benefit, but those of all their relatives and ancestors. The foundation of the abbey was not a relationship between an individual and God, it was a whole family or kin entering the relationship with the Sacrum and benefiting from it. This act united past and present generations of the family and promised patronage and further grants for the monastic community. This was an obligation not only for the people immediately involved in the foundation, but also binding future generations. The effectiveness of this bond was not always as good as the monks might wish for, and this will be discussed in chapter 3.

The precise identity of Hugh de Wildecher, listed as one of the named beneficiaries of the foundation, remains uncertain, although the Wildecher family had tenurial links with the Ros family who were the heirs of Walter Espec.[47] The placement of Hugh's name in the charter after Walter's parents and before his in-laws suggests Wildecher's importance, probably personal, to the founder. It provides a rare glimpse into the realm of personal motivations hidden behind standard formulae and suggests further that the spiritual motivations were genuine. Hugh de Wildecher cannot be classified as one of the standard recipients; he was included in the list at the special request of the founder. Although it is impossible to verify, Hugh may have been a close friend of Walter Espec, possibly one from childhood, or a personal favourite from his close circle of associates, perhaps his favourite steward. His identity would presumably have been obvious to everybody since Hugh is not described by any additional title.

The first endowment by Espec consisted of nine carucates of land of which four were located in the vill of Griff and five in Tileston (present-day Stiltons Farm) with all the rights of pasture, collecting dead wood and timber, water and meadow, and freedom from any secular services. These two properties lay between the east bank of the Rye river and Borobeck stream, which runs through the township of Helmsley. Parts of this land were still covered by a wood; the rest comprised arable and pasture. On the plateau overlooking the river Rye there are remains of medieval earthworks, indicating a possible settlement which may be the remains of the Griff

---

[47] Wildechers appeared in other charters related to Rievaulx, Kirkham, and the Ros family. Stephen de Wildecher witnessed (together with Walter Espec and several other men) in 1145 a grant of Odo de Boltby to Rievaulx Abbey (*Cartulary*, no. 76). Hugh de Wildeker witnessed a confirmation of a donation to Kirkham by William son of Ukke between 1192 and 1198 (*EYC*, I, 501–02). In 1199 Walter de Wildecher witnessed a grant of the advowson of the church of Burythorpe to Kirkham (*EYC*, I, 493), and he witnessed a charter of William de Ros to Rievaulx about 1226 (Bodl. Dodsw. vii, fol. 188v, published incomplete in the *Cartulary*, p. 240). In 1226 Walter de Wildeker appeared in the witness list of Robert II de Ros to the Templars (*EYC*, X, no. 14). Wildechers were tenants of the Ros fee and Walter de Wildeker donated one and a half carucates of his land in the fee of Ros to Kirkham Priory in the first part of the reign of Henry III (*EYC*, II, 382).

vill depopulated by Rievaulx Abbey.[48] The second donation by Espec was made between 1145 and 1153 and was subsequently included in the compilation known as the foundation charter in the cartulary. It consisted of the southern part of Bilsdale, whose borders are described carefully in the charter: from Laskill to the confluence of William and Raisdale Becks except the manor of Stainton and the vill of Raisdale. The grant also included the right to gather wood and pasture pigs in his forest of Helmsley. The location of these grants ensured that the patron and the abbey would be close neighbours and had shared use of the same forest. These circumstances must have been perceived as desirable by the founder, but this was not to be the case in the later generations. This closeness caused significant problems in the mid-thirteenth century and this issue will be discussed later in more detail.

The analysis of the witness list of thirty-nine people in the foundation charter reveals four separate sub-lists containing names of people who attended the foundation ceremony and those who were present when Walter Espec granted Bilsdale. First comes a group of various clergymen — Thomas, Dean of Beverley Minster, Arnald, priest of Beverley, Godfrey chaplain, Walter chaplain, Robert, chaplain of Walter Espec, Geoffrey, clerk from Warter Priory, and five named brethren from this house — plus two laypeople: Eustace FitzJohn (royal justice in the North who operated together with Walter Espec) and Henry de Manferd. Then follow nine of Espec's nephews, who not only acted as witnesses but also gave their consent for the alienation of land. They are listed according to age: William, Jordan, and Roger de Buscy were sons of Hawise, the oldest sister, then Geoffrey, William, Gilbert, and Nicholas de Traili, sons of Albreda, and finally the sons of Adelina, Everard and Robert de Ros. The third group of witnesses consists of the close circle of the members of Walter Espec's retinue and his principal tenants. Their involvement in the foundation and the ceremony was described as giving advice to their lord. This group consisted of William de Stonegrave, Robert Lenveiset, Drew de Harome, Robert de Sproxton, Peter de Surdeval, William Luvel, John Ingram, William son of Amfred, William de Surdeval, Roger de Frammevila, and Hugo Camin. Out of this group, four men were tenants of the Ros fee in 1160: Peter de Surdeval, Drew de Harome, Robert de Sproxton, and William de Stonegrave.[49] Many of them and their children became benefactors of the abbey. Finally the last group in the list is comprised of the neighbours who also acted as witnesses: Henry de Muntfort, Stephen I de Meinil, Geoffrey de Sneit with his son Benedict, Roger de Hiltun, Aschelin son of William son of Aschelin, and many other neighbours and friends.[50]

---

[48] John McDonnell, 'The Evolution of the Monastic Grange', *Journal of the North Yorkshire County Record Office*, 2 (1975), 78–95 (pp. 78–82).

[49] *Red Book of the Exchequer*, vol. I, ed. by Hubert Hall, Rolls Series, 89 (London: Eyre & Spottiswoode, 1896), pp. 432–33.

[50] *Cartulary*, no. 42.

These early grants by Walter Espec were confirmed by the highest authorities to ensure security of the abbey's property. In 1133 King Henry I confirmed the initial grant of four carucates in Griff, five in Tileston, and pasture and forest right in Helmsley.[51] He also included a confirmation of the total of nine carucates given by Espec and immunity from various services and taxes.[52] This confirmation was then reconfirmed by King Stephen in 1136, the first year of his reign. This document was witnessed by, among others, Archbishop Thurstan and the founder's nephew William de Traili.[53] Although this was clearly an important charter, it was not copied in the cartulary, and the original document survived with other remnants of the abbey's archive at Belvoir Castle. This omission may be connected to the political climate towards the end of Walter Espec's life when he became disillusioned with King Stephen (see below). The late 1130s and 1140s were not an easy time for many of Rievaulx's benefactors caught in the violence of the civil war. The core of the cartulary was created at the end of the reign of Henry II, and his favours to the abbey were carefully listed in the volume, but any connection with King Stephen was clearly omitted. However, it is unlikely that the monastic compiler of the cartularies in the 1180s and 1190s was concerned with the politics of fifty years previous. Berman, however suspects this document to be a forgery, but even if this is the case, the possible forged nature does not explain its omission in the cartulary.[54]

There is no indication in the cartulary, or elsewhere, that Walter Espec granted any more land to the abbey, but he witnessed charters to the abbey, particularly those of his neighbours and his men, and influenced his tenants to become benefactors, thereby augmenting the initial donation. Walter Espec witnessed a grant of Odo de Boltby, neighbour of the abbey, between 1142 and 1145, of a portion of the waste below Hesketh bordering with Boltby, and also of the common pasture and woods in his three vills of Boltby, Ravensthorpe, and Thirlby.[55] Walter's influence was the probable reason behind another grant by Odo de Boltby, that of the vill Hesketh recorded in the 'Iste sunt possessiones' section of the cartulary in the same entry as the foundation grant of Walter Espec.[56] These grants were located ten miles west of Rievaulx. Then, between 1145 and 1147 Walter Espec witnessed a grant of Benedict son of Gervase de Wombleton, which consisted of land in Wombleton, where the

---

[51] *Cartulary*, no. 194.

[52] *Cartulary*, no. 196.

[53] Historical Manuscripts Commission, *The Manuscripts of the Duke of Rutland at Belvoir Castle*, vol. IV (London: H.M.S.O., 1905), p. 74; *Regesta regum Anglo-Normannorum 1066–1154*, vol. III, ed. by H. A. Cronne and R. H. C. Davis (Oxford: Clarendon Press, 1968), no. 716.

[54] Constance H. Berman, 'The Cistercian Mystery: How Was the Order Formed and by Whom? Can the Anglo-Norman Sources Elucidate the Problem?', *Haskins Society Journal: Studies in Medieval History*, 13 (1999), 1–19 (p. 5).

[55] *Cartulary*, no. 76; *EYC*, IX, no. 89.

[56] BL, Cotton Julius D. i, fol. 15v [fol. 19v].

abbeys already had some buildings on the land granted earlier by the same Benedict, adding also twelve perches in Spelcross, four perches in Skiplam, and meadows in Rook Barugh and Muscoates.[57]

Beyond these standard acts expected from any patron, there are other indications of a close relationship between Rievaulx Abbey and Espec. The location of the monastery, just two miles from Espec's castle in Helmsley, ensured close contact with the patron. Walter Daniel, the author of Abbot Ailred's vita, explained that the founder was a frequent visitor to the abbey and might, therefore, offer some practical assistance in the crucial years of the abbey's development. When Ailred, a future Abbot of Rievaulx, visited Walter Espec in Helmsley, as a layperson sent by the King of Scotland on a political mission to the Archbishop of York, he went to see the monastery with his host. Walter Daniel wrote: 'Next morning the lord Walter, accompanied by a few people of the vicinity, goes with him to the monks. Ailred meets the prior, the guest-master and the keeper of the gate.'[58] This event took place about two years after the foundation. Walter Daniel's text indicates that Walter Espec took considerable pride in the achievement of his monastery and wanted to show it to the people who were visiting him. Ailred, who came on a political mission to Yorkshire, was exactly the type of person whom Espec wanted to impress with the achievement of 'his monks'. The quality of the religious life of the monastery reflected directly on the position of the founder and patron, which increased not only his chances for salvation, but also his status among the peers.[59] The involvement of the founder in the life of Rievaulx Abbey shows that the Cistercian community there could not refuse their patrons this important privilege. In fact, it was not in its interest to do so. The degree of involvement was a matter of negotiation between both parties, but the protection offered by Espec was valued by the community, and after his death Rievaulx struggled to find a replacement figure having been rather disillusioned with the heirs of the founder.[60]

Walter Espec was strongly committed to the Cistercian ideal, and after the foundation of Rievaulx Abbey he established another house of white monks within his southern lands in Warden (Bedfordshire) in 1136 as a daughter house of Rievaulx. His commitment to the Cistercian order was in fact so strong that he intended to turn his earlier foundation at Kirkham into a Cistercian house as well. On the occasion of the first step towards Rievaulx Abbey's foundation in 1132 a certain reshaping of the priory's property occurred and a revised foundation charter was written for Kirkham to accommodate a transfer of some of its properties to Rievaulx Abbey, namely the

---

[57] *Cartulary*, no. 69; *EYC*, IX, no. 145; *Cartulary*, no. 63; *EYC*, IX, no. 146; Burton, 'Estates and Economy', p. 31.

[58] *Life of Ailred*, p. 14.

[59] *Life of Ailred*, p. 14. Graeme R. Ritchie suggested that Ailred's mission was connected to claims by the Archbishops of York to jurisdiction over Glasgow: *Normans in Scotland* (Edinburgh: Edinburgh University Press, 1966), p. 253.

[60] See below, pp. 45, 185.

tithes of Griff and Tileston.[61] Later, two almost identical charters confirmed the transfer of these tithes to Rievaulx Abbey. The first one was issued by an unidentified Prior of Kirkham in 1135, before the death of King Henry I, or as Burton suggests, prior to 1140.[62] The second one was issued by Prior Waldef not much later.[63] These changes were the direct result of Walter Espec's plans and intentions for his foundations and as such were copied in the Rievaulx cartulary, even though neither of these houses were neighbours.[64] Sometime between 1132 and 1140, a peculiar agreement was drawn up between Rievaulx and Kirkham. The canons agreed to transfer their present house and most of their property to Rievaulx in return for a new residence built on another site within the year by Rievaulx Abbey. The prior and some members of the community would stay behind, in the old house, and be granted the status of Cistercian monks. All of that was done according to the 'will and wish' of the patron as stated in the charter.[65] When for some unknown reason this plan of turning Kirkham Priory into a Cistercian house failed, another charter was issued extending the property of Kirkham Priory.[66]

This attempt to turn an Augustinian house into a Cistercian one indicates not only the founder's strong belief in the quality of Cistercian piety, but also Espec's ideas of lay patronage over religious houses, which as his action shows, could extend as far as changing the order. Not only was Kirkham Priory almost dismantled and the majority of its lands transferred to Rievaulx, but the remaining canons had to be accommodated in the quarters provided by the abbey. The timing of this failed enterprise coincided with the early years of Rievaulx Abbey when the monastic community was probably more interested in creating its own precinct than providing buildings for part of the Kirkham community. Although the Cistercian order had its own ideas about the extent of lay influence over their houses, the lay patrons were not keen to give up what they perceived as their rights. After all, it was Walter Espec himself who gave lands to both religious houses and secured their economic basis, so he must have felt justified in his actions towards Kirkham.

An important indication of the extent of the personal interaction of Walter Espec and Rievaulx Abbey and its wider significance is the role of Abbot William (1131–45)

---

[61] Derek Baker, 'Patronage in the Early Twelfth-Century Church: Walter Espec, Kirkham and Rievaulx', in *Traditio – Krisis – Renovatio aus Theologischer Sicht: Festschrift Winfried Zeller um 65. Geburtstag*, ed. by Bernd Jaspers and Rudolf Mohr (Marburg: Elwert, 1976), pp. 92–100 (p. 96); *Cartulary*, no. 216.

[62] *Cartulary*, no. 234; Janet E. Burton, *Kirkham Priory from Foundation to Dissolution*, Borthwick Paper, no. 86 (York: Borthwick Institute of Historical Research, 1995), p. 8.

[63] *Cartulary*, no. 235.

[64] Baker, 'Patronage', p. 97.

[65] 'pro voluntate et desiderio advocati nostri': *Cartulary*, no. 149; Baker, 'Patronage', p. 94; for the full text of this charter, see ibid. p. 100.

[66] The difference between these two endowments of Kirkham Priory is presented in tabular form in Burton, *Kirkham Priory*, pp. 4–6.

in the negotiation to surrender Walter's castle in Wark (Northumberland) after the battle of Standard.[67] This battle between English forces gathered by Archbishop Thurstan and King David I's army supported by many northern magnates, including Eustace FitzJohn, took place in 1138. The Scots were defeated, but King Stephen did not come to help the English forces and Walter surrendered his castle at Wark.[68] Abbot William was chosen as negotiator to this surrender to the Scottish king. It is likely that he was accompanied by Ailred who, after all, knew King David personally. Because of his monastic position, Abbot William was an ideal choice for an intermediary: he was a skilful negotiator respected by both sides in the conflict and had not been directly involved in either the military or political aspects of the event.[69]

In addition, one of the literary works of Abbot Ailred, *Relatio de Standardo*, gives a testimony to the political importance of Walter Espec as seen by the Abbot of Rievaulx.[70] There are several contemporary accounts of the battle of Standard, but this particular one provides further evidence of the relationship between Rievaulx Abbey and its patron. The *Relatio de Standardo* celebrates the military achievement of Walter Espec, his standing among the northern nobility, and even his physical strength. Ailred employed many literary techniques including oration by Walter Espec as a principal character to comply with the rules of romances and histories.[71] Literary conventions aside, this poem shows that the Abbot of Rievaulx was not only aware of the political role of the abbey's patron, but also believed that it should be celebrated and remembered. Even if the text was written with the monastic audience in mind as Antonia Gransden asserts, the *Relatio* was intended as commemoration of the abbey's founder to keep his memory alive.[72]

Remembering and commemorating was not restricted to the founder figure. The early support group of the abbey which formed around him also had an important role for Rievaulx and it is reflected in the composition of the cartulary.

---

[67] *Symonis Monachis Opera Omnia*, vol. II, ed. by Thomas Arnold, Rolls Series, 75 (London: Longman, 1885), pp. 291–92; 'Historia Ricardi Prioris Ecclesiae Haugustaldensis, de Gesti Regis Stephani', in *Chronicles of the Reigns*, vol. III, ed. by Howlett, pp. 137–78 (pp. 171–72).

[68] Dalton, *Conquest, Anarchy and Lordship*, p. 151.

[69] *Life of Ailred*, p. xlvi.

[70] Ailred, 'Relatio de Standardo', pp. 181–99.

[71] Inclusion of direct speech was a common aesthetic element of medieval literary composition, and also in the historical works. Nancy Partner, *Serious Entertainments: The Writing of History in Twelfth-Century England* (Chicago: University of Chicago Press, 1977), pp. 26–27, 207.

[72] Derek Baker, 'Ailred of Rievaulx and Walter Espec', *Haskins Society Journal: Studies in Medieval History*, 1 (1989), 91–98 (93–96); Antonia Gransden, *Historical Writing in England c. 550 to c. 1307* (London: Routledge, 1974), pp. 212–16; Aelred Glidden, 'Aelred the Historian: The Account of the Battle of Standard', in *Erudition at God's Service*, ed. by John R. Sommerfeldt, Studies in Medieval Cistercian History, 11 (Kalamazoo: Cistercian Publications, 1987), pp. 175–84 (pp. 180–83). Freeman, *Narratives of a New Order*, pp. 32–37.

Building Relationships: Family and Locality

The continuity in the relationship between a religious house and its benefactors was important for the enlargement and security of its property, but the continuity, or lack of it, between the patron and the monastery also had a significant impact on the successful functioning of the religious institution. The participation of the patron's relatives not only would ensure a larger pool of benefactors, but also created a group of people who could claim particularly strong attachment to the abbey. The foundation of the abbey was not the act of one sole individual, and Walter Espec's family was involved in it from the very beginning. As we have seen, many members of his family, some close (including his nephews) and some more distant, appeared in the witness list; one nephew, Jordan de Buscy, became a benefactor of Rievaulx, and another, Nicholas de Traili, who was a Canon of York, witnessed various charters to the abbey.[73] This activity was probably connected to both his position in the Church and his family ties with Espec. Canons were valued as witnesses, and the chapter of York provided many confirmations for this abbey and many others in Yorkshire. Nevertheless, Nicholas's involvement with Rievaulx Abbey must have been deeper than that suggested by his appearances as a witness alone. He was also concerned with the preservation of the abbey's interest. This is indicated by a note added in the thirteenth century on one of the empty folios at the beginning of the cartulary.[74] This memorandum is a declaration by Nicholas de Traili that his maternal uncle Walter Espec gave the abbey a piece of land in Tileston, which corresponds with a description in the foundation charter. The witness list of this document suggests a period between the death of Walter Espec and the late 1170s, but it is puzzling why this note was copied so late. It could be that a long forgotten document of Nicholas de Traili surfaced in the thirteenth century and was copied to the cartulary during the disputes with William de Ros, the patron of the abbey who questioned the abbey's rights to many of its properties (see chapter 3).

Nicholas de Traili was also a supporter of his uncle's other foundation, Kirkham Priory. His special position in relation to this institution was recognized in 1180 when he gave testimony to the justiciar, Ranulf de Glanville, on the election procedure of the prior at Kirkham, which stated that only after a suitable candidate was elected unanimously by the convent was he to be presented to the patron for approval and then finally to the Archbishop of York for the benediction.[75] Nicholas de Traili's knowledge of the election procedure at Kirkham Priory was most likely derived from his family connections with the patrons of this house, but the reasons behind writing this letter are unclear. It is possible that Everard II de Ros, the patron

[73] *Cartulary*, nos 43, 45, 129, 189, 219.

[74] BL, Cotton Julius D. i, fol. 1^{v} [fol. 5^{v}]; *Cartulary*, no. 5.

[75] *EYC*, x, nos 105–06.

of the house, might have interfered beyond his role in the election process, and the testimony of Nicholas, his great-uncle, was to clarify the situation.[76]

On both occasions Nicholas de Traili acted as a reliable repository of information about the religious foundations of his uncle. He outlived many of his cousins and could provide information about events occurring fifty years previously; being a canon gave him further authority in matters of Church rights. Although he did not give anything to Rievaulx Abbey he was thus an important figure for this relatively young institution. Religious houses needed supporters in various matters, not just donors of further pieces of land.

Jordan de Buscy, a younger nephew of Walter Espec, became a benefactor of the abbey and a witness to its charters.[77] In the mid-twelfth century his relative Oliver de Buscy granted all his meadow in Silton to Rievaulx, with the right of passage through his property, but requested one penny yearly for the services. His charter contains an interesting passage explaining the reasons for his grant:

> You should know that I have given and granted and by this present charter confirmed, to the abbot and the convent of Rievaulx, for the certain sum of money, which I had received from them in my great necessity, my whole meadow in the territory of Silton.[78]

This phrase can be interpreted in various ways, as a cover-up sale or as a return payment for a loan, but more importantly, this charter indicates that Rievaulx Abbey developed close links with its neighbours not only as a recipient of the grants; it was also able to give financial help to those of the patrons' family experiencing difficulties. This was a common practice among the religious houses, and Cistercians often provided this service to its patrons and key benefactors. For example, Roger de Mowbray mortgaged in 1172 a large piece of land in Nidderdale to Byland Abbey for three hundred marks. The agreement between them stated that if Roger failed to pay the monks were to keep the land. Among the loans from Fountains Abbey, Roger de Mowbray also received twenty-eight marks for his 'great necessity'.[79] Such actions, that is, lending money to benefactors, gave monastic houses an opportunity to foster mutually beneficial relations with these people and the possibility of more bargaining power in the future.

Walter Espec's influence prompted not only his relatives to become benefactors, but also members of his tenurial group. These people were close neighbours of the abbey and their day-to-day contacts with the new abbey might have been rather

[76] Burton, *Kirkham Priory*, p. 22.

[77] *Cartulary*, nos 76, 103; Burton, 'Estates and Economy', p. 67.

[78] 'Noveritis me dedisse et conciesse et hac presenti carta confirmasse abbati et conventui de Rievalle, pro quadam summa pecunie, quam recepit ab eisdem in necessitate mea, totum pratum meum in territorio de Siltona': Bodl. Dodsw. vii, fol. 152; published incomplete in the *Cartulary*, p. 234.

[79] *Charters of Mowbray*, nos 120, 54.

regular. A passage from *Life of Ailred* mentions a group of men from the neighbourhood who went to visit the abbey with Espec and Ailred.[80] Among them might have been Uctret son of Orm and Ralph son of Serlo, both men of Walter Espec, who in the mid-1150s quitclaimed their alleged rights to Griff and Tileston.[81] In return Ralph received a promise that if either he or one of his heirs wanted to become a monk, they would be admitted to Rievaulx.[82] It is likely that these men were holding Griff and Tileston from Walter Espec prior to the abbey foundation but had to give them up in 1132. Later they became close neighbours of the abbey and as such showed an interest in their lord's foundation. Unfortunately, we do not know if Ralph son of Serlo or any of his relatives entered Rievaulx Abbey, but if so, monks recruited from within the local community provided further strong links between the neighbourhood and the monastery.

Although Walter Espec did not have children, his relatives, particularly his nephews, had shown some interest in Rievaulx Abbey. Despite positive gestures from the relatives and tenants of Espec, his heirs in the Ros family did not become the kind of patrons he must have wished for his favourite foundation. Even so Rievaulx Abbey was not a passive object of laypeople's benefaction or abuse. It was actively responding to both positive and negative signals and actions from its patrons. The remaining part of this chapter traces the changing and often uneasy relations between the abbey and the Ros family in the twelfth and thirteenth centuries.

A fundamental change in the abbey's relationship with its patrons came with the death of its founder. Walter Espec died *c.* 1153, and because he did not leave a direct heir, his estates were divided between his sisters' sons. The Yorkshire estates were granted to Adelina's son Robert I de Ros and the Bedfordshire lands were divided in half between Hawise and Albreda.[83] The patronage of the monastic houses in Rievaulx and Kirkham was inherited by the Ros family together with the estates. Walter's childlessness has been noted by Abbot Ailred who, in his *Relatio de Standardo*, explained the foundations of Kirkham and Rievaulx as a result of both his piety and the lack of heirs, stating that Walter chose, for that reason, to leave his property to Christ.[84] This is a conventional explanation and may not be related to the personal motivation of Espec, who in fact left most of his lands to his nephews. However, a lack of a direct heir to continue his father's patronage over Rievaulx Abbey created considerable problems for the institution. There are strong indications that the abbey

[80] *Life of Ailred*, p. 14.

[81] *Cartulary*, nos 228, 227.

[82] 'si ipse vel aliquis suorum heredum vitam mutare voluerit, ab abbate et conventu loci illius suscipiatur': *Cartulary*, no. 227.

[83] Sanders, *English Baronies*, pp. 133–34.

[84] 'Erat praeterae nobilis carne, sed Christiana pietate longe nobilior. Nempe cum liberis careret haeredibus, licet ei nepotes strenui non deessent, de optimis tamen quibusque possessionibus suis Christum fecit haeredem': Ailred, 'Relatio de Standardo', p. 183.

looked for Walter Espec's replacement elsewhere, and this role was taken, at some point, by the Bishop of Durham; this will be discussed in the fifth chapter.

The new patrons of Rievaulx Abbey, the Ros family, originated from Holderness and, more precisely, from Roos village. The first recorded member of this family was Peter de Ros who was a steward of the Count of Aumâle at the beginning of the twelfth century. His son Everard inherited this rank, but in 1130 paid the King two marks to be freed from this obligation. By that time the Ros family was a leading tenant family in Holderness and remained connected to the Aumâle family.[85] Therefore, a considerable turn in the family fortune came as a result of the marriage of Peter de Ros to Adelina sister of Walter Espec. Peter de Ros and Adelina Espec had two sons.[86] The elder one, Everard, inherited family property in Holderness and had already become a benefactor of religious houses, albeit in a rather limited capacity. Between 1138 and 1140 he is known to have granted the church of Atwick to the Augustinian priory in Bridlington, for his own soul and that of his wife Eustachia.[87] Everard died shortly before or just after his uncle Walter, in or before 1153.[88] The main share of Walter's inheritance was therefore acquired by the younger brother, Robert I de Ros.

The changing fortunes of the abbey's relationship with its new patrons were also influenced by the careers of the heads of the Ros family, who advanced their status from tenants of the great lord to noblemen directly involved in the politics of the royal courts. Their estates were also significantly enlarged by marriages to wealthy heiresses. This could have been very beneficial for Rievaulx, but by the time the Ros family reached this status, ideas and expectations about religious patronage had changed, and the attitude of subsequent generations of the Ros family towards Rievaulx and Kirkham illustrates this process.

The first significant step in the rise of the family was made by Robert's son, Everard II de Ros. He married Roese Trussebut who was the eldest of three sisters and heirs to William Trussebut, Lord of Warter. This marriage gave Everard a substantial increase in his economic power. His son Robert II de Ros inherited Helmsley and other Yorkshire estates from his father and married Isabel, an illegitimate daughter of the Scottish King William the Lion thereby strengthening family links with Scotland. When Roese de Ros died in 1194 Robert II inherited from his mother her portion of the Trussebut fee as well as patronage of the Augustinian house at Warter, although the Templars were his favourite object of patronage and he even considered

[85] Barbara English, *The Lords of Holderness 1086–1260: A Study in Feudal Society* (Oxford: Oxford University Press, 1979), p. 151; Green, *Aristocracy*, p. 208.

[86] For a genealogical table of the Espec-Ros family, see Emilia Jamroziak, 'Rievaulx Abbey and its Patrons: Between Cooperation and Conflict', *Cîteaux: Commentarii Cistercienses,* 53 (2002), 51–71 (p. 59).

[87] *EYC*, III, no. 1330.

[88] *Peerage*, XI, 90.

going to Jerusalem himself.[89] Upon the death of Hilary Trussebut and her sister Agatha in 1241 and 1247 respectively, the whole of the Trussebut fee came into the possession of William de Ros of Helmsley, the son of Robert II.[90] In contrast to his father, who never fulfilled his plans for pilgrimage to Jerusalem, William went to Santiago di Compostela in 1252. He died in 1264 and was buried at Kirkham.[91] Robert III de Ros, his son and heir, married Isabel, daughter and heir of William d'Aubigny, who brought him Belvoir Castle in inheritance. Robert died in 1285 and was buried, like his father, in Kirkham Priory.[92]

The transition from one patron to another was often a difficult time for a monastery. Robert I de Ros was a nephew of the founder, and his attachment to the house established by his uncle was not necessarily as close as that of Walter's son might have been, especially one that would have grown up in the family seat at Helmsley and accompanied his father on visits to the abbey. There are not many indications of the interaction between Rievaulx Abbey and Robert I de Ros either during the life of his uncle or afterwards. He was patron for a relatively short time, probably less then ten years until his death in 1162/3, and may simply not have had enough time to develop an attachment to the monastic house founded by his uncle. Robert I de Ros appeared as a witness in charters of other Yorkshire benefactors to abbeys and priories, but this may indicate more his social position and affinities to the leading families in the area than an interest in pious donations to any particular house.[93] Initially the first of the patrons from the Ros family restricted his contacts with the abbey to the confirmation of his uncle's grants.[94] The second of his confirmations, issued between January 1151 and 14 October 1153, conveys the particular solemnity of his promises. During the ceremony, in the presence of Archbishop Henry of York, Espec's charter was read, and Robert took an oath to protect the abbey and made a pledge to the Archbishop:

> Moreover he [Robert] promised to that house and to the brothers all support, and first he strengthened all these things by an oath, and then he gave his oath as a Christian [and] himself as a hostage into my hand [the Archbishop's], and made me a pledge in all these matters.[95]

---

[89] *EYC*, X, 13.

[90] *EYC*, X, 25.

[91] Burton, *Kirkham Priory*, p. 23.

[92] *Peerage*, XI, 93–96; Burton, *Kirkham Priory*, p. 23.

[93] Robert witnessed a grant to Meaux Abbey by William, Earl of Aumâle, *c.* 1150 (*EYC*, III, no. 1380) and a confirmation grant by William de Vescy to Watton Priory *c.* 1150–57 (*EYC*, III, no. 1884).

[94] *Cartulary*, no. 43; Historical Manuscripts Commission, *Manuscripts at Belvoir Castle*, IV, 75.

[95] 'Insuper promisit domui illi et fratribus omnem manutenentiam; et primum hec omnia sacramento firmavit, deinde Christianitatem in manu mea qua se obsidem dedit, et me plegium constituit de his omnibus': *Cartulary*, no. 219; dated by Burton in *EEA*, V, 99.

Although this statement does reveal more than conventional reaffirmation of the patron's responsibilities, the final clause states that any trespass on the abbey's rights by the patron will be prosecuted by the Church authority. Such provision does not indicate any great personal connection between Rievaulx Abbey and Robert I de Ros, but rather a cautious approach by the monks who wanted to minimize possible damage, rather than to develop close cooperation with the patron. The Archbishop appears here as a go-between of the layman and the monastery, who could intervene if things went wrong between them. Later, between 1158 and 1163, Robert quitclaimed all the rights he might have had to the parts of the waste below Pickering with the assent of his wife and children, as well as brothers Peter and William, who were his tenants in 'Theokmarais', and Robert Luvel, his tenant in 'Loftmarish'.[96]

The importance of tenurial and family connections was particularly crucial if the patrons themselves did not show much interest in their religious houses. Robert I de Ros never showed much generosity toward Rievaulx Abbey but some of his connections, chiefly those established by the marriage of his daughter Joan to Stephen II de Meinil, brought new benefactors to the abbey. Stephen II de Meinil, grandson of Stephen I de Meinil who witnessed the 'foundation charter' of Rievaulx Abbey, granted to Rievaulx between 1175 and 1189 forest in Greenhowe (east of Great Broughton) and a right of way through his property towards Bilsdale which was west of the said forest, for the soul of his wife Joan, his own, and those of his parents and ancestors.[97] This pattern of establishing new connections between the abbey and potential benefactors by means of marriage was present among the abbey's benefactors on many levels and helped the abbey to attract new donations throughout the twelfth century.

The next generation of the Ros family brought some changes to their relationship with Rievaulx. Robert's son and heir, Everard II, interacted much more with the abbey than his father had, although he acted as the abbey's patron for not much longer than Robert. He confirmed his great-uncle's and father's grant to the abbey, probably soon after he took his inheritance.[98] Later he donated an additional grant in Helmsley consisting of wood on the west side of the vill and a common pasture in the wood of Pockley vill.[99] This grant was significant for the abbey, and Rievaulx acquired a specific royal confirmation for it.[100] Besides this donation, Everard made an affidavit to the charter of one of his tenants, William Ingram, which indicates his active participation in local politics, as much as his interest in the prosperity and security of Rievaulx property. His steward, William, also witnessed two charters for the abbey.[101]

[96] *Cartulary*, no. 180.

[97] *Cartulary*, no. 164; *EYC*, II, no. 799.

[98] *Cartulary*, no. 45.

[99] *Cartulary*, no. 44.

[100] *Cartulary*, no. 211.

[101] *Cartulary*, nos 59, 144; *EYC*, IV, no. 95.

Despite these positive gestures, there are strong indications that Everard II was trying to reclaim some of the abbey's properties in the late 1160s or early 1170s. He was not alone in his actions, as several prominent noblemen tried to do the same. They were all benefactors or relatives of the benefactors of the abbey. Their actions must have been considered a serious threat to the abbey as the monks turned to Pope Alexander III for help. The Pope sent a mandate to the Bishop of Exeter, the Abbot of St Mary's York, and the Dean of York to investigate the matter and restore the properties unjustly occupied.[102] At this time the main aggressors were Robert de Stuteville and William, his son, who encroached on Rievaulx property in the vills of Hoveton (forest and newly cultivated land) and Middlehead (forest and land). Other men, Roger de Mowbray and his son Nigel, Alan de Bowforth, Robert de Vado and his brother Ralph, Everard de Ros, and Robert son of Ernisius, were also accused by the Pope of encroachments on the abbey's lands. These conflicts were, to a large extent, related to the changes in possession and royal actions, which originally had nothing to do with the religious houses. William and Robert de Stuteville had a long-standing dispute with Roger de Mowbray about the lands of the Stuteville family, which had been given to the Mowbrays by King Henry I after the battle of Tinchebrai (1106). By the time the Stuteville family returned to the royal favour, some of their lands had already been alienated by the Mowbrays to many religious houses, including Rievaulx.[103] This inadvertently caused problems to Rievaulx who had its rights to particular properties questioned by the Stutevilles who did not want to part with the lands they considered to be theirs. Although the papal mandate does not specify on this occasion which lands were encroached on by Everard de Ros, it is possible that he tried to regain some properties given by his ancestors to Rievaulx Abbey or to invade the land located conveniently close to his own property, for example the forest of Helmsley, which featured prominently in later disputes.

Following the earlier example of his father, Robert II de Ros confirmed before 1198 the grants of his great-grand uncle Walter, grandfather Robert I, and father Everard II to Rievaulx Abbey.[104] In contrast to his father, Robert II was less aggressive towards the abbey, although not overly generous either. Two grants by Robert II to the abbey were not particularly substantial. One of them consisted of the property previously held by Simon de Hale in Lebberston (one carucate with eight tofts) and Cayton (four bovates), along with two parts of the mill in Cayton. He also rendered a service payment for Lebberston of twelve shillings and five pence and added a pittance to be distributed yearly in the abbey on All Saints Day.[105] Robert's second grant consisted of one silver mark which Robert had been receiving yearly as a service payment from Bilsdale, but now surrendered and added to the monetary grant which the

---

[102] *Cartulary*, no. 262; *EYC*, IX, no. 132; *PU*, I, no. 191,

[103] Burton, 'Estates and Economy', pp. 44–45.

[104] *Cartulary*, no. 46.

[105] *Cartulary*, no. 47.

abbey received yearly on All Saints Day.[106] As a part of his patron's duties Robert II also witnessed, with his sons William and Robert, the confirmation of an important grant of Crosby and Cowton by Bishop Richard March of Durham on 1 July 1217, which was given by his predecessors, Bishops William and Hugh of Durham.[107]

Despite these gestures, Robert's main gifts went elsewhere. It is likely that his crusading intentions prompted his generosity to the Knights Templar, and he seems to have been reluctant to give any more land to Rievaulx Abbey. Between 1206 and 1212 Robert II granted the vill of Hunsingore to the Templars for the salvation of his own soul and that of his wife Isabel.[108] Shortly before his death another grant was given to the Templars, comprising the manor of Great Ribston, the advowson of the church there, and the hamlet of Wilshford in exchange for Robert's burial in the Templars' church.[109] It appears that the Cistercian abbey of Rievaulx did not appeal to Robert's pious taste as he became a Templar in old age and was buried in their London church.[110]

Upon the death of Robert II in 1227 and taking his inheritance, William confirmed his father's monetary grant received yearly by the monks on All Saints Day.[111] More importantly, in 1228 William with his brother Robert quitclaimed a debt, of unknown size, which was due in the name of their father from the abbey of Rievaulx. They received a considerable compensation of 250 marks for their quitclaim.[112] This loan was almost certainly taken by the abbey for the financial support of the building programme carried out during the abbacy of Roger II (1225–35) when the monastic church was rebuilt in the Gothic style and extensive works were carried out on the monastic choir, presbytery, and the new eastern chapel.[113] This information indicates that the relationship of the abbey with the patrons was not limited to sporadic confirmation charters, but also had a practical dimension. It appears that, although he gave little further land, Robert II de Ros supported the abbey on a practical level by lending money and that his sons were prepared to make a compromise beneficial to both sides; the abbey did not have to give back the whole sum, and William and Robert received some financial compensation.

Despite this initial goodwill gesture by William de Ros, his subsequent relationship with Rievaulx Abbey was very turbulent. He was also involved in some dis-

[106] *Cartulary*, no. 48.

[107] Bodl. Dodsw. vii, fol. 136; published incomplete in *Cartulary*, pp. 222–23.

[108] *EYC*, X, no. 13.

[109] *EYC*, X, no. 14.

[110] *DNB*, XLIX, 218.

[111] Bodl. Dodsw. vii, fol. 188; published incomplete in *Cartulary*, p. 240.

[112] *Excerpta e rotulis finium in turri londonensi asservatis Henrico regis A.D. 1216–1272*, vol. I, ed. by Charles Roberts, Record Commission (London: G. Eyre, 1835), p. 169.

[113] Fergusson, Harrison, and Coppack, *Rievaulx Abbey*, p. 172.

agreements with Kirkham Priory over the use of the forest of Helmsley in the 1250s and 1260s.[114] The new patron became one of Rievaulx's most persistent 'difficult neighbours', and this part of the relationship between the abbey and William will be discussed in chapter 3.

Regardless of this temporary upheaval in the mid-thirteenth century though, it is quite clear that Kirkham Priory was the family monastery, with several burials in the church as well as the Ros arms on the gatehouse.[115] And like many other Augustinian houses, Kirkham was closely dependant on its patrons. The Ros family as the heirs of Walter Espec had chosen the Augustinian priory in Kirkham rather than Rievaulx as their favourite object of patronage. This much smaller and less famous house was preferred not only because the patrons had more power over the canons than over the Cistercian monks, but also because Kirkham Priory had agreed to a display of the status and position of the family in the decoration of the priory's gatehouse and lavish burials, which Rievaulx, as a Cistercian house, was far more reluctant to follow. Robert III de Ros, son of the quarrelsome William, who was himself buried in front of the altar, was buried in a marble tomb in the south part of the priory's church. Several other patrons were also buried at Kirkham.[116] The late thirteenth-century gatehouse of the priory was decorated with the Ros coats of arms. The gatehouse, apart from its practical function of controlling entry and exit to the monastic precinct, also had a symbolic function. The portal was meant to impress passers-by and visitors and to convey an impression of the status and splendour of the house.[117] However, the coats of arms on the gatehouse say even more about the status of Kirkham Priory. They indicate that the patrons wanted to be closely associated with this religious institution, but also that the Ros family had considerable influence over the house. The absence of such manifestations at Rievaulx Abbey confirms the much cooler relationship between this house and its patrons, but also indicates that Cistercians did not want to be associated with the lay world in the way Augustinian canons did.[118] The white monks wanted to convey the image of a certain separation and independence from the lay world. Newman describes this image building as a conscious differentiation of the monks' social role from those of the lay aristocrat and secular clergy,

[114] Burton, *Kirkham Priory*, p. 23.

[115] Burton, *Monastic Order in Yorkshire*, p. 195.

[116] Burton, *Kirkham Priory*, p. 23.

[117] R. W. Morant, *The Monastic Gatehouse and Other Types of Portal of Medieval Religious Houses* (Lewes: Book Guild, 1995), pp. 12–13, 81.

[118] The gatehouse of Rievaulx Abbey has not been excavated, but the sixteenth-century Dissolution inventory describes it as a substantial building, two storeys high. Glyn Coppack, 'Some Descriptions of Rievaulx Abbey in 1538–39: The Disposition of a Major Cistercian Precinct in the Early Sixteenth Century', *Journal of British Archaeological Association*, 139 (1986), 100–33.

but not a rejection of social involvement as such.[119] The use of physical space mirrors the image presented in the cartulary of Rievaulx which carefully delineates both worlds. The monks wanted to know about the lay world that surrounded them, but interacted with it only selectively. As for the Ros family, while the patronage of a great Cistercian house could give public prestige, at the same time the size and importance of the abbey might have been a deterrent for the patrons, particularly those who inherited patronage rights from more distant relatives, as in the case of the Ros family. The steady social advancement of this family throughout the late twelfth and thirteenth centuries, due to very advantageous marriages and inheritances, needed its reaffirmation in visual manifestation such as the gatehouse in Kirkham Priory, something that we can suggest that Rievaulx did not want to provide.[120]

The provision of burials in the monastic church and sometimes even in the chapter houses was a common expectation of patrons and significant benefactors.[121] Being buried in a holy place was not only an issue of commemoration and prestige, but also a matter of the increased chances for salvation. Although Walter Espec is said to be buried at Rievaulx, the first member of the patron's family certainly buried in the church was Isabel d'Aubeney, wife of Robert III de Ros, who died in 1264. Her grave was located in the galilee porch, in the western part of the church, which was considered to be a more 'secular' space than the liturgical east end, and thus permissible for lay burials.[122] This rather humble location was not satisfactory for later generations, who wanted more prominent locations for their graves. Thomas de Ros (d. 1384) as well as John de Ros (d. 1393) and his wife, Maria, were buried at Rievaulx, in front of the high altar and to the south of it, respectively.[123] While the location of lay burials was a controversial issue within the Cistercian order, those graves were also an indication of the dynamics of lay-religious relationships (see chapter 5). As Brian Golding has shown, the choice of family burial was intended to express the stability and permanence of the attachments.[124] In the light of this assertion, the change of locations of family burials from Kirkham Priory to Rievaulx Abbey in the fourteenth century indicates a new phase in the relationship between

---

[119] Newman, *Boundaries of Charity*, p. 2.

[120] For information about the possible appearance of the Rievaulx gatehouse, see Peter Fergusson, '"Porta Patens Esto": Notes on Early Cistercian Gatehouses in the North of England', in *Medieval Architecture and its Intellectual Context: Studies in Honour of Peter Kidson*, ed. by Eric Fernie and Paul Crossley (London: Hambledon Press, 1990), pp. 47–59 (pp. 51–52, 58).

[121] See chapter 6 for further discussion.

[122] Megan Cassidy-Welch, *Monastic Spaces and their Meanings: Thirteenth-Century English Cistercian Monasteries*, Medieval Church Studies, 1 (Turnhout: Brepols, 2001), pp. 233–34.

[123] Fergusson, Harrison, and Coppack, *Rievaulx Abbey*, p. 242 n. 5 and pp. 250–51 n. 28.

[124] Brian Golding, 'Burials and Benefactors: An Aspect of Monastic Patronage in Thirteenth-Century England', in *Symposium on England in the Thirteenth Century: Harlaxton Conference Proceedings*, ed. by Mark Ormrod (Harlaxton: Harlaxton College, 1995), pp. 64–75 (p. 74).

the Ros family and Rievaulx Abbey. The old loyalty to Kirkham Priory was weakened, and the prestigious monastic church of Rievaulx Abbey became the burial place for the Ros family. By the late fourteenth century the family's position was assured and the splendour of the Cistercian church became a more appropriate burial ground than a small Augustinian house. The late dating of the patrons' graves could also be a result of the early Cistercian prohibition on lay burials within the monastic church.[125] However, in numerous cases particularly prominent benefactors were allowed to be buried in their favourite monasteries, and the prohibitions of the Chapter General were broken by many Yorkshire houses including Fountains, Sallay, and Kirkstall.[126] In comparison with other Cistercian houses in the region, Rievaulx Abbey was rather resistant to pressure by laypeople for burials within the monastic church; by the thirteenth century smaller houses, for example Sallay and Meaux, were much more accommodating to the wishes of their benefactors.[127] This great variety of relationships between Cistercian houses and their patrons indicates not only the difference in the socio-economic position of these houses, but also the highly personal, and therefore difficult to regulate, character and expression of these contacts. I will return to the issue of burials in the final chapter.

Although the Ros family never displayed much generosity towards the abbey, they did perform one of the duties of the patrons and kept reconfirming over several generations what was already given. In none of the confirmation charters, however, appears the phrase 'my monk' which, on one hand, signifies a proprietary attitude in patrons but, on the other, indicates warm and personal connections. Examples of such manifestations of close connections between patrons and their monasteries in Yorkshire come from both Cistercian (Kirkstall) and Augustinian (Bridlington, Newburgh, Malton) houses.[128] This may indicate that it was not the character of the order as such which hampered the possibility of close connections between the patrons and the monastic convent, but rather particular circumstances and personal choice in the case of Rievaulx and the Ros family. The absence of any closer relationship between Rievaulx and the Ros family manifested itself in the lack of commemoration in some form, particularly writing, of the patrons. Often Cistercian monastic cartularies incorporated histories or genealogies of the patron's family, and monastic houses were often 'repositories of family tradition'.[129] At Rievaulx, this business-like approach to the issue of patrons, the lack of sentimentality or even commemorative attempts, appears to reflect their distant relationship. Although there is a genealogy of the Ros

[125] *Twelfth-Century Statutes from the Cistercian General Chapter*, ed. by Chrysogonus Waddell, Studia et Documenta, 12 (Brecht: Cîteaux-Commentarii Cistercienses, 2002), 1180/86, pp. 542–43; 1157/79: 63, p. 606.

[126] Burton, *Monastic Order in Yorkshire*, p. 209.

[127] Cassidy-Welch, *Monastic Spaces*, p. 236.

[128] Burton, *Monastic Order in Yorkshire*, p. 199.

[129] Wood, *English Monasteries*, p. 124.

family attributed to a monastic writer, it is more likely to originate from Kirkham than from Rievaulx.[130]

While the relationship between the heirs of Walter Espec and the abbey was difficult, Espec's inheritance brought several tenurial links to the Ros family, which provided Rievaulx Abbey with a strong group of benefactors. Some of them kept the links with Rievaulx for several generations either as donors or simply as neighbours. Among these families were the Surdevals, Sproxtons, Haromes, and Ingrams who were witnesses to the foundation ceremony in 1132 and to further grants by the founder between 1145 and 1153. The patterns of their interactions with Rievaulx Abbey over the course of the twelfth and thirteenth centuries shows a mixture of pious donations and rather undignified squabbles, but also reveals the mechanisms of creating and sustaining these connections in close vicinity.

The Surdeval family were relatively local as tenants of the Ros family and became one of the closest neighbours of the abbey. Their grants were not particularly substantial, but they frequently acted as witnesses to the grants of other benefactors as a way of expressing their affinity to this monastic house.[131] They continued to live in the vicinity of the core estates of the abbey, and some members donated further properties to the abbey, including Robert de Surdeval's substantial grant, in the late twelfth century, of the whole of the vill of Newton, a pasture for three hundred sheep, and a free passage to the abbey's sheepfolds of Skiplam.[132] By the mid-thirteenth century there are also indications of the typical neighbourhood-type of disputes between the abbey and the Surdevals; for example, in 1259 John de Surdeval was sued by the Abbot for trespasses on Rievaulx property.[133]

The association of the Sproxton and Harome families with both Walter Espec and the Ros family illustrates again the complexity of association between laypeople and the abbey which was related to the tenurial connections. Members of the Harome family witnessed numerous charters for the abbey in the twelfth century, but they did not become substantial benefactors of the abbey.[134] Instead, their pious gifts went to Kirkham Priory, the favourite house of their lord, where Drew de Harome received

---

[130] William Dugdale, *Monasticon Anglicanum*, rev. by J. Caley, H. Ellis, and B. Bandinel, vol. V (London, 1846), p. 280.

[131] Charters witnessed by the members of the Surdeval family: *Cartulary*, nos 43, 45, 88, 120, 123, 127, 129, 130, 132, 133, 152, 153, 162, 163, 180, 182, 191, 239.

[132] *EYC*, IX, no. 141.

[133] *Yorkshire Assize Rolls, for the Reign of King John and King Henry III*, ed. by C. T. Clay, Yorkshire Archaeological Society Record Series, 44 (Leeds: Yorkshire Archaeological Society, 1911), p. 134.

[134] *Cartulary*, nos 43, 45, 73, 76, 104, 132, 134, 140, 152, 153, 162, 182, 187. Donations of the Harome family to the abbey: Bodl. Dodsw. vii, fols 96^{v}, 153^{v}; published incomplete in *Cartulary*, pp. 519, 236.

the right to have a chantry chapel.[135] Similarly, despite their close affinity with the Augustinian house, the Sproxton family continued to witness charters for Rievaulx Abbey throughout the twelfth century.[136] But in the thirteenth century members of this family became rather difficult neighbours. In 1226 Richard de Sproxton had a lawsuit with the abbey concerning his alleged rights to the Griff forest, and his relative Robert de Sproxton was sued by the Abbot in 1233 for obstructing the passage for the abbey's cattle to the common pasture in West Newton.[137] This rather mixed range of contacts between this family and Rievaulx Abbey was a typical experience for the close neighbours of monastic houses. On the one hand, these people were often the core group who witnessed monastic donation charters on a regular basis, sometimes becoming benefactors themselves, but on the other hand, the reality of sharing the same common pastures or forest generated many conflicts.

The Ingrams were a family who had an early connection with the patron family but later became donors to the abbey in their own right. Like other tenants of Walter Espec and the Ros family they witnessed charters for the abbey, but many fewer than the Surdevals or Sproxtons. However, in contrast to those two families they were also more generous.[138] Walter Ingram, a son of John, one of Walter Espec's men, not only confirmed a donation by his mother granting her demesne vill of Heslerton (between 1160 and 1170), but also gave to the abbey thirty acres of common pasture for one thousand sheep in East Heslerton.[139] In the same time span Walter together with his wife Holdierda gave five bovates in Welbury near Northallerton in the parish of East Harlsey (Holdierda was the heiress of Welbury) which were held previously by his tenant John Tort, as well as a meadow in Arncliff and pasture for five hundred sheep, ten cows, and a bull. Walter also acknowledged in his charter that the monks gave him, in return, fifteen marks, a golden ring for his wife, and two shillings for their sons.[140] This grant placed him among the most valued benefactors of the abbey, but later generations of the Ingram family were much more cautious in alienating their property. William, the son of Walter and Holdierda Ingram, confirmed his parents'

[135] Burton, *Kirkham Priory*, p. 14; Oxford, Bodleian Library, MS Fairfax 7, fol. 67.

[136] Burton, *Kirkham Priory*, p. 14. *Cartulary*, nos 59, 104, 105, 127, 128, 129, 132, 153, 162, 163, 182, 184, 186.

[137] *Feet of Fine for the County of York from 1218 to 1231*, ed. by John Parker, Yorkshire Archaeological Society Record Series, 62 (Leeds: Yorkshire Archaeological Society, 1921), p. 82; *PR 1225–1232*, p. 222; *CRR*, XV, 25–26; *CRR*, XVI, 66–67; *Feet of Fines for the County of York from 1232 to 1246*, ed. by John Parker, Yorkshire Archaeological Society Record Series, 67 (Leeds: Yorkshire Archaeological Society, 1925), pp. 105–06.

[138] *Cartulary*, nos 90, 118, 123, 164.

[139] *Cartulary*, no. 85, *EYC*, II, no. 713.

[140] *Cartulary*, no. 90; *EYC*, II, no. 710.

donations and those of his tenants, but his son Robert Ingram tried, in the 1230s, to reclaim his grandfather's donation to the abbey in East Heslerton.[141]

It is clear that Walter Espec's men, who were close neighbours of the abbey, formed recurring groups of witnesses on the abbey's charters. Although their relationship with the house originated from tenurial links with Walter Espec, it was developed and sustained by the physical proximity of their own lands and the abbey's estates. Espec's men such as Robert de Sproxton, John Ingram, and Drew de Harome witnessed the foundation charter of Rievaulx Abbey. From then on, the relationship between these families and the abbey continued to develop. Many families displayed varying degrees of generosity, which indicates not only the amount of land that could be disposed of, but also the levels of their attachment to Rievaulx Abbey. The pasture grants of the Ingram family exemplify a strong affinity to this Cistercian house. Some individuals acted very much in accordance to their tenurial connections; for example, Drew de Harome witnessed charters to Rievaulx Abbey and granted land to Kirkham. By the middle of the next century, however, these families showed the same tendency to dispute predecessors' grants as did many other benefactors, whilst being a neighbour was likely to aggravate this situation. Being the neighbour of Rievaulx Abbey was not always an easy role, and many neighbours felt a considerable economic pressure from the abbey. Its estates dwarfed the properties of its immediate lay neighbours. In addition, many of the thirteenth-century disputes between the abbey and its neighbours were a result of laypeople's desire to reclaim properties alienated by their ancestors, which they considered to be excessive and damaging to their economic interests.

The foundation of Rievaulx Abbey by Walter Espec exemplified the role of the 'new men' in the expansion of the Cistercian order and the interdependence between the needs and expectations of the order and the patron's desires for public display and conspicuous acknowledgment of their piety. Although Espec as a patron of the Cistercian houses had much less formal power over these institutions, his actions towards Kirkham Priory showed that he had very clear ideas about the role of the patron and did not hesitate to interfere in the life of the priory. His relationship with Rievaulx Abbey shows that this monastery was his favourite foundation located conveniently close to his residence, thus allowing for frequent visits. Moreover, Rievaulx very soon was able to play an important role in Walter Espec's political life, particularly in the early years of King Stephen's reign. The help which the founder offered to Rievaulx in the early years was reciprocated at the time of the battle of Standard.

The lack of direct heirs broke the close relationship which developed between the founder and Rievaulx Abbey. Although the majority of the patrons from the Ros

[141] Charters of William Ingram: *Cartulary*, no. 120; *EYC*, II, no. 716; *Cartulary*, no. 122; BL, Cotton Julius D. i, fol. 88^{v} [fol. 92^{v}]; published incomplete in *Cartulary*, no. 137. Robert Ingram's disputes with Rievaulx Abbey: *CRR*, XIV, 519; *CRR*, XV, 21, 219.

family did perform basic duties towards the house, neither Robert I, Everard II, nor Robert II showed any signs of personal interest or attachment to the abbey. The series of conflicts between Rievaulx and William de Ros in the mid-thirteenth century, to which I will come back in the third chapter, exemplified the changing expectations of noblemen and the changing socio-economic conditions in the area, particularly the increasing competition for forest resources.

The founder, his family, and their tenurial group played an important role in the formative years of the abbey, but they were, by no means, the only laypeople around Rievaulx. A number of prominent and more local noblemen became by the mid-twelfth century supportive benefactors of this house. Their relationships with Rievaulx will be analysed in the next chapter.

CHAPTER 2

Good Neighbours: Benefactors and Supporters

The lay benefactors and neighbours of the abbey were a large and diverse group of people consisting of families ranging from barons to the tenants of small plots. What was their experience of being a neighbour of the abbey? Why did they give donations to this house? What did these people expect from Rievaulx? To what extent did the fact that Rievaulx was a Cistercian house influence its relationships with these benefactors and neighbours? This chapter seeks to answer these questions by examining a variety of positive contacts between Rievaulx Abbey and its neighbours and benefactors. Such contacts will also be considered in chapter 6 which concentrates on the symbolic aspects of the lay-religious interactions, whilst this section explores the practical dimensions. The introduction outlined how modern historiography explains the reasons and motivations for grants to religious houses; this chapter explores this issue through the particular example of Rievaulx Abbey. The next chapter examines negative aspects, broken relationships and conflicts between Rievaulx and its neighbours and benefactors. In some respects, this distinction is artificial because often one family, or even one individual, could be a good neighbour at one point in time but a bad one at another. Reaffirmation and redefinition of the relationships between the abbey and its benefactors was a continuous process throughout the period analysed.

The reasons for contacts between the monastery and laypeople can be divided, somewhat artificially, into two groups. Firstly, there were interactions related to the spiritual mission of the abbey — Divine Service and prayer — that were rooted in the monastic character of this institution, exemplified by donations from laypeople given in exchange for spiritual benefits. Secondly, there were contacts related to the economic activities of the abbey, which resulted from Rievaulx Abbey's position as a large landowner, and therefore the monks and laypeople had to negotiate terms of landholding and their subsequent contacts as neighbours. Many grants of pasture to the abbey show the concern by donors to delineate precisely what was given and how the use of common pasture should be organized to prevent any possible disputes. Some such cases will be discussed in this chapter. These two groups of reasons were by no means separate, and people would have interacted and did interact with the abbey on both levels simultaneously. Being a neighbour increased the chances of donating land by following the example of relatives, lords, or other important people in the locality. Large monastic houses, and Rievaulx was undoubtedly one of them, influenced the social and economic landscape around them. Indeed it would have been difficult to ignore their presence. The Cistercians preferred to have land free from secular obligations, and this often led to complex negotiations between religious houses and their lay neighbours. Despite Cistercian regulations concerning grants in free alms, it was not often possible to secure them, and Cistercian monks routinely accepted land with 'feudal' obligations. The earliest examples of such donations to Rievaulx Abbey come from the 1150s, but some houses, for example Mortemer in Normandy, received land in tenure as early as 1146, ten years after its foundation.[1] But the majority of the grants recorded in Rievaulx's cartulary, similar to those made to Fountains Abbey, were made with a clause providing freedom from all services.[2] Out of the total of 133 charters of grants from laypeople entered into the cartulary, 105 contain this clause (79 per cent). Among the remaining charters which specify payments in respect of services, the majority do not actually indicate the type of service for which the abbey was liable to pay. The annual amount varied between as little as twelve pence up to two marks, the most common being the upper limit paid in biannual instalments.

Although by the early statute of the Chapter General, dated by Chrysogonus Waddell to 1147, the Cistercians rejected donations in the form of manors, rents, mills, churches, and tithes, that is, income from the work of others, they did not reject the basic economic assumption of Benedictine monasteries about the donation of land from laypeople in return for prayers.[3] Those 'spiritual services' were always assumed and not necessarily spelled out in donation charters. Like those of many other Cistercian houses, the cartulary of Rievaulx Abbey does not contain many direct requests for prayers. Among the 147 charters of grants copied into the Rievaulx cartulary, ninety-seven have the phrase *pro anima* (66 per cent), which indicated that these donations were made with the specific intention of gaining salvation, but explicit requests for prayers were rare. Some historians interpret the phrase *pro anima* to

---

[1] Philip F. Gallagher, 'Conditions of Land Tenure and their Religious Implications', in *Studies in Medieval Cistercian History*, vol. II, ed. by John R. Sommerfeldt (Kalamazoo: Cistercian Publications, 1976), pp. 106–22 (p. 113).

[2] Joan Wardrop, *Fountains Abbey and its Benefactors 1132–1300* (Kalamazoo: Cistercian Publications, 1987), p. 31.

[3] *Narrative and Legislative Texts from Early Cîteaux*, ed. and trans. by Chrysogonus Waddell, Studia et Documenta, 9 (Pontigny: Cîteaux-Commentarii Cistercienses, 1999), p. 460; Constance H. Berman, *The Cistercian Evolution: The Invention of a Religious Order in Twelfth-Century Europe* (Philadelphia: University of Pennsylvania Press, 2000), pp. 48–51.

imply prayers, even if only as the cumulative prayers for all the benefactors of the house.[4] This may be true, although the spiritual benefit of the grant came not only from the prayers of the monks, but more fundamentally from the grant itself, that is, donating property to the religious institution was a good work in itself.

The contacts resulting from the landowning status of the abbey were in a way a by-product of the spiritual services expected from and grants given to the house. With the enlargements of its estates Rievaulx came into contact with an ever-growing group of people who become its neighbours or, in most cases, neighbours of the monastic granges. The necessity of accumulating the amount of land which would support the community of monks was a natural requirement of the land-based economy, but very soon this necessity was transformed into the desire for growth and expansion. The pragmatic consideration for the sustenance of the community and the physical aspects of the abbey's existence, such as building maintenance, food provisions, and daily running costs, forced this house to act like any other landowner interested in maintaining a successful estate in order to support a large community and to finance costly building projects. It is therefore very easy to confuse rational (in the modern sense of the word) economic expectations and actions with irrational (also in the modern sense) religious ideology. As the grant to the monastery was in fact a grant to God, the abbey should be interested in the endless expansion of its properties as a part of their pious mission and a visible sign of the religiously endorsed prosperity; on the other hand, expansion was also motivated by purely economic reasons.[5]

Even more than in the case of the abbey's contact with patrons and their relatives and associates, Rievaulx faced, in its interactions with neighbours and benefactors, not only individuals, but predominantly families and pre-existing networks of tenants and their lords. As I argued in the previous chapter in connection with the founder, grants were rarely given in isolation from the family or tenurial context. Tenants customarily donated grants to monastic houses which were already benefiting from the generosity of their lords. Similarly marriages between families brought people into contact with monasteries which they had not previously supported. Therefore information about formal and informal connections between the people interacting with the abbey, both current and potential donors, was crucial for the effectiveness of the abbey's efforts to acquire further properties. This knowledge of the abbey's neighbourhood was preserved in the structure of the cartulary. This map-like form of the cartulary allows us to examine the abbey's perception of its neighbours, the relative importance of the particular individuals, and the significance of social networks in the locality for the development of the estates of Rievaulx Abbey.

---

[4] Wardrop, *Fountains Abbey*, p. 242.

[5] The same idea of a connection between economic and religious elements in monasticism is expressed in Jack Goody, *The European Family: An Historico-Anthropological Essay* (Oxford: Blackwell, 2000), p. 40.

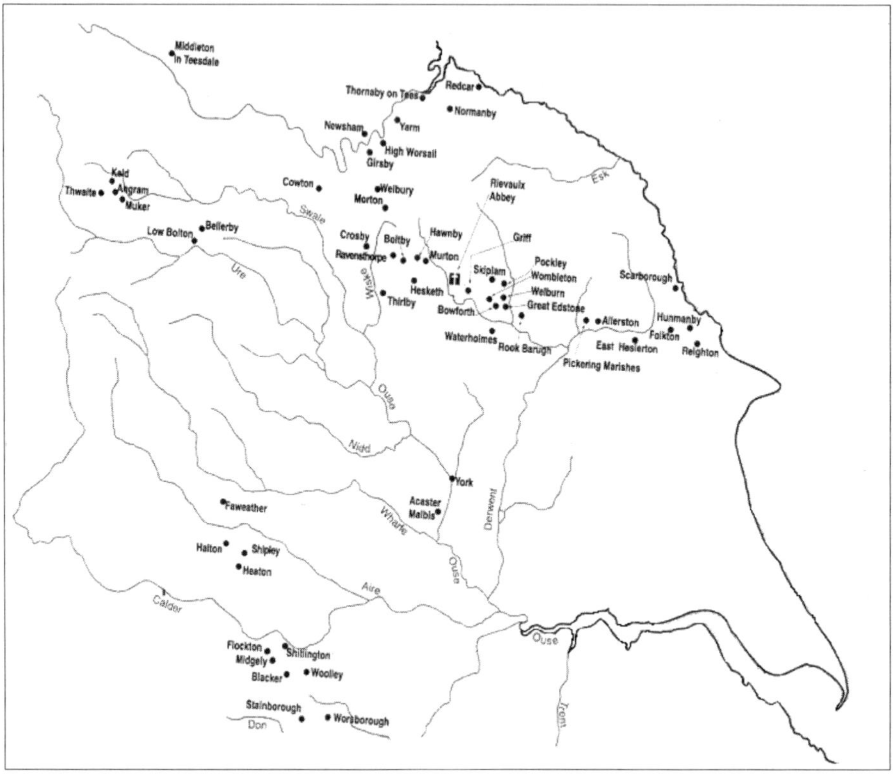

Map 1. The estates of Rievaulx Abbey. From Janet Burton, 'The Estates and Economy of Rievaulx Abbey in Yorkshire', *Cîteaux: Commentarii Cistercienses*, 49 (1998), 36 (reprinted with permission with minor alternations).

A grant of a property, regardless of its size, to a religious house was not an action confined, in time, to the actual transmission of property from the hands of one owner to another. In the great majority of cases, a grant created a continuum, that is, a relationship between the donor and the grantor which lasted for more than one generation.[6] On the religious level, for donors as well as founders, the spiritual benefits of the grants were intended to last for generations, both past and those to come. One of the most common formulae used in charters, 'for the salvation of my soul and all my ancestors and heirs', expresses this wish. The act of giving was therefore a bridge between generations, an act performed not between an individual and a monastery, but between kin as a community of relatives, dead, living, and not yet born, and the

[6] Arnoud-Jan A. Bijsterveld, 'The Medieval Gift as Agent of Social Bonding and Political Power: A Comparative Approach', in *Medieval Transformations: Text, Power, and Gifts in Context*, ed. by Esther Cohen and Mayke B. de Jong (Leiden: Brill, 2001), pp. 124–56 (pp. 144–48).

religious house. This concept of continuity was pertinent not only to the spiritual services offered by the abbey but also to the holding of the land given to the monastery, yet in practice this continuity was often questioned. Why and how the relationships with benefactors were broken will be examined further in the next chapter.

Repeated gestures of support by heirs were very much desired by the abbey, because in this way the security of the possession was maintained and consecutive generations of the benefactors reaffirmed their affinity to the monastery. There are two types of documents which expressed continuity of support for a grant given by a family member or other closely connected person in the past — confirmation and quitclaims — but they have different emphases. Confirmations were more common, but less secure than quitclaims because persons giving them merely approved of their predecessors' donations, while retaining the claim to the property. Quitclaim gave a complete transfer of all the rights to a given property, but were not necessarily created as a result of conflict.[7] Sometimes the wording of the charters gives some hints to the circumstances of the quitclaims, and often these acts were performed publicly with great solemnity. A third party, for example a lord of the person giving the quitclaim or a locally important ecclesiastical figure, could act as a recipient of the guarantees of the layperson. As we will see later, the charters of Rievaulx Abbey contain numerous records of such acts.

One of the most important characteristics of the twelfth-century social world which had a fundamental impact on the relationships between religious houses, Cistercian and other, and laypeople was the multitude of vertical and horizontal connections existing between individuals and across the social strata. While discussing formal and informal ties among the benefactors of Rievaulx Abbey, it is convenient to use the term 'affinity' introduced by David Crouch in the context of twelfth-century society. Many tenants held land from several lords but followed only one of them. This link to a particular lord was not necessarily motivated by ties of homage, but often common interest. Many of the lords' followers did not hold any substantial lands or offices, but nevertheless were counted as 'their men'. These informal links, which contributed to the power of barons, without being grounded in the legal framework of the honorial system, can be called affinity.[8] Although the honorial system was the most important manifestation of local power, other informal structures, such as locality and neighbourhood, played a crucial role in social organization.[9] The natural centres of such communities were great abbeys, large trading centres, and the comparatively more ephemeral powers of the great barons. Ultimately, in Crouch's interpretation, the social organization of twelfth- and thirteenth-century England was

---

[7] Raymond V. Lavoie, Jr, 'English Monasteries' Techniques for Avoiding Property Disputes, 1250–1380', *Comitatus*, 23 (1992), 46–63 (pp. 49–52).

[8] David Crouch, *The Reign of King Stephen, 1135–1154* (London: Harlow, 2000), p. 166.

[9] Peter Coss, *Lordship, Knighthood and Locality: A Study in English Society, c. 1180–1280* (Cambridge: Cambridge University Press, 1991), p. 8.

not based in reality on the geography of honours, counties, and fees; rather power in each region was sought by an individual who was dominant enough to control it and built around himself a network of followers and tenants.[10] This fluidity of power among the aristocracy of Anglo-Norman England had an impact on the religious houses supported by them. A sudden shift of power could, and often did, influence the material security of the abbey. The specific case of the shifting powers of the Mowbray and Stuteville families who were benefactors of Rievaulx Abbey will be discussed later in this and the next chapter.

Although the social structure of twelfth- and thirteenth-century Yorkshire was by no means fixed, it is possible to distinguish two broad groups among the benefactors of Rievaulx Abbey — noble members of the aristocracy and knights — who played important but different roles as benefactors and neighbours. The first part of this chapter is devoted to the analysis of the interactions between Rievaulx and members of the top social stratum. The second part is concerned with those knightly families who held land from the lords but who, as benefactors of Rievaulx Abbey, should be considered in their own right due to the scale and importance of their donations.

Aristocratic Families and Rievaulx Abbey

In comparison to Fountains Abbey, Rievaulx did not attract a large number of benefactors from the top ranks of the aristocracy, and only one family — the Mowbrays — gave substantial amounts of land. These people from the highest ranks of society were particularly significant in the formative years of the abbey. Aristocrats were important, not only because they could afford to be more generous than anybody else, but their powerful position could bring further benefits. The example of many of the aristocratic benefactors of Rievaulx Abbey shows that they encouraged their tenants to give grants to this house. On the other hand, such powerful individuals could put a lot of pressure on the monastery, alienate parts of its land, or cause other damages, and it was not easy for the abbey to find locally sufficiently strong protection to counterbalance the power of the aristocrats, so that by the end of the twelfth century the monks had to seek papal protection against them.

In the middle of the twelfth century, after the upheaval of the postconquest period, the political and social make-up of Yorkshire stabilized and several leading families who held large honours from the king established their own networks of knightly tenants, members of their retinue, and honorial officials. Among these families were the Mowbrays, Stutevilles, Gants, Lacys, Bruses, and Aumâles. Some of them became benefactors of Rievaulx and played a significant role in the history of this

[10] David Crouch, 'From Stenton to McFarlane: Models of Societies of the Twelfth and Thirteenth Centuries', *Transactions of the Royal Historical Society*, 6th series, 5 (1995), 179–200 (p. 194).

institution, while those who for various reasons did not have any interest in Rievaulx Abbey were patrons and benefactors of many other religious houses, some of which became Rievaulx Abbey's competitors.

It was not only political power that mattered: the physical location of a religious house in relation to the lands of local barons also had a fundamental impact on the range and volume of grants. One of the smaller Cistercian abbeys in Yorkshire, Jervaulx (formerly a Savigniac house), was located within the lands of the Earls of Richmond and never managed to obtain substantial donations from other lords apart from the earls and Roger de Mowbray. Similarly the benefactors of Sallay Abbey were restricted almost exclusively to the Percy fee.[11] In that sense diversity of neighbours was very desirable, because it could potentially bring further grants and prevent the monastery from being dependant on one family or one tenurial group.

The most important benefactors of aristocratic status to Rievaulx Abbey were, without doubt, the Mowbray family who donated large amounts of land in the early stages of Rievaulx's development. They also encouraged and influenced their numerous tenants to give land. The generosity displayed by the Mowbrays was particularly valuable for Rievaulx Abbey which lacked supportive patrons after the death of Walter Espec. For many generations the Mowbray family played a very considerable role in Yorkshire's social and religious development. They supported numerous monastic institutions over several generations and the pattern of their actions well illustrates how patronage developed and changed in the course of the twelfth and thirteenth centuries. The rise and fall of the Mowbrays' fortune and the individual careers of family members had a significant impact on their attitude towards religious houses. Monasteries were aware of these implications and had to respond to the changing status of their benefactors. A closer look at the careers of the Mowbrays and their enemies the Stutevilles illustrates the opportunities and problems for Rievaulx Abbey which association with these people brought.

The family fortune of the Mowbrays was established by Nigel d'Aubigny. Although Nigel was only the younger son of Roger d'Aubigny, himself a small Norman landowner, with no rights to the family inheritance, he became a frequent member of the royal court, alongside Walter Espec, and was one of the most prominent and rewarded among the new men of Henry I. As a loyal supporter of Henry I, he was granted some of the extensive lands of Robert de Stuteville, a supporter of Robert Curthose, after the battle of Tinchebrai in 1106 and after 1114. Nigel's continued service to the King was also rewarded by the additional grant of the Norman lands of Robert de Mowbray, Earl of Northumberland, through his marriage to Robert's divorced wife Maud. He assumed the name of Mowbray after the Montbrai estate and subsequently received six lordships in the North. Later he divorced his wife, claiming that they were too closely related, but kept the lands; in 1118 he

[11] Janet E. Burton, *The Monastic Order in Yorkshire, 1069–1215* (Cambridge: Cambridge University Press, 1999), pp. 120, 124.

married Gundreda de Gournay who outlived him.[12] From about the time of his second marriage Nigel was a justiciar for Yorkshire and Northumberland, but he also remained a member of the royal court. His son and heir, Roger de Mowbray, was still a child at the time of his father's death in 1129. The large estates which Roger inherited were spread over Yorkshire, Lincolnshire, and the Midlands. In 1166 these estates consisted of sixty fees. He acquired an additional twenty-eight fees, and his son added a further eleven and three-quarters.[13] An estate of nearly one hundred fees put them amongst the wealthiest families in England. The young Roger participated in the battle of Standard in 1138, alongside Walter Espec, on the side of the barons loyal to the English King Stephen.[14] He did not join other northern barons, such as Eustace FitzJohn, who took the side of King David, and remained Stephen's supporter and a frequent member of his court. The Mowbrays were one of the most influential families not only in Yorkshire, but also in the whole country, and their political ambitions were national, not local. However, the economic basis of their power was located primarily in the North and any shift in their economic and political power was likely to affect monasteries located there.

The source of inspiration for Roger's grants to the various monasteries was his mother, Gundreda, a prolific patron of monasteries throughout the North of England.[15] Mother and son together took care of the monks from Calder escaping from the Scots in 1138 and granted them land in Old Byland. In 1147 Roger refounded this monastery on a new site. In 1145 he founded the Augustinian Priory at Newburgh, although it was first set up at Hood three years earlier.[16] Rievaulx Abbey was another prominent recipient of his grants together with a further twenty-one monastic houses, Bridlington, Burton Lazars, Combe, Fountains, Furness, Saint Andre-en-Gouffern (arr. Caen), Hirst, Jervaulx, Malton, Newburgh, Nostell, North Ormsby, Pipewell, Selby, Welford, Whitby, Vaudey, Villers-Canivet (arr. Caen), St Leonard's York, St Mary's York, and St Peter's York, and also the Hospitallers and Templars.[17] His generosity

[12] *Peerage*, IX, 367–69; *Charters of Mowbray*, pp. xviii, xxiv.

[13] Judith Green, *The Aristocracy of Norman England* (Cambridge: Cambridge University Press, 1997), p. 166.

[14] Ailred of Rievaulx, 'Relatio de Standardo', in *Chronicles of the Reigns of Stephen, Henry II and Richard I*, vol. III, ed. by Richard Howlett, Rolls Series, 82 (London: Longman, 1886), pp. 181–99 (pp. 184–85).

[15] Grants to Byland, Rievaulx, Whitby. *Charters of Mowbray*, nos 47, 155, 156, 160, 201, 232, 235, 236, 237, 300, 302.

[16] For an extensive discussion of the foundation of Byland Abbey, see Burton, *Monastic Order in Yorkshire*, pp. 110–12.

[17] *Charters of Mowbray*, nos 21–24, 26, 27, 77, 79, 84, 85, 95, 98, 102, 103, 105, 110, 114, 118, 119, 122, 125, 126, 128, 129, 130, 132, 134–40, 145, 150, 162, 163, 170, 172, 185–99, 202, 208, 210, 211, 215–17, 220, 223–26, 228, 251, 255–57, 270, 272–76, 278, 279, 280, 282, 283, 288, 289, 294, 296, 299, 306, 307, 313, 316–19, 322, 324–27.

to monastic houses was matched by his enthusiasm for the crusades. He took part in the Second Crusade of 1147, and upon his return he granted lands to the Templars in Balshall (Warwickshire), Axholme, and other places and founded a hospital for lepers in Burton Lazars (Leicestershire). This interest in crusading was typical for his time and social position. After all, Robert II de Ros, Rievaulx Abbey's patron, directed more pious gifts to the Knights Templars than to the Cistercian house.

An important turn in Roger's fortune, which directly influenced some possessions of the religious houses listed above, came after 1154 when eight of his fees were given by King Henry II to Robert III de Stuteville. The Stutevilles had become royal supporters, and the King rewarded them with a regrant of their ancestral lands.[18] This arbitrary act by the ruler endangered the possessions of several Yorkshire houses, including Rievaulx, which had received some of the Stutevilles' lands from the Mowbrays in donations. Roger's fortune changed even further after he and his two sons, Nigel and Robert, frustrated with the renewed political and material rise of the Stuteville family, joined young Henry against the King in 1173.[19] After the defeat of the rebels Roger surrendered in 1176 and was pardoned by the King, but had to give back even more of his lands to Robert de Stuteville. This was a significant setback for Roger and subsequently caused problems for the monastic houses in the area. Roger's life was marked by many religiously motivated acts, although towards the end of his life his interest shifted from the local monastic institutions to the Holy Land. In 1177 and again in 1186 he went on the crusade to Jerusalem, but was captured at the battle of Hattin on 4 July 1187.[20] Nigel, his elder son, who succeeded him, was already politically active during his father's life and confirmed many of his grants to religious houses. Nigel took over the family's Norman lands in 1172 and joined his father in the rebellion of 1173. He too was a crusader and died at Acre in 1191.[21]

The comparison between Roger and Nigel de Mowbray reveals how over two generations the pattern of the patrons' behaviour changed, under the influence of the changing fortunes of their political careers and new fashions. Roger was the founder and patron of Byland Abbey and Newburgh Priory and the generous benefactor of several other Yorkshire houses. Following a common pattern, his son Nigel mainly re-confirmed or restored his predecessors' grants.[22] William de Mowbray represented yet another generation of benefactors, who were even more reluctant than their fathers and grandfathers to alienate more land from the family inheritance. This shift in the form of the aristocratic donations has been summarized by Wardrop in the following way:

---

[18] Green, *Aristocracy*, p. 166.

[19] *Charters of Mowbray*, pp. xxix–xxx.

[20] *DNB*, XXXIX, 227–30; *Peerage*, IX, 269–72.

[21] *Peerage*, IX, 372–73.

[22] *Charters of Mowbray*, p. xli.

> Rather than continuing in his predecessor's footsteps and granting lands and rights to the house, he became to a certain extent its protector, confirming earlier grants and acting as a witness to other of the house's transactions at a time when the status of a witness and his potential for protecting a particular agreement was becoming ever more important, while yet being assiduous in the protection of his own rights.[23]

William, the son of Nigel, who succeeded his father to the Mowbray estates, continued to be politically active but remained under pressure from the Stutevilles' claims. His family fortune was seriously threatened when William de Stuteville (the great-grandson of Robert whose lands after Tinchebrai were given to Nigel d'Aubigny, great-grandfather of William de Mowbray) claimed his right to certain lands in 1200. According to the settlement reached by Mowbray and Stuteville, the latter received twelve liberates of land in Bricklow (Warwickshire) and the service of nine knights augmenting ten knightly fees which Robert de Stuteville had held from William.[24] Another loss for the family came in 1204 when the whole of Normandy was taken by the French king and the Mowbrays lost all their properties there, as William remained loyal to King John. Just like previous generations of the Mowbray family, William too was a benefactor of many monastic houses including Rievaulx. His charters were mainly confirmations of his predecessors' grants, but his main object of benefaction and pious interest was Fountains Abbey, where he was finally buried.[25] William died in March 1224, and the barony was inherited by his son Nigel de Mowbray; upon Nigel's death in October 1240 it passed to his brother Roger. Although William's sons continued to be active political figures, their interest in the patronage of monastic houses was now diminishing. Roger confirmed several of his father's charters to various monasteries, but did not give any additional land.

The actions of these subsequent generations of Mowbrays, their religious foundations and grants to numerous houses, as well as their participation in the crusades, indicate their strongly conventional piety. All these pursuits had a high visibility factor, which helped the Mowbrays to maintain signs of their social status, even if in reality their position was under considerable pressure. The spectacular generosity of Roger de Mowbray must also have been motivated by strong spiritual considerations which he owed to the influence of his mother, Gundreda. From this brief look at the political careers of the several generations of the Mowbray family, it can be seen that the scale and scope of their activities was far wider than Yorkshire. They were, indeed, far more important politically than Rievaulx's founder, Espec, and the heirs and descendents of Nigel d'Aubigny were active in the top stratum of the political élite. Although later generations of the Mowbrays were not generous, monastic foundations were a significant element in the political and social rise of the earlier generations of the family in the first half of the twelfth century. Their donations were important to them

---

[23] Wardrop, *Fountains Abbey*, p. 146.

[24] *EYC*, IX, 100.

[25] Wardrop, *Fountains Abbey*, pp. 151–52; *EYC*, IX, nos 99–104.

as one of the expressions of their social status, but to the monasteries their protection and patronage was not only important, but crucial for their continued successful existence. If the aristocratic benefactors lost power, or were in any way weaker than their rivals, this could seriously threaten monastic possession. In this particular case, the Mowbray-Stuteville conflict had a significant impact on Rievaulx Abbey which had to struggle to keep some of the lands belonging to the Mowbray fee.[26] Similarly, Fountains Abbey lost some of the Mowbrays' grants which were successfully claimed by William de Stuteville.[27] Sudden changes on the baronial level often had an impact on religious houses. Sometimes people who succeeded to particular lands by royal will continued the benefactions of their predecessors to whom they were not related. Hugh de Laval, who was granted the Lacy's honour of Pontefract in 1118 supported Pontefract and Nostell Priories, but his successor William Maltravers was openly hostile to these institutions.[28] The security of the grant might be challenged not only by the heir of the original benefactor but also, as in the case of Rievaulx Abbey, by somebody who was in a conflict with the donor or his heirs. The complexity of land-holding and the dominance of possession (actually holding the land) over ownership (having a legal right to it) meant that once the overlord changed, the position of the previously secure grant, and the monastery's possession, might be endangered. Once the Stutevilles received parts of their lands back from the Mowbrays they tried to reverse some of the donations to the ecclesiastical institutions given by the Mowbrays. Yet the religious houses were not completely powerless, and Rievaulx Abbey managed to defend its possessions against the Stutevilles, as I will explain later.

It is often asserted in the literature that the foundation of a monastery was 'a tried and tested method of consolidating power in the areas of territorial dispute or doubtful political allegiance'.[29] In Yorkshire, behind-the-scene control of monastic property by the patron or donor could have been more effective in times of serious crisis than direct possession. If the property given to the abbey was subsequently claimed by a third party, it was an attack on a religious institution, rather than a lay individual, with all the spiritual consequences. Often, as the case of Rievaulx Abbey suggests, the misfortune or loss of political influence by the protector would directly influence the security of the abbey holdings since many barons did not hesitate to

---

[26] See conflicts over Hoveton and Welburn below. *Cartulary*, no. 131; *EYC*, IX, no. 10.

[27] *EYC*, IX, nos 10, 126, 129, 132, 157, 158, 161; *Charters of Mowbray*, p. xxviii, n. 6; *Abstracts of the Charters and other Documents contained in the Chartulary of the Cistercian Abbey of Fountains*, ed. by W. T. Lancaster, vol. I (Leeds: J. Whitehead & Son, 1915), no. 215.

[28] W. E. Wightman, *The Lacy Family in England and Normandy 1066–1194* (Oxford: Oxford University Press, 1966), pp. 67–71.

[29] Paul Dalton, *Conquest, Anarchy and Lordship: Yorkshire, 1066–1154* (Cambridge: Cambridge University Press, 1994), p. 135; Janet E. Burton, 'The Foundation of the British Cistercian Houses', in *Cistercian Art and Architecture in the British Isles*, ed. by Christopher Norton and David Park (Cambridge: Cambridge University Press, 1986), pp. 24–39 (p. 35).

seize or at least encroach on monastic land. While the benefaction and protection of powerful patrons or benefactors were desired, the political fall of those patrons often brought a material loss to religious houses. However, monasteries had their own ways to fight back against greedy laymen.

A closer analysis of the Mowbray charters in the abbey's cartulary illustrates how important this family was for Rievaulx, not only as a source of donations but also as a supporter on other levels. The grants and confirmations of the three generations of the Mowbray family greatly outnumber those of the Ros family — the actual patrons of the abbey. The majority of Mowbray charters in the cartulary are grouped in the early, prominent part of the volume, in two clusters: from no. 55 to no. 71 (charters of Gundreda and Roger de Mowbray), close to the patrons' charters, and from no. 153 to no. 157 (charters of Roger and Nigel de Mowbray). The creators of the cartulary linked the Mowbrays' charters spatially with the charters of their tenants also copied in the cartulary.

The donations to Rievaulx Abbey were initiated by Gundreda, wife of Nigel d'Aubigny, in the crucial early stage of the abbey's development. She was a benefactor of many monastic houses, including Rievaulx's closest neighbour — Byland. The most active period of her independent religious patronage occurred after the death of her second husband and before her son Roger came to age. During her widowhood, between 1129 and 1138, Gundreda granted to Rievaulx a part of her demesne in Welburn in the western part of the Vale of Pickering, a common pasture and a meadow there called 'Gildelmsdale'.[30] A few years later, between 1144 and 1154, this grant was augmented by the donation of her demesne in Skiplam and the property of her and her son, being a part of their fee, between the vills of Welburn, Wombleton, and Fadmoor. She reserved her rights and those of her men of Welburn to the common pasture and the right to collect firewood and materials for building. Gundreda also added an important confirmation clause of any grant, sale, or exchange made by her men of Welburn to the abbey.[31] This indicates that she encouraged her tenants to give more land to the abbey, even if it meant a financial loss to herself. This act went further than the standard approach of the majority of the benefactors. Many lords would confirm grants by their tenants, but giving a blanket permission was an act of very positive encouragement. Gundreda's tenants could give plots of land to Rievaulx Abbey without her further permission in each individual case, thereby streamlining the process. Such clauses were significant for the further expansion of the abbey's property and could provide a large number of small but useful grants, which would round off the larger chunks of land given by her. Indeed, Gundreda's grant in Welburn was the beginning of grange development due to subsequent donations by her son Roger de Mowbray and his tenants.[32]

---

[30] *Cartulary*, no. 56.

[31] *Cartulary*, no. 55.

[32] *EYC*, IX, 231.

The importance of Gundreda to the monastic community has been preserved in a small but significant way. On the margin of fol. 34 [new fol. 38] in the cartulary the name Gundreda is written in red ink. No other individual benefactor has been singled out in that way. This little note could have been used as an aid to locating the copies of Gundreda's charters, but it could also have been a way of bringing her name to the attention of the future readers of the cartulary and ensuring her commemoration.

At the end of Gundreda's life in 1154 Roger confirmed her grants with the consent of his heirs, Nigel and Robert. It was a clear endorsement of her generosity to the abbey and a promise of the continuation of support.[33] In later years he became one of the most prolific benefactors of Rievaulx Abbey, and there are no fewer than seventeen of his charters copied in its cartulary. They spread over Welburn, 'Hoveton', Bowforth, Wombleton, the vicinity of Hesketh and Boltby, and the Farndale valley. They are not only simple grants of land but also confirmations of grants previously given by him, confirmations of other people's grants, conflict settlements, exchanges, and concessions.

The role of the aristocratic benefactors of the abbey was not restricted to simply giving large grants to the abbey, but took many other forms. The courts of great magnates were a form of 'clearing house' for all the legal affairs of their tenants including their dealings with the monastic houses. Great lords were also instrumental in securing undisputed possession of particular properties by religious houses. Sometimes this was a long and multistage process, as the story of 'Hoveton' vill illustrates. It began with a grant by Roger de Mowbray between 1163 and 1169. The charter copied in the cartulary illustrates the consecutive stages of this process. First, it contains confirmation of the grant of the vill of 'Hoveton', including four bovates of land in the said vill which Samson of Cornwall had held as a gift from Gundreda de Gournay. Roger bought this land from Samson and his wife for twenty marks. Then this transaction was legally confirmed by Ralph de Belvoir, a steward of Roger de Mowbray, and the couple solemnly promised that neither they nor their descendants would dispute ownership. After that they made a similar pledge in Roger's court, in the presence of Sheriff Ranulf de Glanville, and finally it was legally affirmed by the York chapter.[34] The aim of the ceremony at Roger's court was similar to a warranty clause and was probably initiated by the abbey, although there are similar contemporary examples of pledges in the private charters of laypeople.[35] The pledge in hand resembles much earlier practices of oath-helping, but it is not very clear how the donors chose a particular individual to receive their pledge, and it is also unknown if these people were also expected to oversee the fulfilment of the

---

[33] *Cartulary*, nos 57, 60; *EYC*, IX, no. 151.

[34] *Cartulary*, no. 67; *EYC*, IX, no. 126; between 1163 and 1169.

[35] David Postles, 'Pledge of Faith in Transactions in Land', *Journal of the Society of Archivists*, 7 (1982–85), 295–98.

pledge.[36] This ceremony was intended to put pressure on Samson and his wife to honour their promises. High-status witnesses and the ecclesiastical authority of the York chapter were used as an additional social pressure. It is left to speculation why Samson of Cornwall and his wife were asked formally to affirm their quitclaim so many times. Maybe the couple already enjoyed some notoriety when it came to disputes, or maybe Roger was just acting as the protective lord keen to ensure the strength of the abbey's rights to 'Hoveton'. A separate charter of quitclaim by Samson and his wife, Hestilde, to Rievaulx Abbey, issued by the Dean and chapter of York (between 1163 and 1169), for the same four bovates of land in 'Hoveton', indicates that they did indeed try to reclaim what they sold to Roger de Mowbray.[37] It is probably a further indication of insecurity of the abbey's possession that Nigel de Mowbray, Roger's son, specifically confirmed this charter, and the confirmation was copied in the cartulary just after his father's charter.[38]

A convincing explanation for this string of confirmations is offered by Marie Lovatt. 'Hoveton' might have been a part of the feoffment of ten knights' fees transferred from Roger de Mowbray to Robert III de Stuteville, discussed above.[39] The uncertainty of the possession rights incited Samson and his wife to claim their rights to parts of it, hoping that the lack of consensus over the lordship of this area would help them to retain some of the land in their own hand. Meanwhile, the abbey kept acquiring more land in 'Hoveton' to strengthen its own holdings in the area by the means of quasi-sales or, more accurately, compensation to these individuals who still claimed rights in the area and needed some material encouragement for their quitclaim.[40] By securing quitclaims and offering compensations, Rievaulx was able to acquire desirable properties, which would not be given otherwise, and could also reduce possible antagonisms in the future.

Despite the multitude of documents issued in order to secure the abbey's possession of 'Hoveton', this did not stop further disputes which emerged in the 1170s. At some point between February 1171 and the beginning of 1181, Pope Alexander III issued a mandate to Bishop Bartholomew of Exeter (1161–84), Abbot Clement of St Mary's York (*c.* 1161–84), and Dean Robert Butevilain of York. He ordered these men to investigate and correct all the injustices caused to Rievaulx properties in 'Hoveton'. If the properties in question were not returned to the monks, the Pope threatened to

---

[36] *Rufford Charters*, ed. by C. J. Holdsworth, vol. I, Thoroton Society Record Series, 29 (Nottingham: Thoroton Society, 1972), pp. lxi–lxii.

[37] *Cartulary*, no. 232; *EYC*, IX, no. 129; *PU*, I, no. 191.

[38] *Cartulary*, no. 68; *Charter of Mowbray*, no. 250; between 1163 and 1169. There is also another confirmation by Nigel of his father's grant in Hoveton, copied further down in the *Cartulary*, no. 157, but dated identically by Clay to between 1163 and 1169.

[39] *EEA*, XX, 86.

[40] *Cartulary*, nos 231, 239; *EYC*, IX, nos 130, 131.

excommunicate the offenders. Among the accused group were Robert de Stuteville and his son William, who illegally took a wood and newly cultivated land in 'Hoveton' as well as land and wood called Middlehead in Farndale.[41] The timing of the papal letter also indicates that towards the end of the twelfth century the amount of disposable land was shrinking and the barons became anxious not to lose any more. The changes in the overlordship aggravated the anxieties of laypeople over the integrity of their estates and made religious houses fear for their own rights. This combination led to a number of open conflicts between Yorkshire monasteries and their benefactors, in which monks called upon the external authority of the Pope for help. Meaux Abbey, a fellow Cistercian abbey, suffered problems similar to Rievaulx's in the 1180s–90s when its benefactors successfully reclaimed parts of the abbey's land.[42]

To put it in simple terms, the enemy of a baron was often the enemy of the religious house of his patronage or supported by him. One of the reasons that Welburn and 'Hoveton' were particularly disputable properties among the abbey's estates was their uncertain property rights. Because both vills were included in the ten knightly fees which Roger de Mowbray was forced to return to Robert III de Stuteville in 1176, the security of the grant was endangered. However, as I indicated earlier, the religious houses were not completely defenceless; besides calling upon papal help, they could also strike a deal with an aggressive baron. When finally Robert confirmed Rievaulx's possession of Welburn and 'Hoveton' between *c.* 1176 and 1183, the document does not say that Robert de Stuteville was not an original donor of these vills, but it does state clearly that the confirmation was given by Robert de Stuteville for the salvation of his own soul and those of his father, mother, grandfather, and wife.[43] The name of the original grantor, Roger de Mowbray, was eliminated from this document, which likely reflects the fact that this charter was an outcome of some deal between Rievaulx and Robert. In this case, prayers for Robert's soul were rather a moderate price to pay for the abbey to keep 'Hoveton' and Welburn. This was not, however, strictly a transaction because normally donors could not legally demand spiritual services, such as prayers in order to acquire salvation, in the same way that they could make demands in a commercial transaction when buying material goods. This was nevertheless a compromise which diverted the potential danger of losing an important property by Rievaulx Abbey, and Robert de Stuteville eventually became its benefactor and not its persecutor.

Among the grants of Roger de Mowbray to Rievaulx Abbey are some interesting and unusual cases illustrating the way in which property was transferred to religious houses. His grant of the vill of Welburn (between 1154 and 1157) is the first documented case of a grant of land with its serfs to a Cistercian house in England, a type

---

[41] *Cartulary*, no. 262; *EYC*, IX, no. 132.

[42] *Chronica Monasterii de Melsa: A fundatione usque annum 1396 auctore Thoma de Burton, abbate*, vol. I, ed. by E. A. Bond, Rolls Series, 43 (London: Longman, 1866), pp. 231–32.

[43] *Cartulary*, no. 131; *EYC*, IX, no. 10.

of gift which was forbidden by the internal regulations of the order, but was nevertheless broken elsewhere particularly in areas where there was a shortage of labour.[44] This brings us again to the debate among the historians of the order outlined in the introduction, and in particular to the question of how far the local conditions shaped Cistercian practice. The majority of the Cistercian houses in Central-Eastern Europe (in Poland and Bohemia in particular) had scarcely any lay brothers, and the workforce of the granges consisted of paid labourers and serfs. This was accompanied, particularly from the early thirteenth century, by a process of setting up villages on the monastic estates according to the *ius Teutonicum*.[45] In Yorkshire the shortage of labour was less acute, but it was nevertheless a concern of all landholders. Although Roger de Mowbray granted a whole vill with its people, he also included a clause stating that the serfs might stay or leave as they wanted:

> Let it be known that I give all my serfs in Welburn to the Abbot of Rievaulx, without restrictions. I permit to them all freedom and to go or stay whichever they want and to whatever place they want.[46]

The significance of the grant of land with people should first of all be considered in terms of the availability of labour. The land could only generate income if there was enough labour to work on it. Indeed, the practice of the Cistercian order of forbidding the possession of serfs was not uniform throughout Europe and reflected this fundamental concern of the availability of labour. The grant of Roger de Mowbray to Rievaulx Abbey is also related to this issue. Not only had he given to Rievaulx Abbey land that was already cultivated and populated, but the clause of free choice for the serfs allowed them to continue to work on this land, probably as paid labourers.

Aristocratic benefactors were also useful in helping to secure the other rights of religious houses. The exemption from the tithe payment on their own produce, an early privilege of the Cistercian order granted in 1132, caused many disputes between the white monks and bishops and other religious orders. These concerns and conflicts over tithe payments by Rievaulx are discussed in chapter 4 in the context of the abbey's interactions with the ecclesiastical world. However, Rievaulx also enlisted the help of laypeople in preserving its exemption. The name of Roger de Mowbray, the supportive benefactor, again appears in this context. His charter granting particular plots of land in Welburn and 'Hoveton', between 1154 and 1166,

---

[44] *Narrative and Legislative Texts*, ed. and trans. by Waddell, p. 460; Janet E. Burton, 'The Estates and Economy of Rievaulx Abbey in Yorkshire', *Cîteaux: Commentarii Cistercienses*, 49 (1998), 29–94 (p. 55); Bennett D. Hill, *English Cistercian Monasteries and their Patrons in the Twelfth Century* (Urbana: University of Illinois Press, 1968), p. 67.

[45] *Monasticon Cisterciense Poloniae*, I, ed. by Andrzej Wyrwa, Jerzy Strzelczyk, and Krzysztof Kaczmarek (Poznań: Wydawnictwo Poznańskie, 1999), pp. 205–06.

[46] 'Sciatis quod omnes rusticos meos de Wellebruna concedo abbati de Rievalle quietos, et ipsis de omnem libertatem eundi et remanendi quocunque voluerint, et ubi locum invenerint': *Cartulary*, no. 64; *EYC*, IX, no. 152.

contains an important clause that he will not try to extract tithes from these vills himself nor help anyone to do so:

> Concerning their tithes, that is, from Welburn and from 'Hoveton', if anybody should trouble them and extract tithes from them, neither I nor my heirs will interfere there, or on anyone's behalf, and we will do what we can to hold them back, nor will we encourage or help anybody speaking against them in that matter.[47]

Rievaulx Abbey had a series of conflicts with other religious institutions, particularly Augustinian houses, concerning the payment of tithes, so the support of the lay lords in such matters could make a difference. Freedom from the payment of tithes was not only an important financial privilege which marked off the Cistercian order. It allowed for a better practical and symbolic separation of the monastic economies from their environment. It is not an accident that Mowbray's help was requested in connection with two important granges in Welburn and 'Hoveton', which Rievaulx was building up in the second half of the twelfth century. The abbey's concern over the tithes exemption there had, of course, a practical dimension of profit maximization, but was also a way of emphasizing its Cistercian exempted character.

A great baron could act not only as a protector of the abbey and its interests, but also as an intermediary between the religious community and his tenants. The tenants on the extensive estates of the Mowbray family were a varied social group. Almost all of them were of Norman descent, with the exception of two who were English. The scale of holdings varied enormously. Such prominent noblemen as Stuteville, Vescy, Bulmer, and Vere held, apart from fiefs within Mowbray honour, lands in chief from the King and lands from other lords, but the majority of his tenants had much less. By the time that Roger de Mowbray came into possession of the honour, fees were routinely inheritable, but lords still had the power to exchange tenancies, and this often occurred in connection with grants to religious houses. In terms of the social and economic standing there was a distinct difference between the tenants who provided service to the amount of one or two knights and the smaller tenants whose service was a fraction of a fee, usually in monetary form.[48] Among both the prominent and smaller tenants of the Mowbrays were those who became benefactors of Rievaulx Abbey. Their example, in turn, prompted their subtenants to make similar gestures, usually on a small scale. Among this diverse group of Rievaulx benefactors who had tenurial bonds with the Mowbrays, some of the individuals and families should be discussed in more detail because the character of their contacts with the abbey exemplifies the importance of both horizontal and vertical connections within the family and tenurial groups.

---

[47] 'De decimis suis, hoc est de Wellebr[una], et de Houet[una], si quis eos vexaverit et decimas ab eis exegerit nec ego nec heredes mei inde intromittemus nec aliquis per nos vel quem inde retrahere poterimus nec aliquem contra eos inde loquentem adjuvabimus vel manutenebimus': *Cartulary*, no. 154; *EYC*, IX, no. 154.

[48] *Charters of Mowbray*, pp. xxxv–xli.

Hugh de Malebisse, a steward of Roger de Mowbray, had been the founder of the Malebisse family fortune and acquired fees from various lords, mainly the Mowbrays and the Arches. Members of the Malebisse family remained in the Mowbrays' retinues for four generations serving from Nigel d'Aubigny to his great-grandson William de Mowbray.[49] Hugh de Malebisse's son, also called Hugh, was a generous donor to Rievaulx and Byland, both houses which benefited from the generosity of his lord, Roger de Mowbray.[50] One of Hugh's grants to Rievaulx involved a substantial reciprocity on the part of the abbey. A countergift was not given to each benefactor, and the abbey carefully selected individuals to be rewarded in this way. Between 1160 and 1165 Hugh de Malebisse gave to Rievaulx Abbey a meadow called Oswaldenges in Scawton, which was part of Malebisse's fee, with the permission to use a pasture in Scawton and an adjoining piece of land called 'Brochesholes', located between the hill of that name and the river Rye, for the animals which ploughed the fields at Griff.[51] This grant was then confirmed by his lord, Roger de Mowbray.[52] The grantor, Hugh de Malebisse, received twenty shillings of compensation from the monks in a special ceremony in the abbey church witnessed by many people:

> So, however, that I should make this grant more willingly, the monks gave me twenty shillings for love; and I presented it [the charter] by my own hand on the high altar of [the church] of St Mary's Rievaulx, where also in the presence of many, monks as well as laypeople, I agreed, in truth, the attestation of this charter in good faith, to be kept by me in perpetuity and said land to be guaranteed to the house of Rievaulx against all men.[53]

This case is a good illustration of how religious and economic interests were linked together. This grant was not a secret sale, but a donation from which Hugh de Malebisse wanted to benefit on both a material and a spiritual level. The ceremony took place in the most sacred part of the church, which was normally out of bounds for laymen. Hugh placed his charter on the altar to strengthen his commitment. By this

---

[49] Hugh M. Thomas, *Vassals, Heiresses, Crusaders and Thugs: The Gentry of Angevin Yorkshire, 1154–1216* (Philadelphia: University of Pennsylvania Press, 1993), p. 24.

[50] Wardrop, *Fountains Abbey*, p. 194; *EYC*, III, 452, the editor's comment. *Cartulary*, nos 70, 71, 72, 73; *EYC*, III, nos 1842, 1843, 1844.

[51] *Cartulary*, no. 74. This grant of land in Scawton and Oswaldenges was probably a source of later conflict between Rievaulx and Byland Abbey about the tithes from these locations. *EEA*, XX, 88–89.

[52] *Cartulary*, no. 156; *Charters of Mowbray*, no. 244.

[53] 'Ut autem hanc elemosinam libentius facerem dederunt michi monachi xx solidos pro caritate; et ego eam propria manu mea supra altare Sancte Marie Rievallis obtuli ubi etiam coram multis tam monachis quam secularibus conventionavi in veritate hujus carte attestationem sine malo ingenio me in perpetuum servaturum et terram prefatam domui Rievallis contra omnes homines warantizaturum': *Cartulary*, no. 75.

act, he became elevated above his peers watching him from the nave, and the solemnity of this occasion put pressure on Hugh to honour his grant in the future. The substantial reciprocal gift of twenty shillings was handed to the benefactor in a religious ceremony, and this was proudly noted in the charter. This act was not something to be ashamed of, but a part of the process of establishing good mutual relations. A public ceremony of this kind reinforced ties between the monastery and its benefactors and neighbours present there. The phrase used by many historians in such cases, 'disguised sale', hints at some dishonesty of both parties; it is therefore a misleading term that also serves to hide the active role of religious houses in procuring grants in particularly desirable locations.[54] Compensation for a benefactor was often a tool enabling a grant in cases where the potential donor could not afford an alienation. Reciprocity was an important element of the relationship between monastic communities and laypeople; by the twelfth century, it had a long tradition which Cistercian houses could not ignore or reject. Although the white monks modified some of its elements, for Rievaulx Abbey and other houses of that order, reciprocity continued to be a key building block of relationships between the white monks and their benefactors.

After the death of Hugh de Malebisse *c.* 1188 the leading position in the family was taken by his nephew Richard son of William de Malebisse of Acaster. Richard became a generous benefactor of several houses including Byland, Newburgh, and Fountains, as well as Rievaulx, but achieved a status of significant notoriety for his leading role in the massacre of Jews in York in 1190.[55] Despite Richard's generosity to Rievaulx, their relationship was not always smooth. The object of one recorded dispute, on 23 January 1201, was the border between Hawnby (near Helmsley) and Laskill and the right to Stainton granted by his uncle Hugh de Malebisse. Richard quitclaimed all his demands to the said properties and Abbot William II Punchard (1199–1203), who was the plaintiff, paid £100 of compensation.[56] Although Richard de Malebisse and the abbey had what appears to be a dispute, it might have been a fictitious lawsuit. Both parties might simply have wanted to legalize the status quo and to obtain a permanent record of an exchange or sale by the means of a court record. Written evidence was becoming more important than the oral testimony of the witnesses. This practice provided interested parties with a record of their holding from the King's court. It was employed by religious houses and laypeople alike from

[54] Berman, *Cistercian Evolution*, pp. 171–72. 'Disguised sales' did exist, but as a way of preventing secular powers to appropriate monastic income, as shown in the example of Kaisheim monastery in Bavaria in the early modern period. Klaus Wollenberg, 'The Cistercian Monastery of Kaisheim: Aspects of its Economic and Social History', paper presented at the 36th International Congress on Medieval Studies, Kalamazoo, 3 May 2001.

[55] R. B. Dobson, *The Jews of Medieval York and the Massacre of March 1190*, Borthwick Paper, no. 45 (York: St Anthony's Press, 1974), p. 33.

[56] *Pedes Finium Eboracensium Regente Johanne* AD *MCXCIX – AD MCCXIV*, Surtees Society, 94 (Durham: Andrews, 1897), p. 7.

the early thirteenth century and became common during the early reign of King Henry III. Wardrop identified similar cases among the conflicts between Fountains Abbey and its neighbours.[57] A fictitious lawsuit seems to be rather plausible in the case of Rievaulx versus Malebisse considering the substantial compensation paid by the Abbot and Richard's generosity to the abbey on later occasions.[58]

The example of another significant family of tenants shows that status and role within the tenurial group had no straightforward connection to the scale and intensity of the relationship with the religious institution patronized by the lord. Roger de Flamvill, one of the more important knightly tenants of Roger de Mowbray, established the family fortune. His son Hugh de Flamvill (d. 1212) succeeded him no later than 1169 and witnessed several charters of Roger and Nigel de Mowbray between 1180 and 1189 as a member of Roger's retinue.[59] Hugh did not give any land to the abbey himself, but he did donate a mill in Fryton called 'Poketo' (parish of Hovingham), as well as strips of land on the sides of a canal to improve the flow in the pond, and he gave permission to use his forest in the same vill to obtain material for the repair of the mill.[60] Although it was forbidden by Cistercian regulations unless used solely by the community, a grant of a mill was not an unusual form of donation and it was potentially a very generous one, since it guaranteed a steady income from the payments for grinding corn.[61] The subsequent conflict over the mill shows that Rievaulx was particularly interested in holding the mill monopoly. Since Hugh de Flamvill did not leave an heir, his sisters Maud de Hastings and Agnes de Percy inherited his holdings. This broke the affinity between the Flamvill family and the abbey. In the next generation, Walter de Percy, the son and heir of Agnes disputed Rievaulx Abbey's rights to the mill in Fryton given by his uncle. There is no record of the means by which this conflict was resolved, but we know that Walter confirmed in 1224 not only the abbey's possession of the mill, but also the monopoly in the vill of Fryton.[62]

Although Alan de Ryedale, another tenant of the Mowbrays, was one of the most troublesome neighbours of the abbey, and will be discussed in the next chapter, his wife came from a family of its early benefactors. Her father Gervase and brother Benedict (with Hugh de Tuit) gave the meadow of Rokesbergh between 1145 and 1152.[63]

---

[57] Wardrop, *Fountains Abbey*, p. 126.

[58] *Cartulary*, no. 74; Bodl. Dodsw. vii, fols 96, 107; published incomplete in *Cartulary*, pp. 211, 213.

[59] *Early Yorkshire Families*, ed. by Charles Clay and Diane E. Greenway, Yorkshire Archaeological Society Record Series, 85 (Leeds: Yorkshire Archaeological Society, 1973), p. 30.

[60] Bodl. Dodsw. vii, fols 116^{v}–117; published incomplete in *Cartulary*, p. 218.

[61] *Narrative and Legislative Texts*, ed. and trans. by Waddell, p. 460.

[62] *Early Yorkshire Families*, ed. by Clay and Greenway, p. 31; *Cartulary*, p. 219; Burton, 'Estates and Economy', p. 56.

[63] This is known from 'Iste sunt possessiones', London, British Library, Cotton Julius D. i, fol. 15^{v} [fol. 19^{v}]; identification of persons in the *EYC*, IX, 228.

Benedict son of Gervase was also a tenant of the Mowbrays and he had shown considerable generosity to the abbey. Benedict granted a part of Wombleton with buildings, ten and a half acres of plough land, and the common pasture of the vill. His lord, Roger de Mowbray, confirmed this grant between 1142 and *c.* 1152 and added an important clause of protection for peasants living in Wombleton with particular respect to the common pasture to protect the legal extent of 'the common pasture of that vill, according to legal consideration, so that the people of that vill are not to be harmed'.[64] This short passage gives an insight into the practical side of the abbey's coexistence with its neighbours and benefactors with whom it shared the use of common pastures. The clause indicates an attempt to stop the stronger side, the abbey, from pushing the weaker party, the peasants, out of the common pasture which they were entitled to use. This must have been a more acute problem in the cases of common pastures located near vills or on lowlands used regularly by the inhabitants of those vills than on the pastures on the moors which had a much bigger capacity, but either way, an introduction of another flock of animals must have affected established users of the pasture.[65] It is also a direct example of the economic impact of the monastery on its neighbours and their attempt to prevent its negative effect.

Despite their lords' peculiar relationship with Rievaulx Abbey, the Stutevilles' tenants were no exception to the pattern of grant giving and also donated parts of their land to Rievaulx Abbey. Among them, the Boltby and Etton families had shown a similar pattern of interaction to the tenants of the Mowbray family.

The Boltby family were tenants of Robert de Stuteville in 1166, holding ten carucates in Boltby, Thirlby (parish of Felixkirk), and Borrowby (parish of Leake). They gave to Rievaulx Abbey substantial grants in those vills. In the first half of the 1140s Odo de Boltby gave a large donation consisting of Hesketh, a part of the waste below Hesketh bordering on Boltby, and wood and common pastures in his three vills of Boltby, Ravensthorpe, and Thirlby. The donation was given with the explicit consent of his lord, Robert de Stuteville, and Robert's wife, Helewise, for the salvation of Odo himself, his wife Judith, and their fathers and mothers.[66] His son Adam de Boltby between 1154 and 1160 augmented his father's grant by giving the abbey land between Hesketh, previously acquired by the monks, and a plot of land called 'Guthalgillesiche'.[67] Despite this initial generosity Adam seemed to regret his father's benevolence to Rievaulx Abbey, and in the following decade he disputed the abbey's

---

[64] 'et communem pasturam ipsius ville secundum legalem considerationem ut homines illius ville non graventur': *Cartulary*, no. 63; *EYC*, IX, no. 146.

[65] Benedict gave further land to Rievaulx Abbey: one tillage in Wiresdale, twelve perches of land in Spelcrose (Stony Cross), four perches in Skiplam, meadow at Rook Barugh and Muscoates, and the common pasture of Wombleton. BL, Cotton Julius D. i, fol. 43 [fol. 47]; *Cartulary*, no. 69; *EYC*, IX, no. 228.

[66] *Cartulary*, no. 76; *EYC*, IX, no. 89.

[67] *Cartulary*, no. 77; *EYC*, IX, no. 90.

right to the pastures of Boltby, Ravensthorpe, and Thirlby. He might also have been influenced by the actions of his lords, the Stutevilles, or other people in the locality who claimed right to various lands in the possession of Rievaulx Abbey throughout the 1170s. Whatever was the motivation, Adam and the abbey of Rievaulx managed to reach an agreement at Doncaster on 8 September 1178, before the royal justices. Adam confirmed his father's grant; additionally, he confirmed the donation of common pastures in Boltby, Ravensthorpe, and Thirlby with the capacity for four hundred sheep and other animals (cows, bulls, and oxen) and unrestricted entry and exit from these.[68]

The interest in Rievaulx Abbey filtered down among the Boltbys' tenants, providing further useful donations. One of the undertenancies was held by the Borrowby family from the Boltby fee. In the late twelfth century (between 1183 and 1203) Ralph son of Uctred de Borrowby granted eleven acres of meadow in Leake, located between the meadows of the Bishop of Durham, and added permission to make a channel for water from the spring on his land to the grange of Crosby.[69] His overlord, William de Stuteville, brother of Robert III de Stuteville, gave his consent for the alienation as did Ralph son of Uctred's sons Roger, Richard, and Nicholas.[70]

A similar pattern of donations was exhibited by the Etton family, who supported religious houses which were favoured by their lords. The Ettons branched out in the late twelfth century or early thirteenth century in two lines, one of Etton and the second of Gilling Castle. The first line held a tenancy under the Stutevilles and were recorded as generous benefactors of Meaux Abbey.[71] The confirmation charter to Rievaulx Abbey of William de Etton was witnessed by Ernald, Abbot of Melrose (a daughter house of Rievaulx), and several members of the Etton family. This grant, originally given by William's father, Walter, consisted of a meadow in Layerthorpe outside York's city walls. The charter contains an interesting clause:

> If indeed, I or my heirs in any way get back our inheritance in Hambleton, for which we have, in exchange, the above said Layerthorpe, from the abbot and the monks of Selby, and if we therefore demise that Layerthorpe with the meadow, we will give without delay to the monks of Rievaulx an exchange elsewhere to the value of the said meadow.[72]

Unfortunately there is no indication if William de Etton received Hambleton from Selby Abbey or if he ever fulfilled his promise of providing a 'replacement grant' for

[68] *Cartulary*, no. 112; *EYC*, IX, no. 91.

[69] *EYC*, IX, no. 93.

[70] *EYC*, IX, no. 93; *VCH*, I, 412.

[71] John Bison, 'Gilling Castle', *Yorkshire Archaeological Journal*, 19 (1906–07), 105–92 (pp. 105–20).

[72] 'Si autem ego vel heredes mei aliquando recuperaverimus hereditatem nostram de Hamelt[ona] pro qua habemus in escambium predictam Thorpe ab abbate et monachis de Selebi et dimiserimus eandem Thorpe cum prato dabimus sine mora monachis Rieuallensibus alibi escambium ad valentiam predicti prati sui': *Cartulary*, no. 166.

Rievaulx Abbey. Nevertheless this clause provides an indication of the pragmatic approach of both laypeople and the monks who, on the bases of earlier experiences, wanted to avoid possible disputes should the material situation of the benefactor change in the future. There are also indications that the area around York was important for the abbey, and it clearly wanted to establish a strong presence there. Holdings in Layerthorpe were augmented by Rievaulx Abbey in the early thirteenth century when it acquired a plot of land and a house there from the convent of St Andrews in York.[73]

Grants from barons were important to the abbey not only because their donations were larger, but because they helped to create connections with other people, mainly their tenants and subtenants. The eschatological value of donation to the Church was a universally shared belief in medieval society, but giving land to a particular order or house was determined by more transient trends. Lords would set a fashion for monastic benefaction among their knights and permit them to alienate their own lands. However, as the examples of many of Rievaulx's benefactors show, this was often a complex decision process and tenants did not simply follow the choices of their lords. As for the abbey, the greater differentiation of the benefactors group offered a greater variety of possible grants, in terms of location, type, and size. Although, as Green asserts, the reasons and influences behind grants from aristocrats were more likely to be explained in the charters than the motivations of the lesser men, it does not mean that the lesser men were only motivated by their affinities and not by the religious considerations.[74]

Spectacular generosity and extensive alienations of land were characteristic of the 'first generation' of benefactors up until the late twelfth century. In the thirteenth century large grants became rare and noblemen would rather confirm their predecessors' donations than alienate any more of their own land, but even confirmations were highly valued. Disputes over land possession were a routine part of life, and protective lords were a great advantage. In many cases though, the same people would be protectors at one time and would try to reclaim their previous grants at another, when their own situation had changed. An important indication of the mutual dependence of Cistercian abbeys and their baronial protectors is the entry in the Roll of Pipe for the year 1209:

> The abbots of Fountains and Rievaulx and Byland rendered account of £100 for having the advice of the king's court as to whether they should give help to William de Mowbray for acquitting himself against the king of the fine which he had made with the

---

[73] *York Minster Fasti being notes on the dignitaries, archdeacons and prebendaries in the church of York prior to the year 1307*, vol. II, ed. by Charles Travis Clay, Yorkshire Archaeological Society Record Series, 124 (Wakefield: Yorkshire Archaeological Society, 1959), no. 75.

[74] Green, *Aristocracy*, p. 413.

> king when he was impleaded by William de Stuteville about the lands which he claimed against him. In the treasury, nothing; to the king himself in his chamber £100.[75]

The large sum of £100 paid by the monks of these three Cistercian abbeys to the King for advice as to whether they should help William de Mowbray whose lands were claimed by William de Stuteville indicates that they considered that their benefactors' fortune was important and could influence their own. The Mowbray family was exceptional in Yorkshire for the number and scale of their grants and charters of protection to a variety of abbeys and priories. It is impossible to establish precisely what exactly motivated the Abbots of Rievaulx, Byland, and Fountains to make this request; was it their fear of losing an important benefactor, concerns over the security of their property, or more an expression of their loyalty to the people whose generosity helped to establish those institutions but who were now in financial troubles? It is likely that the abbots were worried, on the basis of the experiences of their predecessors, that if William de Stuteville took over they might suffer losses and the new lord might reclaim grants made by the Mowbrays. Wardrop saw it as an expression of the ties of reciprocity between the Cistercian houses and their benefactors.

> It also indicates the extent to which the fortunes of the cistercian houses of the north and those of their benefactors were, by the early thirteenth century, inextricably entwined. The powerful layman had his role in defending the rights of a religious house; the house too had a responsibility towards its benefactors, even if only from a sense of self-interest.[76]

The interdependence between the Cistercians and the lay lords has been correctly identified by Wardrop, but it was not an exclusive feature of the early thirteenth century. The close connection between Rievaulx and its powerful benefactors was a direct result of their donations. The new dimension of these relationships indicated by Wardrop became obvious by the 1170s when Rievaulx, and many other Yorkshire Cistercian houses, went through a period of conflicts and disagreements with the baronial benefactors. The external pressures on the lay lords and their attempts at estate consolidation put a strain on the relationships with religious houses. Already by the mid-twelfth century monastic communities were fully aware of the double edged impact of the close association with aristocratic families. Burton asserts that some of the Yorkshire houses (Pontefract, Nostell, Bridlington, Selby, and St Mary's York) were particularly damaged by their closeness to particular patrons and benefactors,

[75] 'Abbates de Fontibus et Riuall' et Beiland' r.c. de c. li. pro habenda consideratione curia regis utrum debeant auxilium facere Willelmo de Molbrai ad acquietandum eum versus regis de fine quem fecit cum regis quando inplaciatus fuit per Willelmum de Stuteuill' de terris quas adversus eum clamauit. In thes. Nichil. Et ipsi R. In camera sua c. li.': *The Great Roll of the Pipe 11th year of John*, ed. by Doris Stenton, Pipe Roll Society, n.s., 24 (London: Pipe Roll Society, 1949), p. 139.

[76] Wardrop, *Fountains Abbey*, p. 144.

namely Henry de Lacy, Gilbert de Gant, and William, Earl of Aumâle, who were involved in 'local warfare'.[77] None of these houses belonged to the Cistercian order. As we have seen, Rievaulx Abbey maintained a certain distance from its powerful benefactors. Although the monastic community knew how to enlist their help in various matters (disputes over borders, tithes conflicts, or clashes with other benefactors and neighbours), they also did not make themselves too closely attached or reliant on just one family or individual. This perhaps should be seen as the manifestation of their Cistercian identity as much as practical thinking.

The Mowbrays, despite their generosity to Rievaulx Abbey, were not the only benefactors of baronial status. The remaining part of this section discusses other baronial families who were benefactors of Rievaulx, paying particular attention to their expectations towards the abbey and vice versa. Other important benefactors coming from the highest stratum of Anglo-Norman society were Gilbert de Gant, Earl of Lincoln (who was also a brother-in-law of Roger de Mowbray), his daughter Alice, married to Earl Simon de St Liz, and his nephew also called Gilbert. In contrast to the Mowbray family, who gave land to a whole range of religious institutions, the Gants were particularly interested in the new orders, primarily Cistercian and Augustinian houses.

The Gants' fortune had been established by the Earl's grandfather and father, but Gilbert was the first one to obtain the title, from King Stephen in 1149, and he further expanded the family estates. His wife Rohaise, daughter of Richard son of Gilbert, came from the prominent de Clare family. Their only child, Alice, married Simon de St Liz, Earl of Northampton, but they died without any issue (Simon in 1184 and his wife in the following year). The family inheritance passed to Robert, brother of Earl Gilbert de Gant, and after his death in 1191 to his son Gilbert, who took the title of Earl of Lincoln in 1216.[78]

The first member of the Gant family to make a donation to Rievaulx was Walter de Gant (d. 1139). He was, in fact, one of the earliest important benefactors of this house. The only remaining record of his grant is an entry in the list 'Iste sunt possessiones' from the cartulary:

> In the year of the Lord's incarnation 1158 King Henry II gave us the waste below Pickering, in exchange for Stainton, which Walter de Gant gave us for the purpose of the construction of an abbey.[79]

The mysterious 'for the purpose of the construction of an abbey' may mean two different things. It may refer to the income derived from this property, which was then used for the building of the precinct, rather than for erecting any buildings in Stainton

[77] Burton, *Monastic Order in Yorkshire*, p. 205.

[78] *EYC*, II, 432–34.

[79] 'Anno ab Incarnatione Domini M° clviii dedit nobis Rex Henricus Secundus vastum subtus Pikering in escambio pro Steintona quam nobis dedit Walterus de Gant ad abbatiam construendam ibi': BL, Cotton Julius D. i, fol. 15ᵛ [fol. 19ᵛ]; *Cartulary*, p. 261.

as such. It is also possible that this note indicates that Walter de Gant might originally have intended to establish a daughter house of Rievaulx there, an idea which was never accomplished.[80] If this was the case, such grand plans would place Walter among the most important benefactors of Rievaulx with a particular commitment to the Cistercian order. This special interest in the order continued in the next generation of the Gant family. His son Earl Gilbert de Gant was the patron of Bridlington Priory (founded *c.* 1113 by his father, Walter) and gave donations to the Benedictine abbey of Bardney, the Augustinian canons in Thornton, the hospital of St Peter in York, and two Cistercian houses, Rievaulx and Vaudey (Lincolnshire). Gilbert's grant to Rievaulx consisted of two bovates in Hunmanby given in 1147.[81] There must have been more connections between Earl Gilbert de Gant and Rievaulx than this rather unimpressive grant of two bovates, as revealed by another entry in the 'Iste sunt possessiones': 'At the time of Lord Ailred, the abbot, Gilbert de Gant gave us the grange of Hunmanby with all that belongs to it.'[82] Information about the creation of the grange was added *post factum*, but what it basically means is that the Earl's grant was large enough to establish the abbey's grange in Hunmanby. However, it is not certain how long this grange functioned or even if it went beyond a planning stage as the comprehensive confirmation of the abbey's estates in 1332 does not mention it.[83]

Just before receiving his title from the King, Gilbert founded in 1146 or 1148 a Cistercian abbey in Rufford as a daughter house of Rievaulx. Firstly, the choice of the order and the mother house is a clear indication of his attachment to Rievaulx, and secondly, the time of the foundation coincided with his rise in status to become an earl; thus the foundation of Rufford is likely to be a manifestation of his advancement. The choice of the order was also motivated politically, as a gesture towards his powerful father-in-law, Earl Ranulf of Chester, who founded Pipewell Abbey, and Gilbert's step-uncle William de Roumare, Earl of Lincoln, who established Revesby.[84]

In his role as the patron of the new abbey, Gilbert de Gant continued his relations with the community of Rievaulx, the initial contingent of the monks being sent to Rufford from the mother house.[85] Soon after the foundation, in 1149 or 1150, the

---

[80] *Rufford Charters*, ed. by Holdsworth, I, p. xxii; *VHC*, III, 149; Burton, *Monastic Order in Yorkshire*, p. 122.

[81] *Cartulary*, no. 78; *EYC*, II, no. 1182. His confirmation of this grant, *Cartulary*, no. 79.

[82] 'Tempore Domini Ailredi Abbatis dedit nobis Gilbertus de Gant grangiam de Hundemandebi cum pertinenciis suis': BL, Cotton Julius D. i, fol. 15^{v} [fol. 19^{v}]; *Cartulary*, p. 260.

[83] Burton, 'Estates and Economy', p. 80.

[84] *Rufford Charters*, ed. by Holdsworth, I, p. xxiii. The Earl of Chester was one of the most prominent patrons of the Cistercian order in Britain. David Crouch, *The Beaumont Twins: The Roots and Branches of Power in the Twelfth Century* (Cambridge: Cambridge University Press, 1986), p. 202. Burton, *Monastic Order in Yorkshire*, p. 123.

[85] The close and formal link between Rievaulx and the daughter house in Rufford is also acknowledged in the conformation charter of King Stephen: '[Ego] concedo et confirmo illam

new abbey had a conflict with Ralph son of Wichard, Gilbert's tenant, who claimed unjustly some property which was given by the founder to Rufford and generally harassed the monks. This conflict developed for some time before Gilbert intervened; the monks at first looked for justice without consulting the patron. The reaction of the Earl is a very clear indication of how a lord of high status saw his own position towards 'his monastery' and how he understood his role of protector. In the charter issued by Gilbert de Gant between 1148 and 1150 he addressed the community of Rufford as 'my brothers of Rievaulx living in Rufford', which indicates warm attachment, but at the same time, in the light of the rest of the document, a rather proprietary attitude towards the object of his patronage.[86] Gilbert then went on to reprimand Ralph son of Wichard for interfering with his prerogative and forbade any encroachment on the land given by himself, as his lord, to the third parties, reminding Ralph that he also depended on Gilbert's generosity and the good will of his lord. The most important clause of this document refers to both sides of the conflict — Ralph and the monks:

> Thus I forbid the above-mentioned Ralph, for the love of me and all that he holds from me, to act in any way against my generosity. Similarly I forbid the abbot and brothers to quarrel against Ralph or anybody else about my property or my generosity, but he should come to me and I will do justice.[87]

In this way Gilbert asserted his position as the authority over the abbey and ensured that he would not lose control over his property, which although alienated to the monastic institution, remained partly controllable via informal links with 'his monks'. His response to his tenant's encroachment on the abbey's property resembles to some extent Roger de Mowbray's position in the conflict between Rievaulx Abbey and his tenants in Welburn, although Gilbert appears to be much more decisive in dealing with a difficult tenant.

Gilbert de Gant's daughter Alice had also shown an interest in Rievaulx Abbey but, as far as we know, completely ignored her father's foundation in Rufford. She confirmed grants of men holding lands from her to Rievaulx Abbey: Ralph de Nevill and Ranulf son of Walter (in Hunmanby) between 1160 and *c.* 1175 and Henry de

---

donationem [quam] Gilb(er)tus de Ga(n)t fecit deo et ecclesie Beate Marie Rievall(ensis) et monachis ibidem deo servientibus de manerio de Ruf(ford).' *Regesta regum Anglo-Normannorum 1066–1154*, vol. III, ed. by H. A. Cronne and R. H. C. Davis (Oxford: Clarendon Press, 1968), no. 736.

[86] 'fratribus meis de Rievalle apud Rucforda habitantibus': London, British Library, Harleian Charter 83 E. 52.

[87] 'Quamobrem Radulfo predicto prohibeo super amorem meum et sicut diligit quicquid de me tenet quod nullo modo amodo se intromittat de elemosina mea. Et eciam abbati et fratribus meis predictis similiter prohibeo ne aliquam loquelam versus Radulfum vel aliquis alius calumpniatur aliquid de meo dominio vel de mea elemosina, coram me ipso veniat et plenum rectum ei teneam': BL, Harleian Charter 83 E. 52.

Willerby's grant and sale between 1170 and 1184.[88] Together with her husband, Earl Simon de St Liz, she gave permission to alienate land held from them by their men to Rievaulx Abbey by sale or gift.[89] Independently from his wife, Earl Simon confirmed his father-in-law's grants and those of his men Ralph de Nevill and Ranulf son of Walter de Greystoke to Rievaulx Abbey between 1160 and *c.* 1175.[90] Simon's personal interest in the Cistercian order was so substantial that he founded a Cistercian house in Sawtry (Huntingdonshire) in 1147 as a daughter house of Warden.[91] This new house was a granddaughter of Rievaulx. The founder of Warden and Rievaulx, Walter Espec, was still alive in 1147, and Simon's foundation might have been a gesture towards him. Importantly, Sawtry Abbey was established on the land which Simon received from King Stephen soon after he was established as a lord of the Huntingdon honour. Keith Stringer suggests the founder wanted in this way to assert his grip on this new acquisition in the face of the rival claims to the honour of Huntingdon by King David I.[92]

After Alice's and Simon's deaths, the family inheritance went to Gilbert's brother Robert and then his son Gilbert (died *c.* 1241), who continued the tradition of supporting Rievaulx Abbey. Gilbert gave pasture in Grinton together with several rights in Swaledale with specific privileges (sheep folds, hunting, building lodging for the staff), including a right to catch wolves by any method.[93] This was then confirmed by his son, also called Gilbert, in the second half of the thirteenth century.[94]

The Gant family became important for Rievaulx Abbey in the first decades of its existence and continued to be so for a number of generations with varying intensity. In contrast to the Mowbrays, they had a particular interest in the Cistercian order, and this was the most likely reason behind their initial connection to Rievaulx. The political and tenurial dimension of the Gants' foundations and donations to the Cistercian monasteries did not necessarily have a negative impact on them, but as a patron of Rufford, Gilbert de Gant had shown a very 'hands-on' approach, which Rievaulx Abbey might not tolerate itself. The community of Rievaulx, although welcoming his grants, never developed a particular dependence on Gilbert, preferring to keep a variety of connections with a number of prominent aristocrats.

The tenants of the Gants, just like those of the Mowbrays, followed the example of their lords in supporting Rievaulx Abbey, and this connection was clearly understood

---

[88] *Cartulary*, no. 159; *EYC*, II, no. 1188; *Cartulary*, no. 160.

[89] *Cartulary*, no. 158; *EYC*, II, no. 1232.

[90] *Cartulary*, no. 80; *EYC*, II, no. 1187.

[91] *Rufford Charters*, ed. by Holdsworth, I, p. xxi.

[92] Keith Stringer, 'A Cistercian Archive: The Earliest Charters of Sawtry Abbey', *Journal of the Society of Archivists*, 6 (1980), 325–34.

[93] *CPR 1330–1334*, p. 316; published in *Cartulary*, pp. 304–05 and 307.

[94] *CPR 1330–1334*, p. 316; published in *Cartulary*, p. 305.

and recognized by the abbey. The copies of the charters of the Gants' men in general followed those of their lords in the cartulary. The status of many of those men was relatively high at the time of donations, but changed in the period after they became benefactors of Rievaulx. The Nevill family was prudent in their pious donations, rising in social status throughout the twelfth and thirteenth centuries, whilst the Willerby family became too generous to Bridlington Priory, their lord's foundation, alienated most of their lands, and lost their position in consequence.[95]

Another family of benefactors who displayed generosity to the religious institutions supported by the Gants were the Chambords.[96] The pattern of their donations had also shown a strong correlation between the direction of their grants and their lords' interests. In the mid-twelfth century Simon and Alan de Chambord gave two bovates of land in East Cowton, which were later confirmed by their brother Robert.[97] Robert de Chambord witnessed other charters for Rievaulx Abbey, which also indicates his interest in this institution.[98] Several other members of the Chambord family made grants to Bridlington Priory, which reveals the influence of the Gants, the hereditary patrons of Bridlington.

An altogether different case of a tenant family of the Gants were the Greystokes. They had identifiably native roots, a rare case among the benefactors of Rievaulx. The Greystokes were also generous beyond what was given to Rievaulx Abbey by their wealthier peers. They had been a family of some standing in Yorkshire since the first recorded member of the family, Forne son of Sigulf, received a small fee in Nunburnholme and Greystoke in the second decade of Henry I's reign.[99] Subsequently, they were tenants of the Gants in Folkton. Forne's son Ivo inherited his father's land in 1130 and died no later than 1156. The family had a long tradition of pious donations. Both father and son were benefactors of St Mary's York and Hexham Priory.[100] This interest continued in the next generation, although it shifted from the Benedictine and Augustinian to the new and fashionable Cistercian houses.

[95] *Peerage*, IX, 476; Thomas, *Vassals, Heiresses, Crusaders and Thugs*, p. 163. Grants of the Nevilles: *Cartulary*, no. 159; *EYC*, II, no. 1188. Grants of Willerby family: *EYC*, II, no. 1228, from Cartulary of Bridlington, London, British Library, Additional MS 40008, fol. 86; *Cartulary*, no. 158; *EYC*, II, no. 1232; *Cartulary*, no. 147; *EYC*, II, no. 1229; also copied in the Cartulary of Bridlington, fol. 86d.

[96] Simon's and Alan's brother Robert is known to have held half of a knight's fee from Robert de Gant in 1166 in Great and Little Barugh. *Red Book of the Exchequer*, vol. I, ed. by Hubert Hall, Rolls Series, 89 (London: Eyre & Spottiswoode, 1896), p. 433.

[97] *Collectanae Topographica et Genealogica*, vol. V (London: Nichols, 1838), p. 110. This charter was dated by Clay, *EYC*, V, 283; see also p. 184. London, British Library, Additional Charter 20564; published incomplete in *Cartulary*, p. 253.

[98] *Cartulary*, nos 43, 162; *EYC*, II, no. 1249.

[99] *EYC*, II, 503–04.

[100] *Early Yorkshire Families*, ed. by Clay and Greenway, p. 38.

Walter son of Ivo de Greystoke gave at least two grants to Rievaulx, as is testified by the charters of his son Ralph (d. *c.* 1190) and widow Beatrice which were copied into the cartulary. In 1158 Walter gave half a carucate of land in Folkton near Scarborough to the abbey, and his son added to this, between 1162 and 1175, the tillage of Rainsdale, a pasture for one thousand sheep and the animals plowing that land.[101] Beatrice, the widow of Walter, confirmed after his death between 1162 and *c.* 1175 a grant of land and pasture in Folkton.[102] This large pasture grant was very valuable for the abbey, which was in the process of creating and expanding its pastoral granges.

The interest in donating land to Rievaulx filtered down even lower in the tenurial web to the subtenants who were holding land from the Greystokes. Like his overlords the Gants, Ranulf de Greystoke gave permission, between 1162 and 1175, for transactions between his tenants and the abbey. However, he cautiously gave consent not for their permanent alienation, but for a lease or a grant for a limited time only.[103] This is symptomatic of a broader trend. The wealthy aristocrats, such as Gundreda de Gournay or Gilbert de Gant, could afford substantial alienations, but for their knightly tenants this was not possible without losing their status and income. There were, however, ways of decreasing the damage done by the alienation to a small landholder by offering compensation or regular tenure payment. Between 1162 and 1167 William son of Theobald granted sixteen acres of land in Folkton in three separate plots: four acres in Camb in Whitefield, seven acres in Aldefeld, and the rest in Sternekelde. In fact, eleven acres of this grant was a part of his wife's marriage portion. In return the monks paid eight marks to William who also compensated his wife, and they formally acknowledged that they held this land from William:

> And because the eleven acres were of the dower of my wife, I have given an exchange to my wife the value of these eleven acres, so that the whole above said land would remain in the house of Rievaulx free from all the secular services and secular customs, except that each year the monks should give me or my heirs one pound of cumin as recognition of their tenure.[104]

Between 1162 and 1167 Ralph son of Walter confirmed this grant of sixteen acres of land in Folkton by William son of Theobald, his man. Because there was service due from this land to Ralph, he agreed that if William failed to pay it, he would not

[101] *Cartulary*, no. 82, 161; *EYC*, II, nos 1247, 1248.

[102] *Cartulary*, no. 162; *EYC*, II, no. 1249.

[103] *Cartulary*, no. 83; *EYC*, II, no. 1245.

[104] 'Et quia de dote uxoris mee erant xj acre, dedi excambium uxori mee ad valentiam ipsarum xj acrarum, ut tota terra predicta quieta remaneret domui Rievallis et libera ab omni servitio terreno et seculari consuetudine excepto quod singulis annis dabunt michi monachi vel heredibus meis libram unam cimini pro recognitione ejusdem tenure': *Cartulary*, no. 84; *EYC*, II, no. 1250.

bother the monks but claim this payment directly from William.[105] This agreement between Ralph and the abbey was, in Paul Dalton's interpretation, a clear indication of the erosion of the lord's power over his tenant and the relatively strong position of the abbey. Rievaulx secured firm possession of Folkton, confirmed by Ranulf and the canons of York, and was obliged to pay only a nominal service.[106] The cost of the transfer of this property into the hand of Rievaulx Abbey was taken up by the lord, not his tenant, who in fact was the benefactor.

The example of the Gant family and their tenants indicates how intertwined were tenurial connections in the spread of patterns for pious donations. It was very common to hold land from several lords, often each of the land portions being relatively small, and it may not be clear which of these connections provided an individual with the idea of becoming a benefactor of Rievaulx. Walter son of Asketil de Grimston held land from Robert de Gant, but also parts of the Bulmer fee, and members of these families were also benefactors of Rievaulx. Similarly, the Colvilles held lands from both the Gants and the Mowbrays, but only one member of the Colville family, Philip, made a donation to Rievaulx.[107] Having many lords might give a kind of choice about which house or which lord's foundation to support, but ultimately the decision would be influenced by a mixture of reasons embedded in local politics. Indeed, some historians point out that the patterns of religious benefactions do not correspond with the pattern of tenurial landholding, that those who held land from a number of honours did not make donations to all the religious houses of their lords. These decisions about religious benefaction were not based simply on arithmetic; that is, the amount of land held from one lord did not always predetermine pious donations. Often the location of the religious houses in relation to the held property mattered more.[108]

While the Mowbray family had a rather eclectic taste in religious patronage, and the Gant family clearly preferred Cistercian and Augustinian houses, the religious patronage of other families reveals a multiplicity of connections which might influence the direction of their grant giving. The example of William de Vescy, another aristocratic benefactor of the abbey, shows strong family background in making decisions about pious grants. William was a son of Eustace FitzJohn, a royal justice of the North working closely with Walter Espec. Like Espec, Eustace was also a benefactor of several religious houses, the founder of a Premonstratensian house in Alnwick and Gilbertine houses in Watton and Malton, and an early benefactor of Fountains Abbey. His son William's marriage to Burga, a daughter of Robert de

[105] *Cartulary*, no. 148; *EYC*, II, no. 1251.

[106] Dalton, *Conquest, Anarchy and Lordship*, p. 287.

[107] Bodl. Dodsw. xciv, fol. 137^{v}; published incomplete in *Cartulary*, p. 248.

[108] Emma Cownie, *Religious Patronage in Anglo-Norman England 1066–1135* (Woodbridge: Boydell, 1998), p. 176.

Stuteville, brought another set of high connections and was, in fact, an alliance between two powerful and antagonistic tenants of the Mowbrays. William de Vescy was the Sheriff of Northumberland (1150–70) and held the honour of Lancaster (1160–70). He is known to have been a benefactor of many religious houses: Brinkburn, Selby, Alnwick, and Old Malton.[109] Unfortunately it is not known what exactly William de Vescy granted to Rievaulx Abbey because only a general confirmation by Archbishop Roger of York survives, issued between 1164 and 1174.[110]

A manifestation of the continuing relationship between the Vescy family and the abbey, on different terms, is the memorandum of an agreement between William de Vescy (d. 1253) and Abbot Adam de Tilletai (1240–60) copied into the cartulary in the thirteenth century.[111] This William was a grandson of the William discussed in the previous paragraph and a son of Eustace de Vescy (d. 1216). William de Vescy, like many of his contemporaries, was concerned with securing appropriate hunting grounds and having the animals there protected from poaching. According to this document the Abbot gave permission to William to enclose a park in Castle Ings ('Eduimersch') within the waste below Pickering:

> Let it be known, that we without a claim and any lawsuit or any charge in future, have granted to the lord William de Vescy and his heirs a free park to be enclosed wherever they wish of the length of sixty feet and the same breadth, in his meadow of Castle Ings on the little hill next to the border of the meadow, opposite the bridge of Houm, so that the park has two exits, in which it was legitimate for him and his heirs to empark it according to what is contained more fully in the document of agreement made between us.[112]

This memorandum was copied into the final sections of the cartulary in a thirteenth-century cursive hand, and the wording of this document suggests it might have been the outcome of a conflict. The text was also copied into the cartulary of Malton, a

---

[109] *EYC*, III, 199; *Peerage*, XII.2, 275. For an analysis of the political background of William de Vescy, see Paul Dalton, 'Eustace Fitz John and the Politics of Anglo-Norman England: The Rise and Survival of a Twelfth-Century Royal Servant', *Speculum*, 71 (1996), 358–83 (pp. 363–80).

[110] *Cartulary*, no. 237; dating in *EEA*, V, no. 82, pp. 93–94.

[111] This abbot is incorrectly identified as Abbot Ailred by the editor of the cartulary: *Cartulary*, no. 279.

[112] 'Noveritis nos, absque reclamatione et ullius objectione calumpnie in futurum, concessisse Domino Willelmo de Vescy et heredibus suis liberum parcum undecunque voluerint includendum, longitudinis sexaginta pedum et ejusdem latitudinis, in prato suo de Eduiemersc in monticulo juxta divisam ejusdem prati versus pontem de Hou, ita quod parcus ille duos habeat exitus, in quo licebat illi et heredibus suis rationabiliter inparcare secundum quod in scriptis conventionis inter nos confectis plenius continetur': BL, Cotton Julius D. i, fol. 174 [fol. 191]; *Cartulary*, no. 279.

house founded by Eustace FitzJohn, which had holdings in the same area.[113] This was then followed by a more specific agreement on 22 March 1244 between William and the abbey. It was decided that the pasture should be unavailable to both parties between 1 March and 22 August, but after that until the following March, the abbey's flock should be given common pasture elsewhere and the enclosed pasture should be used by Vescy's demesne cattle. This routine should be repeated yearly. The parties also set up a procedure for resolving future problems, for example if the abbey's cattle happen to be on Castle Ings pasture during the close time.[114] This shift from grants of land in the twelfth century to elaborate agreements about the use of forests and pastures in the thirteenth century, as exemplified by the Vescy case, repeats itself among many aristocratic benefactors of Rievaulx and took an even more dramatic turn in the case of its quarrelsome patron William de Ros, discussed in the next chapter.

In the course of this discussion about the great lords who became benefactors of Rievaulx it has become apparent that the abbey attracted only a relatively small number of great lords, and none of them appeared to choose this abbey as a favourite house or to be buried there, manifesting a special attachment, which remains in striking contrast to the situation at Fountains Abbey.[115] The most important characteristic of this group for Rievaulx Abbey was not just the amount of land given, but the great number of donations from their tenants and subtenants. These small grants were almost always located close to each other or even bordering, which helped the abbey to built compact estates. This tendency became even more pronounced in the case of other baronial families: Lacys, Bruses, and Aumâles whose donations to Rievaulx Abbey were only on a very small scale. Their generosity was directed towards different monastic houses although their tenants had various contacts with Rievaulx Abbey.

Henry de Lacy was one of the important Yorkshire noblemen who stood by Stephen against Empress Matilda and became one of the most prominent barons of the realm after the battle of Lincoln in 1141. He was not, however, particularly generous to Rievaulx Abbey, but actively supported other foundations, including Cistercian houses.[116] Two of these were family foundations, the Cluniac house in Pontefract and the Augustinian priory of Nostell. In 1147 Henry de Lacy himself founded a Cistercian house in Kirkstall, of which he was a generous patron, but Rievaulx was beyond the area of his influence and interest. There is only one charter copied into the cartulary that was issued by him for the abbey. It is a confirmation of a grant made by his

---

[113] Malton Register, London, British Library, Cotton Claudius D. xi, fols 37^{v}–38; published in *The Honour and Forest of Pickering*, ed. by Robert Bell Turton, North Riding Record Society, n.s., 4 (London: North Riding Record Society, 1897), pp. 185–86.

[114] Malton Register, BL, Cotton Claudius D. xi, fol. 38, published in *Honour of Pickering*, ed. by Turton, pp. 186–88.

[115] Wardrop, *Fountains Abbey*, pp. 133–70.

[116] *EYC*, III, 49.

man Adam son of Peter de Birkin of land in Oggethwaite with the iron ore and dead wood for smelting near Stainborough.[117] This confirmation was issued between 1158 and 1177 and was placed by the creator of the cartulary together with other charters of the Birkin family. Adam son of Peter, unlike his lord, was one of the most generous benefactors of Rievaulx, and he will be discussed later in detail. His lord, Henry de Lacy, appears in the cartulary only in the context of his tenant, a much more prominent figure for the abbey, which is reflected in the organization of the charters.

Another important Yorkshire family, the Brus family, known as generous patrons of Guisborough Priory, also interacted on a limited level with the house of Rievaulx.[118] Parts of their extensive honour were held by a great number of knights of various standings, including important benefactors of the abbey: Lasceles and Ingrams among others. There are two confirmation charters by Adam II de Brus in the cartulary, and although they are very typical documents, the transfer of properties which are described in them is worth a more detailed examination. The tenants of the Bruses who were related to each other alienated to Rievaulx Abbey a substantial, compact territory in a process which resembles piecing together a puzzle. The first of the documents was a confirmation of the grant by Adam II de Brus's tenant Richard de Losth of thirty-three acres of land in Normanby with Saltcote-hill and fisheries in the Tees, which was issued between 1175 and 1185.[119] Adam also confirmed his other grant of a fishery in Normanby with eight acres of land, also between 1175 and 1185.[120] The grants of Richard de Losth were not isolated acts, since he had pre-existing family links with Rievaulx. His uncle Richard son of Thurstan de Normanby granted to Rievaulx an important property in Normanby, some time earlier than his nephew's grant, between 1170 and 1180. It consisted of a tillage at Saltcote-flat in Normanby, the water of Tees in his fee in Normanby for making fisheries, pasture for carriers' horses, and the right of way through his property in Normanby.[121] His son Robert, a cousin of Richard de Losth, confirmed his father's grant soon after.[122] Between 1185 and 1195 Robert gave a stretch of land in Normanby lying between the property which the abbey held from Richard de Losth, Fleet and 'domum monachorum', meaning probably buildings of the grange, and the river Tees.[123] Later on, between 1189 and 1199, he also confirmed agreements on the lease of the fisheries made by Walter priest of Eston with Abbot Ernald (1189–99).[124]

---

[117] *Cartulary*, no. 98; *EYC*, III, no. 1507.

[118] Guisborough was founded and richly endowed in 1119 by Robert de Brus.

[119] *Cartulary*, no. 119; *EYC*, II, no. 744.

[120] *EYC*, II, no. 664.

[121] *Cartulary*, no. 116; *EYC*, II, no. 739.

[122] *Cartulary*, no. 117; *EYC*, II, no. 740.

[123] *Cartulary*, no. 169; *EYC*, II, no. 742.

[124] *EYC*, II, no. 741.

Richard de Losth himself added a missing part of the puzzle of the property in Normanby, namely his inheritance bordering with those of his uncle. This donation consisted of several small grants helping the monks to round off what they had already accumulated in the area: thirty acres of land in Saltcote-flat in Normanby, lying between the river Tees and land which Richard son of Thurstan, his uncle, gave them, and between Wrange Flat on the east and Saltcote-hills on the west, and in five other places. He also gave his land in Saltcote-hills, his part of the water of Tees for fisheries, and pasture for one hundred ewes. Richard's sons Roger and Ernald gave their consent for this alienation.[125] Afterwards, between 1175 and 1190, Richard de Losth gave, again with the consent of his sons, one bovate of land and one acre for building purposes in Normanby.[126] This cluster of grants is a prime example of how family connections were important in securing desirable properties by the abbey. This was the most effective way of creating compact estates. Once the tradition of being a benefactor to a particular house had been established and sustained beyond the first generation, the likelihood of future donations or at least confirmations increased. Besides, grants from one family had another advantage for the recipient as they were usually located close to each other.

Another confirmation charter, dated somewhere between 1178 and about 1190, was issued by Adam II de Brus for Rievaulx Abbey, to confirm a substantial grant by William Ingram, from this family of active benefactors of Rievaulx. This donation consisted originally of five bovates in Welburn, the site of a sheep fold and pasture for five hundred sheep, and a meadow below Arncliffe.[127] In this case, though, Brus's charter is copied among other grants of the Ingram family. This manoeuvre indicates that the Ingram family, although of lower standing, were more important as benefactors, and their connections with the abbey were more important than their tenancy of Brus. Therefore the compiler of the cartulary grouped the Ingram charters in a distinctive set and was not concerned with their tenurial connections with the Bruses.

If we look at the distribution of the charters in the cartulary discussed above it is clear that the abbey was aware of the connections between those individuals, both familial (Richard son of Thurstan, Robert son of Richard, and Richard de Losth) and tenurial (Adam II de Brus and Richard de Losth). Connections acquired via marriages, cousins, and siblings were recognized by the compiler of the cartulary by placing the charters of related individuals together. Similarly, the confirmation charters granted by tenants accompany donations of lords. In some of these cases donated properties were adjacent or located in close vicinity, so the organization of the cartulary mirrors the social and topographical organization of the locality in which Rievaulx was located.

---

[125] *Cartulary*, no. 118; *EYC*, II, no. 743.

[126] *EYC*, II, no. 745.

[127] *Cartulary*, no. 121; *EYC*, II, no. 121.

By the early thirteenth century the generosity of the richest men was very much restricted, rarely stretching beyond confirmations or small value grants. In 1233 Peter III de Brus son of Peter confirmed several grants by his tenants, mainly to Guisborough Priory. Among them was a grant by Stephen, Richard, and Dionisius de Eston originally given by their father, Walter, of two carucates of land in Cargo Fleet, York, which he bought from Rievaulx Abbey. Peter de Brus, as their overlord, rendered to the abbey the two shillings yearly due to him from the said property.[128]

The last of the great barons, discussed here, who was connected to Rievaulx Abbey was William, Lord of Holderness and Earl of York, one of the most powerful magnates in the North during the reign of King Stephen. William, Earl of Aumâle was the overlord of the Ros family, hereditary patrons of Rievaulx Abbey. As a benefactor of religious houses he particularly favoured the Cistercian order and founded two daughter houses of Fountains Abbey at Meaux and Vaudey (Lincolnshire). William's involvement with Rievaulx Abbey was limited to only one quitclaim of his rights to 'Micleholme' between 1166 and 1184. This charter was copied into the cartulary together with the other documents related to the dispute about the waste below Pickering, thus the involvement of William was motivated, in the compiler's understanding, by the economic conflict rather then any possible links through the Ros family, although the Earl took the abbey into his special protection: 'Therefore I have taken the said house into my protection and custody, and similarly the monks and lay brothers of this house, just as my brothers.'[129] None of the other quitclaimants of the waste below Pickering made similar gestures. There are several possible explanations for this special relationship. Firstly, William, Earl of Aumâle, as the founder of Meaux and Vaudey Abbeys had a special interest in the Cistercian order; secondly, as a great lord, he was expected to be a protector of religious houses; and thirdly, the favour shown to Rievaulx might have been motivated by the tenurial links with the Ros family, although this last explanation is the least likely considering that the hereditary patrons of Rievaulx were very reluctant benefactors themselves.

The cartulary provides excellent evidence that, in the first hundred and fifty years of its existence, Rievaulx Abbey secured the patronage of several prominent earls and barons, of whom Roger de Mowbray and Gilbert de Gant were the most generous. Furthermore, the services of protection and arbitration also offered by the noblemen to the abbey played an important role for Rievaulx. Crucially, this house remained cautious in becoming particularly dependent on one individual or one family. In contrast to Fountains Abbey, this monastery had fewer benefactors from the top stratum of society, but these benefactors were important for Rievaulx, nevertheless, and this is reflected in the organization of the cartulary. Fountains Abbey

---

[128] London, British Library, Additional Charter 20578.

[129] 'Ego etiam recepi eandem domum in meam protectionem et custodiam et monachos et conversos ejusdem domus similiter sicut fratres meos': *Cartulary*, no. 185.

had built the core of its estates on grants from the Percys, Mowbrays, Rumillies, and Stutevilles, but like Rievaulx, it was the multitude of donations from knights that gave this house its extensive estates.[130] Even if the other wealthy benefactors of Rievaulx were not particularly generous themselves, some of their tenants often were, and the lords, if they did not encourage, at least did not object to these alienations. Some of the donors clearly favoured certain orders, such as the Gant family who preferred Augustinian and Cistercian monks as the recipients of their grants; others such as the Bruses spread their grants over several orders; but in all cases Rievaulx benefited from the donations of their tenants. Besides, many of the wealthy knights who were less connected to the great families gave more to Rievaulx with much greater loss for themselves.

Knightly Families and Rievaulx Abbey

The middle rank of benefactors played a significant role in the development of the abbey's estates as these people constituted the majority of the abbey's benefactors and surpassed, collectively, the generosity of the barons. Knights were based locally and were more accessible than the great lords who often spent considerable time with the royal court and were engaged in political and military campaigns far from their northern estates. The knights' status came below the aristocrats discussed in the earlier part of this chapter and was defined by the possession of a knight's fee or fees; holdings could vary in size from several, often held from a number of lords, to a fraction of a fee. Like their lords, knights often sub-infeudated their holding to other people and built their own networks of tenants. Knights were a very diverse social class, and the status of many families changed over the generations by means of advantageous marriages, land acquisition, or patronage, any of which could boost the economic power of the family. In Yorkshire there were several locally important families, many of them connected to each other by kinship and marriage.[131] Over the years many families acquired substantial holdings and political significance and broke through to baronial level; others lost their status altogether due to excessive alienations or misfortunes. In their quest for social advancement, many knightly families tried to emulate those above them. Since religious patronage was so widespread among the aristocrats, in the twelfth century knights increasingly followed their example. However, this does not mean that all the grants from knights were given purely for the sake of social elevation; other reasons such as piety or personal motivations also played an important role.

Among the knightly benefactors of Rievaulx there were clear examples of strong and personal religious motivation behind the donation. The participation of knights,

[130] Wardrop, *Fountains Abbey,* pp. 133–70.

[131] Green, *Aristocracy*, p. 414.

for whatever reason, in the foundation of and donation to Cistercian houses was common throughout Europe and significantly helped the expansion of the order. One knightly family in particular displayed an unparalleled generosity to Rievaulx Abbey. The Birkin family remained generous benefactors of the abbey for four generations, although there was no clear tenurial reason for the grants.[132] The Lacy family who were their lords founded, among other houses, Pontefract Priory and Kirkstall Abbey but did not show much interest in Rievaulx. However, many of the marriages of the Birkins created links with families who already supported the abbey. The first member of the Birkin family who became a benefactor of Rievaulx Abbey was Emma, wife of Peter (sister of John de Lasceles, from a family of neighbours and early benefactors of the abbey). Her favourite monastic house was Selby, but she also granted to Rievaulx two carucates in Shitlington and Flockton (south-west of Wakefield) with their respective common pastures between 1145 and 1160.[133]

Her son Adam son of Peter married twice, firstly with Matilda, probably a sister of Adam son of Swane, also a benefactor of Rievaulx. Their son Robert died without an heir. From the second marriage, also to a woman called Matilda, who was a coheir of Robert de Caux, there were five children: John (the heir), Peter, Roger, William, and Juliana.[134] When Adam son of Peter died in 1184 John succeeded him in the office of the forestership of Sherwood.[135] Although Adam son of Peter was a benefactor of several houses — Selby, Monk Bretton, Pontefract, Kirkstall, Headley, Esholt, and Hampole, due to tenurial and family connections with the first five houses and physical proximity with the last two houses — his donations to Rievaulx appear to be motivated by a strong personal choice.[136] His charters also have an individual touch which is lacking in many other charters for Rievaulx Abbey. Apart from the conventional request for the salvation of the souls of his relatives and his own, there is a recurring request in his charters for salvation of those who 'may have sinned for me and because of me'. This phrase also appears in Adam's charters to other monasteries as well.[137] Although the phrase in itself is conventional, it did not appear in the charters of any other benefactor of Rievaulx Abbey. It might have been suggested by the scribe of Adam son of Peter's charters, but it is unlikely that the scribe would do it without Adam's request for a wording somehow reflecting his concerns. There was clearly something in his past, something which he had done, which he deeply regretted, so his donations to monasteries had strong expiatory

---

[132] For the genealogical table, see *EYC*, III, 359.

[133] *EYC*, III, no. 1724.

[134] *EYC*, III, 358–59.

[135] *EYC*, X, 170.

[136] Burton, *Monastic Order in Yorkshire*, p. 212.

[137] 'illiorum qui peccaverit per me et pro me'; see discussion of the phrase in Burton, *Monastic Order in Yorkshire*, pp. 214–15.

overtones. It is likely that the unknown sins of Adam son of Peter were related to the unstable years of King Stephen's reign, a difficult time in the northern peripheries, marked by violence and fast-changing alliances. It is possible that Adam had betrayed somebody or acted against his principles in this difficult political climate and still felt guilty in his later life.[138] It is also important to ask why Rievaulx Abbey, not Fountains or other Cistercian houses in the region, should have become the recipient of Adam's donations. Was it the spiritual reputation of the house or the high profile of Abbot Ailred? Unfortunately, his charters do not provide any clue, but some pre-existing family tradition (the grant of his mother, Emma) might have influenced his choice. The donation to religious houses as an expiatory act has a long tradition, and the church clearly encouraged such ideas. For example, Meaux Abbey was founded in 1151 by William, Earl of Aumâle, as a compensation for not fulfilling a vow to go on a crusade. According to the Meaux chronicle this expiatory gesture was suggested to William by a monk from Fountains Abbey.[139] Although the scale of Adam son of Peter's generosity for Rievaulx was unusual, the gesture itself was within the established convention.

The copies of his charters in the cartulary are numerous and consistently placed together with other documents issued by members of his family. The first charter, dated between 1142 and 1150, comprises the grant of a smithy in Stainborough (near Barnsley) by the river Dove (in Farndale), a riding called Oggethwaite with the right to extract iron ore, dead wood for charcoal, and a common pasture there.[140] His next charter, issued before 1160, indicates how competition for benefactors and their grants had intensified between the religious houses by the mid-twelfth century. In this document, Adam son of Peter promised that he would not grant any property to other monastic houses apart from Rievaulx in the places where he had already given them some land:

> Let it be known that I have granted and established and confirmed, [. . .] that I and my heirs will never accept any other men of any other religious order in any vill, or land, or pasture, wherever I have given them land or pasture or mining rights, except the said monks of Rievaulx.[141]

---

[138] On the influences on the phraseology and composition of the charters, see David Postles, 'Country *Clerici* and the Composition of English Twelfth- and Thirteenth-Century Charters', in *Charters and the Use of the Written Word in Medieval Society*, ed. by Karl Heidecker, Utrecht Studies in Medieval Literacy, 5 (Turnhout: Brepols, 2000), pp. 27–42. I would like to thank Dr Janet Burton for her suggestions concerning this peculiar phrase.

[139] Burton, *Monastic Order in Yorkshire*, p. 121.

[140] *Cartulary*, no. 91; *EYC*, III, no. 1725.

[141] 'Sciatis me concessisse ac statuisse ac confirmasse [. . .] quod ego et heredes mei nunquam recolligemus alicujus religionis homines in villa aliqua vel terra vel pastura, ubicunque dedi eis terram vel pasturam vel mineriam preter eosdem monachos Rievallenses': *Cartulary*, no. 92.

Although Adam was exceptionally generous to Rievaulx Abbey, this particular promise was not fulfilled as he gave land there to many other houses.[142] Later grants by Adam to Rievaulx consisted of valuable properties in Faweather (Rumbolds Moor, parish of Bingley) and in Stainborough — for building smithies and wood for making charcoal, essential in iron production — as well as iron-rich land and woods in Shitlington and Flockton.[143] Between late 1170 and 1180 he increased the abbey's holdings in the West Riding and added further clauses of iron production monopoly in the five vills in the parish of Bradford:

> I have given [. . .] all the dead wood and the whole minerals rights in Halton and Shipley, and in Heaton and in Chellow, so that nobody in these above said places should build a forge, except the said monks.[144]

The recurrence of such clauses seems rather puzzling, since Adam's generosity was not restricted to one house only, as Rievaulx Abbey and other interested monastic houses knew very well. In the area of Adam's earlier grant to Bolton Priory, he also gave to Rievaulx the whole vill of Halton between 1166 and 1185 with the exception of one carucate which he had granted previously to the canons of Bolton. The abbey of Rievaulx promised to pay six shillings of annual service, which were previously paid by William de Kasteleia and Thomas de Mohaut. The grantor also added an annual pittance of bread and fish to be given on the anniversary of his death.[145] Such a request ensured continuous commemoration of his name in the abbey and was often requested by the benefactors of Benedictine as well as Cistercian monasteries. In the context of the unusual generosity of Adam son of Peter, it indicates his desire for particular commemoration by the monastic community and his personal concern for salvation. This will be discussed in more detail in the last chapter.

---

[142] Adam son of Peter was also benefactor of Esholt, Hampole, Headley, Kirkstall, Monk Bretton, Pontefract, Selby: *EYC*, I, no. 201, III, nos 1730, 1701, 1732–34, 1739–42, 1735, 1738, 1452; VI, no. 67. For discussion of Adam's donation activities, see Burton, *Monastic Order in Yorkshire*, pp. 211–15.

[143] *Cartulary*, no. 94; *EYC*, III, no. 1726; dated 1150–60. *Cartulary*, no. 95; *EYC*, III, no. 1728; dated 1150–70. *Cartulary*, no. 99; *EYC*, III, no. 1727; dated 1150–60.

[144] 'me dedisse [. . .] totum mortuum boscum et totam mineriam de Hageltune et Schipeleia et de Hetune et de Chelleslawa, ita ut nullus in his predictis locis favercam faciat nisi predicti monachi': *Cartulary*, no. 100; *YD*, I, no. 210; dated 1166; *West Yorkshire: An Archaeological Survey to A.D. 1500*, vol. III, *The Rural Medieval Landscape*, ed. by M. L. Faull and S. A. Moorhouse (Wakefield: West Yorkshire Metropolitan County Council, 1981), pp. 774, 788.

[145] London, British Library, Egerton Charter 2247; for an English summary of this charter see, *YD*, I, no. 211. There were further accessions in the vill of Halton at the end of twelfth century, for example, a grant of Walter Grimet later confirmed by his widow Johanna: London, British Library, Egerton Charter 2248.

The pious interest of Adam son of Peter was shared by other members of his family as Adam's younger brother Roger was also a benefactor of Rievaulx Abbey. He confirmed his brother's grant of fifteen acres in Blacker.[146] Roger is also known to have given some land in Shitlington and Flockton, which was confirmed by his brother.[147] In contrast with many other families of benefactors, the first dispute between Rievaulx and the Birkins occurred only in the early thirteenth century, although it was primarily an inheritance dispute within the family in which Rievaulx Abbey was caught up. In 1204 the younger son of Adam son of Peter, Peter de Birkin, sued his brother Roger in an assize of *mort d'ancestor* and the Abbot of Rievaulx as Roger's tenant for one and a half carucates in Shitlington. The case remained unresolved because Peter and Roger were brothers from the same parents, but Peter was allowed to seek a writ of right and the Abbot a separate writ.[148] Adam's son and heir, John de Birkin (d. 1227), appeared in numerous charters by his father, giving consent to the alienation of family property. Between 1207 and 1227 he also gave the wood in Harden after his father's death for the salvation of his soul, his mother's, and those of all his relatives. And as his father's grant he restricted the building of forges in Harden to Rievaulx Abbey only.[149]

The Birkin family was also exceptional in the fact that their generosity continued beyond the first two generations, allowing the abbey to strengthen its holdings in the West Riding. The grandson of Adam son of Peter, Thomas de Birkin (d. 1230), a son of John, granted to the abbey his lands and wood in Harden located between Halton and Cullingworth between 1227 and 1230.[150] His sister and heiress, Isabel, married Robert Everingham and they also confirmed, between 1230 and 1235 the grants by Adam and John de Birkin of Halton vill, wood in Harden, twelve bovates in Cullingworth, three bovates in Faweather, all their grants in Rumbolds Moor, and common pasture in Stainborough (near Barnsley).[151] The same couple confirmed the right of the abbey in 1235 to hold the vill of Halton given previously by Adam son of Peter, grandfather of Isabel, sixteen bovates given by John de Casteleya, nine bovates and the mill in Cullingworth (a gift of Robert de Meinil), three bovates there given by Esholt nunnery, as well as other properties in Rumbolds Moor and Stainborough

[146] *Cartulary*, no. 96.

[147] *Cartulary*, no. 97.

[148] *Yorkshire Assize Rolls, for the Reign of King John and King Henry III*, ed. by C. T. Clay, Yorkshire Archaeological Society Record Series, 44 (Leeds: Yorkshire Archaeological Society, 1911), p. 23; also published in *Pleas before the King or his Justices 1198–1212*, ed. by Doris M. Stenton, Selden Society, 83 (London: Bernard Quaritch, 1967), no. 1007.

[149] *YD*, I, no. 212.

[150] London, British Library, Egerton Charter 2249; for an English summary of this charter, see *YD*, I, no. 213.

[151] London, British Library, Egerton Charter 2250; for an English summery of this charter, see *YD*, I, no. 214.

(common pastures) and wood in Harden, which Adam and his son John had donated to the abbey.[152]

The grants of the Birkin family and their tenants were the bases of the extensive iron works of Rievaulx Abbey in Chellow, Flockton, Halton, Harden, Heaton, Shipley, and Shitlington. These areas, all in the West Riding, were a considerable distance from Rievaulx, but this was not a deterrent for the abbey which recognized their commercial value. Other houses, Byland (Bentley and Denby granges), Fountains (Bradley and Ainley granges), and Selby (Chellow grange), also established their iron works in close proximity to each other in this area.[153] These important holdings by the abbey were the result of a donation from one family and some of their tenants who had shown an unparalleled generosity to Rievaulx. Adam son of Peter had strong personal reasons for the donations; his pious gestures appear to be underlined by some sort of personal grief and guilt. But his sons and grandsons continued donations to Rievaulx Abbey as the family tradition without the strong expiatory motivation which underpinned the actions of their ancestor.

Another interesting example of lay generosity extending over several generations comes from the Tunstall family and their tenants in East (Low) Bolton in Wensleydale. They cannot be compared with the Birkins in their generosity, but the pattern of their donations needs to be discussed in more detail because it gives a good insight into the mechanism of building up supportive groups of benefactors within a closely connected community. The Tunstall family relationship with Rievaulx Abbey spanned several generations, and a great number of other individuals connected to this family augmented lands originally granted by Acaris de Tunstall. As a testimony to this family's importance to the abbey, Acaris's charters and confirmations were copied into the cartulary in a single cluster. However, the printed edition of the cartulary incorporated additional charters connected to the Tunstall family, which were never a part of the original cartulary, potentially misleading the reader. These additional documents, dating from the late twelfth and early thirteenth centuries, were at the time of the cartulary edition at Bolton Hall and remained there until they were deposited in 1982 in North Yorkshire County Record Office, Northallerton with the rest of the Orde-Powlett family (Lords of Bolton) archive.[154] It seems that this group of charters, many of them with seals still attached, were handed over by Rievaulx Abbey to Henry le Scrop in 1315 when Abbot Thomas III exchanged with him the lands in East Bolton for land in Newsam on Tees.[155]

---

152 *The Feet of Fines for the County York from 1232 to 1246*, ed. by John Parker, Yorkshire Archaeological Society Record Series, 67 (Leeds: Yorkshire Archaeological Society, 1925), pp. 39–40.

153 *West Yorkshire*, ed. by Faull and Moorhouse, III, 779.

154 ZDO1/0208–0256.

155 Burton, 'Estates and Economy', p. 40; ZDO1/0252–0256.

Acaris granted, in 1173–74, twenty-five and a half acres of land in East Bolton and the right of pasture in the territory of that vill for a limited number of animals, reserving a service payment of a half mark yearly, although the monks gave a lump sum of ten marks to cover payments until 1194.[156] This arrangement may have helped Acaris to pay off his debts or acquire some other land. Even if material consideration played some role in his initial grant, he continued his support for Rievaulx Abbey. In the same year he gave, or rather added, one house and several plots of land in East Bolton and the right to use the common pasture for a limited number of animals.[157] In the late 1170s he added a further grant of arable land and a meadow in the same vill.[158]

Like the cases discussed in the earlier parts of this chapter, the idea of becoming a donor of Rievaulx Abbey spread throughout the tenurial group of the Tunstall family providing Rievaulx Abbey with a selection of small but useful properties. Dolfin de Bolton and William son of Humphrey gave more lands in the vicinity of their lord Acaris's grants and with his explicit permission.[159] The lord made sure that he had control over what was given to Rievaulx Abbey, and each donation from his tenant required his sanction. Occasionally other individuals whose property rights were affected had to give their authorization. One of his tenants, Peter son of Gilo de Bolton, donated to the abbey his rights to the land and park in Depedale, also in East Bolton. This land was given to Peter by his lord, Acaris de Tunstall, and Peter's sister Sigerid and her husband gave consent to the alienation.[160] The same Peter, with the consent of his lord, exchanged half an acre in Bolton for another plot and payment of twelve pence.[161] Another neighbour, Adam son of Ralph de Bolton, who also might have been a tenant of Acaris de Tunstall and certainly had an interest in the same area, quitclaimed, after Acaris's death, any possible rights he might have to the land in East Bolton which Acaris had granted to Rievaulx.[162] Adam also exchange one perch and six and half rods of land there with the abbey for another plot in the same vill and received the additional compensation of two shillings.[163]

In the early thirteenth century Acaris de Tunstall was succeeded by his son Roger in the lands in Tunstall and Appleton, and the family and its tenants retained their interest

[156] *Cartulary*, no. 139; *EYC*, IV, no. 91.

[157] *Cartulary*, no. 140; *EYC*, IV, no. 92.

[158] *Cartulary*, no. 141; *EYC*, IV, no. 93. The full extent of Acaris's grants from the fee of his lord, Ralph son of Roger, in East Bolton was confirmed by Ralph in the charter copied into the cartulary immediately after Acaris's charters. *Cartulary*, no. 142; *EYC*, V, no. 142.

[159] *Cartulary*, nos 143, 144; *EYC*, IV, nos 94, 95.

[160] ZDO1/0222; published incomplete in *Cartulary*, p. 100–01.

[161] ZDO1/0218; published incomplete in *Cartulary*, p. 100.

[162] ZDO1/0208; published incomplete in *Cartulary*, pp. 101–02.

[163] ZDO1/0216; published incomplete in *Cartulary*, p. 102.

in East Bolton.[164] The younger son of Acaris, Richard de Tunstall, was not entirely happy with his father's alienations in favour of Rievaulx Abbey but eventually confirmed his father's donations in 1192, including twelve acres and a small meadow in East Bolton which were previously the object of a lawsuit between Richard and the abbey at the court of royal justices at York.[165] He also granted three rods in East Bolton between the land already belonging to the abbey and properties belonging to other individuals.[166] This example was followed by tenants in East Bolton. Richard son of Wimar donated to Rievaulx all those lands in East Bolton which he received from Acaris de Tunstall, Acaris's son Richard, and Emma, daughter of Richard de Bolton.[167] Alda, a daughter of the previously mentioned Peter son of Gilo de Bolton, as a widow with the consent of her son and heir, William son of Ulf, quitclaimed all her rights to the lands in East Bolton held by the abbey. The grant was sealed and confirmed at the court of their lord, Richard son of Acaris de Tunstall.[168]

In the third generation of the Tunstall family the links with Rievaulx Abbey and further grants continued. Ismania, daughter Richard de Tunstall, married first Peter son of William de Bolton and then Reginald son of Walter de Bolton and became the heiress when her brother, Conan, died without issue. Ismania followed the example of her father, uncle, and grandfather, became a benefactor of Rievaulx Abbey, and gave properties and rights to the abbey with both of her husbands and also independently as a widow. Ismania gave, jointly with her first husband, their mill in East Bolton with the monopoly in that vill.[169] They also confirmed her father's grant in East Bolton, but for an annual service payment of two shillings and six pence.[170] During her widowhood Ismania independently granted to the abbey a rent, described in the previous charter, and additionally confirmed all her previous donations and added one penny of rent which she received from her brother, Conan.[171] After her second marriage to Reginald, the couple confirmed her father's and her own earlier grants. Ismania also pledged in the hand of Ellis de Bellerby that, if she survived her husband Reginald, she would not claim any land back from the abbey and would confirm all the grants before getting married again.[172] This interesting clause shows again the concern of the abbey to secure any legal and practical loophole if the

[164] *EYC*, IV, 123.

[165] ZDO1/0214; dated in *EYC*, IV, no. 98; printed incomplete in *Cartulary*, pp. 91–92.

[166] ZDO1/0220; published incomplete in *Cartulary*, p. 96.

[167] ZDO1/0250; published incomplete in *Cartulary*, p. 93.

[168] ZDO1/0246; published incomplete in *Cartulary*, pp. 102–03.

[169] ZDO1/0224; published incomplete in *Cartulary*, p. 93.

[170] ZDO1/0226; published incomplete in *Cartulary*, p. 94.

[171] ZDO1/0240 and 0242; published incomplete in *Cartulary*, pp. 94–95.

[172] ZDO1/0244; published incomplete in *Cartulary*, pp. 95–96.

donor's circumstances would change in the future. This was one of the methods of preventing disputes and will be discussed further in the next chapter.

This sequence of donations given over several generations in the East Bolton area illustrates how a group of relatives and their tenants would slowly, but effectively, alienate large parts of their holdings to the abbey. These kinds of grants, not large in themselves, were very important for the abbey, because they helped to build compact estates. Grants were rarely given in isolation by one individual. Donations had a collective character and could either unite members of a family in a pious gesture or cause dissatisfaction among heirs who objected to the decrease of their holdings. This shared nature of the donations is reinforced by the witness lists on the Tunstall charters. They consist of relatives, neighbours, members of the tenurial group, and local clergy.

The generosity of the benefactors could take different forms. The type of their donation depended very much on the location and character of their own properties; it could consist of pastures, arable lands, or forests or other income-generating properties such as iron ore deposits, mills, and inland waters suitable for setting up fisheries. In the North Yorkshire setting the grants of pasture were not only fairly common, but also desirable. The harsh climatic conditions favoured pastoral economy, and by the late twelfth century, many of the local monastic houses became successful wool producers. Torphin de Allerston was one of the early donors responsible for the grant of extensive pasture rights in Allerston within the waste below Pickering. The charters of his grants contain some interesting clauses shedding light on the practice of neighbourly coexistence. Between 1160 and 1175 Torphin gave some land on the east side of Allerston and the adjoining meadow, which Richard son of Gil held from him, as well as a meadow in the direction of Derwent, previously held by the same Richard.[173] Other family members also joined in his donations. Together with his wife, Matilda de Fribois, and their son Alan, they granted in 1160 five acres of land and a site for the buildings in Gindale in Allerston, a pasture, and sheep folds for five hundred sheep. This grant also had a clause by which the grantors reserved half of the manure for themselves and one toft. The monks were also obliged to pay a rent of twenty shillings annually to Matilda and her heirs. In return, the grantor promised not to allow sheep belonging to anybody else on this pasture. This appears to be a sensible precaution, since this particular location was already occupied by the animals of the donors and the abbey, which was probably the maximum amount of grazing this pasture could sustain.[174]

Between 1154 and 1174 Torphin and his son Alan gave another pasture for five hundred sheep in Allerston, a sheep fold near Morehow, and a portion of land in the Westerdale. The donors also added one acre of meadow to collect hay for the sheep

[173] *Cartulary*, no. 138; *EYC*, I, no. 388.

[174] *Cartulary*, no. 167; *EYC*, I, no. 386; *Cartulary*, no. 86.

folds, but again reserved half of the manure for themselves.[175] Sheep dung was an important fertilizer, and many monastic grants had a clause reserving all or some of the dung for the benefactor.[176] A further grant in Allerston, of much smaller value, was given to the abbey in the early thirteenth century by John son of Baldwin de Allerston (who was not related to this family) of free passage through his territory in Allerston called Greenhill.[177] Such a grant of passage, small in itself, was very important to the abbey. Since the estates of Rievaulx and many other houses were spread throughout the region, rights of way were crucial for the efficient running of their economy.[178]

The charters of the Allerston family contain some of the most specific arrangements of the use of pasture among the twelfth-century grants to the abbey. These documents give a good insight into the practical side of grant giving and the subsequent relationship between the donor and the recipient which was the result of sharing the same pasture or becoming close neighbours. The shared use of common pasture as described in the Allerston charters necessitated cooperation on a daily basis between these two parties, and in practice these were probably the employees of the Allerston family and the abbey. The more detailed the agreement was, the less likely conflict was to arise because the initial document specified the practice of dealing with potentially conflicting interests.

As we have seen so far, family and tenurial connections mattered a great deal in securing new benefactors among the neighbours of the abbey. These could include contacts established via marriages, and vertical or horizontal affinities across social strata. In some cases, lay neighbours of Rievaulx Abbey had multiple connections, all of which could influence them to become benefactors of a particular institution. These social ties were often the first steps in securing donations by the abbey, but the continuity of pious gifts within families required a favourable set of circumstances over a longer period of time, stretching beyond the first generation. The relationship between Rievaulx Abbey and the Bulmer family exemplifies how these mechanisms worked in practice.

Bertram de Bulmer's brother-in-law, Stephen I de Meinil, was connected to Rievaulx Abbey in many ways. He was a neighbour of Walter Espec, and his name appears in the so-called foundation charter in the second place on the list of neighbours

---

[175] *Cartulary*, no. 168; *EYC*, I, no. 387.

[176] *West Yorkshire*, ed. by Faull and Moorhouse, III, 764–65.

[177] Bodl. Dodsw. vii, fol. 93^{v}; published incomplete in *Cartulary*, p. 209. Allerston was inherited by the Hastings family in the early thirteenth century: *Early Yorkshire Families*, ed. by Clay and Greenway, p. 1.

[178] Stephen Moorhouse, 'Monastic Estates: Their Composition and Development', in *The Archaeology of Rural Monasteries*, ed. by Roberta Gilchrist and Harold Mytum, British Archaeological Reports, 203 (Oxford: B.A.R., 1989), pp. 29–81 (p. 59).

witnessing the act.[179] It is important to remember at this point that this charter is in fact a compilation of two documents, one related to the actual foundation ceremony and the second one to the augmentation of the foundation grant which took place between 1145 and 1153. Stephen I de Meinil was therefore a witness at one or both of these ceremonies, and as a neighbour, he was understandably interested in the new monastic house.

Stephen I de Meinil was a prominent individual in his own right, connected to Eustace FitzJohn and also appearing as a witness on many important monastic charters between 1120 and 1140.[180] His gift to Rievaulx was made towards the end of Walter Espec's life, between 1145 and 1152, and consisted of the vill of Stainton.[181] This land was given with the consent of Sibil his wife and his sons Robert and Henry, but the donor reserved the right to take timber from Stainton and requested one mark yearly of service payment from the monks.[182] The younger son of Stephen I, Henry de Meinil, did not add anything to his father's donation, but confirmed grants by his men in Broughton (Cleveland) given by Jordan Pain, Alan Barn, and Bernard.[183] The donor also reserved his right of arbitration in the case of conflicts between his tenant Jordan, or his heirs, and the monastery. This clause appears to copy the behaviour of the great barons, such as the Mowbrays or Gants, whose courts were a legal arena in case of disputes between their tenants and their monasteries:

> And if by chance it should happen that Jordan or his heirs would wish to trouble the said monks on the account of the said charitable grant, I and my heirs will perform full justice for them in this.[184]

In this way, even if Henry de Meinil lost direct control over the alienated property, he could exert some degree of control over its future by acting as a mediator between the abbey and any potential layperson infringing on its rights to the Meinil's donation.

The next generation of the Meinil family, represented by Stephen II (d. 1188), continued to support Rievaulx Abbey. Stephen II was the grandson of Stephen I and the son of Robert de Meinil, the older brother of Henry. Between 1175 and 1185 he gave part of the woodland of Greenhove bordering Great Broughton to the east and to the west Bilsdale (already in the hands of Rievaulx), for the salvation of his own soul, his

---

[179] *Cartulary*, no. 42.

[180] *EYC*, II, 137.

[181] BL, Cotton Julius D. i, fol. 15^{v} [fol. 19^{v}].

[182] *Cartulary*, no. 72; *EYC*, III, no. 1842; dated 1145–52.

[183] The original grant of Jordan Pain was given between *c.* 1180 and 1188. *Cartulary*, no. 123; *EYC*, I, no. 580.

[184] 'Et si forte contigerit quod Jordanus vel heredes ejus de ipsa elemosina molestiam eisdem monachis inferre voluerint, ego et heredes mei plenariam inde illis justitiam exhibebimus': *Cartulary*, no. 125; *EYC*, II, no. 775; dated 1175–85.

wife's, and those of all their relatives.[185] Although he came from a family of generous benefactors to the abbey, it is worth pointing out another connection to the abbey created by his marriage. Stephen II's wife was Joan, a daughter of Robert I de Ros, patron of the abbey. Robert was not particularly generous towards Rievaulx Abbey, but his son-in-law might have wanted to show support for the family foundation of his in-laws. Surprisingly, Stephen II did not show any interest in Kirkham Priory, their favourite house, so the donation to Rievaulx Abbey was his personal choice, not just a sign of asserting his affinities to the family of his wife. Besides, Kirkham was located further away geographically from his area of interest than Rievaulx.

More than one hundred years after the death of Stephen II, when his great-grandson Nicholas de Meinil died, the connection of the family with Rievaulx Abbey was still evident. The inquisition into the lands of Nicholas, who died on 28 May 1299, revealed that the Abbot of Rievaulx held from him four carucates in Little Broughton (near Stokesley) in frankalmoign, each worth forty shillings yearly.[186]

The Meinil family particularly favoured white monks and were also long-standing benefactors of another Cistercian house, Fountains Abbey. Although Stephen II requested spiritual benefits from the monks of Rievaulx, he planned to enter Fountains Abbey as a monk in old age, and for that purpose, he granted the latter land in Eston for building fisheries.[187] What is important to stress about the contact between Rievaulx Abbey and the Meinils is the multiplicity of their links with the abbey: tenurial links to a close associate of Walter Espec and marriage to a daughter of a patron of Rievaulx. Yet this would not have sustained this family's long relationship with the abbey if the Meinils had no personal commitment to the Cistercian order.

Although there was no simple correlation between the wealth of a knightly family and their generosity to religious institutions, those who controlled large estates could aspire to emulate aristocratic families in their pious donations. Donations to monasteries were an important element in asserting social status. Among the knightly benefactors of Rievaulx Abbey the Bulmers were certainly the wealthiest and most prominent family. The first noted member of this family was Ansketil (died *c.* 1129), a native Anglo-Scandinavian landowner who secured a sheriffdom and royal grants, held mainly in-chief, and also occupied a number of subtenancies from the Rumilly and Mowbray families. Ansketil belonged to the group of new men benefiting from royal patronage.[188] His son Bertram de Bulmer became Sheriff of York in 1130 and again between 1155 and 1163. Bertram held, besides what he already inherited from

---

[185] *Cartulary*, no. 164; *EYC*, II, no. 799.

[186] *Yorkshire Inquisitions*, vol. III, ed. by William Brown, Yorkshire Archaeological Society Record Series, 31 (Leeds: Yorkshire Archaeological Society, 1902), p. 117.

[187] Wardrop, *Fountains Abbey*, p. 167.

[188] Dalton, *Conquest, Anarchy and Lordship*, p. 100; Judith Green, *The Government of England under Henry I* (Cambridge: Cambridge University Press, 1986), p. 248.

his father, a tenancy of the honour of Skipton and probably some subtenancies of the Percy fee. Following the example of many other people of his standing and above, Bertram founded an Augustinian house in Marton during the reign of King Stephen, and he was also a benefactor of Byland Abbey.[189] His marriage to Emma, a daughter of Robert Fossard, brought very desirable connections for a family keen to preserve and advance its position. Bertram's sister Sibil married Stephen I de Meinil, who was present at the foundation of Rievaulx Abbey and later became its benefactor.[190] The early career of the family shows many similarities with the aristocratic benefactors of Rievaulx who benefited from royal patronage and entered advantageous marriages. The grants of the Bulmer family to the houses of the new orders — Cistercian and Augustinian houses — were also in line with the fashion for monastic patronage showed by the aristocrats.

The Bulmer family was closely associated with Rievaulx Abbey in a number of ways. Stephen de Bulmer, who died in 1171/72, the brother of Bertram de Bulmer, was the first member of this family to be connected to Rievaulx Abbey.[191] Stephen de Bulmer confirmed, on behalf of his son and heir, Thomas de Muschamps, an arrangement between their man Walter de Stainesby and Rievaulx Abbey about the fishery on the river Tees with eight acres of land belonging to it of which no details are given. As a part of the deal Stephen and Thomas, with their wives and children, were admitted into the confraternity of the house and promised prayers.[192] The connection between the Bulmer and Meinil families by marriage and shared tenants might have influenced Bertram de Bulmer to give Rievaulx one carucate in Welburn, which was until then held from him by Ansketil son of Gospatric de Brawby. The former tenant received in exchange some other land in an unspecified location.[193] Such a grant always had the potential for causing future trouble, particularly from the heirs of Ansketil who might dispute the rights of the abbey to the part of Welburn which used to belong to their ancestors. The lords still had the power to change the location of the tenancies, but compensation was not always considered adequate by the recipients. Bertram de Bulmer's grant, however small, must have been valued by Rievaulx as it was located in an area of great interest to the abbey. Larger parts of Welburn had already been given to the abbey by Gundreda de Mowbray and augmented later by her son Roger.[194] A clear sign of the monks' concern over the security of the grant was the fact that they copied into the cartulary the charter of the grant of Bertram de Bulmer to his tenant Ansketil son of Gospatric of eleven bovates

[189] *EYC*, XI, 180.

[190] For all the family connection, see *EYC*, II, 128.

[191] My identification is based on the genealogical table in *EYC*, II, 128.

[192] *EYC*, III, no. 907.

[193] *Cartulary*, no. 104; *EYC*, II, no. 1049; dated 1154–57.

[194] *Cartulary*, nos 56, 64.

in Flockton being exchanged for this one carucate in Welburn given to the abbey. The witness list of this charter opens with the name of Abbot Ailred of Rievaulx, which proves the strong interest of the abbey in securing this deal. Bertram de Bulmer had to accommodate the cost of the exchange or rather buy the permission of Ansketil. He did not increase the service payment from the new plot of land, although it was three bovates larger than the property in Welburn.

> Therefore I wish and grant that the said Ansketil and his heirs should hold eleven bovates in the fee and inheritance of me and my heirs, with all the free customs and that service which they used to do for the said carucate of land in Welburn, and there should be in no way any increase in service, which should belong to me or to my heirs on the account of the addition of the three bovates of land.[195]

Like many other lords, including Roger de Mowbray, Bertram had to make a compromise at his own expense to satisfy the rights of his tenant and to support the abbey at the same time. The potential for a dispute between Ansketil and the abbey was diverted, but the expense was borne by his lord, Bertram. This was another valuable service which the lay lords could offer to religious houses.

The Bulmer family is a good example of a wealthy family on the rise who had given generously to a number of religious houses and encouraged their tenants to do the same, even if this meant a material loss for them. The Bulmers were a part of the network of benefactors of Rievaulx Abbey connected by marriages, landholdings, and political affinities between the new men who lived or settled in the area to become not only neighbours but also benefactors of the Cistercian monks.

The spatial closeness between the abbey estates and the laypeople, in other words, being each other's neighbours, could result in a whole range of interactions from becoming benefactors and supporting the abbey as a witness at donation ceremonies to a high degree of hostility, acts of encroachment, or even physical violence against the property and employees of the abbey, as we will see in the next chapter. Despite these variations, the neighbours of the abbey seem to have held in common the longevity of their contacts. Its intensity and character often changed over the generations, but the relationship itself was not easily broken.

Among the longest lasting relationships between the abbey and a knightly family in the neighbourhood was the one with the Lasceles of Bordelby. They were knightly tenants of the Brus fee in Morton, Bordelby, East Harlsey with hamlets of Salcoc and Siddall. Although the family was large, the main branch of the kin, which had substantial holdings in the honour of Richmond and advanced its position considerably

---

[195] 'itaque volo et concedo quod ipse Aschetillus et heredes sui teneant xj bovatas in feodo et hereditate de me et de heredibus meis et cum omnibus liberis consuetudinibus et eodem servitio quod faciebant de predicta carrucata terre de Welleburn et nullo modo crescet aliquid servitium quod michi vel heredibus meis pertineat propter iij bovatas terre de incremento': *Cartulary*, no. 214; *EYC*, II, no. 782; dated 1147–63.

in the thirteenth and fourteenth centuries, did not form any relationships with Rievaulx Abbey, in contrast to the lesser branches of the kin.

Robert de Lasceles of Bordelby was one of the early benefactors of the house in the areas of Cowton and East Harlsey. Between 1154 and 1159 he gave one carucate in Morton in the parish of East Harlsey.[196] In the 1160s Robert gave to the abbey another small grant, an income of one mark from his mill in Bordelby.[197] Robert's grants were not the sole act of one individual. Before 1162 his cousin William de Lasceles of Cowton added a meadow in Cowton, which he acquired from the exchange with Robert de Ros and his wife for one bovate of land in the same vill, which another William the carpenter had held previously.[198] None of these grants was large but all were located in areas where the abbey was receiving donations from other individuals and hoped for further acquisitions. This was to remain a characteristic of Rievaulx's contacts with the Lasceles, although some of the family members were more generous than others, particularly in terms of pasture grants.

The next charter copied into the cartulary after Robert's grant, in the section devoted to this family, is his son's confirmation given between 1170 and 1176. Geoffrey de Lasceles, with the consent of his brothers Robert and William, confirmed half of the vill, but also other properties given by his father, namely the common pasture of East Harlsey and Bordelby for four hundred sheep, ten cows, a bull, and oxen sufficient to till that land, one carucate consisting of eight perches lying on the south side with toft and croft. The donor placed a restriction on the use of common pasture by himself and his people to give a favourable treatment to the flocks of the abbey.

> Within and outside, wherever my cattle and those of the people of these vills should be pastured, provided that nevertheless, their lambs should not be pastured in stubble after harvest of the above said vills, neither should my sheep nor those [belonging] to the people of these vills be pastured in their stubble.[199]

This clause is one of many indications of practical difficulties faced by users of common pastures when new flocks belonging to a third party were introduced to a common pasture. At the point of donating pasture rights to the abbey, the donors wanted to secure some consensus and prevent future disputes by putting in place clear guidelines concerning the use of pasture. In this case, however, the arrangement

---

196 *Cartulary*, no. 87; *EYC*, II, no. 727; *Cartulary*, no. 212.

197 Bodl. Dodsw. vii, fol. 51^{v}; published incomplete in *Cartulary*, p. 206.

198 Bodl. Dodsw. vii, fols 152^{v}–153; published incomplete and with mistakes (Robert de Ros is transcribed as Richard de Ros) in *Cartulary*, p. 207.

199 'intus et extra, ubicunque pecora mea et hominum earundem villarum pascuntur, ita tamen quod agni eorum non pascentur in bladis predictarum villarum, nec agni mei nec hominum earundem villarum pascentur in bladis illorum': *Cartulary*, no. 88; *EYC*, II, no. 728.

favours one user of the common pasture, the abbey, and puts restrictions on its use by other parties.

Between 1170 and 1176 Geoffrey de Lasceles also confirmed his father's grant of a tillage on the south side of Morton given by Robert in return for admittance into the fraternity of Rievaulx Abbey. Similarly, he confirmed his father's grant, for the purpose of the salvation of his own soul and his father's fraternity of the abbey, of the tenement of the late Robert de Hernievill.[200] This type of countergift was important in the process of building lasting contacts between the abbey and its neighbours; the promise of perpetual prayers performed by the monks had a high value in the eyes of people for whom the idea of hell and damnation was a very real threat. I will come back to this issue in the last chapter.

Parallel to the Lasceles grants, their tenants also gave land to Rievaulx Abbey, which effectively augmented their lords' donations. Between 1166 and 1176 Jocelin de Harsley, with the permission of Geoffrey de Lasceles, gave the abbey three acres in Harlsey, located to the east of the town, on the south side of the land belonging to his lord.[201] These grants continued in the next generation and beyond; William son of Jocelin gave to the abbey one more acre in Harlsey, and his son Ralph, Jocelin's grandson, added sixteen acres in the same vill.[202]

In 1185 Geoffrey made an agreement with the abbey, but the details are not known except that the monks paid one mark for the licence to make a settlement with him.[203] After his death, Geoffrey was succeeded by his brother Robert de Lasceles.[204] This Robert son of Robert gave thirteen acres in Harlsey to the abbey, in the vicinity of the donations of his predecessors.[205] The large amount of land held already by the abbey in East Harlsey was further augmented by grants from other members of the Lasceles family in the late twelfth and early thirteenth centuries: William son of Andrew de Lasceles gave four acres in Harlsey, and Gerard son of Adam de Lasceles gave six acres there.[206]

These donations from the Lasceles family are a good, but not isolated, example of the generosity of one family of moderate standing who remained generous to the abbey for several generations. The value of these grants lay in their location, in their close vicinity to each other and in their closeness to the core estates of the abbey.

---

200 *Cartulary*, no. 88; *EYC*, II, no. 728.

201 *Cartulary*, no. 170; *EYC*, II, no. 962; royal confirmation in *CChR 1226–1257*, p. 397.

202 *CPR 1330–1334*, p. 316; published in *Cartulary*, p. 287.

203 'Et de .j. m. de monachis de Rieuall' pro licentia concordandi cum Galfrido de Lacell': *The Great Roll of the Pipe for the Thirty-First Year of the Reign of King Henry the Second, A.D. 1184–1185*, Publications of the Pipe Roll Society, 34 (London: St Catherine Press, 1913), p. 72.

204 *EYC*, II, 71.

205 Bodl. Dodsw. vii, fols 143–143v; published incomplete in *Cartulary*, p. 207.

206 Bodl. Dodsw. vii, fols 52, 142v; published incomplete in *Cartulary*, pp. 206–07.

East Harlsey thereby became a grange; this was first recorded in 1301, but must have existed much earlier.[207]

In the thirteenth century, however, some members of the Lasceles family disputed some grants of their predecessors following the steps of many other benefactors of Rievaulx. In 1205 the monks paid for the aid of the royal court to secure possession of their farm of the demesne of East Harlsey until the end of its term, but it did not prevent further disputes.[208] On 6 October 1251 Abbot Adam de Tilletai of Rievaulx paid one hundred shillings for leave to make an agreement with Robert de Lasceles in a plea of warranty of charter.[209] Then, on 13 October of the same year, Abbot Adam brought a case against the same Robert de Lasceles. The objects of the dispute were two carucates, fifteen acres, one rod, three perches of land in Morton (East Harsley) and one bovate, one hundred and seventy-eight acres of land, and five tofts in Harlsey, and also the pasture for six hundred sheep, ten cows, and one bull in Harlsey and Bordelby. After a lengthy hearing Robert de Lasceles recognized the right of the abbey to hold the above-listed properties which were given to the monks by his ancestors.[210]

The long-lasting relationship between the Lasceles family and the abbey was acknowledged again in the later part of the thirteenth century. According to the writ issued on 28 April 1285 to the Sheriff of Yorkshire, a messuage and two bovates of land in East Harlsey were held by William de Lasceles from the Abbot of Rievaulx 'by homage and service'. As William was illegitimate offspring and had no heirs, this land would return to the Abbot on his death.[211] This connection is important to consider because it points to the changing attitude by the monastic community to its lands and the ways in which they were utilized. By the late thirteenth century the abbey was much more flexible in maintaining the integrity of its estates. Various forms of lease became a viable option to the abbey, particularly in the light of the increasing problems in the recruitment of lay brothers.

---

[207] *Yorkshire Lay Subsidy being a Fifteenth Collected 30 Edward I (1301)*, ed. by William Brown, Yorkshire Archaeological Society Record Series, 21 (Leeds: Yorkshire Archaeological Society, 1897), pp. 85–86.

[208] *EYC*, II, 295; *Great Roll of the Pipe, 7th year of John, Michaelmas 1205*, ed. by Sidney Smith, n.s., 19 (London: Pipe Roll Society, 1941), p. 60.

[209] *Feet of Fines from 1246 to 1272*, ed. by John Parker, Yorkshire Archaeological Society Record Series, 82 (Leeds: Yorkshire Archaeological Society, 1932), p. 24, n. 1.

[210] *Feet of Fines from 1246 to 1272*, ed. by Parker, p. 24.

[211] *Yorkshire Inquisitions*, vol. II, ed. by William Brown, Yorkshire Archaeological Society Record Series, 23 (Leeds: Yorkshire Archaeological Society, 1898), p. 26; *Notes on the Religious and Secular Houses of Yorkshire*, vol. II, ed. by William P. Baildon, Yorkshire Archaeological Society Record Series, 81 (London: Yorkshire Archaeological Society, 1931), pp. 34–35.

Although the Lasceles family was not an isolated case, their generosity to the abbey is particularly well documented. Despite their relatively low status, a large number of Lasceles gave land to Rievaulx Abbey; some of these grants were not larger than a few acres, but their location in Harlsey and its vicinity made them very attractive to the abbey. Although their status was much lower than, for example, the Meinil family's, in contrast to the latter, the Lasceles charters that were copied into the cartulary were placed in a rather prominent position. This again indicates the relative importance of the family to the monastic community, which was not necessarily equal to its standing in the social hierarchy.

The group of the abbey's benefactors of knightly status was by no means uniform, either in the scale of their wealth, in political and local importance, or in the amount of land that each of these individuals and families gave to Rievaulx. Their motivations for becoming benefactors were also extremely varied, ranging from very personal piety to family tradition to the emulation of those above them in the social hierarchy. Often all these motivations were present at the same time in the actions of the people examined in this section. Although members of the nobility, holding broad-ranging powers, were particularly valuable as benefactors, the knightly families often retained their loyalties and interest in the abbey for far longer. The ups and downs of aristocratic careers often took the former away from Yorkshire and the horizon of the religious house, but for the immediate neighbours of the abbey, the connection with Rievaulx was often still strong in the late thirteenth century. As indicated earlier, these relationships were not easily broken, although they often took a different, sometimes negative turn. Why good neighbours sometimes became bad neighbours is the subject of the next chapter.

CHAPTER 3

Bad Neighbours: Disputes and Conflict Resolution

As we have seen in the previous chapter, it is often impossible to separate conflict from other modes of interaction, simply because the same people were often at one time generous benefactors and quarrelsome neighbours at another. This phenomenon was not unique to Rievaulx Abbey, but was a common experience of religious institutions. However, just as this monastery did not attract a great number of important aristocratic benefactors, in the way that can be seen in the case of Fountains, it also did not draw particularly vehement enemies. This I am inclined to explain by a certain aloofness displayed by Rievaulx and its policy of limited closeness to its most powerful benefactors, particularly the Mowbrays and the Gants.

Conflicts and their Mechanisms

The great majority of the conflicts between the abbey and its benefactors had their origins in the grants given either by them or by their predecessors. Cistercian insistence on the freedom from services on the donated land as well as the explicit consent of the heirs in the donation charters were intended to minimize the interference of donors and the possibility of future resumption of grants. A grant alone, without hope for its continued confirmation and protection, was under threat of being challenged, particularly if the circumstances of the donor's family had changed. Apart from the legal considerations, the participation of the whole family in a grant of a property, and the consent of the heirs, was also an important expression of family solidarity, which was often reinforced after the death of the original grantor. 'The son who did not confirm his father's gift was sinning not only against God, the saints, and the Church, but also against his father.'[1] The inherent contradiction contained in an act of taking away land from the members of one's family to give it as a pious gift to a religious institution created potential conflicts.

> If a son acted ill by disinheriting his father of his heavenly inheritance, his father acted ill by depriving his heir of an earthly one. He did so if he alienated too much of the family land, particularly if the gift was made for reduced or no worldly service.[2]

As we will see below, Rievaulx Abbey had to struggle with many dissatisfied heirs, who clearly did not fear spiritual punishment for their attempts to reclaim the gifts of their fathers and grandfathers.

Immediate reasons behind disputes between the abbey and its neighbours and benefactors are manifold. Most commonly, they took the form of quarrels over possession of particular properties or the shape of the borders dividing the estates of Rievaulx and those of the laypeople. The majority of conflicts seem to originate in a sudden change of the financial circumstances of the donors or their heirs. However, sometimes it is difficult not to see greed as a primary reason, particularly if there was a sharp difference of attitude within one family unit. The case of Jocelin and Helewise de Arecy illustrates this trend. This couple had a conflict with the abbey about their possession of Loftmarish and Theokemarais within the waste below Pickering. Their quitclaim was made on condition that the monks give Jocelin fifteen marks. It seems that the husband was the aggressive party in this dispute, joining other individuals trying to snatch the wasteland from Rievaulx (see below). His wife, Helewise, the foundress of Yedingham Priory, also known as Little Mareis, was an ardent supporter of monasteries and did not join her husband in his campaign against Rievaulx. After her death, the monks were concerned that Jocelin might start the conflict again, so they gave him further compensation in the form of two calves, twenty shillings, and one cow to secure his goodwill. Also, as a part of the agreement, conducted in public, he promised not to cause any damage to the abbey's property. In return, the monks bound themselves to pray for Jocelin after his death as they would for a monk or a lay brother of the abbey. The charter finishes with this declaration:

> I, Jocelin, swear in the presence of Dean Robert and many other clerical and laypeople, by my own hand, that I will never make any claim or change in future against the said monks concerning that land, or these agreements, either for myself or others, but I will support them just as a faithful and devoted brother of this house and I will stand with them loyally and faithfully in their lawsuits and business.[3]

---

[1] John Hudson, *Land, Law, and Lordship in Anglo-Norman England* (Oxford: Clarendon Press, 1994), p. 189.

[2] Hudson, *Land*, p. 192.

[3] 'Ego vero Gocelinus coram Roberto decano et multis aliis clericis et laicis propria manu affidavi quod nunquam in posterum movebo adversus prefatos monachos de terra illa vel de illis conventionibus aliquam querelam vel calumpniam vel per me vel per aliquem alium, sed

In this context the acceptance to a fraternity was often seen as a legitimate return on a grant.[4] However, it remains unanswered whether and how the monks used Jocelin's declaration of assistance in the abbey's business and legal affairs. In any case, this was seen as a mutually useful solution to a long-lasting hostility.

Sometimes the conflicts between the abbey and its neighbours or benefactors were resolved much more quickly if some form of monetary compensation was offered to its quarrelling neighbour. If they were in financial difficulties the compensation would be particularly welcomed, especially if the dispute was caused by material problems in the first place. In the Welburn area, discussed in the previous chapter, Walter son of Asketil de Grimston quitclaimed between 1162 and *c.* 1176 any rights which he or his heirs might have to Welburn, granted by his lord Roger de Mowbray to Rievaulx. There was nothing unusual about this case, although his charter contains an interesting phrase:

> Let it be known to you that I gave and quitclaimed to God and the monks of Rievaulx from me and my heirs [. . .], for the love of God and for the charity which these monks gave me.[5]

This unspecified charity of the monks for Walter may indicate some form of compensation; although many other charters of quitclaim spell out clearly any payment given by the abbey, this charter merely suggests it. It is possible that Walter tried to dispute the abbey's right to a certain part of Welburn, just like many other tenants of Roger de Mowbray discussed earlier, but in the meantime had fallen into financial troubles and was very keen to settle his dispute with the abbey so he could benefit from Rievaulx's compensation.

Walter son of Asketil de Grimston was not the only neighbour of Rievaulx who resolved a conflict with the abbey in a rather swift manner, although, as often, we know only the outcome of the negotiation, not the details of the negotiation process. Between about 1160 and 1176 Ralph de Wath and his brothers, Richard, Gerard, and Gervase, quitclaimed in the court of Roger de Mowbray, their lord, any rights they might have claimed to Welburn.[6] Later on, Ralph de Wath developed closer and

---

sicut frater domus illius fidelis et benevolus juvabo illos et stabo cum ipsis legittime et fideliter in eorum causis et negotiis': *Cartulary*, no. 181; *EYC*, I, no. 611.

[4] Benjamin Thompson, 'From "Alms" to "Spiritual Services": The Function and Status of Monastic Property in Medieval England', in *Monastic Studies: The Continuity of Tradition*, vol. II, ed. by Judith Loades (Bangor: Headstart History, 1991), pp. 227–61 (p. 237).

[5] 'Notum sit vobis me dedisse et quietum clamasse Deo et monachis Rieuallis de me et heredibus meis [. . .] pro Dei amore et pro caritate quam monachi dederunt michi': *Cartulary*, no. 59.

[6] Charles Clay suspected that 'Richard' in the charter should be 'Robert' since Robert de Vado and Ralph his brother are mentioned in the papal letter of Alexander III reprimanding several people for damaging the abbey. If this identification is correct, this quitclaim might have been a result of the papal intervention. *Cartulary*, no. 152; *EYC*, IX, 161.

more pragmatic ties with the abbey. In the later part of Henry II's reign he exchanged five acres of land bordering the monastic grange in Skiplam for ten acres in Wombleton. Additionally, as part of the deal, Ralph and his heir promised to go on the abbey's business within Yorkshire, with their expenses paid by the abbey.

> Therefore I and my heirs will go to act in their business just as their brothers, wherever the need shall be in Yorkshire, at their expense, even if [we have] no reason [ourselves to go].[7]

This agreement is an interesting indication of the practical cooperation occasionally to be found between the abbey and its neighbours. The type of business is not specified, but it might have been anything to do with the running of granges, selling produce, and negotiating with buyers. The majority of the day-to-day business of the abbey which required contact with the outside world was conducted by the lay brothers, but the agreement with Ralph de Wath indicates that such tasks might have been performed by laymen as well. The abbey must have had considerable trust in the abilities and integrity of Ralph to entrust him with their business affairs.

The charters recording conflict resolutions between the abbey and its neighbours suggest that trust was a particularly desirable quality in their mutual relationship. The mechanisms to develop it were built into the agreements. This explains fraternity admissions and promises of help and assistance offered to and by Jocelin de Arecy and Ralph de Wath. A sum of money offered a simple solution to a conflict, but the formation of a mutually profitable relationship based on trust was worth more to the abbey in the long term, particularly if it involved individuals living in the vicinity of the abbey and its estates.

Paradoxically, the generosity of great lords could also lead to potential disputes, not just from their heirs but, more immediately, from their tenants. There were various reasons why they did so. Firstly, the grants from their lords to religious institutions might deprive them of part of their landholding. They were particularly unhappy if the compensation which they received from the lord was considered unsatisfactory. Secondly, even if the grants of their lords did not directly affect their holdings, the shift in the use of a common pasture or forest or a new mill monopoly in their neighbourhood could affect their financial well-being. Thirdly, many tenants followed the example of their lords and offered donations to the religious houses of their patronage. Although their donations were much smaller than those of the barons, it was much easier for them to be affected by the consequences of the alienation of the family property. This could lead to disputes with the descendants of the original benefactors.

---

[7] 'Ego autem et heredes mei ibimus in negotiis illorum agendis sicut fratres eorum ubicunque opus fuerit in Eboracensi sciria ad illorum expensas sine occasione tamen': *Cartulary*, no. 129; *EYC*, IX, no. 148.

In a case of disputes between the abbey and its benefactors or neighbours, the baronial benefactors were often instrumental in helping to settle these conflicts. They acted as mediators or judges between the tenants and 'their monasteries'. Sometimes they compensated the disgruntled tenants in order to protect the holdings of the abbey. A very spectacular conflict over Welburn between Rievaulx Abbey and Roger de Mowbray's tenants illustrates the role of the lord as mediator between the religious institutions and his tenants, and shows the growing cost of being a protector of the abbey. The conflict started in the mid-twelfth century with a dispute between Roger de Mowbray himself and his tenant Alan de Ryedale over the stretch of moor between Welburn and Bowforth and towards Cowldyke, which was a common pasture for the vills of Welburn, Hoveton, and Bowforth. Between 1160 and 1169 Roger de Mowbray made a notification of the perambulation made by him, unspecified barons, his men, and neighbours of the moor before Bowforth. These people declared that according to their knowledge it had been given by Roger to Rievaulx Abbey and the lord again explicitly forbade, on this occasion, Alan de Ryedale or anybody else to 'trouble or oppress' this property.[8] The evidence given by the neighbours did not stop Alan's claims that this pasture was a part of his demesne, while his lord insisted that it was a common pasture on the moorland which he had given to Rievaulx Abbey. When Alan started to obstruct passage for the monks to the moor, Roger actively took the side of the abbey. He called Alan to his court to resolve the conflict in the presence of his knights, neighbours, and royal officials. Among the neighbours listed as witnesses there were several benefactors of the abbey, also some of the members of Roger's court, particularly Hugh de Malebisse, and relatives of the benefactors: Peter de Surdeval, Robert de Sproxton, Thomas de Colevilla, and Robert de Buscy, which shows once again the importance of the local community in settling conflicts.

This dispute was solved by a trial of battle between the champions of Roger de Mowbray and Alan de Ryedale. When Roger's champion started to win, Alan's friends persuaded him to abandon his claims to his lord's grants to Rievaulx Abbey. In return, Roger agreed to put the case into the judgement of twelve knights from the neighbourhood to decide whether or not the moor should be common. These men decided that the moor was indeed common, but they declared that the unspecified constructions on the moor erected by Alan should be left standing there.[9] The inclusion of the people from outside Roger's court may be a symptom of the weakening position of the lord's court as a legal authority for his tenants. It also

[8] *Cartulary*, no. 61; *EYC*, IX, no. 158.

[9] *Cartulary*, no. 153; *EYC*, IX, no. 157. This charter was discussed by W. H. Galbraith, 'The Death of a Champion', in *Studies in Medieval History Presented to Frederick Maurice Powicke*, ed. by R. W. Hunt, W. A. Pantin, and R. W. Southern (Oxford: Clarendon Press, 1948), pp. 283–95 (p. 290).

indicates the importance of the local community in establishing the correct running of the borders. It was established by the consensus of the neighbourhood, not by the sole decision of Roger de Mowbray. Since the abbey was a part of the community, it had to find its place within it, not act against it.

As a donation created a tenurial relationship between the grantor and recipient, the lord's court was a place to solve all the disputes related to it.[10] In consequence, the lords could become, as this example illustrates, sometimes more go-betweens for their tenants than final authorities. The case of the dispute over Welburn shows that the lord might be put in a difficult position as a benefactor of an abbey when one of his men decided to dispute a particular grant. If he wanted to remain loyal to his object of patronage, yet did not want or could not be harsh to his tenant, he might be forced to make a compromise which would undermine his own position. In the opinion of Hugh Thomas, Roger had to make 'a compromise at his own expense' even after winning the trial and the arbitration of the neighbours.[11]

Despite the efforts of Roger, Alan de Ryedale continued to dispute Rievaulx's rights to the common pasture of Welburn. Another settlement was made on 24 March 1176 in the presence of Gregory, Prior of Bridlington, in Nottingham.[12] The choice of the authority to resolve this long-lasting dispute was not accidental. Bridlington Priory was among the houses benefiting from the Mowbrays' generosity and from this priory came the first canons to live in Newburgh Priory, a house founded by Roger de Mowbray.[13] Additionally, on the same day and place, Alan de Ryedale and his wife, Maud, quitclaimed to Roger de Mowbray, their lord, any claims which Alan, Maud, or their heirs might have to the property of Rievaulx Abbey in Welburn.[14] In response, Roger released Alan and his heirs from paying ten shillings of annual rent from Bowforth. The tenant was to pay only a pound of pepper per year for all the services.[15] Roger de Mowbray was forced again to make a concession at his own expense to secure peace between his tenants and the abbey.

---

[10] Thompson, 'From "Alms"', p. 242.

[11] Hugh M. Thomas, *Vassals, Heiresses, Crusaders and Thugs: The Gentry of Angevin Yorkshire, 1154–1216* (Philadelphia: University of Pennsylvania Press, 1993), p. 53.

[12] *Cartulary*, no. 133; *EYC*, IX, no. 159.

[13] Janet E. Burton, *The Monastic Order in Yorkshire, 1069–1215* (Cambridge: Cambridge University Press, 1999), p. 192.

[14] 'Sciatis quod ego Alanus de Ridale et Matilda uxor mea fide interposita quietum clamavimus de nobis et heredibus nostris domino nostro Rogero de Molbrai et monachis Rieuall[ensibus] quicquid juris habuimus vel unde calumpniam movimus predictis monachis de terris et aliis rebus que continentur infra metas que in cartis eorundem monachorum de donatione predicti domini nostri Rogeri nominantur': *Cartulary*, no. 132; *EYC*, IX, no. 160.

[15] *Cartulary*, no. 132; *EYC*, IX, no. 160.

Families and tenurial groups were the most common forms of social organization encountered by the abbey in their dealings with laypeople. However in its early history Rievaulx Abbey was already confronted with conflicts not related to any of the above. Sometimes difficult neighbours could appear in groups and as such were much harder to deal with, in particular if the dispute were related to a coveted property. A very direct reflection of such a conflict, and Rievaulx concern about it, is recorded in the structure of the cartulary. Just before the royal and ecclesiastical section of the volume, on fols 117–125^{v} [new fols 121–129^{v}], there is a distinct grouping of charters related to the waste of Pickering. It was a substantial property located east of the abbey, demarcated by Costa Beck to the east and Allerston Beck to the west, and north of the Derwent. It came into the abbey's possession as a grant from King Henry II in 1158 with permission to use it in any way they wanted, including erecting sheep folds and buildings, free from all services, in exchange for Stainton given to the abbey by Walter de Gant.[16] His son, King Richard I, confirmed this grant.[17] Much of this area was covered by a marsh, which was used as a pasture. Conflicts over Pickering occurring throughout the late 1150s up to the early 1190s pushed the abbey into contact with large and diverse groups of laypeople. There were no apparent links between those individuals; some of them were already benefactors of the abbey or related to such individuals, but for some it was the only contact they may have had with Rievaulx.

There are twenty-two copies of charters related to the disputed possession of the waste below Pickering. These entries are grouped in a few clusters in the cartulary: nos 150–51 (quitclaim charters of Manuivelains), nos 163 and 165 (quitclaims of Roger de Clere and William de Mandeville), nos 180–88, 190–91 (quitclaims of various individuals), and nos 205–10 (royal charters). It is clear that the organizing theme for these entries is the property. These conflicts were the sole reason that some people came into close contact with the abbey, and for those who already interacted with Rievaulx it added another dimension to their contacts, as their tenurial or family connections were disregarded by the cartulary compiler. Although such connections must have played some role in the process of settling the disagreements, the charters of quitclaim related to this waste are all grouped together. Charters of those individuals who were already benefactors of the abbey were placed in this sequence and not dispersed throughout the volume. This editorial manoeuvre indicates that the community of Rievaulx clearly associated these people and their actions with the conflict over the Pickering waste. Table 2 below gives a brief summary of these charters, but it is worth examining some of the quitclaims in greater detail.

---

[16] *Cartulary*, nos 205–10. The last charter in this sequence was also copied to the Coucher Book of the Duchy of Lancaster: *The Honour and Forest of Pickering*, ed. by Robert Bell Turton, North Riding Record Society, n.s., 4 (London: North Riding Record Society, 1897), pp. 75–77.

[17] *Cartulary*, no. 173.

Table 2. Charters Related to the Pickering Dispute

Printed edition reference	Grantor	Type	Property	Others involved	Date
Cart. no. 150	Stephen Manuivelain	Quitclaim	Rights to a waste below Pickering	With the consent of his son Roger	1170–80
Cart. no. 151	Roger Manuivelain	Confirmation of the above	Rights to a waste below Pickering	Originally granted by his father Stephen	1170–80
Cart. no. 163, *EYC*, I, no. 610	Roger de Clere	Quitclaim	A ditch between the waste below Pickering and his town of Wilton, with the land between that ditch and the waste	before king's justices in Doncaster	1180
Cart. no. 164, *EYC*, II, no. 799	Stephen II de Meinil	Grant	Woodland of Greenhove on the western side of 'Haggesgate' and below that gate (or way) westward to the bounds of Bilsdale and eastward to the bounds of Great Broughton		*c*. 1175–89
Cart. no. 165, *EYC*, I, no. 617	William de Mandeville, Earl of Essex	Quitclaim	The ditch made by the monks between the waste below Pickering and his territory of Thornton (Dale), and the land between that ditch and the waste	before king's justices in Westminster	1181
Cart. no. 180	Robert I de Ros	Quitclaim	Of all his rights he may have to 'Theokmarais' and 'Loftmarish' on the waste below Pickering	With the consent of his wife, sons, and tenants Peter and William de Surdeval	1158–63
Cart. no. 181, *EYC*, I, no. 611	Jocelin de Arecy and his wife Helewise de Clere	Quitclaim and affirmation	Of their rights in 'Loftmarish' and 'Theokemarais' for 15 marks + other gifts from the monks	in the presence of Robert, Dean of York	*c*. 1170–76
Cart. no. 182	Peter de Surdeval and his brother William	Quitclaim	Of their rights to 12 bovates of land in 'Theokemarais'	With the confirmation of their lord Robert I de Ros	1158–63
Cart. no. 183	William son of Levoch	Quitclaim	The rights to a waste below Pickering, as described in the charter of King Henry	No witnesses	
Cart. no. 184, *EYC*, I, no. 412	Walter Bardolf	Quitclaim	Of his rights in the waste below Pickering on the south side of 'Midsyke' towards		1170–80

Printed edition reference	Grantor	Type	Property	Others involved	Date
			'Erneshow' or within the bounds as in Henry II charter		
Cart., no. 185	William, Earl of Aumâle	Quitclaim	Of his rights in 'Micleholme'	in the presence of king's steward William	1166–84
Cart. no. 186, *EYC*, I, no. 409	Asketin son of Roger de Thornton	Quitclaim	Of his rights in 'Micleholme' and in the waste below Pickering	Affidation by his son Jollan	1160–70
Cart. no. 187	Alan Forester son of Roger de Thornton	Quitclaim	Of his rights in 'Micleholme' and in the waste below Pickering	Affidation by his son Alan	1160–70
Cart. no. 188, *EYC*, I, no. 410	Hugh Brun	Quitclaim	Of his rights in 'Micleholme' and in the waste below Pickering		1165–75
Cart. no. 189, *EYC*, I, no. 402	Torphin de Allerston and his nephew Geoffrey	Acknowledgement	upon an oath of the borders of the king's waste below Pickering	Lists people who made the oath	1158
Cart. no. 190	William de Vescy	Quitclaim	Rights to the waste below Pickering with some reservation to a pasture within it (borders described)		1166–83
Cart. no. 191, *EYC*, I, no. 411	Stephen de Manuivelain and his son Roger	Quitclaim	Rights in 'Micleholme' in the waste below Pickering	Pledge made in the hand of Hugh de Malebisse	1170–80
Cart. no. 205	King Henry II	Grant and Confirmation	Of 2 carucates in Kilverdmersch Of all the pasture in the waste below Pickering		1158
Cart. no. 206	King Henry II	Precept	To secure formal recognition of Henry's I grant of the waste below Pickering	To the Sheriff of Yorkshire	1158
Cart. no. 207	King Henry II	Precept	Not to permit anybody to infringe rights of the abbey to the waste below Pickering	To the Sheriff of Yorkshire	After 1158
Cart. no. 208	King Henry II	Precept	That the monks should hold waste below Pickering in peace	To the Sheriff of Yorkshire	After 1158
Cart. no. 209	King Henry II	Precept	the waste below Pickering within specified boundaries	To the Sheriff of Yorkshire	After 1158
Cart. no. 210	King Henry II	Renewal of the grant	Of the waste below Pickering, the boundaries are specified		1158–79

The time span between the earliest and the latest quitclaim in this group is over twenty years, from 1158 to 1184. The majority of the documents were issued in the 1170s, which indicates that the peak of the conflicts occurred at that time. The oldest document was issued, almost parallel to the royal grant of the waste below Pickering, by Torphin de Allerston, with his nephew Geoffrey, a generous benefactor of Rievaulx Abbey. His charter is a solemn recognition of the described boundaries of the waste as testified by the important men from the neighbourhood. Although the charter characterizes the waste as being in royal hands, and does not mention Rievaulx Abbey at all, it has been preserved in the cartulary of this institution. The abbey had a vested interest in securing the consensus as to what constituted the boundaries of the area which it was about to acquire. The later charters in the same group were clearly issued after it came into the possession of Rievaulx. They show a range of methods used to either prevent or resolve disputes with neighbours encroaching on the borders of the waste. Three of these charters contain information that the quitclaims were accompanied by a solemn oath in front of the altar in the monastic church at Rievaulx. The charters of Asketin son of Roger de Thornton, Alan Forester son of Roger de Thornton, and Hugh Brun declared that each of them placed the charter, by hand, on the altar of the abbey.[18] Other ways of making quitclaim more secure included an affidavit to the lord of the person making quitclaim, and attaching an additional seal of a mutual neighbour, as in the charters of Stephen Manuivelain and his son Roger.[19] Roger de Clere made an oath to an external authority — the Royal Justice at Doncaster. William de Mandeville, Earl of Essex, a frequent visitor to the royal court, made a similar oath to the royal justice at Westminster. In two cases the quitclaimants chose a religious authority for that purpose. Peter and William de Surdeval and Jocelin de Arecy and his wife, Helewise, swore in the presence of Dean and chapter of York to honour their promise. These entries in the cartulary emphasize the variety of methods of securing a lasting conclusion to a conflict, in particular solemnity of oaths, ritual gestures, and external lay and ecclesiastical authorities. In fact, in this particular instance, the abbey was successful in its strategy, and there are no further indications, beyond the late twelfth century, that any of these individuals or their heirs made any further claims to the Pickering waste.

However, the thirteenth century saw an increase of conflicts between Rievaulx and its neighbours on a very basic level. The families of the oldest benefactors, the tenants of the founder who continued to live and own land in its vicinity — the Ingram, Surdeval, Sproxton, and Harum families — had an increasing number of disputes with Rievaulx from the early thirteenth century onwards. These squabbles, described in the first chapter, were very much a result of the physical closeness of their properties and the growing economic pressure for land. Also, in the thirteenth century both

---

[18] *Cartulary*, nos 186, 187, 188.

[19] *Cartulary*, no. 191.

laypeople and the monks were more inclined to use formal channels for resolving their disputes, the courts in particular, which left documentary traces, whilst earlier forms of local arbitration did not. A good indication of this type of neighbourhood conflict in which Rievaulx was engaged occurred in 1300. William de Sproxton brought a formal complaint against Henry II, Abbot of Rievaulx, and several named monks, who assaulted him in Sproxton and 'consumed and spoiled his corn there to the value of twenty pounds'.[20] The attack on William might have been a retaliation for some actions of his against the abbey, or was perhaps part of some other disagreement which was not recorded otherwise. Either way, the triviality of it exemplifies the type of everyday problems that might occur between any type of neighbours, with no connection to the religious character or mission of Rievaulx.

In the same period the abbey also experienced another type of conflict, originating from new forms of landholding. The abbey became much more liberal in terms of entering economic relationships with laypeople than in the twelfth century. Land which would be previously accepted by the abbey only as a grant, preferably in free alms, was often wrestled from neighbours with the help of some form of payment or simply held for rent. Once the core of the abbey estates was formed by the late twelfth century, the later accessions, on the fringes of the existing granges, were smaller and more transient and often held in return for some form of payment and for limited periods of time. This often led to prolonged and convoluted conflict which often involved a number of interlinked interests. For example, in 1241 the manor of Foxton was given by William de Mowbray to William de Grey the husband of Agnes, the widow of William of Taunton (an uncle of Walter de Mowbray), a former tenant of this property. The couple then granted this property to Rievaulx Abbey in 1246, for a yearly rent of two shillings and the obligation of forinsec service. Agnes quitclaimed her rights to the manor, and the Abbot gave the couple a substantial compensation of one hundred marks.[21] On the same day Abbot Adam and the Greys resolved another of their disputes over the manors of Ryedale and Busby. Both manors were given to the abbey in exchange for forty shillings yearly for the term of Agnes's life, and with the clause that they should be returned afterwards to Walter de Mowbray.[22] The situation became really complicated when William de Mowbray of Tameton lodged a plea, with the support of his lord Simon de Vere, against Adam, Abbot of Rievaulx in 1251. The object of the conflict was the manors of Great

---

[20] *Notes on the Religious and Secular Houses of Yorkshire*, vol. I, ed. by William P. Baildon, Yorkshire Archaeological Society Record Series, 81 (London: Yorkshire Archaeological Society, 1931), no. 12, p. 179.

[21] *Feet of Fines from 1232 to 1246*, ed. by John Parker, Yorkshire Archaeological Society Record Series, 67 (Leeds: Yorkshire Archaeological Society, 1925), pp. 165; Bodl. Dodsw. xcviii, fol. 138; published incomplete in the *Cartulary*, p. 249.

[22] *Feet of Fines from 1232 to 1246*, ed. by Parker, pp. 165–66.

Rythesdale and Little Rythesdale, a half carucate and three tofts in Little Busby. The litigant explained that these properties were held by the Abbot for the term of the Abbot's life from William and Agnes de Grey. These properties were Agnes's dower, an inheritance from William de Mowbray of the freehold of William of Taunton, her former husband. This dispute was resolved by means of a complicated deal involving at least three distinct parties — William de Mowbray, his lord, and the abbey. The court decided that the manors in Rythesdale should be returned to the Abbot after the death of Agnes, to be held from William de Mowbray for half a carucate with forinsec service and another payment of eleven shillings and eight pence to Simon de Vere the lord. Another yearly payment of service of half a mark from the same manors was due to William de Malebisse. In addition, the Abbot quitclaimed to William de Mowbray the manors of Foxton in Cleveland.[23]

This case, although particularly complex, was by no means unique for the situation of Rievaulx Abbey by the mid-thirteenth century. It shows how fragmented were fees and how complicated were the landholdings. One individual usually held lands from several people, to whom he or she might also be related, causing additional rights and obligations. Besides, the abbey was more liberal in terms of form of acquisition and held these lands with secular obligations, often for a term only. As a result, Rievaulx Abbey became entangled with several families and their lords and tenants and participated in the quest for more land and rights, even if the stake was relatively small in comparison with the twelfth century. Parts of the abbey's possession became much more transient than its core estates acquired in the twelfth century. Land might be held for a limited time under the obligation of secular services or easily exchanged for a more useful plot of land elsewhere to augment particular granges and streamline existing landholdings.

Bad neighbours came in different forms. In the second half of the twelfth century they were often former benefactors in financial difficulties, heirs who regretted their fathers' generosity, or simply opportunists who wanted to try their luck in gaining some more land. By the mid-thirteenth century the pattern had changed, showing the influence of a more transient form of landholding favoured by the abbey, which often caused prolonged disputes. In the twelfth century many cases were resolve by a gift from the abbey and a solemn ritual in the abbey's church; in the following century, the court became the most popular arena for settling disagreements. This shows that in the eyes of many of its neighbours the abbey came to be seen more as any other powerful landowner, and the attraction and power of the Sacrum did not play such a prominent role in the settlements as it did in the twelfth century.

---

[23] *Feet of Fines from 1246 to 1272*, ed. by John Parker, Yorkshire Archaeological Society Record Series, 82 (Leeds: Yorkshire Archaeological Society, 1925), pp. 59–60.

The 'Bad' Patron

The thirteenth century also brought another significant challenge to Rievaulx in the form of a patron who turned out be one of its most difficult neighbours. I have discussed the relationship between the Ros family and the abbey in the first chapter. Although up to the early thirteenth century their mutual contacts were on the whole distant, these patrons did not show open hostility. As Thompson asserts,

> [r]eligious houses, like other tenants, depended upon the renewal of the relationship between them and their founders' and benefactors' heirs (although clearly it would be much less easy for an heir of a founder to remove his support from a religious house, and thus destroy the institution, than for the heir of a minor donor to do so).[24]

Again, hostile patrons were not a unique feature, yet the intensity of the conflict between William de Ros and the abbey shows what might happen when an heir of a founder tried to remove his support and illustrates how the abbey developed tactics to avert the very real danger of losing some of its core properties.

The conflict, which began in the late 1220s and lasted until the early 1250s, was essentially a series of attempts by William de Ros to reclaim the properties granted to the abbey by his ancestors, or at least to change the conditions of these donations. There was nothing unusual about the dispute. There are many cases of donors and their heirs trying to reclaim properties given previously, but William displayed a great persistence in his actions. There is good evidence for many stages of this conflict, which exposes William's attitude to the abbey but also the Abbot's strategy in the court and the defendant's responses to it. Above all, this conflict shows why and how a conflict between a patron and a monastic institution could develop and why the expectations of the laypeople towards 'their' monasteries changed by the mid-thirteenth century.

The object of the dispute was four carucates of land in Griff and five carucates in Tileston, as well as the common pastures and woods of Helmsley and Pockley. These properties were parts of the initial grants of the founder and the early grants of the patron's family to the abbey and were located in close proximity to both the abbey and the family seat at Helmsley castle. The lands in Griff and Tileston were parts of the original endowment; the right of common pasture and woods had been extended by Everard II. The core of the conflict was a disagreement about the hunting rights which William claimed to possess in the forest of Helmsley. At the time when this grant was given in the twelfth century, all the component rights were handed over to the monks, except hunting. It was simply of no concern then, but with the changing conditions of the land use and lifestyle of both noblemen and the monks, hunting rights became a very vexatious issue.

---

[24] Thompson, 'From "Alms"', p. 243.

In 1213 William de Ros sued the Abbot of Rievaulx for the first time, but the plea does not specify the reason.[25] The first more detailed indication of the conflict is the information that Roger, Abbot of Rievaulx, had appointed brother Jordan of Wardon or brother Alan of Rievaulx as his representative in the case against William de Ros in 1229.[26] The lawsuit went ahead in the same year, and Abbot Roger II (1224–39) sued William for the warranty of four carucates of land in Griff and five in Tileston and common pasture and forest in Helmsley and Pockley, which the abbey held from Robert II according to his charter. Because William did not come to the court, he was summoned to appear later.[27] This tactic of absenteeism became part of William's strategy throughout the conflict. When both sides met again, later the same year, the Abbot listed all the legal rights of the abbey to the disputed property. He asserted that

> William acted against the charter of his father, which witnesses that the said Robert father of the said William granted and confirmed to God and the church of Holy Mary of Rievaulx four carucates of land in Griff and land in Tileston where there are five carucates, and through which he confirmed to them all his easements in the manor and his forest of Helmsley, namely the timber and wood for his own use, and pasture land and panage free from all custom in the whole forest of Helmsley, and through which he confirmed to them the common pasture in Pockley in wood and open land for his sheep and his other cattle and timber and wood for his own use in the whole forest of that vill and pasture and panage free from all customs, and that he himself and his heirs will never welcome men of any religion into the above said pasture except the same monks, just as the charter of Everard de Ros father of the said Robert better testifies.[28]

Not only did William act against the charter of his father, but he also obstructed in many ways the monks' use of the land. The Abbot listed all the damages caused by William, who became increasingly more aggressive:

---

[25] *Cartulary*, p. 382.

[26] *CRR*, XIII, 380. Rievaulx Abbey had a number of cases against several noblemen in that year. The Abbot appointed brother Alan to act as his attorney in these cases. *CR 1227–1231*, p. 240.

[27] *CRR*, XIII, 423.

[28] 'Willelmus contra cartam patris sui, que testatur quod idem Robertus pater predicti Willelmi concedit et confirmat Deo et ecclesie Beate Marie Ryavall' iiii. carucatas terre in Grif et terram de Tillonestun', ubi sunt v. carucate terre, et preterea per quam concedit eis omnia aisiamenta sua in maneria [*sic*] et foresta sua de Hamlec, scilicet materiam et ligno ad suos proprios usus et pascua et pannagia ab omni consuetudine quieta in omnibus boscis de Hammelac, et per quam concedit eis communam pasture in Pockele in bosco et plano ad oves suas et cetera pecora sua et materiam [et] ligna ad suos proprios usus in omnibus boscis ejusdem ville et pascua et pannagia quieta ab omni consuetudine, et quod ipse et heredes sui nunquam recolligent alicujus religionis homines in predictam pasturam preter eosdem monachos, sicut carta Eborardi de Ros patris ipsius Roberti melius testatur': *CRR*, XIII, 556–57.

> he hindered him [the Abbot] and his people from making entry within the above said nine carucates of land from making hay and from having timber and wood for their own use and from having common in the wood in Helmsley and there impounded his draught animals, so that an ox died in his enclosure, and besides that he shot with arrows dogs of the said Abbot and of his people [. . .] to the value of fifteen marks.[29]

Because William denied all the charges, the court ordered another hearing. The case was scheduled to be tried in three weeks from Easter and in the meantime, the Abbot and William remained in possession of exactly what they had at that point.[30]

That was, however, not the end. On 4 July 1231 the itinerant justices in York received a royal mandate that the case between Rievaulx Abbey and William de Ros about the dispute over Helmsley forest was to be heard in Westminster a fortnight after Michaelmas.[31] Finally, in January of 1232, Abbot Roger (the plaintiff) and William de Ros (the defendant) reached an agreement, probably after several sessions, in Westminster. William dropped his claims to the four carucates in Griff and five in Tileston and the common pasture and forest in Helmsley and Pockley, as described in the charters of his ancestors. Particular attention was given to the hunting rights within this territory contested so fiercely by William:

> And they [the monks] may take the same wild animals, and all kinds of wild beasts, by their dogs and hare-hounds, and by bow and arrows and by all other means which they can, at their will, without any hindrance or objection of the said William or his heir and his people.[32]

In return the Abbot acknowledged William's right to the park on the eastern side of Helmsley, another park there called Le Haye, and the common pasture of 'Plocwude', to which the abbey did not have any rights. William gave a warranty for the agreement, and the Abbot presented him with two hundred silver marks.[33] This large sum of money indicates that William pressed a hard bargain and wanted substantial compensation for his quitclaim. Even if all the legal rights were on the abbey's side, the settlement still required considerable financial compensation for the patron,

[29] 'Inpendit eum et homines suos infra predictas ix. carucatas terre secare et habere materiam et ligna ad proprios usus et habere communam in bosco de Hammelac et ibi inparcat averia sua, ita quod quidam bos mortuus fuit in parco suo; et preterea sagittat canes ipsius abbatis et hominum suorum [. . .] ad valentiam xv marcarum': *CRR*, XIII, 557.

[30] *CRR*, XIII, 557.

[31] *CR 1227–31*, p. 522.

[32] 'Et easdem feras et omnimodam salvaginam, capiant per canes et leporarios suos, et per arcus et sagittas et omnibus aliis modis quibuscunque poterunt, pro voluntate eorum, sine omni impedimento vel contradictione ipsius Willelmi vel heredum suorum et hominum suorum': *Cartulary*, no. 217.

[33] *Cartulary*, no. 217.

whose strategy of obstruction and persistency proved to be very effective. The ability to push his claims so successfully also indicates how strong William's position was in relation to the abbey, which could not easily defend its property against the claims of a powerful nobleman.

Despite that, the abbey was not going to give up what it considered to be its rightful possession. In particular the many uses of forest resources were singled out. On 27 March, very soon after this agreement was settled, the Abbot contested specific parts of the agreement claiming that the abbey had had from the beginnings of its existence 'possession of winter food for oxen and cows and sheep, collecting nuts, burning heath in the pasture within the said woods, and making charcoal for their own use'.[34] It was then agreed that the Abbot could collect animal fodder and nuts, but should not cut too many trees in one place.

In Michaelmas term of the same year, 1232, the Abbot of Rievaulx again sued several noblemen (including William de Ros) for breaking the previous agreement over common pasture and rights of pasture and wood gathering in the forest of Helmsley and Pockley. The patron had obstructed the monks' passage against the agreement reached only a year earlier.[35] Yet again, in 1233, the Abbot sued William for not adhering to the recently signed agreement concerning forest and pastures in Helmsley and Pockley. At the hearing the Abbot gave more evidence of William's tactics, which continued to be based on violence against the abbey's property:

> The same William had his oxen and cows taken, that is to the number of three hundred sheep and eighteen cows, and he held them enclosed until all became useless and near death, and that he had his [the Abbot's] people distrained and took their carts, on the account of which he sustained damages, amounting to the value of ten marks.[36]

William's attorney came to the court, examined displayed charters of grants, and confirmed their validity, but denied all the accusations. The court decided that the attorney should wage his law by the oaths of twelve men, but there is no record of this action taking place.

The next court case in the same year, about the common pasture of 'Plocwude', was in Westminster, but William did not attend and the sheriff was not able to bring him to the court.[37] The conflict surfaced again in 1239 when Abbot Roger sued William de Ros for the warranty of four carucates in Griff and five carucates in

---

[34] *Cartulary*, no. 217.

[35] *CRR*, XIV, 519–20.

[36] 'Idem Willelmus capi facit averia sua et pecora, scilicet semel usque ad trecentas oves et bo[ves] suos usque ad xviij et detinet inclusa donec omnino inutiles fiunt et usque ad mortem, et quod devadiari facit homines suos et capi facit charettas suas, propter quod deterioratus est et dampnum habet ad valentiam x marcarum': *CRR*, XV, 23–24.

[37] *CRR*, XV, 63.

Tileston and, again, the common pasture and wood of Helmsley and Pockley. As in previous years, William did not appear in the court.[38]

The last indications of the dispute between Rievaulx and William and its final resolution are two thirteenth-century entries in the first pages of the cartulary left empty by the original scribe.[39] The first one suggests that there was another agreement between the Abbot and William in the presence of judges in York, Bishop Sylvester Everdon of Carlisle, and Roger de Thirkleby in 1252.[40] The second document, issued in the same year, was also copied on the front folios of the cartulary, which indicated that the monastic community considered it of highest importance. According to this text William appeared to have been monitoring the activities of the monks in the forests of Helmsley and Pockley and to have come to the conclusion that these were excessive:

> The said Abbot against the said fine [the agreement of 1232] has winter fodder cut for their oxen and cows at some times round about thirty carts full, or other times about forty carts full, and has these carried away, and also has acorns and hazels collected in the said wood, round about twelve quarters, and sometimes round about ten quarters, and has them taken away, and similarly has trees cut down in the above said woods, and makes charcoal from the said trees in diverse places; and similarly has round about thirty oaks or more cut down at the time for sap, and strips them of the bark to sell the bark, and leaves those oaks to lie in the above said woods until they should be dried. He said, also, that against that fine he has heath burned in the pasture within the above said woods to the great damage of the above said pasture. He [William] said from that, that by doing this he [the Abbot] did not keep the above said fine, he [William] was harmed, and sustained damage to the value of one hundred pounds.[41]

The Abbot denied these charges and repeated the earlier argument of the abbey's right received from the ancestors of the present patron. In addition, the Abbot presented a written proof of his rights to the court. He

---

[38] *Cartulary*, p. 390, published from *Coram Rege: Henry III*, 1239, no. 32, m. 11.

[39] London, British Library, Cotton Julius D. i, fols 1^{v}–2^{v} [fols 5^{v}–6^{v}].

[40] *Cartulary*, no. 6.

[41] 'Predictus abbas contra predictum finem scindere facit husagium ad boves et vaccas suas, aliquando circiter xxx carettatas, aliquando circiter xl carettatas, et illis asportare facit et etiam colligere facit de glanis, et nucibus in predictis bosci circiter xij quarteria, et aliquando circiter x quarteria et asportare facit; et similiter prosternere facit arbores in predictis boscis et facit carbones de predictis arboribus in diversis locis; et similiter prosternere facit circiter xxx quercus vel amplius tempore seve, et eas excoriat, et vendere corticem, et dimittit illas quercus jacere in predictis boscis quousque fuerint desiccate. Dicit ergo quod contra eundem finem comburi facit brueriam in pastura infra predictos boscos ad magnum detrimentum predictae pasture: unde dicit quod per hoc quod non tenuit predictum finem deterioratus est et habet dampnum ad valorem c librarum': *Cartulary*, no. 8.

> brought out a charter under the name of Robert son of Everard de Ros in which it is contained that the said Robert gave and by his charter confirmed to God and the church of Holy Mary of Rievaulx and the monks serving God there, [. . .] that place in Ricalf for charcoal and charcoal-burners, which they held in the time of Everard his father.[42]

It must have become obvious to both parties that unless they removed the reason for the conflict, no amount of promises would solve the dispute. Finally William de Ros and the abbey settled this conflict by means of exchange, which would eliminate constant interference between them. William

> gave them [the monks] a piece of land in exchange for all the common which they quitclaimed him in the wood and in the land next to Helmsley as far as the south part of the road which goes to Helmsley and to Rievaulx beyond their ditch and wall, beyond the ditch of their main assart as from the bank of Helmsley to the River Rye. He also granted to them that they may enclose by wall and ditch that place where waters of Deepdale and Litelbee come into confluence.[43]

This document appears to finish this long dispute, and William did not achieve what he wanted, which appeared to be the eviction of the abbey from the lands he wanted so badly, but had to settle for a compromise. The exchange between the parties appeared the most sensible option open to them. The issue of common in the forest of Helmsley was so vexatious that only elimination of the abbey's claim to it could finish the dispute once and for all.

Throughout this conflict, lasting for three decades, William's tactics were persistence and the boldness of his actions. Even the fact that William signed an extensive agreement in 1232 with the abbey did not stop him from breaching it soon afterwards. The Abbot had all the legal rights to hold the disputed properties, and appropriate charters were displayed in the court on several occasions. The Abbot also had powerful tools on his side — memory and tradition. The argument that the abbey possessed certain rights from its foundation and had had them during the life of the previous abbots was invoked by Abbot Roger on several occasions.[44] From the

---

[42] 'profert quandam cartam sub nomine Roberti filli Everardi de Ros in qua continetur quod [idem] Robertus dedit et carta sua confirmavit Deo et Ecclesie Beate Marie de Ryevalle et monachis ibidem Deo servientibus, [. . .] locum illum in Rycalvegray[ne] ad carbones et carbonarios suos, quem tenuerunt tempore Everardi patris sui': *Cartulary*, no. 8. Ricalf, a lost vill, was located half way between Muscoates and Harome.

[43] 'Hunc autem locum dedit eis pro escambia totius commune quam sibi quietam clamaverunt in bosco et in terra juxta villam de Hamelec, ad australem partem vie que itur ad Halmelak et ad Ryevallem extram fossatum et murum eorum extra fossatum sarti eorum sicut nemus tendit a barra de Halmelak usque ad Ryam. Concessit etiam illis claudere muro vel fossato locum illum divise sue ubi aqua de Dipedale et Litelbee simul veniunt de qua conventio fuerat inter eos': *Cartulary*, no. 8.

[44] 'dicit predictus Abbas quod ipse et omnes predecessores sui a fundatione Domus sue': *Cartulary*, no. 8.

records of the legal proceedings it appears that the tactic of the abbey was consistent; the plaintiff, the Abbot or his representative, steadily referred to the charters of Everard II de Ros and Robert II de Ros and to William's legal obligations as their heir. The appropriate charters were displayed in court, which again indicated the abbey's reliance on the written documents. William's tactic, as the defendant, was denying the accusations or simply not turning up to court, which was, after all, very effective, not least because he was a wealthy and important individual and even a powerful institution, such as Rievaulx Abbey, could not stand up to him. Consequently, because William was the patron of the abbey, his withdrawal of support from Rievaulx and his open aggression were more damaging than similar actions by any other benefactor. The object of the dispute was the properties and rights within the core of the abbey's estates in the areas where the community wanted to maintain complete control of the economic resources.

The son and heir of William de Ros, Robert III, continued his father's quarrel about pastures and forests in Helmsley and Pockley, but with less persistence. In 1282 Abbot William IV de Ellerbeck of Rievaulx sued Robert de Ros and two other men for breaking the agreement and taking away the abbey's sheep grazing in the pastures of the said vills.[45] This case indicates that the problem of close proximity between the abbey and the patron's residence, and the shared use of the pasture, continued to be the cause of conflicts. This proximity, understood by the founder and the monastic community as beneficial for both sides, turned out to be a real burden in the changed circumstances.

William de Ros was a difficult patron not only for Rievaulx Abbey but also for Kirkham Priory, which otherwise had a very positive relationship with the Ros family. In 1251 Prior Roger and the convent reached an agreement with William concerning the same forest of Helmsley, in which Kirkham had certain rights, breached by the patron. The Prior was promised estovers for husbote and heybote, as well as fishing in the river Rye east from the bridge. In 1261 the next Prior, Hugh, sued William de Ros for the right of hunting in Helmsley wood and moor.[46] As a settlement compensation William granted one toft in Pockley, right of passage through the woods and moors of Helmsley, and three animals yearly in lieu of the tithes of hunting. Since the right of hunting was very important for a thirteenth-century nobleman, William did not want to share his forest resources with anybody. The location of Helmsley wood in the vicinity of William's residence was a reason for his persistence in trying to secure this title for himself against the rights of both

[45] *Notes on the Religious and Secular Houses of Yorkshire*, vol. I, ed. by William P. Baildon, Yorkshire Archaeological Society Record Series, 17 (London: Yorkshire Archaeological Society, 1895), no. 9, p. 178.

[46] Janet E. Burton, *Kirkham Priory from Foundation to Dissolution*, Borthwick Paper, no. 86 (York: Borthwick Institute of Historical Research, 1995), p. 23.

religious houses. He saw some of the donations of his ancestors to Rievaulx and Kirkham as an inconvenient infringement on his rights and tried to rectify them.

The prolonged conflict in which the abbey of Rievaulx was involved with its patron was symptomatic of a number of issues affecting religious houses at that time, namely the increased competition for land and forest rights. In addition, the response of the abbey indicates how, by the first half of the thirteenth century, the courts surpassed the arbitration of the local community as a location for resolving conflicts, and moreover, written documents came to be seen as important evidence.[47] However, the final outcome was a compromise between the demands and rights of both parties. The desire to separate the abbey's economic interests and spheres of influence from those of its quarrelsome patron was not just a practical issue; it was also a manifestation of the Cistercian approach to dealing with laypeople. It was not turning away from them, but rather drawing a line of separation.

Once more the cartulary provides useful background for the understanding of the conflicts between Rievaulx and it neighbours. This volume recorded many of the quitclaims and conflict settlements in the context of other actions, often positive, of these individuals towards the abbey. Besides, the cartulary gives an important tenurial and family context to these events, showing how arbitration and influence of the immediate social environment helped to resolve many of the neighbourhood disputes. But in the thirteenth century, the changing economic format of the abbey landholding gave a way to new types of connections with laypeople, and, in consequence, also new forms of conflict resolution, based to a much greater extent on the official power and authority of the courts.

The ability to negotiate and compromise was also a very important element of the interaction between Rievaulx and the broader ecclesiastic world. The next chapter examines the character of contact between this Cistercian house and its various monastic neighbours, then moves on to the complex politics of gaining supporters at a high level of the ecclesiastical hierarchy, in particular among the Archbishops of York and Bishops of Durham.

---

[47] For the relationship between oral and written evidence, see M. T. Clanchy, *From Memory to Written Records: England 1066–1307*, 2nd edn (Oxford: Blackwell, 1993), pp. 272–78.

CHAPTER 4

Rievaulx Abbey and the Monastic World

The web of connections between Rievaulx Abbey and its lay benefactors was not the only network of which this monastic house became a part. Other religious institutions and ecclesiastical figures also played a significant role in its life on many levels. Being a Cistercian house gave Rievaulx access to important international links and provided not just guidelines of how to conduct its affairs but also practical assistance in many situations. On the institutional level Rievaulx had been assisted by the Chapter General but also by important churchmen. Ultimately, these contacts were not only a matter of practical solutions, but also of building long-lasting connections. The problem of friendship, examined by a number of historians of the order in relation to Cistercian spirituality, will be considered here in relation to the personal contacts between Yorkshire monastic communities, abbots, and issues they had to deal with.[1] As Julian Haseldine observes,

> *amicitia* and its attendant obligations explain or illuminate many bonds between monasteries of different orders, and show up the operations of the twelfth-century monastic world in a more realistic way than the traditional picture of rival groups of institutions.[2]

This statement is certainly applicable to the particular case of Rievaulx Abbey which had a number of monastic neighbours belonging to the Cistercian and other orders, which were often competitors of Rievaulx on the donation market, but also important allies and even friends. The issue of tithes payment became in the second half of the twelfth century a major cause of conflicts between Rievaulx and Augustinian houses in Yorkshire. The severity of many of these disputes shows that payment of

---

[1] For the most comprehensive analysis of the spirituality of friendship in the Cistercian context, see Brian Patrick McGuire, *Friendship and Community: The Monastic Experience, 350–1250* (Kalamazoo: Cistercian Publications, 1988).

[2] Julian Haseldine, 'Friendship and Rivalry: The Role of *Amicitia* in Twelfth-Century Monastic Relations', *Journal of Ecclesiastical History*, 44 (1993), 390–414 (p. 393).

tithes was a matter of principle, upholding Cistercian right to the exemption, not purely a financial issue.

Among the neighbours of Rievaulx Abbey, other monastic houses had a special place. They shared with Rievaulx the same corporate nature and mission, but were also competing for grants from the same pool of potential donors. Similarly to the contacts with lay neighbours, relationships between various houses formed a web of intertwined connections. However, for purpose of clarity, these relations are divided here into six groups: Rievaulx Abbey's relationship or contacts with close neighbours, with the houses which had the same founder as Rievaulx, with other Cistercian houses, with Augustinian monasteries, with houses belonging to the order of Sempringham, and finally with other religious institutions. This division points to several crucial reasons for the intermonastic connections. Firstly, houses were either located in close vicinity or their granges might border even if the precincts were at a considerable distance. Secondly, many houses had mutual contacts, both positive and negative, due to having the same patrons or receiving grants from the same people in the vicinity of each other. Thirdly, some of the connections occurred due to the personal involvement of the particular abbots in the interorder politics. All these issues are visible in the case of Rievaulx Abbey and will be discussed in this chapter. It is important, however, to stress that often all these reasons were intertwined and occurred at the same time. For example, Byland and Rievaulx, both Cistercian abbeys, were close neighbours and received, to a large extent, grants from the same people.

In the early twelfth century, the North of England experienced a revival of religious life, beginning with the resurgence of Selby Abbey, Monkwearmouth, and Durham monastic communities. In 1113 the church of Hexham in Northumbria was given by Archbishop Thomas II of York to the canons regular. Moreover, several Augustinian houses were founded by local noblemen, with the encouragement or advice of Archbishop Thurstan, in Guisborough, Drax, Bolton, Kirkham in Yorkshire, and Thurgarton in Nottinghamshire. Although Waverley Abbey in Surrey was the first Cistercian house in England, it was the North of the country which experienced the foundation of eight houses of this order in a quick succession between 1132 and 1150, in Rievaulx, Fountains, Kirkstall, Roche, Salley, Byland, Jervaulx, and Meaux.[3] With the growing numbers of religious foundations in Yorkshire, it became more common for many monasteries to have other religious institutions as neighbours or neighbours of their granges.

Despite the theological doctrines and the ideology of monasticism expressed in the language of *caritas*, friendship and cooperation between various monastic

[3] Janet E. Burton, *Monastic and Religious Orders in Britain 1000–1300* (Cambridge: Cambridge University Press, 1994), pp. 31–32, 48. Although several of the Yorkshire Cistercian houses, among them Rievaulx and Fountains, became the most prominent within the Cistercian order in England, Yorkshire did not have particularly high concentration of monasteries of this order. Bennett D. Hill, *English Cistercian Monasteries and their Patrons in the Twelfth Century* (Urbana: University of Illinois Press, 1968), p. 36.

communities, many of the relationships not only between houses of different orders but even between those belonging to the same order were not always peaceful. Cistercian authors particularly stressed the importance of friendship within and between the monastic communities. The idea of *caritas* was understood on two levels: as a spiritual union with the divine and as a spirit which should bind monastic communities and other members of the Church.[4] This ideal had its practical application in the contacts and connections between Rievaulx and its monastic neighbours; it was a tool and a guiding principle for the communities and their leaders.

Although Rievaulx Abbey was the first and one of the most important Cistercian houses in the North of England, it had many monastic neighbours both in its immediate vicinity and further afield. Within a radius of fifteen miles of Rievaulx Abbey were the houses of three orders; the closest one was Byland (originally Savigniac, then Cistercian), then two Augustinian houses in Newburgh and Kirkham, and one Gilbertine house in Malton.[5] Within the wider radius of thirty miles there were two Benedictine houses in Whitby and St Mary's York, one Premonstratensian in Easby, two Cistercian in Fountains and Jervaulx, and one Augustinian in Guisborough. The majority of these neighbours had similar rural-based economic foundations, although Guisborough, Bridlington, and Selby also established towns in their close vicinity.[6]

There were two distinct geographical areas where the majority of their estates were concentrated and even overlapped. The lands of Rievaulx, Byland, Guisborough, Fountains, Newburgh, and Whitby were concentrated in Cleveland. In the Vale of Pickering donations, exchanges, and purchases created the estates of Malton, Rievaulx, Whitby, Byland, Newburgh, and Bridlington.[7] The majority of Yorkshire religious houses also acquired town properties, particularly in York and Beverley, and these properties often bordered each other. A grant of land and buildings to Rievaulx Abbey in the early thirteenth century in Aldwark illustrates this trend. The property given to Rievaulx was located opposite the houses belonging to Guisborough Priory and next to the property of Marton Priory.[8]

The direction of growth of the monastic estates was the result of several factors. The foundation grants and initial donations gave each abbey its base and a direction

[4] Martha G. Newman, *The Boundaries of Charity: Cistercian Culture and Ecclesiastical Reform 1099–1150* (Stanford: Stanford University Press, 1996), pp. 97–105.

[5] Janet E. Burton, 'The Estates and Economy of Rievaulx Abbey in Yorkshire', *Cîteaux: Commentarii Cistercienses*, 49 (1998), 29–94 (p. 44).

[6] Lawrence Butler, 'The Archaeology of Rural Monasteries in England and Wales', in *The Archaeology of Rural Monasteries*, ed. by Roberta Gilchrist and Harold Mytum, British Archaeological Reports, 203 (Oxford: B.A.R., 1989), pp. 1–28 (p. 1).

[7] Bryan Waites, 'The Monastic Settlement of North-East Yorkshire', *Yorkshire Archaeological Journal*, 40 (1962), 478–95 (p. 492).

[8] *Charters of the Vicar Choral of York Minster: City of York and its Suburbs to 1546*, ed. by Nigel J. Tringham, Yorkshire Archaeological Society Record Series, 148 (Leeds: Yorkshire Archaeological Society, 1993), no. 5.

for further expansion. Subsequent acquisitions of land by each house were limited by the geographical conditions in the area and the willingness of the benefactors to alienate their own property, but monasteries often had a conscious policy of expansion in particular directions and concentrated on building granges in particular places. Early on in their existence religious houses focused on building up their core estates near the actual administrative centre of the monastic precinct, but later on many houses diversified their holdings both in terms of type, for example arable, pasture, or ironworks, as well as location.[9] From the late twelfth century many Cistercian monasteries in Yorkshire began a consolidation of their estates to create more compact holdings. Particularly distant or small lands were sold or exchanged for properties located nearer the abbey and its existing granges. Many Cistercian houses began to hold more land for rent from the laypeople or other monasteries for a limited time only. The consequences of this process have been discussed in the third chapter.

Paradoxically, many links between religious houses were also a result of their involvement with the lay world, particularly through their patrons. The majority of benefactors gave grants to more than one house and often these acts created links between houses which otherwise might have never occurred.[10] Not surprisingly, most of the conflicts resulted from overlapping areas of economic interest and disputed borders. This was typical for any kind of neighbours, not necessarily ecclesiastical, but in the case of conflicts between monasteries disputes might take a different form from cases of confrontation with lay neighbours. The monks or canons were also more likely to ask abbots of other houses or other Church officials for arbitration.

Conflicts of an economic nature occurred because, in practice, the role of any Cistercian monastery was dual, consisting of spiritual pursuits on the one hand and economic activities on the other. This dualism, so clear to us, was probably not perceived so strongly by contemporaries, particularly by members of the Church, for whom economic pursuits were probably identified more closely with the need for expansion for the glory of God. In order to attract donations monastic houses needed to establish and cultivate a reputation of spiritual excellence and to develop relationships with existing donors and also neighbours or tenants who were also potential benefactors. Thus Rievaulx competed with other monasteries for the land and donations which were given by the laypeople for the salvation of their souls and the glory of God. The growing properties of these institutions were not only a proof of the 'endorsement from above', but also a necessary base for their successful functioning. As the economic bases of every monastery were confined almost exclusively to the land, the expansion of a monastery's holdings was usually the only way in which it

[9] R. I. Hodgson, 'Medieval Colonisation of Northern Ryedale', *Ryedale Historian*, 10 (1980), 47–62 (p. 57).

[10] This is true in the case of not only Cistercian houses, but many other monastic orders. A rivalry or at least competitiveness between houses was often fostered by the lay patrons. Penelope D. Johnson, *Prayer, Patronage and Power: The Abbey of la Trinité, Vendôme, 1032–1187* (New York: New York University Press, 1981), pp. 103–04.

could secure and develop successful functioning on a material level. This area of monastic history, crossing both religious and economic spheres, remains one of the most puzzling, not only due to the common application of the modern notion of rationality as confined to the material spheres of human activities, but also due to the perception of religious motivations as intrinsically irrational.[11] An economically successful house with a big church was more likely to attract donations than a small and visibly poor establishment. To put it in rather crude terms, the wealthy house stood a good chance of becoming even richer by further donations and purchases, but a poor monastery was unlikely to improve significantly its material assets. Some interesting answers to this problem have been provided by recent studies on the economic behaviour of the medieval Church in which its religious function is analyzed in the terms of rational choice made by religious institutions wanting to satisfy simultaneously economic and non-economic goals.[12] Robert B. Ekelund tries to explain inter-Church mechanisms, which created conflicts between individual monasteries, by comparing its structure and functioning to that of a modern firm. He sees medieval monasteries, Cistercian houses in particular, as franchise monopolists within the organizational framework of the Church. They were, according to this model, distributors or retailers of salvation, and it was in their interest to keep the competitors — alternative religious institutions — away as well as to reduce intrabrand competition between the houses belonging to the same order. So maintaining a monopoly was fundamental for their success in accumulating, shaping, and retaining land.[13]

This desire for territorial exclusiveness is testified to by the Cistercian regulations, in particular 'Instituta Generalis Capituli', *c.* 1147. The distance between the granges of two houses should be at least two leagues (*c.* 5 miles) and every new house should be at a distance of at least ten leagues (*c.* 25 miles) from existing monasteries.[14] In some parts of Yorkshire, maintaining this territorial exclusiveness proved to be difficult, despite the clauses in many donation charters against grants to other orders. Repeated conflicts over landholding testify that maintaining a monopoly in terms of grants was almost impossible, because benefactors rarely kept their promises of exclusive grants. Certain areas, such as the West Riding which was rich in minerals, were very popular among religious houses, and the benefactors, of

[11] David A. Postles, 'Heads of Religious Houses as Administrators', in *England in the Thirteenth Century. Proceedings of the 1989 Harlaxton Symposium*, ed. by W. M. Ormrod (Stamford: Watkins, 1991), pp. 37–50 (p. 37), considers investments in the religious side of the monastic houses, for example buildings 'for the glory of God', as directly opposite to the rational investments in the estates.

[12] *Sacred Trust: The Medieval Church as an Economic Firm*, ed. by Robert B. Ekelund and others (New York: Oxford University Press, 1996), p. 46.

[13] *Sacred Trust*, ed. by Ekelund and others, pp. 3–5.

[14] *Narrative and Legislative Texts from Early Cîteaux*, ed. and trans. by Chrysogonus Waddell, Studia et Documenta, 9 (Pontigny: Cîteaux-Commentarii Cistercienses, 1999), pp. 469–70.

whom Adam son of Peter de Birkin, discussed in the second chapter, was probably the most extreme example, rarely restricted their generosity to one house only.

While this comparison between the medieval Church and modern market organizations may appear far-fetched to many historians, it provides a tangible explanation as to why the monasteries were involved in so many conflicts, despite the genuine belief in charity and cooperation. Many monasteries behaved in a monopolistic fashion, trying to ensure their dominant position in certain territories by pushing weaker houses out of their area. An expression of these monopolistic tendencies are the clauses in some donation charters preventing the benefactors giving land to other religious houses in the same area. Rievaulx obtained, for example, a special agreement with Adam son of Peter that he would not grant any property to other monastic houses in the vicinity of Rievaulx's lands given by him.[15] Such action was most likely motivated by the fact that Adam son of Peter and his wife, Matilda, were prominent benefactors of the Cluniac priory in Pontefract, and the Cistercian monks were concerned that Adam and Matilda might be tempted to grant something in the area of Rievaulx's interest to Pontefract Priory.[16] Some smaller houses, in particular nunneries, discussed later in this chapter, were also on the receiving end of Rievaulx's monopolistic tendencies and often had to make way for the expansion of this already successful institution.

Conflict was not, of course, the only mode of interaction. The regulations of the Cistercian order stated that if a disagreement arose between two abbots, they should ask a neighbouring abbot from the same order for arbitration, and if that failed, they should bring the issue to the Chapter General.[17] The statutes of the order reveal that Rievaulx was involved in such cases on several occasions, acting as an investigator or mediator at the request of the Chapter General. This was related to its prominent position among English Cistercian houses, and therefore the Chapter General was inclined to ask Rievaulx for arbitration between fellow Cistercian communities. Significantly, Rievaulx Abbey acted often as mediator in this way, but much less as an open party involved in conflict. Between 1191 and 1292 the Abbots of Rievaulx mediated or reported, together with other abbots, nineteen times to the Chapter General about situations in several English Cistercian houses, but Rievaulx itself was involved in only seven conflicts, out of which four were with its closest neighbour, Byland. In comparison, Fountains Abbey seemed to be a more aggressive institution: it acted between 1191 and 1278 as a mediator or investigator only ten times, but was

---

[15] *Cartulary*, no. 92.

[16] *The Cartulary of St John of Pontefract*, vol. II, ed. by Richard Holmes, Yorkshire Archaeological Society Record Series, 30 (Leeds: Yorkshire Archaeological Society, 1902), p. 397.

[17] This regulation is contained in the 'Instituta Generalis Capituli', *c.* 1147, but evolved in the twelfth century in keeping with the expansion of the order. By the 1190s the statutes ordered that conflicts should be resolved by the designated abbots. *Narrative and Legislative Texts*, ed. and trans. by Waddell, pp. 488–89.

involved in conflicts with Byland, Melrose, Furness, and Archbishop Roger of York eighteen times. This difference between the situations of Rievaulx and Fountains might have been caused by the appropriation of churches by the latter monastery, which caused this high number of disputes with the Archbishop. Disagreements of Fountains with its monastic neighbours also had a financial character.[18]

Cartularies of Yorkshire monastic houses and papal letters provide testimony for the active role of the Abbots of Rievaulx as mediators among religious houses in the region. In 1154 or 1155 Abbot Ailred mediated between the abbey of Savigny in Normandy and its daughter, Furness in Lancashire, in their dispute over the control of Byland Abbey.[19] Abbot Sylvan of Rievaulx (1167–88) was appointed among other high ecclesiastics to resolve conflict between the priory of Guisborough and Robert priest of Glemham over the church in Crathorne.[20] In 1223 the Abbots of Rievaulx and Byland were appointed by the pope to hear an appeal of the Prior and convent of Durham against the rector of Embleton church in their dispute concerning tithes. The abbots were given power to either settle the matter finally or return it to the papal curia for further consideration.[21] In 1251 the Abbots of Rievaulx and Rufford (a daughter house of Rievaulx) were called to arbitrate between Fountains and Sallay Abbeys. More then twenty years later in 1279 Abbots William of Rievaulx and Adam of Byland were appointed by the Chapter General to resolve a further conflict between Fountains and Sallay.[22]

In the twelfth century English monasteries, not only Cistercian, seem to have relied heavily on the mediation of other religious houses, and in more severe cases asked bishops or other ecclesiastical authorities for assistance. Mediation by the abbots of other local houses, not involved in the case, was done either on an informal basis or by the formal appointment by the Church authorities.[23] Often Archbishops of York and Canterbury asked the Abbots of Rievaulx to investigate disputes in the houses

---

[18] Joan Wardrop, *Fountains Abbey and its Benefactors 1132–1300* (Kalamazoo: Cistercian Publications, 1987), pp. 60, 95–99.

[19] *Life of Ailred*, p. xcii. This conflict was probably related to the wider issue of the merger of the Savigniac with the Cistercian order. Furness Abbey resented the growing Cistercian control over internal issues of the former Savigniac houses. Janet E. Burton, *The Monastic Order in Yorkshire, 1069–1215* (Cambridge: Cambridge University Press, 1999), pp. 116–17.

[20] *Cartularium Prioratus de Gyseburne Eboracensis Dioeceseos Ordinis S. Augustini*, vol. I, ed. by W. Brown, Surtees Society, 86 (Durham: Andrews, 1889–94), no. 592.

[21] Jane E. Sayers, *Papal Government and England during the Pontificate of Honorius III (1216–1227)* (Cambridge: Cambridge University Press, 1984), p. 119 and Appendix 2, no. 28.

[22] *The Cartulary of the Cistercian Abbey of St Mary of Sallay in Craven*, vol. II, ed. by Joseph McNulty, Yorkshire Archaeological Society Record Series, 90 (Wakefield: Yorkshire Archaeological Society, 1934), no. 412.

[23] Jane Sayers, 'English Cistercian Cases and their Delegation in the First Half of the Thirteenth Century', *Analecta Sacri Ordinis Cisterciensis*, 20 (1964), 85–102 (pp. 87–90).

under their jurisdiction. For example, in 1177 Archbishop Richard of Canterbury (1173–84) appointed the Abbot of Rievaulx to investigate a disagreement between Malton and Elstow Priories.[24] Soon afterward, the same Archbishop gave a mandate to the Abbot of Rievaulx and the Prior of Bridlington to examine a conflict over the church of St Peter in Halton (Lincolnshire) between Elstow Priory and Malton.[25]

In the late twelfth century popes often delegated Abbots of Rievaulx to oversee the implementation of their mandates concerning other religious institutions.[26] For example, in 1226 the Abbots of Rievaulx and Fountains were appointed to oversee the restoration of the financial solvency of the Yorkshire nunneries.[27] In 1231 Archbishop Walter Gray of York and a monk of Rievaulx, whose initial was 'S', were ordered by Pope Gregory IX to investigate clerical non-residency in the diocese of York.[28] In 1253 Abbot Adam de Tilletai of Rievaulx and Prior John of Newburgh were appointed by Pope Innocent IV to ensure that the Cistercian abbey of Meaux received the chapel of Skyren and its yearly income of eight marks, given to them by Thomas de Etton.[29]

The large number of arbitrations, investigations, and verdicts passed upon other religious houses in the North of England by the Abbots of Rievaulx shows that various authorities in the wider Church (popes, Chapter General, archbishops) recognized the abbey's high standing. These services for their fellow religious houses were also an important element and expression of brotherhood and care among the monastic communities. It was important that the abbots involved in the investigations and arbitrations knew the local situation and conditions, but at the same time were respected by the parties involved. It is clear that many Abbots of Rievaulx had both qualities.

Another important indication of the extent of the positive contacts between Rievaulx and its monastic neighbours are the witness lists. Of the 245 charters which constituted the original twelfth-century cartulary of Rievaulx Abbey, as many as fifty-four (22 per cent) contain the names of abbots, priors, monks, or canons from other houses. Not surprisingly, the single most frequently recorded individual witness was the Abbot of neighbouring Byland, Roger (1142–94), who appeared five times, but Priors and Canons of Bridlington witnessed nine charters, more than the representatives of any single Cistercian house: Priors Roger (1149–53) and Gregory

[24] London, British Library, Harleian Charter 43 G. 23.

[25] London, British Library, Harleian Charter 43 G. 24.

[26] *Papal Decretals Relating to the Diocese of Lincoln in the Twelfth Century*, ed. by W. Holzman and R. Kemp, Lincoln Record Society, 47 (Lincoln: Lincoln Record Society, 1954), pp. 6–9, 12–17, 40–41; *PU*, III, 445.

[27] *CPL*, p. 114.

[28] *The Register of Rolls of Walter Gray Lord Archbishop of York 1215–1255*, ed. by J. Raine, Surtees Society, 56 (Durham: Andrews, 1872), p. 165.

[29] *CPL*, pp. 114, 129, 292.

(1154–81) and the Canons Gregory, Ralph, Gilbert, Reginald, Baldwin de Gant, and Geoffrey the cellarer. Priors of Newburgh, another Augustinian house, witnessed five charters: Prior Augustin (1142/3–54) witnessed three charters and Richard (1155–86) two charters. The Abbots of Rievaulx performed reciprocal gestures, acting as witnesses for other religious houses, among them Rufford, Beggan Abbey (Brittany) for Kirkstead Abbey, and Newburgh Priory.[30] The witnessing of charters was an important activity in helping to establish and sustain friendly relationships between monastic houses and their neighbours, both lay and religious. By the act of witnessing a donation or other legal act, the witnesses became bonded with the grantee; their memory had a legal value and could be used in any future dispute. As the occasions of witnessing the charter required the physical presence of these individuals, so this practice fostered further friendly contacts between the religious houses and no doubt the abbots and priors used such events to discuss various issues of mutual importance or to exchange useful information.[31]

Letters, a valuable source for reconstructing monastic networks of alliance and friendships, can also be a help in examining contacts of the Rievaulx community with other religious institutions and individuals. Although letters of Abbot Ailred did not survive, another monk from Rievaulx, Matthew, a member of the community during the abbacy of Sylvan, who held an office of precentor and was still active in the first decade of the thirteenth century, left some correspondence (ten letters), mainly with other ecclesiastics, and a number of literary works.[32] A collection of letters written by Matthew shows a range of recipients including William, Prior of Byland, and a canon of the Beverley Minster, which indicates the abbey's connection within the Yorkshire ecclesiastical scene.[33]

As we have seen so far, the connections between Rievaulx Abbey and other religious houses in Yorkshire developed for a variety of reasons, but the physical proximity between two monastic precincts was the most direct one.

---

[30] London, British Library, Harleian Charter 83 G. 38 (1200–23); Harleian Charter 43 B. 47 (1215); Cotton Charter V 13 (1186). The last of those documents is an agreement between William de Mowbray and Newburgh Priory, concerning financing of St Nicholas chapel in Thirsk. It has attached seals of the Abbots of Rievaulx and Byland and the Priors of Kirkham and Malton.

[31] John R. Senior suggests for example that the abbots of Yorkshire monasteries exchanged information and advice on the building materials. John A. Senior, 'The Selection of Dimensional and Ornamental Stone Types Used in Some Northern Monasteries – the Exploitation and Distribution of a Natural Resource', in *Archaeology of Rural Monasteries*, ed. by Gilchrist and Mytum, pp. 223–50 (pp. 230–36).

[32] McGuire, *Friendship and Community*, pp. 369–70.

[33] André Wilmart, 'Les Mélanges de Mathieu Préchantre de Rievaulx au Début du XIIIe Siécle', *Revue Bénédictine*, 52 (1940), 15–84 (pp. 39–41 (nos 62–65), 72–83 (nos 30–33)).

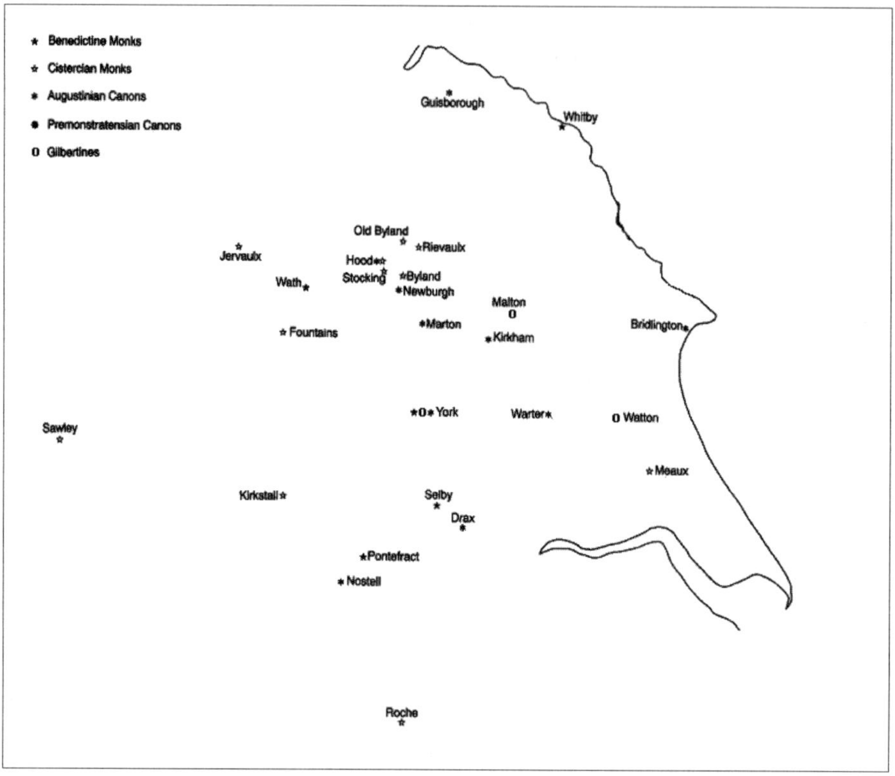

Map 2. Rievaulx Abbey and selected religious houses in Yorkshire before 1300.

Close Neighbours

Physically, the closest monastic neighbour of Rievaulx was Byland, initially located only one and a half miles away from Rievaulx. This abbey was founded in 1138 by Roger de Mowbray, also an important benefactor of Rievaulx Abbey, and had a very turbulent early history. The house changed its location four times in the first thirty-three years. Originally established as a Savigniac house in Calder (Cumberland) in 1134 by Ranulf Meschin, in 1137 the abbey was destroyed by a Scottish raid. The monks escaped to Furness, their mother house, but were refused entry there. At this point the desperate monks travelled to York to seek help from Archbishop Thurstan, who was known as a protector of monks. There they received help from Roger de Mowbray and his mother, Gundreda, in 1138 who gave them Hood as their new site and the tithes of food, which were replaced in 1140 by the lands in Cam, Wildon, Scackleton, and Airyholme. According to the *Historia Fundationis* compiled by Abbot Philip of Byland (1196–98), the site in Hood was intended only as a temporary residence. The growth of the community prompted Gundreda and Roger to grant them a new site in Old Byland (vill and a church) in September 1142.[34] This new location created conflict with Rievaulx Abbey, which was so close that the monks were confused by the sound of each other's bells signalling the differing daily routines, as Byland was at this point still a Savigniac house. As a result, in 1147 the congregation of Byland was moved again, first to Stocking (parish of Kilburn) and finally in 1177 to New Byland where it remained.[35]

Essentially, conflicts between Rievaulx and Byland derived from the proximity of the houses and from the fact that their properties bordered. Although the dating of the documents related to contacts between Rievaulx and Byland copied into the cartulary is approximate, the earliest one dates from the time when the Byland community was still living in Old Byland. Between 1142 and 1145 Abbot Roger of Byland agreed that Rievaulx Abbey could dig a ditch to the river Rye, at the foot of Ashberry Hill, which overlooks Rievaulx's precinct, on the property belonging to Byland. The Abbot of Byland granted to Rievaulx a right to use land which the said ditch enclosed.[36] This grant, particularly the enclosed land, caused further disagreements soon after between Abbot Roger of Byland and Abbot Ailred of Rievaulx. A comprehensive agreement dated 1147–67 (probably closer to 1147 than the later date), although copied with some additions into the cartulary only after 1170, regulated various disagreements concerning the borders of the properties of both houses.[37] The preamble of this charter emphasizes the intention of both communities to maintain mutual peace and love. They promised each other reciprocal prayers and, on a more practical level, to support and advise in case of hostility or persecution by the patrons, powerful noblemen, or neighbours.

> And therefore, brothers from Byland should perform for any brother of Rievaulx in respect of masses and psalms and other prayers just as they would for a brother of their house; and those of Rievaulx should give what is due to themselves to any brother of Byland. If indeed any oppression or persecution by advocates or powerful men or neighbours should occur for one house, then they should stand together in advice and help, supporting each other in all things.[38]

---

[34] 'Historia Fundationis', in William Dugdale, *Monasticon Anglicanum*, rev. by J. Caley, H. Ellis, and B. Bandinel, vol. V (London, 1846), p. 350; *EYC*, III, no. 1833. This is a simplified account of the early history of Byland; for a detailed account, see Burton, *Monastic Order in Yorkshire*, pp. 110–12.

[35] Janet E. Burton, 'The Settlement of Disputes between Byland Abbey and Newburgh Priory', *Yorkshire Archaeological Journal*, 55 (1983), 67–72 (pp. 67–68); Burton, 'The Abbeys of Byland and Jervaulx and the Problem of the English Savigniacs, 1134–1156', in *Monastic Studies: Continuity and Tradition*, vol. II, ed. by Judith Loades (Bangor: Headstart History, 1991), pp. 119–31 (pp. 119–24).

[36] *Cartulary*, no. 244.

[37] Burton, 'Estates and Economy', p. 47.

[38] 'Et ideo, obeunte aliquo fratre Rievallensi, fratres de Bellelanda in missis et psalmis ceterisque orationibus sicut pro fratre ipsius domus faciant, quod et ipsum, obeunte aliquo

The expression used in this case is vague and does not refer to any specific occasion or person, but the clause is an essential part of the contract; it was not a decorative feature and was put there on purpose. By establishing a community of prayers the monks set up a system of reciprocity and remembrance between both houses. For a monastic community such a declaration carried a significant practical and ideological dimension; the exchange of prayers expressed the idea of monastic brotherhood. Often these mutual commemorations were the result of friendships between the abbots or marked the end of disputes between houses, just as in the case of Rievaulx and Byland. The personal friendships were also a common ground helping to resolve disputes.[39]

This lengthy agreement, entitled in the cartulary as 'Cyrographum pacis inter nos et Bellalandes', was intended as a permanent solution. It stipulates all the points of controversy between Byland and Rievaulx and aims to solve all the areas of conflict, not only the borders, but also usage of particular properties and their possible changes in the future. The agreement marked the eastern side of the Vale of Pickering as the area for expansion for Rievaulx Abbey, from which the other house was excluded.[40] Finally both sides agreed to an arbitration procedure if any problem should arise in the future:

> That if even after that a dispute ever would arise, it should be resolved by four monks, according to the above said method. If any of the brothers should overstep the above said boundaries, on account of his carelessness and negligence he should be flogged in the Chapter of the brothers on the next Sunday, and that day he should not eat with others at the table, but on the floor. However, the negligence should be examined, to see if while he himself was ignorant and occupied by other things, the cattle which he watched [are] into strange pastures. If, in fact, he did it knowingly, that is seeing it while lying down, sitting, or standing, they should be found in unknown pastures, he should be punished on three Sundays by the above said punishment. Moreover, if having been seen by another brother and ordered to leave, he should not obey, he should be banished from his order, and should be the lowest of all until the previous punishment has been completed on three Sundays, so that on these three days he should drink only water. The boys who may be in the monastery, should be flogged for such fault until the blood [appears]. If a hired labourer should commit such a crime, the master should be warned a first and second time. If once more he should not improve, the master of hired labourers should suffer the above said punishment as if he himself had done it, This charter has been read in both Chapters, in the presence of the

---

fratre Bellelande, Rievallenses pro ipso persolvent. Si vero aliquid adversi vel prosecutionis ab advocatis vel a potentibus vel vicinis uni domui emerserit, per invicem stabunt consilio et auxilio, sibi in omnibus adherentes': *Cartulary*, no. 243.

[39] Newman, *Boundaries of Charity*, pp. 124–25; Haseldine, 'Friendship and Rivalry', p. 413.

[40] For the details of the agreement, see Emilia Jamroziak, 'Considerate Brothers or Predatory Neighbours? Rievaulx Abbey and Other Monastic Houses in the Twelfth and Thirteenth Centuries', *Yorkshire Archaeological Journal*, 73 (2001), 39–40 (pp. 32–33).

abbots, lord Silvan of Rievaulx and Roger of Byland, is made in perpetuity and having made so in the respect by them as well as by both Chapters.[41]

This lengthy description of the procedure to curb any future disputes not only shows how monasteries dealt with these issues, but also indicates how conflicts might occur in the first place. Human error or simple ignorance of the borders of pastures caused trespasses on to the lands of neighbours, which could in turn produce a full-scale dispute. The punishment procedures established in this agreement indicate the personal responsibilities of the monks for maintaining good relations with neighbours. The error of one individual could cause problems for the whole convent, therefore a rather severe physical and public punishment was meant to be a deterrent for the monks and lay brothers. The detailed nature of the agreement between Rievaulx and Byland Abbeys indicates also a delicate balance between these institutions and the extent of the actual or possible areas where disagreements could occur. It can also be seen as a delineation of the spheres of influence of each institution. Within those territories each house had a monopoly for the land acquisition and freedom to undertake economic activities. The language of friendship and compromise was not an empty rhetorical device, but a reflection of the reconciliation process between both institutions. Developing friendships was a key element of conflict resolution as shown by Brian Patrick McGuire on the example of correspondence between the Danish Cistercian Abbot of Esrum and the Abbot of the Augustinian house at Æbelholt.[42]

Although this lengthy agreement between Rievaulx and Byland settled several issues, there were still other areas which caused further conflict between both houses. The tithes payment, a common cause for disputes, was at the bottom of it. The question of payment of tithes of Oswaldenges and Stainton due to the church in Scawton was resolved by a separate agreement, probably parallel to the one discussed above. Those properties were in the hands of Rievaulx, but the church in Scawton was controlled by Byland. Between 1154 and 1160, Rievaulx and Byland reached an agreement

---

[41] 'Quod si aliquando inde controversia aliquando exorta fuerit, per iiii^or monachos, secundum modum predictum pacificetur. Si quis fratrum metas predictas transgressus fuerit, [propter] negligentiam suam et incuriam, proxima dominica in capitulo fratrum verberetur, et ea die non cum aliis ad mensam sed in terra comedat. Negligentia autem judicabitur si, ipso nesciente et in aliis rebus occupato, pecora que custodit in alienis pascuis paverint. Si vero scienter id fecerit — id est, supino vidente et sedente vel stante, in alienis pascuis inventa fuerint, tribus dominicis predicta poena plectetur. Si vero, visus ab aliquo fratre, et jussus exire, non obedierit amoveatur ab ordine suo et ultimus omnium sit donec premissam poenitentiam perfecerit tribus dominicis, ita ut ipsis tribus diebus non nisi aquam bibat. Pueri qui de domo sint, pro tale culpa vapulent usque ad sanguinem. Conductitius, si talia commiserit, magister ejus moneatur semel et iterum. Si denuo non correxerit, magister conductitii, ac si ipse fecisset, predictam poenam sustineat. Hec carta lecta est in utroque capitulo, presentibus Abbatibus, Domino Silvano Rievallensi, et Rogero Bellelandensi et tam ab ipsis quam utroque capitulo in perpetuum confecta': *Cartulary*, no. 243.

[42] McGuire, *Friendship and Community*, pp. 356–57.

according to which Rievaulx agreed to pay twenty pence yearly as compensation to the church of Scawton for the loss of tithes.[43] This agreement did not end this conflict. Archbishop Roger of York, after his appointment in 1154, and later Archdeacon Ralph Baro, in 1157–58, issued separate charters concerning these tithes.[44] The conflict did not even finish then, but lasted well into the 1160s when Pope Alexander III gave his ruling concerning payment of the tithes.[45] The protracted character of this case was typical for disputes about tithes. This became a particularly controversial issue between Cistercian houses and the secular church, and Rievaulx became entangled in a number of such disputes in the second half of the twelfth century. They were important not only from a financial point of view, but also with regard to defining Cistercian identity. I will come back to this issue further in the chapter.

Whilst Byland and Rievaulx Abbeys were engaged in these conflicts, another neighbour of Byland, Newburgh Priory, carried out a successful collaborative drainage project with Byland. The flows of Holbeck stream, Thorpe Beck, and Long Beck were altered to provide better water delivery to Byland's precinct and a better current for Newburgh's mills.[46] This example of cooperation indicates that conflict was not inevitable between religious houses, although Rievaulx Abbey was not as willing as Newburgh to cooperate for mutual benefit. Having said that, we should remember that the land which was the object of dispute between Rievaulx and Byland was crucial for Rievaulx's expansion of its precinct and shaping of its estates in the most desirable way, and the community was not prepared to compromise on that.

Despite this seemingly endless stream of conflict between Rievaulx and Byland, personal contacts between the abbots of both houses were very good. After all, it was Abbot Roger of Byland who brought his monastic community into the Cistercian order and may have consulted Ailred on many issues pertinent to this move. It was also Abbot Roger who anointed the dying Ailred and kept the vigil, with other abbots, on his last days.[47] Personal friendship between abbots of various houses were part of the Cistercian ideology of *caritas* and played an important role in the order's life. As we will see below, personal contact also had a strong impact on the early relationship between Rievaulx and the order of Sempringham.

A conflict between two Cistercian houses was not just their internal matter, but an issue of concern for the whole Cistercian community. So the prolonged conflicts between Rievaulx and Byland Abbeys prompted their superiors in the Cistercian order to intervene. Between 1162 and 1165 Geoffrey, Abbot of Clairvaux, and G. (either Gariaumer or Gilbert le Grand), Abbot of Cîteaux, sent a letter, later copied

---

[43] *Cartulary*, no. 242.

[44] *Cartulary*, nos 225, 226; published and dated in *EEA*, XX, 88.

[45] *PU*, I, no. 104.

[46] C. J. Bond, 'Water Management in the Rural Monastery', in *Archaeology of Rural Monasteries*, ed. by Gilchrist and Mytum, pp. 83–111 (pp. 97–98).

[47] *Life of Ailred*, pp. 59–60.

into the cartulary, expressing their concern about preserving 'brotherly peace and love' between Byland and Rievaulx. The French abbots strongly reinforced the order's prohibition on the acceptance of certain lands, by forbidding the communities of Rievaulx and Byland to accept any lands against the order's rules.[48] The charter does not specify to which rules and decrees of the order the Abbots of Cîteaux and Clairvaux were referring, but it may well be one of the early regulations of the *Summa Cartae Caritatis* or legislation of the early Chapter General (now dated by Waddell to 1133/4–50 and 1147 respectively) prohibiting acceptance of churches and income from the altars, tithes, manors, serfs, rents from the land, and mills, all of which Rievaulx and Byland held to some extent.[49] These forbidden types of income were seen by the superiors in the Cistercian order as a cause of conflicts between the individual monasteries. But the attitude of the Abbots of Cîteaux and Clairvaux was rather pragmatic. They understood that being close neighbours caused problems and advised both abbots to be cautious in their actions towards each other. It is also possible that this letter was related to some arbitration between Rievaulx and Byland undertaken by the Abbots of Cîteaux and Clairvaux of which no other record has been preserved. The help of the Chapter General was sought by both houses in later conflicts; there is no reason to doubt that Yorkshire Cistercians might ask prominent persons within the order for arbitration.

Despite the detailed agreements and involvement of other abbots, further conflicts took place as times and circumstances changed. A series of conflicts between Rievaulx and Byland recorded in the *Statuta Capitulorum* occurred in 1236, 1238, 1252, and 1253; unfortunately these entries are very laconic and do not provide information about the reasons for these conflicts.[50] In the first instance Byland complained against Rievaulx; then in 1238 the statutes indicate a quarrel without pointing to the offending party. In the last two cases Rievaulx complained against Byland. On the first occasion the Chapter General designated the Abbots of Roche, Kirkstall, and Meaux to investigate the matter and resolve it by arbitration or judgement; and then in 1238 the Abbots of Furness, Combermere, and Beaulieu were called to inspect the situation. In the last two cases, of 1252 and 1253, the Chapter General appointed the Abbots of Furness, Fountains, and Merevale to examine the situation; the first of these three abbots was also designated to report back to the Chapter General about their arbitration. Although all these entries are very laconic, there is a considerable change in tone of the 1253 decision of the Chapter General. Instead of just appointing another team to investigate, the Chapter urged designated abbots to give judgement without delay and resolve the matter so there would be no need for further investigation:

---

[48] 'Ea propter prohibemus vobis et omnimodis intericimus quatinus non grangiam nec terram nec pasturam ab aliquo requiratis vel accipiatis contra formam ordinis et terminos constitutos': *Cartulary*, no. 245.

[49] *Narrative and Legislative Texts*, ed. and trans. by Waddell, pp. 191, 460.

[50] *Statuta*, II, 1236: 48; 1252: 35; 1253: 18.

> A complaint of the abbot of Rievaulx against the abbot and convent of Byland is committed to the abbots of Furness, Fountains, and Merevale again by the full power of the order, to determine judgement, who without cost of delay, if they find one has transgressed against the other, paying attention to what is fair, should proceed quickly to judge and remedy, so that it will not be necessary to repeat its instruction for the commission.[51]

The wording of this entry may indicate that the disagreement between both houses was prolonged and probably related to the earlier cases from the 1230s. The arbitration mentioned in the entry, by Abbots, from within the order, of Furness, Fountains, and Merevale, ensured that the investigating team knew the background and local aspects of the conflict and would not have to travel very far to examine the matter. On other occasions the Abbots of Rievaulx were appointed by the Chapter General to investigate and mediate in both Furness and Fountains Abbey, so this was a mutual service performed by Cistercian communities for each other and another practical application of the ideology of friendship and brotherhood.

In the course of the twelfth and thirteenth centuries Rievaulx and Byland Abbeys had to develop strategies for dealing with difficulties arising from the physical proximity of the houses and estates. Not only were their precincts nearby, but both monasteries tried to attract donations from the same people, which generated direct competition for properties in particular areas, specifically in the West Riding. One of the ways of dealing with the overlapping interests attempted by Rievaulx and Byland was to secure a monopoly of grants from a particular donor, or to establish clear spheres of expansion for each monastery. The string of conflicts between Rievaulx and Byland also shows the importance of the mechanism of arbitration within the Cistercian order and the concern by the Abbots of Cîteaux and Clairvaux over the events in Yorkshire. It was the mixture of pragmatism and the ideology of brotherly love that appears to guide the communities of Rievaulx and Byland and their arbiters in the efforts to resolve the conflicts. This approach was particularly effective if there was no direct lay involvement, but in other situations either patrons or benefactor played some role in generating conflicts between the houses.

Houses Sharing the Same Founder

Moving on from Byland to other neighbours, it is important to point out that the relationship between Rievaulx and Kirkham Priory of Augustinian canons had a particular dimension lacking in other cases discussed here, due to the fact that both houses

[51] 'Querela abbatis de Rievalle contra abbatem et conventum de Bellalanda, de Furnesio, de Fontibus et de Mira valle abbatibus iterato committitur in plenaria Ordinis potestate iudicio terminanda, qui sine morae dispendio si alteram partium contra alteram invenerint excessisse, iuris ordine servato procedant celeriter et emendent in qua super hiis de cetero non oporteat commissionis mandatum innovari, et quid inde, etc': *Statuta*, II, 1253: 18.

had the same founder. Kirkham Priory was founded *c.* 1122 by Walter Espec and located about seven miles from Rievaulx. Walter Espec's treatment of Rievaulx and Kirkham Priory, discussed in the first chapter, showed how a powerful lay nobleman could fundamentally alter the functioning of the house of his patronage. Espec's intention was to turn Kirkham Priory into a Cistercian house, and despite the failure of his plan, the actions undertaken for that purpose had a significant impact on Rievaulx Abbey and Kirkham Priory and their subsequent relationship.

Another reason for the early animosity between both houses might have originated from the desertion of Waldef, then Prior of Kirkham, a friend of Ailred, in the 1140s to become a Cistercian monk. He became the Abbot of Melrose, a daughter house of Rievaulx, in 1148.[52] Marsha Dutton suggests that the 'Letter to Maurice' written by Walter Daniel after Ailred's death was directed to the Prior of Kirkham who harboured resentment towards the abbot of the successful Cistercian house. Prior Maurice questioned the claims of the Rievaulx community for Ailred's sanctity, but his scepticism was also an expression of the animosity between both houses, which had earlier roots.[53] The personal nature of the early contacts between the houses and their respective abbots and priors, originating in the fact of having a common founder, did not last beyond the first half of the twelfth century. Their later relationship continued to involve laypeople, but on different terms.

After this early period of contacts between Rievaulx and Kirkham there is a large gap in the sources, and not until 150 years later is there further indication of more mundane contacts. In 1276 Prior William of Kirkham issued a plea of trespass against the Abbot of Rievaulx. Unfortunately the location of this trespass was not specified.[54] It is likely that it occurred in Bilsdale, where the north-eastern part was in the possession of Kirkham and where, by 1274, the priory acquired control of the whole manor, while the southern part was in the hands of Rievaulx.[55] It might have been an early stage of the conflict which surfaced between 1279 and 1281, when William, Prior of Kirkham, issued a plea against William, Abbot of Rievaulx, about common pasture in Bilsdale. The Prior accused Abbot Adam of Rievaulx of unjustly dispossessing Richard, then the Prior of Kirkham, of the right to a common pasture in Bilsdale. The Abbot of Rievaulx denied the charges and claimed judgement by his peers.[56] The assize was issued, and at the new hearing brother John Wlveley from Kirkham Priory gave evidence against the right of Rievaulx Abbey to the common pasture in Bilsdale.

---

[52] *Life of Ailred*, pp. xxx–xxxi.

[53] Marsha L. Dutton, 'Introduction' to *Life of Ailred*, p. 67.

[54] *Notes on the Religious and Secular Houses of Yorkshire*, vol. I, ed. by William P. Baildon, Yorkshire Archaeological Society Record Series, 17 (London: Yorkshire Archaeological Society, 1895), 103, no. 5.

[55] John McDonnell, 'Medieval Assarting Hamlets in Bilsdale, North-East Yorkshire', *Northern History*, 22 (1986), 269–79 (p. 271).

[56] *Cartulary*, p. 404, published from Placita Ebor, 8–9 Edw. I.

> [H]e said that the assize ought not to be done, because he said that the above said prior is the head lord of the vill of Bilsdale, and that he himself appropriated from the above said place, just as it was legal for him by the provision of Merton etc. And the abbot said that the above said provision does not lie between them, because he said that he was not in the possession of the above said common for forty years before the said prior acquired the lordship of the said vill; and that the said prior acquired the said lordship from the one Simon de Ver, only five years ago. He said also, that he holds this in free alms, and that he himself is not holding of the above said prior by the said alms.[57]

The nature of the dispute is again typical for neighbours, not necessarily ecclesiastical, and involves one of the most important resources, use of a common pasture. What is also important to observe here is that the parties did not look for arbitration among their monastic colleagues, but in a court of law and among those in the vicinity who knew the complexities of the land possession. Simon de Vere, mentioned in the court hearing, was a neighbour of Rievaulx Abbey and a benefactor of Kirkham. Simon himself, like his tenants discussed in the previous chapter, had a long dispute with Rievaulx Abbey. After several years of trespasses and lawsuits Simon de Vere finished formally in 1260 several conflicts with the Cistercian house.[58] The memorandum of this agreement was written in the Kirkham cartulary, which shows that this institution had an interest not only in the area of the dispute but also in the contacts between Simon de Vere, its benefactor, and Rievaulx Abbey.[59] Just as Rievaulx Abbey preserved information about its benefactors in the cartulary, the Augustinian priory also kept documents which, although the events described did not involve them directly, provided important information about the situation in the neighbourhood.

Although the relationship between Rievaulx Abbey and Kirkham Priory is known rather fragmentarily, it indicates strongly that their mutual contacts were to a large extent the result of their involvement in the lay world. The episode of the near disappearance and re-endowment of Kirkham Priory at the beginning of its existence indicates how a powerful founder could intervene in the life of his monastery and create links between the houses of different orders which might not have come into being without his actions. Their bordering Bilsdale properties, given to both houses by their founder Walter Espec, created the usual problems which could occur between

---

[57] 'Et dicit quod assisa [non] debet inde fieri, quia dicit quod predictus Prior est capitalis Dominus de villa de Bildesdale, et quod ipse appropriavit de predicta placea, sicut ei bene licuit per provisionem de Mertona etc. Et Abbas dicit quod predicta provisio non jacet inter eos, quia dicit quod non fuit seissitus de predicta communa quadraginta annis antequam praedictus Prior dominus ejusdem ville perquisierat; et quod predictus Prior perquisivit predictum dominium de quodam Simone de Ver, jam quinque annis elapsis. Dicit etiam quod ipse tenet in liberam elemosinam, et quod ipse non [est] tenens predicti Prioris de predicta elemosina': *Cartulary*, p. 405, published from Placita Ebor, 8–9 Edw. I.

[58] Bodl. Dodsw. vii, fol. 140; published incomplete in the *Cartulary*, pp. 226–27.

[59] Kirkham Cartulary, Oxford, Bodleian Library, MS Fairfax 7, fol. 51^{v}; published in the *Cartulary*, pp. 254–55.

any neighbours.[60] Later contacts between Rievaulx and Kirkham, particularly in the 1280s, were also strongly related to their roles as tenants, lords, and landholders, which entangled them in the web of disputes among not only religious institutions, but lay neighbours as well.

Other Cistercian Houses

Once we get beyond the abbey's immediate monastic neighbours, relationships become calmer and often related to the wider role of Rievaulx Abbey in the Cistercian arena in Yorkshire and beyond. The Abbots of Rievaulx were often called by the Chapter General to intervene in the internal matters of other houses of this order, and their names often appeared in the witness lists of charters from other Cistercian houses. To see more clearly the multidimensional character of these contacts within the order, it is worth examining contacts between Rievaulx and Fountains. Their economic interests generally did not overlap, and their joint position as the most important, richest, and most influential of the northern Cistercian houses was not questioned. During the time when the Abbot Henry Murdac of Fountains was the Archbishop of York, the first two abbot-suffragans at Fountains were monks of Rievaulx: Maurice and Thorald.[61] Throughout the twelfth and thirteenth centuries the relationship of the two monasteries was more often one of working together and mediating for each other than of conflict. The chapters of Rievaulx and Fountains, together with Archbishop Roger of York and lay noblemen, witnessed between 1154 and 1181 an agreement between Byland Abbey and Newburgh Priory.[62] In 1218 the Abbots of Fountains, Rievaulx, Waverley, Margam, and Beaulieu were chosen by the Chapter General to judge serious disorders occurring in English houses which could not wait until the next Chapter General.[63] In 1226 the Abbots of Fountains and Rievaulx were called by Pope Gregory IX to restore the property of several nunneries in Yorkshire which were struggling with poverty and debts.[64]

Although these activities left only dry and fragmentary information in the sources, I am inclined to see them as a continuation of the friendship ideology so central to the Cistercian life in the twelfth century. McGuire elucidates that the absence of the

---

[60] John McDonnell suspected that the remnants of a rampart in Broad Ings were a part of the physical division between sheep pasture of Rievaulx and the northern part of Bilsdale belonging to Kirkham: *A History of Helmsley, Rievaulx and District*, ed. by John McDonnell (York: Stonegate Press, 1963), Appendix A(xv), p. 417.

[61] Burton, *Monastic Order in Yorkshire*, pp. 114, 165.

[62] London, British Library, Egerton Charter 585. For discussion of other documents from the Byland cartulary related to this conflict, but not containing the name of the Abbot of Rievaulx, see Burton, 'Settlement of Disputes', pp. 67–72.

[63] *Statuta*, I, 1218: 74.

[64] *CPL*, p. 114.

language of friendship in the thirteenth-century Cistercian writing is not evidence for the disappearance of the spiritual bonds between the members of the order.[65] I would like to add here another argument to this debate. Not only did the spiritual meaning of the friendships not disappear, but its practical application continued beyond the mid-twelfth century. The involvement of Rievaulx abbots as arbiters and negotiators was its practical expression, even if no longer accompanied by ideological declarations.

At least twice in the thirteenth century Abbots of Rievaulx helped to resolve difficult conflicts in which Fountains Abbey was entangled. In 1251 the Abbots of Rievaulx and Rufford, its daughter house, were called to arbitrate between Fountains and Sallay in their dispute over the changes in the direction of Lonsdale road and pasture rights in that area where properties of both houses were located close to each other.[66] Sallay Abbey was a daughter house of Newminster (which was a daughter of Fountains) and was significantly smaller than its 'grandmother', but its location destined it to be a competitor of Fountains. This road formed a part of the border between the properties of both houses, but the monks from both institutions could not agree what constituted the old road and which was new, an important distinction since the running of the old road was demarcating the border. Originally the case was arbitrated by four knights from the neighbourhood, who declared the precise location of the old road. Both communities made mutual concessions to each other and the document containing this agreement was made and sealed on 14 September 1251 by Abbot Adam of Rievaulx and Abbot Geoffrey of Rufford. Despite the detailed nature of this document, both communities continued to quarrel. More then twenty years later, in 1279, Abbots William of Rievaulx and Adam of Byland were appointed by the Chapter General to resolve a further conflict between Fountains and Sallay about the same road.[67] The aim of the second arbitration was to enforce the previous agreement which was by then broken. The final meeting of all the parties involved, and the sealing of the charter, took place in their fellow Cistercian house of Kirkstall. Since the verdict of the four knights which formed the basis of the previous agreement was given orally and not written down, the Abbots of Rievaulx and Byland ordered that the border between the forest belonging to Fountains and the pasture in the possession of Salley should be perambulated by the monks and lay brothers from both communities and then marked by a series of wooden crosses. In order that this evidence should remain visible for perpetuity, the masters of the neighbouring granges were ordered to replace the wooden crosses by large stones before Michaelmas of the same year. The usage of the common pastures and forests by both communities was described in detail, and the observance of this agreement

---

[65] Brian Patrick McGuire, 'The Cistercians and the Transformation of Monastic Friendships', in his *Friendship and Faith: Cistercian Men, Women, and their Stories, 1100–1250*, Variorum Collected Studies Series (Aldershot: Ashgate, 2002), pp. 1–63 (III) (pp. 3–5).

[66] *Cartulary of Sallay*, II, 13–14, no. 411.

[67] *Cartulary of Sallay*, II, 14–16, no. 412.

was reinforced by the threat of excommunication for anyone who broke it. This case is not very dissimilar to the earlier analysed dispute between Rievaulx and Byland over the running of the border; in both situations one of the houses was also significantly stronger and wealthier. However, a significant difference lies here in the methods of resolving the controversy, manifested by much more active involvement of lay and monastic neighbours at all stages, as witnesses and mediators in particular. This is linked to the more formalized methods of conflict resolution and the more complex landscape of landholdings in the thirteenth century, in contrast to the earlier practice relying primarily on personal connections and involvement of the abbots.

The only documented case of direct conflict between Rievaulx and Fountains occurred between 1170 and 1180, and the cause was rather predictable — conflicting economic interests. It was ended by the agreement between Abbot Sylvan of Rievaulx and Abbot Robert of Fountains, and ratified by Abbot Alexander of Cîteaux and Abbot Henry of Clairvaux in the presence of the abbots of other Cistercian houses: Richard de la Chaussée of Mortemer in Normandy (1174–79), and the Abbots of Byland, Woburn, Sallay, and Jervaulx. Both sides of the conflict agreed that the borders of their unnamed granges in Cleveland should not be changed. The presence of the high rank representatives of the order indicates that the disagreement between Rievaulx and Fountains was taken very seriously by the Chapter General. This appears to be motivated by the status of the houses rather than the gravity of the conflict itself, which was indeed typical. Both communities promised each other not to commit any trespasses, and designated a right of way for the monks of Fountains to the land which they had acquired opposite the property of Everard II de Ros, the patron of Rievaulx Abbey. Both sides had rights to collect wood and salt and to establish fisheries towards the sea.[68] Wardrop suggests that this document refers to Rievaulx's grange in Normanby and Fountains's in Eston. The origin of this conflict lies therefore in Stephen II de Meinil's grant to Fountains Abbey in Eston; he was also an active benefactor of Rievaulx.[69] The grange of Normanby (in the parish of Eston) belonging to Rievaulx was built from the grant from Richard son of Thurstan of Normanby, his son Richard, and his nephew Richard Lost.[70] The considerable distance from the house and the dispute with Fountains prompted Rievaulx Abbey to lease the pastures and fisheries in Normanby to Walter, a priest of Eston church. The money was then spent on the purchase of fifty acres of arable land in Sproxton near Griff and pasture for one hundred sheep and forty-eight head of cattle located close to the abbey.[71]

This conflict between Rievaulx and Fountains Abbeys exemplifies very well the issue of 'spheres of influence' and the process of their negotiation. Rievaulx pulled

---

[68] *Cartulary*, no. 241.

[69] Wardrop, *Fountains Abbey*, p. 167.

[70] *Cartulary*, nos 116, 117, 118; *EYC*, II, no. 739.

[71] Waites, 'Monastic Settlement', p. 493. The article does not specify the source of this information about the land purchase in Sproxton.

out of the Normanby area, allowing Fountains Abbey to secure its domination there, and the funds obtained in this way were spent on expanding property in a more strategically located area. This manoeuvre allowed both houses to maintain the integrity of their estates, and prevented long and possibly costly disputes if both Fountains and Rievaulx tried to expand and consolidate their landholdings in the Normanby area.

Among the Yorkshire houses discussed in this chapter, only Fountains could be compared in scale and importance to Rievaulx Abbey. Their position was recognized also by the Chapter General and officials of the secular Church who often appointed abbots of both houses to investigate problems occurring in other religious communities. The economic interests of Rievaulx and Fountains did not overlap in any significant way, and both communities were keen to preserve this balance, as exemplified by the agreement over Normanby. Both houses maintained a mutually good relationship as key players in the local monastic arena, offering useful mediation services to each other. The same cannot be said about other houses located further away from Rievaulx Abbey.

Augustinian Houses

Among the religious houses in the North of England, the Augustinian priories were well established by the second half of the twelfth century and attracted a large number of donations from laypeople. As a result those houses became competitors of Cistercian monasteries, and their economic interests often overlap as donors to the Cistercian houses were often also donors to the Augustinian priories. The connections between Rievaulx and the Augustinian houses in Bridlington, Newburgh, Guisborough, and Drax were primarily of an economic nature, including disputes over spheres of influence, grange building, and shared common pastures, whilst the disputes over tithes payments remained persistent throughout the second half of the twelfth and early thirteenth centuries. In some instances, which will be discussed later, their granges bordered with those of Rievaulx. Even if each house had a sphere of influence, it was not always possible to maintain a monopoly within such an area; larger and more important houses commanded stronger influences over their environment than their smaller counterparts. A particular group of conflicts between Rievaulx and the Augustinian houses originated from disagreements over tithe payment. Augustinian canons had no prohibition against or reservations about receiving tithes. They were, in fact, an optimal beneficiary for noblemen, who might dispose of their proprietary churches in the later twelfth century due to the growing reform movement in the Church.[72] Cistercian abbeys, although formally prohibited from accepting churches

[72] Janet E. Burton, 'Monasteries and Parish Churches in Eleventh and Twelfth-Century Yorkshire', *Northern History*, 23 (1987), 39–50 (p. 39).

and their tithes, in many instances also controlled such assets.[73] However, the central point of controversy was Cistercian exemption from their payment.[74] This exemption caused a disagreement between Rievaulx Abbey and Newburgh Priory which wanted to assert its right to the tithes from Welburn and Hoveton, properties given to Rievaulx by their mutual benefactors, the Mowbray family.[75] Rievaulx Abbey refused to pay them claiming the Cistercian exemption, a privilege given to the order by Pope Innocent II in 1132.[76] Eventually, between 1189 and *c.* 1210, Rievaulx rendered the tithes due from the abbey's land in Welburn and Hoveton to Newburgh Priory to avoid further disputes. Both houses agreed to which lands were liable for tithes and which were not.[77] The tithe disputes continued in the thirteenth century involving a number of arbiters. In 1239 Rievaulx Abbey petitioned Pope Gregory IX to resolve another conflict between itself and Guisborough about the payment of unspecified tithes. This case had been heard before the officials of the Archdeacon of Cleveland, but no satisfactory resolution was reached. Therefore, the Pope appointed the Abbot of the Premonstratensian house in Croxton (Leicestershire), the Prior of the Augustinian house in Newburgh, and the Prior of Beauver (diocese of Lincoln) to arbitrate between Rievaulx and Guisborough.[78] This conflict was not just about money, although it was of course an important element, but also about asserting rights which were a significant element of being a Cistercian abbey. Freedom from paying the tithes was an important privilege which differentiated communities of white monks from Augustinians, among others, so it was important for Rievaulx Abbey to uphold it in some form as a matter of principle and ideology, not just for financial reasons.

Contacts between Rievaulx Abbey and Guisborough Priory, the wealthiest Augustinian house in Yorkshire, were rather varied. In the early thirteenth century Rievaulx Abbey was appointed to oversee certain interests of Guisborough Priory. In or soon after 1200 the Abbots of Byland, Rievaulx, and Fountains as well as the

---

[73] Among Yorkshire houses Fountains is known to have had possession of three churches: Wardrop, *Fountains Abbey*, pp. 97–99. There was a great variety of practices in this matter in the Cistercian order across Europe. Besides, upon the accession to the Cistercians the Savigniac houses retained control over churches they had held: Constance H. Berman, 'Cistercian Development and the Order's Acquisition of Churches and Tithes in Southwestern France', *Revue Bénédictine*, 91 (1981), 193–203 (p. 196–98); For the situation in Poland and Scandinavia, see *Monasticon Cisterciense Poloniae*, I, ed. by Andrzej Wyrwa, Jerzy Strzelczyk, and Krzysztof Kaczmarek (Poznań: Wydawnictwo Poznańskie, 1999), pp. 202–07; James France, *The Cistercians in Scandinavia* (Kalamazoo: Cistercian Publications, 1992), pp. 208–25.

[74] For further discussion on the tithes controversy, see chapter 5, pp. 180–82 below.

[75] *EYC*, IX, no. 163.

[76] Giles Constable, *Monastic Tithes from their Origins to the Twelfth Century* (Cambridge: Cambridge University Press, 1964), p. 231.

[77] *EYC*, IX, no. 164.

[78] *CPL*, I, 180.

Prior of Kirkham inspected charters of grants of Robert de Brus to Guisborough and reported their findings to Archbishop Geoffrey of York concerning churches and their income given by Robert to this house.[79] In 1210 Pope Innocent III sent a mandate to Abbot Warin of Rievaulx (1208–11) and the Dean and treasurer of York chapter to grant to Guisborough Priory the church of Hessle, for the 'use of hospitality', which had been previously granted to the recently deceased Master Britus, a papal subdeacon and notary.[80] It took eight years for the Pope to confirm Rievaulx Abbey's grant to Guisborough Priory of Hessle church. It is possible either that this long delay was caused by the slow bureaucracy of the papal court or that Rievaulx was trying to delay or even ignore papal orders. If the monks controlled the church of Hessle, as the papal mandate suggests, after the death of its previous holder, they were likely to be reluctant to give away this income.[81]

Although recorded contacts between Rievaulx Abbey and Guisborough Priory are fragmentary, their diversity points to certain characteristics of intermonastic contacts, which consisted of monetary agreements, tithes disputes, and arbitration over these. Like the contacts with lay neighbours, of which conflicts were predominantly recorded, these connections between Rievaulx and its Augustinian neighbours were similarly biased towards disagreements rather than cooperation, presenting a more negative image than it probably was in reality.

Another of the northern Augustinian houses, Bridlington Priory, was founded by Walter de Gant, also a benefactor of Rievaulx Abbey. Although both institutions were located at a considerable distance from each other (forty miles), they received lands in close proximity from their shared benefactors. In order to avoid conflict with Bridlington Priory in Willerby, where the priory owned a church and Rievaulx had a licence to acquire land and pasture, the abbey leased ten and a half acres of land, tenements, and pasture for three hundred sheep to the priory in 1175.[82] Rievaulx's holdings there dated from as early as 1152 and were reconfirmed in 1172 by Henry de Willerby (a tenant of Earl Simon de St Liz, a son-in-law of Gilbert de Gant) with the clause permitting them to build a grange.[83] Rievaulx could technically try to build a grange there, having acquired a licence to purchase or receive grants there from Earl Simon de St Liz and his wife, Alice de Gant, between 1170 and 1184, but decided not to do so.[84] The reason for a compromise so favourable for the canons was probably the possibility of a costly conflict with Bridlington which would arise

[79] London, British Library, Stowe Charter 465.

[80] *CPL*, I, 36.

[81] *CPL*, I, 54.

[82] *EYC*, II, no. 1230.

[83] *EYC*, II, no. 1228. This charter was copied to Bridlington cartulary, not to the cartulary of Rievaulx Abbey which indicated a keen interest of the canons in the matter.

[84] *Cartulary*, no. 158; *EYC*, II, no. 1232.

from attempts to establish a grange there.[85] Rievaulx recognized this area as primarily Bridlington's sphere of expansion and ceased its own territorial growth there before any serious conflict occurred.[86] As any large landowner, religious houses were interested in building not only extensive but also compact estates and usually wanted to secure some form of control over the area in which their properties were located. These spheres of influence had to be recognized by other members of the landowning community if the system was to work smoothly. The ways in which Rievaulx Abbey and Bridlington Priory arranged their economic interests, similarly to the earlier cases between Rievaulx and Fountains, show how conflicts could be prevented.

Drax Priory, also located at a considerable distance from Rievaulx, clashed with the abbey over a grant in Faweather (West Riding, parish of Bingley), an area of a particularly fierce competition for donations between religious houses. Faweather was given to Rievaulx Abbey by Adam son of Peter de Birkin between 1150 and 1160, but Drax Priory's initial endowment was located in that area and the canons claimed rights to the tithes, which Rievaulx refused to pay.[87] Between 1221 and 1223 the abbey agreed to pay an annual compensation to Drax Priory of three shillings for the loss of tithes, although the dispute surfaced again in the early fourteenth century.[88] This way of resolving a dispute over tithes payment by way of paying compensation was characteristic of Rievaulx's dealing with Augustinian houses. The payment of compensation was a clever way of satisfying the financial grievances of the canons without actually agreeing to pay the tithes, and thus asserted the Cistercian right of exemption.

Another West Riding vill, Harden (parish of Bingley), was an area of high concentration of monastic grants from Adam son of Peter, a prolific benefactor of many Yorkshire monasteries. Most of Harden was by the early thirteenth century in the hands of Rievaulx Abbey, and other monastic competitors were pushed out of this attractive area. Rievaulx's methods of asserting its economic position there show that competition between religious institutions was just as fierce as between laypeople, and other monastic rivals were eliminated without much hesitation by this powerful house. Prioress Agnes of Esholt, a small Cistercian nunnery, quitclaimed or rather sold three bovates of land in Cullingworth and the common forest in Harden. The

[85] Waites, 'Monastic Settlement', p. 493; R. A. Donkin, 'The Cistercian Grange in England in the Twelfth and Thirteenth Centuries with Special Reference to Yorkshire', *Studia Monastica*, 6 (1964), 94–144 (p. 103).

[86] *Abstracts of the Charters and other Documents Contained in the Chartulary of the Priory of Bridlington*, ed. by W. T. Lancaster (Leeds: published privately, 1912), pp. 100, 114, 115.

[87] *West Yorkshire: An Archaeological Survey to A.D. 1500*, vol. II, *The Administrative and Tenurial Framework*, ed. by M. L. Faull and S. A. Moorhouse (Wakefield: West Yorkshire Metropolitan County Council, 1981), p. 328.

[88] Burton, 'Estates and Economy', p. 73.

monks paid ten marks in compensation.[89] The common pasture in Harden was also an object of the dispute between Abbot Roger and the Prioress of Esholt in 1231, which the nuns tried unsuccessfully to claim as a part of their freehold.[90] Another nunnery, Kirklees, which also had a right to specific parts of the forest in Harden, quitclaimed it to Rievaulx Abbey.[91] Although these quitclaims concern relatively small properties, they gave the abbey better control of the forest and its resources. Both nunneries, small and poor, stood no chance in confrontation with a large and wealthy house and had to withdraw from the area, which Rievaulx Abbey was determined to monopolize.

Another area where monastic lands were concentrated was East Cowton (parish of Northallerton) including the estates of Rievaulx, Bridlington, Fountains, and Marrick.[92] Just like the localities discussed earlier, it had become a arena of monopolistic expansion, in which smaller monasteries were almost always losers. Marrick, a small Benedictine nunnery, had a conflict with Rievaulx Abbey in the late twelfth century. It resulted from the grant of Simon and Alan de Chambord to Rievaulx Abbey of two bovates which their brother Robert had previously given to the nunnery. Although William de Chambord, son of Robert, confirmed his father's grant to Marrick nunnery, both houses claimed the right to these two bovates.[93] The result of this dispute was an exchange between 1197 and *c.* 1208. Rievaulx Abbey gave to the nunnery its two bovates of land in East Cowton, from the donation of Simon and Alan de Chambord, in exchange for forty-four acres and common pasture for one hundred sheep in Harlsey from the donation of Robert de Lasceles, but in addition the nunnery had to pay the forinsec service from the Cowton property. This charter was witnessed by lay neighbours of both houses and members of the Lasceles family, as well as Richard, seneschal of Philip of Poitiers, Bishop of Durham (1197–1208).[94] Although East Cowton was an attractive area, it was close to the grange of Fountains Abbey, and the acquisition of the pasture in Harlsey helped Rievaulx Abbey to consolidate its grange in Morton with further pastoral components.

---

[89] London, British Library, Egerton Charter 2245; for the English summary, see *YD*, II, no. 143. Adam son of Peter donated three bovates of land in Cullingworth and Harden, between 1180 and 1184, to the nuns of Esholt: *EYC*, III, nos 1785, 1874; IV, no. 67.

[90] *Assize Roll*, no. 1042, m. 16d, in *YD*, II, 57.

[91] London, British Library, Egerton Charter 2254; for an English summary of this charter, see *YD*, I, no. 82.

[92] Burton, 'Estates and Economy', p. 40.

[93] *EEA*, XX, Appendix 2, no. 6.

[94] *Collectanae Topographica et Genealogica*, vol. V (London: Nichols, 1838), p. 110. This charter was dated by Clay, *EYC*, V, 283. The original charter is in the Special Collections, Brotherton Library, University of Leeds and can be viewed online at http://www.leeds.ac.uk/library/spcoll/marrick/rievaulx.htm.

The contacts between Rievaulx Abbey and four Augustinian houses in Bridlington, Newburgh, Guisborough, and Drax had their roots in the grants from the same benefactors located close to each other, which inevitably led to conflicts. Religious houses were prepared to make compromises and often negotiated agreement if such necessity arose. They were realistic and pragmatic in these deals, even if it meant, as in the case of Rievaulx and Bridlington, redirecting the abbey's expansion in another direction. The issue of tithes payment and the Cistercian refusal to pay them triggered many conflicts between Augustinian houses and Rievaulx Abbey. Usually a financial compromise was reached between the parties in the form of either a delimitation of the lands from which the tithes were paid and which were freed, as in the case of Newburgh Priory, or some form of compensation, as in the case of Drax Priory. This mechanism allowed both parties to secure a satisfactory outcome— the canons received financial compensation and the Cistercian house did not, technically, paid the tithes, thus preserving, at least formally, Cistercian exemption.

Contacts with the Order of Sempringham

As we move on to discuss the relationship of Rievaulx Abbey with the Sempringham, also known as the Gilbertine, order, it is important to point out that the early Abbots of Rievaulx displayed a considerable interest in the condition of the Sempringham order which underlie their later contacts. The Sempringham order, as a new addition to the monastic landscape of England, needed to assert its place and role, particularly towards the older and more established institutions; but at the same time, help and advice from the experienced abbots was important to Sempringham's own development. The issue of personal friendship between the communities and abbots was also a key element of these early connections.

The order originated from the Lincolnshire parish of Sempringham where Gilbert of Sempringham established in the 1130s a small house for nuns. After a visit from Abbot William of Rievaulx, and upon his advice, Gilbert introduced lay sisters, a group modelled on the Cistercian example. In the late 1140s, with the advice of Bernard of Clairvaux, Gilbert added canons to the order, creating double houses of both nuns and canons living in separate quarters. The Sempringham order grew in popularity, and before 1154 several double houses were established in and outside Lincolnshire, including Watton in Yorkshire, and single houses for canons only, such as Malton Priory in the same county.[95]

It appears that the situation of the Sempringham order was of concern to Rievaulx, as the charter of protection by King Richard I for this order was copied into Rievaulx's own cartulary.[96] This interest dated from the time of the first Abbot of Rievaulx, William, who visited and advised Gilbert of Sempringham on the organization of his

[95] Burton, *Monastic and Religious*, pp. 98–99.

[96] *Cartulary*, no. 248.

order. Then Ailred, the future Abbot of Rievaulx, became acquainted with Gilbert in 1143 when he was appointed the first Abbot of Revesby in Lincolnshire, which was located only a few miles away from Sempringham.[97]

The personal involvement of Abbot Ailred in the internal issues of the new order is testified by his own account, *De sanctimoniali de Wattun*, of his investigation in the scandal of a Gilbertine nun at the double houses at Watton in the early 1160s.[98] One of the young nuns there became pregnant as a result of an affair with a canon or a lay brother from the same house. Both of them were very severely punished by the nuns, but due to a miraculous intervention the nun's condition disappeared and the chains with which she was bound fell off. Abbot Ailred was called to investigate this miraculous occurrence.[99] Ailred's involvement in this serious and potentially damaging event for the Sempringham order indicates how much he was trusted by Gilbert, master of the order, and how much his spiritual authority and monastic experience were valued in the York diocese. The trust placed in Ailred to resolve this difficult situation must have been based on Master Gilbert's observation of Ailred's success as the first Abbot of Revesby, as an extremely capable manager of estates and director of religious life of its monastic community.[100] This positive picture of the early contacts between both houses has been recently questioned by Berman, who suggests that the rivalry between both orders was already present at this early stage and that Ailred's narrative about the scandal in Watton house was intended to 'reflect badly' on the rival.[101] This suggestion appears unfounded since the focus of the *De sanctimoniali de Wattun* is on the miracle, rather than the event itself or the situation in Watton. While there was some rivalry between the orders, it was a much later development. In the early stages, the friendships between the abbots were the major factor underlying the connection between Cistercian and Gilbertine houses.

---

[97] Brian Golding, *Gilbert of Sempringham and the Gilbertine Order c. 1130–c. 1300* (Oxford: Clarendon Press, 1995), pp. 83, 85.

[98] Ailred of Rievaulx, 'De sanctimoniali de Wattun', *Patrologia Latina Cursus Completus*, ed. by J.-P. Migne, vol. 195 (Paris, 1855), cols 789–96. Watton was founded *c.* 1150/3 by Eustace FitzJohn, who had close connections with Walter Espec. His son William de Vescy was also a benefactor of Rievaulx Abbey.

[99] Giles Constable, 'Aelred of Rievaulx and the Nun of Watton: An Episode in the Early History of the Gilbertine Order', in *Medieval Women: Studies in Church History, Subsidia I*, ed. by Derek Baker (Oxford: Blackwell, 1978), pp. 205–26; Elizabeth Freeman, 'Nuns in the Public Sphere: Ailred of Rievaulx's *De Sanctimoniali de Wattun* and the Gendering of Authority', *Comitatus*, 27 (1996), 55–80.

[100] Dutton, 'Introduction', pp. 29–30. On the friendship between Gilbert and Ailred, see Brian Golding, 'St Bernard and St Gilbert', in *The Influence of Saint Bernard: Anglican Essays*, ed. by Benedicta Ward, Fairacres Publications, 60 (Oxford: S.L.G. Press, 1976), pp. 42–52 (p. 48).

[101] Constance H. Berman, *The Cistercian Evolution: The Invention of a Religious Order in Twelfth-Century Europe* (Philadelphia: University of Pennsylvania Press, 2000), p. 146.

These personal contacts between the leaders fostered more structured contacts between Rievaulx Abbey and houses of the Sempringham order. An agreement of 'societatis et pacis' between the Cistercian and Sempringham orders regulated the relationship between those two orders in England. A copy of it was also inserted in the cartulary of Rievaulx Abbey.[102] This document was witnessed and sealed in 1164 by the abbots and priors of both orders: Abbot Geoffrey of Clairvaux, Ailred of Rievaulx, Richard of Fountains, Walter of Kirkstead, master Philip of St Laurence, Abbot Ralph of Louth Park, Abbot Acius of Vaudey, master Gilbert of the Sempringham order, Prior Thorpin of Sempringham, Alan of Lindesfarne, Adam of Lincoln, Richard of Lindley, Thomas de Ormesby, Hugh of Sixhills, Ralph of Watton, and Robert of Malton. The position of the Abbot of Rievaulx was recognized by the prominent placement of his name in the witness list, in second place after the Abbot of Clairvaux. On the one hand it indicates the personal significance of Ailred, and on the other, it marks the status of Rievaulx Abbey among Cistercian houses in the North of England. This agreement between the Cistercian and Sempringham orders covered procedures for resolving quarrels over property rights and the issue of erecting new buildings. Monks and canons agreed that new granges or buildings belonging to the orders should be at a distance of two leagues from each other (about five miles). Orders were permitted to receive up to one measure of land within this protected area providing that this property was used as a pasture or cultivated by laymen, not by the lay brothers, and under no circumstances should granges be established there. Representatives of the Cistercian and Sempringham orders promised not to accept canons, monks, or novices from each other, nor to hire servants who had not fulfilled their contracts with the other order.[103] Golding interpreted this agreement as symptomatic of the increased competition for people and land. By 1150 the majority of the substantial pieces of property which could have been distributed had already been donated, and the monastic orders were competing for rather meagre leftovers.[104] Recruitment of hired labour was also a vexatious issue and created an additional area of competition between the orders. The creation of this document was an attempt to prevent conflicts between monasteries belonging to both orders. The role of Rievaulx Abbey in this process points again to the personal interest and involvement of its abbots and their adherence to the ideal of brotherhood, care, and love between monastic communities.

However, in the thirteenth century, the personal connection between the abbots of the two orders disappeared, and with it Rievaulx's support diminished, prompting the development of economic conflicts between Rievaulx and Sempringham, as is testified by papal mandates. In 1220 Pope Honorius III issued a mandate to the Abbots of Fountains, Rievaulx, and Byland forbidding them to encroach on the

[102] *Cartulary*, no. 246.

[103] *Cartulary*, no. 246.

[104] Golding, *Gilbert of Sempringham*, pp. 269, 280.

rights of the Canons of Sempringham to the churches and their assets granted to them by patrons.[105] Twenty-six years later, another mandate from Pope Innocent IV urged the Abbots of Byland and Rievaulx to stop harassing the Canons of Sempringham contrary to the licence they had received from the Pope.[106] Next year, in 1247, a similar letter was directed to the Abbots of Rievaulx and Byland and the Prior of Bridlington, although the wording was different. Instead of reproaching the Cistercian abbots for harassing the Sempringham order, the Pope asked them to ensure that nobody encroached on the rights of the canons.[107] It appears that the papal orders were not obeyed, and he had to issue another mandate in 1248 to the Abbot of Rievaulx and the Prior of Kirkham to investigate whether the Sempringham order had been bothered against the papal licence. The Abbot and the Prior were appointed to handle the transfer of two churches and their income in the diocese of Lincoln to the Sempringham order.[108] A year later Pope Innocent IV instructed the Abbots of Byland and Rievaulx to oversee that the privilege of the priors and canons of the Sempringham order not to be summoned away from their houses to places further than two days journey was not broken.[109] Two years later, in 1250, the same abbots received another papal mandate to supervise the implementation of yet another licence for the Sempringham order, concerning the restricted powers of the apostolic legates towards the order.[110]

The number of papal letters directed to the Abbots of Rievaulx and their colleagues in other monasteries concerning various issues related to the rights and privileges of the Sempringham order must have resulted in relatively frequent contacts between these houses. It is impossible to assess why there was such a great number of conflicts between members of the Cistercian, Augustinian. and Sempringham orders in the middle of the thirteenth century, but it is probable that some of these conflicts were related to common pastures in the Vale of Pickering. Both Rievaulx and Bridlington had large sheep flocks there and Malton Priory had the third largest herd there.[111] Many of the papal letters mention churches, and it is therefore likely that Rievaulx Abbey and the Sempringham order clashed over the incomes of these churches or tithes payment. From the 1240s onwards the Abbots of Rievaulx often acted in their capacity as judges or conservators of Sempringham's privileges.

---

[105] *CPL*, I, 76.

[106] *CPL*, I, 230.

[107] *CPL*, I, 233.

[108] *CPL*, I, 258–59.

[109] *Original Papal Documents in England and Wales from the Accession of Pope Innocent III to the Death of Pope Benedict XI (1198–1304)*, ed. by Jane E. Sayers (Oxford: Oxford University Press, 1999), no. 352; London, British Library, Stowe Charter 372.

[110] *Original Papal Documents*, ed. by Sayers, no. 374; London, British Library, Stowe Charter 573.

[111] Golding, *Gilbert of Sempringham*, p. 421.

This change indicated not only that the position of Rievaulx Abbey as a leading religious institution in the North of England was recognized by the Pope, but also that the disagreements between Rievaulx Abbey and the houses of the Sempringham order had ceased.

In their numerous conflicts with monastic neighbours in the late twelfth century, Rievaulx Abbey often looked for help outside the York diocese, even as far as the papal or royal court, just as they appealed for help when a number of powerful aristocrats were trying to wrestle land from the abbey in the same decades (see chapters 2 and 3). An appeal to the highest Church authority was often an indication that other methods, for example local arbitration, had not brought the desired results and that only papal authority could solve the matter. In the attempt to stop the encroachments on Rievaulx's properties by the Canons of Malton, Kirkham, and Sempringham, Pope Alexander III issued a mandate to Bishop Hugh of Durham and Abbot Clement of St Mary's York on 14 March 1174–76. He obviously did not act on his own accord. Monks of Rievaulx must have petitioned the Pope on this matter and asked for help. This mandate urged the above-mentioned ecclesiastics to stop trespasses committed on various properties of Rievaulx Abbey. The Canons of Malton were illegally occupying waste below Pickering, the Canons of Sempringham claimed the right to the property given to the abbey by Adam son of Peter and his mother, and the Canons of Kirkham occupied more than they should of the pasture in Helmsley which Rievaulx and Kirkham had been given for their joint use. The charters do not specify, however, the amount of land taken from Rievaulx by these houses. The Canons of Sempringham and Malton were ordered by the Pope to vacate unjustly taken land, and the Canons of Kirkham were instructed to stick to the portion of pasture granted to them.[112] It is very likely that the disputes described in this charter were not linked to each other. The Pope responded to the request for help from the monks who were troubled by the Canons of Malton, Sempringham, and Kirkham at some point prior to the papal intervention, but these actions were not a joint campaign against Rievaulx Abbey. All three houses had different reasons for their disagreements with Rievaulx. Malton, like many lay individuals, discussed earlier, wanted to get part of the attractive land below Pickering. In contrast, Kirkham shared pasture rights with Rievaulx because these were granted by their founder, and Sempringham wanted a portion of the attractive iron-rich land in Shitlington and Flockton.

The conflict between Malton and Rievaulx remained unresolved until 1175 when King Henry II issued a separate document, copied into the cartulary, which settled it. The monks of Rievaulx permitted thirty oxen belonging to the canons to be pastured between Howe Bridge and Kiptoftleys and from the Costa Beck along the stream past the houses belonging to Rievaulx in perpetuity, and also two bulls and thirty cows with their calves, but the young animals for a year only. In return, Malton

[112] *Cartulary*, no. 267; *PU*, I, no. 188.

Priory quitclaimed all its rights to waste below Pickering.[113] Separately, Simon de Tonei, Bishop of Moray (1171–84), who was a former monk of Melrose, a daughter house of Rievaulx Abbey, and Abbot Richard de la Chaussée of Mortemer issued an attestation of the same agreement, 'Testimonium Symoni episcopi Murefensis et Ricardi abbati Mortum Mari de causa que vertebatur inter nos et Canonicos de Maltona'.[114] The appearance of these non-standard witnesses may indicate that the agreement was made away from Rievaulx and the diocese of York, thus the usual witnesses, such as the Dean and the chapter of York, were not present.[115]

In the first half of the thirteenth century, between 1240 and 1253, Rievaulx Abbey and Malton Priory had another dispute about the particular pasture within the waste below Pickering called Castle Ings ('Eduimersch'). This time lay authority was invoked to solve the conflict. The investigation by the jurors of the Pickering Wapentake revealed that Castle Ings did not belong to the part of the waste given by the King to Rievaulx, but was given by Eustace FitzJohn and his son William de Vescy to Malton Priory. The abbey had to relinquish its claims.[116]

These persistent conflicts between Malton and Rievaulx within the waste below Pickering were a result of several issues. Firstly, the abbey, which held most of the waste, wanted to monopolize the area, although the priory, a great producer of wool, also had a keen interest in the pastures there. Secondly, the founder of Malton Priory and his son were also benefactors of Rievaulx Abbey and granted land to both institutions in close proximity. Two other documents related to the conflicts between William de Vescy and Rievaulx Abbey were copied in the Malton cartulary, which indicated not only that the priory had interests in this area, but also that its cartulary was a repository of important documents for its patron.

On the whole, it appears that the early involvement of Rievaulx Abbey in the affairs of the Sempringham order originated in personal contacts established by its early abbots. They were very much a manifestation of the Cistercian ideology of *caritas* and were only possible in the early stages of monastic development when the personal contacts and friendships were not yet overshadowed by the institutional structures. Later, disputes between Rievaulx and houses belonging to the Sempringham order arose from their conflicting economic interests and possibly some

---

[113] *Cartulary*, no. 192. The same charter was copied to the Malton cartulary, London, British Library, Cotton Claudius D. xi, fol. 28; Coucher Book of the Duchy of Lancaster, in *The Honour and Forest of Pickering*, ed. by Robert Bell Turton, North Riding Record Society, n.s., 4 (London: North Riding Record Society, 1897), p. 122.

[114] London, British Library, Cotton Julius D. i, fol. 125^{v} [fol. 129^{v}]; *Cartulary*, no. 193.

[115] The Cistercian house of Mortemer in Normandy was refounded and moved to a new location from the previous Benedictine establishment by King Henry I about 1134. Its links with the Cistercian houses in England were established by Abbot Richard: Leopoldus Janauschek, *Originum Cisterciensium*, vol. I (Vienna, 1877), pp. 48–49.

[116] *Honour and Forest of Pickering*, ed. by Turton, pp. 184–85.

jealousy over the new and successful order, at the time when the Cistercians became a less fashionable object of donations.

On one level, the contacts between Rievaulx Abbey and other monastic houses discussed here were akin to those between any other neighbours engaging from time to time in conflicts about borders and common pastures. On another level Rievaulx's relationship with its monastic neighbours differed from those with the lay neighbours because all of them were a part of the larger body of the Church. Therefore conflicts between Rievaulx and Byland or disputes with Fountains were not only disputes over borders, but also conflicts within the Cistercian order. The preferred method was arbitration by neighbours, both lay and ecclesiastical, by those who knew the local conditions, as the case of the conflict between Fountains and Sallay Abbey illustrates. If a dispute was not resolved, the Chapter General or a bishop or even the Pope could intervene. Increasingly in the thirteenth century, the courts of law became the arena of conflict resolution between religious houses which had become, by then, deeply involved in complex landholding arrangements, being each other's landlords and tenants. These conflicts had nothing to do with the religious nature of the parties involved, as exemplified by the dispute over Bilsdale between Rievaulx and Kirkham in the late thirteenth century.

In the early years of Rievaulx Abbey the personal contacts with other abbots, primarily due to the high profile of Abbot Ailred, created various links with monastic neighbours. In later years these contacts were formalized by the agreements between Rievaulx and other houses such as Byland or Sempringham to resolve any contentious issue. These agreements show a mixture of pragmatism with the ideology of monastic love and brotherhood, and this reflects how the monastic communities thought about these matters. It would be too simplistic to draw a bipolar picture of idealistic doctrines on the one hand and quarrelling monks on the other. Whilst Cistercian communities tried to conduct their mutual relations in the spirit of brotherly love, the socio-economic context in which those monasteries existed required often rather harsh strategies. Above all, it was the competition for land which left most traces in the sources. The distribution of monastic lands was the product of various factors, most decisively the willingness of laypeople to become patrons and benefactors. This quest for land created competition between the houses and formed relationships which might never have come into being without the lay involvement. Ultimately, conflicts, negotiations, and institutional and personal friendships between various monastic houses were part of a much wider network of relationships across families, tenurial groups, and Church institutions which were intertwined in the system of obligations, dependency, and struggle for position and economic power.

CHAPTER 5

Rievaulx Abbey and the Ecclesiastical World

The most important individuals on the ecclesiastical horizon of Rievaulx were the Archbishops of York and Bishops of Durham, key political figures in the North of England. Their authority was an important reference point for all the religious houses in Yorkshire. Their relationships with Rievaulx altered considerably in the course of the twelfth and thirteenth centuries, and the reasons behind it, and the abbey's strategy to deal with it, will be examined in this chapter. Whilst the chapters of York and Durham had offered important services to the abbey, the tithes payment controversy influenced their later relations. The analysis of Rievaulx's contacts with the Archbishops of York, Bishops of Durham, and their respective chapters, deans, archdeacons, and priors shows how Rievaulx Abbey continued to redefine itself as a Cistercian institution in relation to the secular Church. The issues of friendship, authority, and tithes payment form the core of the discussion.

Power struggles between monasteries and bishops or archbishops who wanted to assert their authorities over monastic communities had been a phenomenon preceding the emergence of the Cistercian order. Many narrative accounts of the eleventh and twelfth centuries produced in Benedictine houses were intended as a tool to assert and protect their rights and privileges against the encroachment of the lay and ecclesiastic power. Memory and tradition were often the key themes of these texts.[1] For the Cistercian order, the relationship with the secular Church was also an important issue. Although the order was independent from the diocesan structure and the bishops did not have the power to appoint Cistercian abbots or make visitations, the order was part of the Church. At the centre of the Cistercian involvement in the

[1] See for example the case of Bec Abbey, Julie Potter, 'Monastic Freedom vs. Episcopal and Aristocratic Power in the Twelfth Century: Context and Analysis of the *De libertate Beccensis*', in *Negotiating Secular and Ecclesiastical Power: Western Europe in the Central Middle Ages*, ed. by Arnoud-Jan A. Bijsterveld, Henk Teunis, and Andrew Wareham (Turnhout: Brepols, 1999), pp. 73–85.

world was the idea of charity as the integral element of the love of God and the love of one's neighbour, which are inseparable. This was an old tradition coming from the writings of St Augustine and St Gregory, but for the Cistercian order, this tradition had practical expressions.[2]

The involvement of monastic communities, usually abbots, in the world outside the monastic precinct was usually related to the land-based economy of the religious house as discussed in earlier chapters. Cistercian involvement in Church politics was motivated not only by the need to protect its material assets or financial freedoms, but also, if not more importantly, by the desire to improve the Church and its officials. This idea was put into practice by the monks of Rievaulx in the first half of the twelfth century, but the later practice was modified in the face of the changing reality of both the secular Church and the Cistercian order. The story of the interaction of Rievaulx Abbey with the Church hierarchy shows a continuous negotiation of the abbey's own place in the ecclesiastical landscape of the North.

The involvement of secular ecclesiastics was important in aiding the spread of the Cistercian order throughout Europe. In the western part of the continent this support was particularly strong before 1152–53. After all, the first British Cistercian house was founded by Bishop William Giffard of Winchester in 1128. The majority of the twelfth-century Cistercian charters in Burgundy were issue by bishops.[3] In the second half of the twelfth century, local bishops assisted Cistercian expansion in Northern and Central Europe: Denmark, Norway, Sweden, Poland, Bohemia, and Hungary. The oldest Cistercian house in Poland in Jedrzejów was founded by Archbishop John of Gniezno in the early 1150s. Even more so, the coming of the white monks to Central Europe, and Poland in particular, is often seen by historians as an attempt to introduce papal reform in the region. In the last pagan territories of the trans-Elba region, the foundations of Doberan monastery near Rostock in 1171 went hand in hand with the Christianization of the region and creation of Church structures.[4] Although in the second half of the twelfth century the involvement of the secular Church in the material development of the Cistercian order in Western Europe diminished, this process was much slower in the eastern part of the continent. Up to the end of the fourteenth century, between 30 and 50 per cent of the land which was given to the Polish Cistercian houses was donated by bishops.

---

[2] David N. Bell, review of Newman, *The Boundaries of Charity*, in *The Medieval Review*, at http://www.hti.umich.edu/t/tmr/ dated 1997.03.10.

[3] Constance B. Bouchard, *Holy Entrepreneurs: Cistercians, Knights and Economic Exchange in Twelfth Century Burgundy* (Ithaca, NY: Cornell University Press, 1991), p. 18.

[4] James France, *The Cistercians in Scandinavia* (Kalamazoo: Cistercian Publications, 1992), pp. 27–98; *Monasticon Cisterciense Poloniae*, vol. I, ed. by Andrzej Wyrwa, Jerzy Strzelczyk, and Krzysztof Kaczmarek (Poznań: Wydawnictwo Poznańskie, 1999), p. 38; Helena Chłopocka and Winfried Schich, 'Die Ausbreitung des Zisterzienserordens östlich von Elbe und Saale', in *Die Zisterzienser: Ordensleben zwischen Ideal und Wirklichkeit* (Cologne: Rheinland-Verlag, 1981), pp. 93–104 (pp. 93–95).

In the first phase of the development of the Cistercian order, during the life of Bernard of Clairvaux, Cistercian monks strove to be reformers of all corruption within the Church and to educate secular clergy in the spirit of ecclesiastical reform. Newman argues that these social concerns of the Cistercians were central to the life of the order in the twelfth century.[5] This idea had also been present in the activities of the Yorkshire Cistercians including the Abbots and monks of Rievaulx Abbey, who took an active part in the reform movement. Abbot Ailred is known to have preached at clerical synods and councils, postulating the necessity for higher standards of prelates' conduct, that those who were responsible for the salvation of others should take responsibility for their own souls first.[6] Between 1139 and 1153, when the popularity and political influence of Bernard of Clairvaux was at its highest point, a large number of Cistercian monks became bishops, among them a former monk of Clairvaux, Henry Murdac, who was elected Archbishop of York in 1147. The significance of the personal connection between Cistercian monks and the prelates who were also white monks remained important throughout most of the twelfth century as a factor in the successful advancement of many houses. Those Cistercians who became bishops remained formally members of the order and often surrounded themselves with white monks as advisors and companions. It is not surprising, therefore, that such prelates assisted houses located in their dioceses. Many bishops were befriended by Cistercians and acted as supporters of the new foundations. It also helped to integrate the Cistercian order closely with the Church.[7] In a society where personal ties were central to any public and political actions, these friendships with churchmen were important for Cistercian houses. Rievaulx secured in this way the protection of important individuals, including Archbishop Thurstan of York and Bishop Hugh du Puiset of Durham.

Cistercian abbeys had particular expectations about their place in the Church; their far-reaching demands for autonomy from bishops' powers and financial immunities shaped the character of Cistercian politics. Although Cistercian abbots had to give an oath of obedience to their bishops, in practice they were independent from bishops' interference in the elections of abbots and free from visitations and participation in the diocesan synods. By the end of the twelfth century many bishops became strongly dissatisfied with the monastic exemptions enjoyed by the Cistercian houses. The major reason for their frustration was monastic control over parish

---

[5] Martha G. Newman, *The Boundaries of Charity: Cistercian Culture and Ecclesiastical Reform 1099–1150* (Stanford: Stanford University Press, 1996), pp. 141–70.

[6] Aelred of Rievaulx, 'Sermo in synodo de pastore et mercenario et fure et lupo', in *Sermones inediti B. Aelredi abbatis Rievallensis*, ed. by C. H. Talbot, Series scriptorum S. Ordinis Cisterciensis, 1 (Rome: Apud Curiam Generalem Sacri Ordinis Cisterciensis, 1952), pp. 150–56; discussed in Newman, *Boundaries of Charity*, pp. 157, 161, 164.

[7] Newman, *Boundaries of Charity*, pp. 141–49, 191–92; Bouchard, *Holy Entrepreneurs*, p. 20.

churches and their income. While the white monks did not conduct pastoral work, they did not abstain from appropriation of the income belonging to these churches.[8] This issue became visible in the late twelfth century in the diocese of York, resulting, among others things, in prolonged conflict between Archbishop Roger de Pont L'Évêque (1154–81) and several monasteries. Although many Cistercian houses, including Fountains, Byland, and Jervaulx did appropriate churches, Rievaulx Abbey did not hold churches or, according to the taxation of Pope Nicholas in 1291–92, any portions or pensions.[9] This can be interpreted, according to the traditional ideas about the order, as Rievaulx remaining, in this aspect, true to the original spirit of the Cistercian order. I am, however, inclined to interpret it as evidence of a pragmatic approach to the acquisition of assets. Possession of tithes and even their payment, although profitable, could also generate numerous difficulties for their monastic owners, as we have already seen in relations between Rievaulx and the Augustinian houses. This problem will be discussed further in this section.

The Cistercian involvement in Church politics was at its highest point during the life of Bernard of Clairvaux, but soon after his death, from the 1150s onwards, these tendencies began to recede.[10] This order-wide trend was also reflected in the early history of Rievaulx Abbey which shows strongly the reformatory tendencies of the Cistercian order and its later gradual acceptance by the monks that a high moral standpoint and direct involvement in Church politics were not always practical. The reality of the local situation required a flexible approach, and this could mean redirecting attention from projects on a grand scale to more immediate concerns. The ideas coming from the Burgundian centre were not always compatible with the situation of the individual institutions. Although the first Abbots of Rievaulx, particularly William, Maurice, and Ailred, were active in the wider Church arena working towards the goals of ecclesiastical reform, the later part of the twelfth century was marked by the much more local concerns of the abbots who had succeeded in building the abbey's estates and also asserting its position and role in relation to a wide range of lay neighbours, other monastic houses, and the representatives of the secular Church.

However, Rievaulx Abbey was not insular or cut off from broader matters of the Church beyond the first half of the twelfth century. The cartulary is, again, the major evidence for it. One of a relatively large number of surviving copies of the decrees of the Third Lateran Council comes from the Rievaulx cartulary, copied on fols 3–14^{v} [new fols 7–18^{v}].[11] It was not an accident that this key Church document made its

---

[8] Giles Constable, *The Reformation of the Twelfth Century* (Cambridge: Cambridge University Press, 1996), pp. 247–48.

[9] *The Taxatio Database*, ed. by Jeff Denton, www.taxatio.man.ac.uk.

[10] For the analysis of the situation within the Cistercian order after the death of Bernard, see Constance H. Berman, *The Cistercian Evolution: The Invention of a Religious Order in Twelfth-Century Europe* (Philadelphia: University of Pennsylvania Press, 2000), pp. 148–51.

[11] *Cartulary*, pp. 362–76.

way into the volume at Rievaulx. As we have seen so far, the cartulary became, over the course of the twelfth century and beyond, the repository of the most important documents which were in some way related to the abbey. The Third Lateran Council was convened by Pope Alexander III in 1179. This Pope was a strong supporter of the Cistercian order and issued a number of bulls in favour of Rievaulx. The council dealt with a number of key issues for the Church, including condemnations of heresy, the manner of bishops' appointments, and clerical celibacy. The inclusion of this document in the Rievaulx cartulary testifies that the monastic community there was interested in, and considered relevant to its own situation, the matters of the Church at the highest level. The number of papal bulls directed to Rievaulx and other Cistercian houses in Yorkshire was high in the last decades of the twelfth century, and the community of Rievaulx was aware of the importance of papal support, particularly by Alexander III, for their order. The presence of the canons in the cartulary was not a simple outcome of their mercenary interest in the affairs of the wider Church, but rather awareness that they are part of it and should participate in its moral and political reform.

On a more local level, an examination of the Rievaulx cartulary reveals that it continued frequent interactions with the prelates and other Church officials beyond the early stage. The very high number of ecclesiastics in all the witness lists in both lay and ecclesiastical charters copied into Rievaulx's cartulary indicates the substantial amount of interaction between the abbey and secular churchmen. The deans and individual canons were considered valuable witnesses for grants by lay donors to the abbey. Among the 245 charters which constituted the twelfth century core of the Rievaulx cartulary, twenty-five have the names of archbishops in the witness list (10 per cent), thirteen documents were witnessed by bishops (5 per cent), and forty charters (16 per cent) contain names of other clergymen: archdeacons, deans, or canons. Archbishop Henry Murdac of York witnessed one charter and Roger de Pont L'Évêque eight; the name of Bishop Hugh du Puiset appeared in the witness lists of seven charters. The relatively high number of Archbishops of Canterbury and other southern bishops in the witness lists comes from the royal grants and confirmations to Rievaulx Abbey. Archbishops and a great number of bishops were frequent members of the royal court, and they witnessed many charters not related to their diocese as a routine part of their duties. The importance of the lay witnesses discussed in the second chapter shows many similarities to the importance of the ecclesiastical witnesses. It was a custom that particularly significant grants to religious institutions were witnessed by ecclesiastical dignitaries.[12] I have argued in relation to the lay witnesses that their participation was a sign of continuing support for monastic house by the later generations of particular families, even if they did not want to, or could not, give any more land to Rievaulx Abbey. Similarly, the participation of the ecclesiastical witnesses was a sign of continuing support of the monastery by these prelates.

---

[12] David Postles, 'Choosing Witnesses in Twelfth Century England', *Irish Jurist*, 23 (1988), 330–46 (p. 339).

Rievaulx Abbey was located in the diocese of York, as were the majority of its estates. The Archbishops of York played a significant role from the beginning of Rievaulx Abbey's history, and later, even if their mutual contacts were not always amicable, they remained important partners both in the wider Church arena and in a more local capacity. The history of the contact between the Archbishops of York and Rievaulx reveals this tension between the ambitions of a prominent monastic community to influence the politics of the secular Church, and the necessity to secure the help of the prelates in the down-to-earth matters of landholding.

The Archbishops of York and Rievaulx Abbey

Episcopal support was significant in the first phase of development of the Cistercian houses in Yorkshire just as anywhere else, bishops being some of the earliest and most important allies of the white monks.[13] Archbishop Thurstan of York was a founder of St Clement's nunnery in York (*c.* 1125/33) and Fountains Abbey (1132). His influence is also attributed to the foundations of the Augustinian houses in Guisborough, Drax, Bolton, and Nostell.[14] Rievaulx, being the oldest Cistercian establishment in the North of England, was also supported by the same Archbishop at a similarly early stage, although his involvement in Rievaulx's foundation had a different character. Archbishop Thurstan was known as a correspondent of Bernard of Clairvaux and they might have talked about the possibility of establishing a Cistercian house in Yorkshire at the Council of Rheims in 1119. Donald Nicholl suggested that the Archbishop of York conducted negotiations between King Henry, Walter Espec, and the delegates of Bernard of Clairvaux.[15] At least official support from the Archbishop was essential since any foundation of a monastic house needed permission from the diocese in which it was located.[16] Thurstan was probably present at the foundation ceremony, and his name was recorded in the foundation charter but, surprisingly, not in the list of witnesses. Although this document is a composite, there are no reasons to doubt his involvement in this act. The closing sentence of the

[13] Newman, *Boundaries of Charity*, p. 142.

[14] *EEA*, v, p. xxix. For the detailed description of Fountains Abbey's foundation, see Joan Wardrop, *Fountains Abbey and its Benefactors 1132–1300* (Kalamazoo: Cistercian Publications, 1987), pp. 13–15; Donald Nicholl, *Thurstan Archbishop of York: 1114–1140* (York: Stonegate Press, 1964), pp. 155–91.

[15] Bernard of Clairvaux, *The Letters of St Bernard*, ed. and trans. by B. Scott James (London: Burns Oates, 1953), nos 170, 176; Nicholl, *Thurstan*, pp. 151–54.

[16] The Cistercian tradition was explicit in stating that bishops should be asked to give permission for the new foundation: 'The Carta Caritatis Prior', in *Narrative and Legislative Texts from Early Cîteaux*, ed. and trans. by Chrysogonus Waddell, Studia et Documenta, 9 (Pontigny: Cîteaux-Commentarii Cistercienses, 1999), p. 442.

foundation charter says explicitly that Thurstan gave permission and advice to the founder to establish the monastery:

> Thus I, Walter Espec, founded the abbey of Rievaulx with the advice and permission of Thurstan, Archbishop of York; with the permission and agreement of Henry, King of the English, and all this confirmed by the apostolic authority of the Lord Pope Innocent.[17]

The Archbishop of York is listed alongside two of the highest authorities, that is, the Pope and the King of England, as being instrumental in the foundation initiative. The permission of Thurstan was an essential formal step of the foundation process. He must also have consecrated the monastic church. Soon after the foundation, between May 1133 and January 1140, Archbishop Thurstan confirmed Walter Espec's grant. The preamble of this document gives, in a conventional form, the Archbishop's motivation for the charter, that it is the duty of the ecclesiastics to protect and support monasteries located in their dioceses.[18] It was very common for Cistercian houses to secure confirmation charters from their diocesan hierarchy. Whilst the monasteries did not want any interference from the secular Church in their internal matters, the authority of the prelates to secure their assets was very much sought after.[19] The relationship between Rievaulx Abbey and the Archbishops of York reveals tension between these two tendencies. On the one hand there was a desire for complete independence from the churchmen's power, but on the other, the recognition that these individuals can be powerful allies, if handled properly.

The importance of the Archbishop of York for Rievaulx Abbey remained significant after the death of Thurstan, its initial supporter, on 6 February 1140. The Yorkshire Cistercians, believing strongly in their mission to improve the secular Church, took an active part in the election process for the new Archbishop and scrutinized all the candidates' moral standing, a right which the monks received at the Lateran Council in 1139.[20] Meanwhile, King Stephen decided upon William FitzHerbert, the

---

[17] 'Hanc abbatiam Rievalensem fundavi ego Walterus Espec, consilio et concessu Turstini Archiepiscopi Eboracensis concessu etiam et consilio Henrici Regis Anglorum, Domino Papa Innocentio Apostolica auctoritate hec omnia confirmante': *Cartulary*, no. 42.

[18] *Cartulary*, no. 218; dated in *EEA*, v, 51.

[19] Constance B. Bouchard, 'Knights and the Foundation of the Cistercian Houses in Burgundy', in *Erudition at God's Service*, ed. by John R. Sommerfeldt, Studies in Medieval Cistercian History, 11 (Kalamazoo: Cistercian Publications, 1987), pp. 315–22 (p. 318).

[20] This right of participation in the diocesan election was given to the monks by the Second Lateran Council of 1139. 'Since the decrees of the fathers prohibit churches to be left vacant for more then three months, we forbid under anathema the canons of the episcopal see to exclude religious men from the election following on the death of the bishop, but let a virtuous and suitable person be elected as bishop with their advice. Because if an election is held with these religious persons excluded, where this is done without their knowledge and consent, it is null and void': *Decrees of the Ecumenical Councils*, vol. I, *Nicea I to Lateran V*, ed. by Norman P. Tanner (London: Sheed and Ward, 1990), p. 203. Nicholl, *Thurstan*, pp, 240–41.

treasurer of York, to be Thurstan's successor.[21] The election of the new Archbishop took place in January 1141, and the majority of York canons voted for the royal protégé. William was also supported by the Benedictine houses of St Mary's York and Whitby Abbey, who perceived the new Cistercian houses at Rievaulx and Fountains as unwelcome competition.[22] The arrival of the white monks undermined the leading role of St Mary's York, the most prestigious monastic house in the North. Not surprisingly, Yorkshire Benedictines were in the opposite camp to Cistercians in the matter of archiepiscopal appointment. Abbot William of Rievaulx, Ailred, monk of this house (and its future abbot), Abbot Richard of Fountains, as well as Waldef, Prior of the Augustinian houses in Kirkham, contested the decision and joined others in accusing William of simony, unchaste conduct, and intrusion. The open involvement of the King, which was against the principles of canonical election, was also criticized by the monks. Although the reforming zeal of the white monks was very visible in this conflict, the local or even personal animosities played, according to Derek Baker, a role here as well. The York chapter was opposed to the royal candidate who by all accounts was an experienced politician, being a treasurer of York, and would not be a puppet of the Archdeacons, Walter of London and Osbert of Bayeux, who probably harboured their own ambitions for the archiepiscopal office.[23]

The analysis of the involvement of the Cistercians in the dispute shows that personal ambitions were not the driving force behind their actions. Ailred of Rievaulx must have been aware of the personal dimension of the dispute, but he and his Cistercian colleagues had a different agenda. Not only were the monks of Rievaulx the prime informants of the Burgundian centre about the contested election, but they also continued to have an active role in the dispute. This was clearly encouraged by Cistercian headquarters. When Abbot William of Rievaulx informed Bernard of Clairvaux about the outcome of the election, Bernard immediately sent several letters to the Pope contesting the suitability of the new Archbishop and the validity of the selection process. Bernard of Clairvaux had full trust in the testimony of the Cistercian monks from Rievaulx and Fountains as being morally superior to William: 'We detect according to the testimony of the truthful men [i.e. Cistercians — EJ], that

---

[21] The genealogy of William FitzHerbert is uncertain, but C. W. Hollister asserted that William was not a nephew of King Stephen as older literature suggested: 'The Origins of English Treasury', in his *Monarchy, Magnates, and Institutions in the Anglo-Norman World* (London: Humbeldon Press, 1986), pp. 209–22 (p. 215).

[22] Reginald L. Poole, 'The Appointment and Deprivation of St William, Archbishop of York', *English Historical Review*, 45 (1930), 273–81 (p. 277).

[23] Derek Baker, '*Viri religiosi* and the York Election Dispute', in *Councils and Assemblies*, ed. by G. J. Cuming and Derek Baker, Studies in Church History, 7 (Cambridge: Cambridge University Press, 1971), pp. 87–100 (pp. 99–100); Janet E. Burton, *The Monastic Order in Yorkshire, 1069–1215* (Cambridge: Cambridge University Press, 1999), p. 113.

there is no purity from the bottom of his feet to the top of his head.'[24] The moral superiority of the monks qualified them, in Bernard's eye, to judge and correct affairs of the secular clergy. Putting this premise into practice posed a broader question as to the place and role of the white monks in the secular Church. The story of the involvement of Rievaulx Abbey in the election dispute at York provides a good example of the reformatory aspirations of the order, but the subsequent change in the character of involvement of the same monastic house in Church politics suggests that these aspirations were not sustainable in the long run on such an intense level.

Still, at the height of the dispute, the monks from Rievaulx Abbey were at the centre of the events. In 1141 monk Ailred of Rievaulx and Archdeacon Walter went to Rome to formally contest William's election, and the new Archbishop of York followed them to fight his case. Both parties managed to gain some support among the cardinals, but due to the lack of evidence and witnesses Ailred and Walter did not fulfil the requirements of the canonical procedure to prove their version of events.[25] The next delegation from York consisted of the Archdeacon of York, Walter of London (1121/28–48), William, precentor of York (1140–64/74), Abbot William of Rievaulx, Abbot Richard of Fountains, and Priors Waldef of Kirkham and Cuthbert of Guisborough. On 7 March 1143 these churchmen presented to the Pope accusations against Archbishop William of unchaste life, simony, and intrusion. Pope Innocent, not wanting to make any decision, referred the matter back to the judges delegate. In 1143 William was consecrated at York by the legate Henry of Winchester with the support of the abbots of the Benedictine houses in York and Whitby. The fortunes of both parties changed again in March 1144 with the election of the new pope, Lucius II (1144–45), who sent the pallium for William with the new legate Imar of Tusculum. Again Bernard of Clairvaux tried unsuccessfully to influence the Pope against the Archbishop. Pope Lucius II died the following year and the new pope, Eugenius III, a former Cistercian monk himself, a firm supporter of Bernard of Clairvaux, and a friend of Henry Murdac, Abbot of Fountains, was urged by the Cistercians to depose William. The Archbishop of York travelled again to Rome, but despite his efforts, the Pope declared William's consecration invalid and he had to return to Winchester where he lived as a monk. In December 1147 Henry Murdac was elected as the new Archbishop of York.[26] The role of the Yorkshire Cistercian order in this election, and the importance of their connections with the key figures, was well known to contemporaries. William of Newburgh summarized these events in the following way:

---

[24] 'Sicut virorum veracium attestatione deprehendimus, a plenta pedis usque ad verticem non est in ea sanitas': *Sancti Bernardi Opera*, ed. by Jean Leclerq, C. H. Talbot, and H. Rochais, vol. VIII (Rome: Editiones Cistercienses, 1977), no. 346.

[25] C. H. Talbot, 'New Documents in the Case of Saint William of York', *Cambridge Historical Journal*, 10 (1950), 1–15 (p. 8).

[26] David Knowles, 'The Case of St William of York', in his *The Historian and Character and Other Essays* (Cambridge: Cambridge University Press, 1963), pp. 76–97 (pp. 82–90).

> William being deposed, Henry, abbot of Fountains, undertook the archbishopric of York through the powerful influence of the venerable Eugenius; who had once been a friend and fellow student with him under father Bernard of Clairvaux and had good knowledge of his life and work.[27]

This dramatic conflict associated with the election of the Archbishop of York indicates that Cistercian monks in Yorkshire believed in their reforming mission in the Church, and that they were guided in this belief by Bernard of Clairvaux. The Abbots of Rievaulx and Fountains were not only willing to openly challenge the position of one of the most important churchmen in England, but also to undertake long, expensive, and difficult journeys to Rome. It must be left to speculation as to what impact such extended absences by the abbots had on the life of these Cistercian houses, which had existed for less then twenty years and were still at the stage of building their core estates. It shows that the priorities of the young monastic communities at Rievaulx and Fountains were not restricted to the development of their own estates, and setting up daughter houses, but also included active participation in the politics of the secular Church. This was part of their mission as a religious order.

Although the struggle of the Yorkshire Cistercians was actively supported by Bernard of Clairvaux, their personal conviction as to the role of white monks as reformers of the Church fuelled their determination to depose Archbishop William. This involvement of Abbot William in the wider Church arena was the peak of Rievaulx's engagement on a national and even European level. A few years later, after the death of Bernard of Clairvaux, these great ambitions were reduced to much more local considerations. The fact that they were local does not mean these issues should be considered less important. On the contrary, in the long run, the success of Rievaulx Abbey as a Cistercian monastery was dependent on its efficiency on the local level. Many of the local issues were concerned with the delineation of the interests of the secular clergy and the monks. The issue of tithes featured prominently in the post-1150s contacts between the Archbishops of York and Rievaulx Abbey. The exemption from paying tithes was one of the cherished privileges of the order and one that was recognized by the members of the secular Church as being distinctively Cistercian. In that way, the strategy of dealing with the tithes exemption by Rievaulx Abbey was also a way of defining its understanding of being a Cistercian house.

The next Archbishop of York, Henry Murdac, a Cistercian himself, likely remained on very friendly terms with Rievaulx considering the recent events and his personal connections with the key members of the Rievaulx community, although there is only one charter of confirmation issued by him preserved in the cartulary, which is an attestation of Robert I de Ros's charter of confirmation of his uncle's

---

[27] William of Newburgh, 'Historia Rerum Anglicarum', in *Chronicles of the Reigns of Stephen, Henry II and Richard I*, vol. I, ed. by Richard Howlett, Rolls Series, 82 (London: Longman, 1884), pp. 20–503 (p. 56); translation in Nancy F. Partner, *Serious Entertainments: The Writing of History in Twelfth-Century England* (Chicago: University of Chicago Press, 1977), p. 76.

grant to Rievaulx Abbey between January 1151 and October 1153.[28] It is possible either that during Henry's time at the see of York Rievaulx Abbey did not need any confirmation charters or that the Archbishop's charters did not survive. It is, however, surprising that there are so few indications of the contacts between Archbishop Henry, a Cistercian himself, and Rievaulx Abbey.

When Henry Murdac died on 14 October 1153, the formerly deposed Archbishop William made another attempt to take the see of York. This time round, the Yorkshire Cistercians abandoned their previous high moral stand-point and did not object to his candidature. Bernard of Clairvaux was dead by then, and the actions of the Cistercian order and many of its houses became more pragmatic. The Archbishop, on his part, made attempts at reconciliation with the white monks in Yorkshire. However, William did not enjoy the office for long and died suddenly, allegedly from poisoning, on 8 June 1154.[29]

The reasons for this decrease in the reforming ambitions of the Yorkshire Cistercians was not a lack of strong personalities to conduct it; after all Abbot Ailred, who held the office from 1147 to 1167, had both political aptitude and contacts in the highest ecclesiastical circles, but he recognized that Rievaulx needed to concentrate on building its estates, not to undertake risky political actions, which might bring more trouble than good to the monastic community and the abbey.[30] His success in soliciting donations for Rievaulx Abbey might have brought criticism in some monastic circles, an echo of which can be found, according to Dutton, in the apologetic tone of the passage in the *Life of Ailred* explaining spiritual benefits to the benefactors of Rievaulx.[31] Indeed a further passage in the same text explicitly states that during the abbacy of Ailred the property of the abbey doubled.[32] This interpretation, however interesting, appears to explain medieval issues by our modern standards. It is possible that Ailred was criticized by other Cistercians for his extensive involvement, particularly political contacts with the royal court, but he could not have been criticized for acquiring land for his abbey. This was part of his role and he was expected to acquire as much land as possible. Although simplicity and poverty were clearly a part of Cistercian ideology, and this often encouraged laypeople to join the order, this was not a deterrent for the land donations. The new formula of spirituality and a strict rule appealed to many people, just like it appealed to Ailred when he first visited Rievaulx with its founder Walter Espec. To use Silber's terminology,

[28] *Cartulary*, no. 219; dated in *EEA*, V, 99.

[29] Knowles, 'Case of St William', pp. 91–92.

[30] Ailred continued to have a very high profile in the court circles. Between 1161 and 1163 he wrote *Vita Sancti Edwardi Regis et Confessoris*, conveying a strong political and ideological message, and dedicated it to King Henry II; Marsha L. Dutton, 'Aelred, Historian: Two Portraits in Plantagenet Myth', *Cistercian Studies Quarterly*, 28 (1993), 113–43.

[31] Marsha L. Dutton, 'Introduction', to *Life of Ailred*, pp. 7–88 (p. 29).

[32] *Life of Ailred*, p. 38.

donations were a way of acknowledging the ideal which the laity could not fulfil personally. Although the precise reasons behind the choice of Rievaulx as an object of pious gift are often obscure, the benefactors had certain preconceived notions and expectations. These will be explored further in the next chapter.

The scale of the shift in the attitude of Yorkshire Cistercians to Archbishop William came into full force during his canonization process. In the early 1220s the Dean and chapter of York petitioned Pope Honorius III to canonize Archbishop William, whose tomb was reported to have healing powers. His predecessor, Pope Innocent III (1198–1216), had codified the canonization procedure and reserved the exclusive papal right to decide who should be venerated as a saint. In April 1223 Pope Honorius III sent a mandate to Bishop John Pherd of Ely (a former Abbot of Fountains) and Abbots John de Cantia of Fountains (1220–47) and William III of Rievaulx (1216–23) to investigate the alleged miracles and report back to Rome.[33] A year later the same Pope sent another mandate to the same addressees, requesting that Bishop John of Ely and Abbots Roger II of Rievaulx (1224–39) and John de Cantia of Fountains should collect statements from witnesses concerning miracles at the tomb of Archbishop William and send it, under the seal, to the Pope.[34] Having received favourable reports from the abbots, Pope Honorius III canonized William in 1227. Finally, in 1284, his relics were translated to a shrine behind the high altar in the York Minster.[35] Thus, over sixty years after the death of Archbishop William, the Abbots of Rievaulx and Fountains acted as independent examiners of his alleged miracles, although their predecessors had fought against William's election. This rather dramatic change illustrates how the abbots of the two largest Cistercian houses in Yorkshire developed their position as the leading religious figures in the diocese of Yorkshire, considered to be suitable for undertaking the delicate task of determining the validity of miracles. Not only did the Abbots of Rievaulx and Fountains not hold a grudge against the man who was considered by their predecessors as unsuitable for the archiepiscopal office, but they also made his canonization possible. Although the comparison of the situation in the twelfth century and in the thirteenth seems to show a completely different attitude of the Cistercian abbots, in fact there are a lot of important similarities in both situations, which tell us not only about the aspirations of the Rievaulx community, but also about its role in the York diocese. To start with, the appointment of the Abbots of Rievaulx and Fountains by Pope Honorius III as the trustworthy investigators of the alleged miracles demonstrates that the twelfth-century ideals of involvement in the lay Church did not disappear, although they became redefined. The local knowledge which the thirteenth-century abbots had was one of the reasons for their appointment to the miracle verification mission by the

[33] *CPL*, p. 90.

[34] *CPL*, p. 96.

[35] *Acta Sanctorum*, ed. by G. Henschen and D. Papenbroch, vol. Julii 6 (Paris: Victor Palmé, 1867), pp. 135–36.

Pope, but the other reason was the abbots' position in the diocese. The Abbots of Rievaulx and Fountains were some of the most respected ecclesiastical figures in the North and in this capacity had considerable influence in the region.

As we return to the events of the twelfth century, it becomes clear that a particularly complex phase in the relationship between Rievaulx and the see of York occurred during the time of Roger de Pont L'Évêque, who has been branded as an enemy of the Cistercian order. The source of Archbishop Roger of York's fame as a monk-hater is an opinion expressed by William of Newburgh:

> He hated Christian philosophers, that is, monks, so much that it was said that he said that Thurstan, once archbishop of York in happy memory, never did anything so bad as when he built that mirror of Christian philosophy, the monastery of Fountains [. . .]. He said ecclesiastical benefices are better conferred even on sensual men than on religious [. . .] and he effected a deterioration in the condition of all the religious in favour of secular clerks.[36]

The extract suggests that one contemporary, at least, identified finance as the cause for the conflict between the Cistercian houses and Roger de Pont L'Évêque. Many historians have followed this claim, identifying the Archbishop's programme of restructuring of the diocesan administration as the centre of the conflict. According to Nicholl the Archbishop was frustrated by the monks who accumulated vast estates with fiscal exemptions, while Archbishop Roger struggled to provide for the diocesan clergy and maintain parish churches.[37] Burton develops this hypothesis further and asserts that the tithes problem was the core of Archbishop Roger's conflicts with Cistercian monks of his diocese. He wanted to establish an efficient organization on the level of the parishes, but without suitable funds this would not be possible, so the monasteries' control of the tithes belonging to the local churches became a major problem in his efforts to develop the structures of the secular Church.[38] The nature of his conflicts with religious houses confirms this hypothesis. Archbishop Roger is known to have clashed with Meaux Abbey about land given to the monks by his predecessor Henry Murdac.[39] His disagreement with Guisborough Priory over the control of churches in Kirklevington and Skelton is known from the papal bulls.[40] Fountains Abbey clashed with the Archbishop over Warsill grange, a dispute which was continued by his successor, Walter de Gray.[41]

[36] William of Newburgh, 'Historia Rerum Anglicarum', p. 226; translation by Partner, *Serious Entertainments*, p. 89.

[37] Nicholl, *Thurstan*, p. 211.

[38] Janet E. Burton, 'Origins and Development of the Religious Orders in Yorkshire c. 1069–1200' (unpublished doctoral thesis, University of York, 1977), pp. 372–73.

[39] *Chronica Monasterii de Melsa: A fundatione usque annum 1396 auctore Thoma de Burton, abbate*, vol. I, ed. by E. A. Bond, Rolls Series, 43 (London: Longman, 1866), p. 94.

[40] *PU*, I, no. 173.

[41] Wardrop, *Fountains Abbey*, p. 60.

Yet, during his rule at York, Archbishop Roger was not indiscriminately hostile to the religious houses in his dioceses. He issued charters of protection for Byland, Marrick, Nunkeeling, Rievaulx, and St Peter (St Leonard) hospital in York.[42] Importantly, two institutions on this list are Cistercian. Although all the charters issued by Roger to Rievaulx were merely confirmations and declarations of protection of monastic properties, a type of action generally expected from a prelate, Roger was not under any obligation to issue them. The Archbishop's positive treatment of Rievaulx, in contrast to his visible hostility towards Fountains Abbey, was partially a result of his respect for Abbot Ailred. This significantly better relationship between Rievaulx Abbey and Archbishop Roger also stems from the simple fact that this house did not appropriate any churches, and thus did not diminish the income of the secular Church, which was a core objection formulated by the Archbishop towards the exempted orders. The refusal of Rievaulx Abbey to possess tithes was a practical as much as ideological choice. Although tithes possession could bring regular and substantial income, Rievaulx Abbey had chosen a different approach. The positive relationship with a powerful Archbishop of York was worth more than the outright monetary income from the tithes, which was often contested and disputed by other claimants.

The evidence from the cartulary of Rievaulx shows the extent of the positive relationship between the abbey and Archbishop Roger. There are copies of eight documents placed in two clusters of six and two charters. Charters 220–25 are placed near the royal charters and those of Archbishops Thurstan and Henry Murdac. Charters 237–38, which are confirmations of laymen's grants, are located near charters issued by the chapter of Durham. The first of the Archbishop's charters, 'De protectione Rogeri Archiepiscopi Rievalle', issued between 1154 and 1164, is a notification to all the rural deans of the Archbishop's protection bestowed on Rievaulx Abbey with the clause of ecclesiastical justice against any trespass on the monks' rights. It was a common type of document issued by bishops in favour of religious houses in their dioceses, but Byland and Rievaulx were the only Cistercian houses which received such documents from the Archbishop.[43] Charters 221 and 225, dated between 1154 and 1160, are confirmations of agreements about the tithes of Crosby, Scawton, and Oswaldenges respectively.[44] Another charter in this sequence (dated between 1164 and 1170) is a precept to Dean Robert Butevilain and the chapter of York and all the diocesan clergy, issued at the King's request, confirming an earlier grant by Bishop Hugh of Durham of East Cowton (parish of Northallerton) to Rievaulx Abbey.[45] The last two charters are confirmations of grants by laymen, two donations of Roger de Mowbray (one in Welburn, one on the opposite side of the river towards Hoveton),

---

[42] *EEA*, XX, pp. xxxii, nos 7, 8, 62, 66, 77, 121, 124.

[43] *Cartulary*, no. 220; dated in *EEA*, XX, 87–88. Marie Lovatt interprets this protection as directly related to the abbey's disputes over tithes payment.

[44] *Cartulary*, no. 221, no. 225; *EYC*, II, no. 955; *EYC*, III, no. 1832.

[45] *Cartulary*, no. 222; *EYC*, II, no. 960. Robert Butevilain was the Archdeacon of York from *c*. 1148 and in 1158 he became the Dean of York: *EEA*, V, 125.

and a confirmation of the grant in Hoveton by Ralph Beler.[46] He was Mowbray's man, therefore the confirmation by the Archbishop of the grant in Hoveton is accompanied by the confirmation of Roger de Mowbray in the presence of the Archbishop, between 1154 and 1159.[47]

Grants of the important lay benefactors were also confirmed by the Archbishop's charters, such as an unspecified donation by William de Vescy, an important northern baron and a benefactor of many religious houses.[48] The grants of the pasture rights in Teesdale and Westerdale by Bernard de Bailliol, a member of a leading knightly family, was also confirmed by the Archbishop of York. During this ceremony, at York, the confirmation charter of Bernard's lord, William de Mandeville, of the above grant was also read in the presence of Archbishop Roger. The Archbishop's confirmation not only added solemnity to the grant, but provided the monastery with a reassurance of the Church's protection, if the heirs of the original donor should try to reclaim this land.[49]

Archbishop Roger was asked to issue a string of confirmations of recent donations by laypeople. Again, this selection and timing were not accidental. The first two charters in this sequence are connected to each other.[50] Roger de Mowbray was one of the most prominent donors of the abbey, and his grants contributed significantly to the development of the abbey's estates. The most likely reason for the archiepiscopal confirmations was the insecurity, in Rievaulx's assessment, of these grants. The borders of Hoveton and Welburn were disputed and encroached upon on several occasions by the members of the Stuteville family, Everard de Ros, and other noblemen, including Roger de Mowbray and his son Nigel.[51]

At first glance, these groups of documents may appear haphazard, but in fact they show what was the major expectation of Rievaulx Abbey from the Archbishop of York. The protection of monastic assets was one of the prime concerns of the monastic community of Rievaulx in the second half of the twelfth century, when a significant number of its neighbours and benefactors tried to reclaim their own grants or those of their predecessors. The obligation to defend the abbey declared by the Archbishop must have been highly valued by the monastery as it was copied into the cartulary in a very prominent place, together with the royal charters, the agreement with the patron William de Ros, and the charters of Archbishop Thurstan. Although such charters of confirmation were conventional and often issued by the bishops at the beginning of their office, Roger did not have to do so, and as his relationship with

---

[46] *Cartulary*, nos 223, 224.

[47] *Cartulary*, no. 224; *EYC*, IX, no. 127.

[48] *Cartulary*, no. 237.

[49] *Cartulary*, no. 238.

[50] *Cartulary*, nos 223 and 224.

[51] Janet E. Burton, 'The Estates and Economy of Rievaulx Abbey in Yorkshire', *Cîteaux: Commentarii Cistercienses*, 49 (1998), 29–94 (pp. 44–45).

Fountains Abbey shows, he made a distinction in his treatment of the monasteries in his diocese. Rievaulx Abbey was the only Cistercian house which had a clearly peaceful relationship with Archbishop Roger. Although the personal friendships with the prelates which were so important in the first half of the twelfth century appear to be replaced by more calculated contacts in the second half of the century, the importance of the Church officials for the Cistercian houses did not disappear.

The documents concerning tithes payment agreements issued by the Archbishop are key evidence for the assessment of the contacts between Archbishop Roger and the abbey. Tithe payment and possession of tithes caused much resentment towards the exempted orders, of which the Cistercians were one. In theory, every Christian, including members of the Church, was obliged to pay them, but in practice many monasteries, including the Cistercian order, received papal exemption from the payment of tithes.[52] Theologically and legally tithes should be paid to the Church in which the sacraments were administered, but the ownership of the tithes could also belong to a layperson or a religious house. In the case of monasteries, the payment and possession of tithes were intertwined due to their historical rights to keep their own tithes. Monks could hold tithes in two ways. Firstly, a monastery could receive tithes from men working on land not belonging to the house as a result of a grant of tithes to the monastery. Secondly, a monastic house could possess tithes owed from its own demesne, that is from the land cultivated by the monks or goods produced for their own use, so they were allowed to keep their own tithes.

The original refusal to take tithes was an important part of the programme of the reformed monastic orders in the late eleventh and twelfth centuries. This was linked to the idea of strict separation from the outside world, including the refusal to perform pastoral work. The founders of the Cistercians believed that the possession of tithes created an unwelcome connection with the outside world. This agenda was, however, according to Giles Constable, unrealistic and backward-looking. No later then by the mid-twelfth century Cistercians and other reformed orders were fully reconciled with the idea and practice of tithes possession. After 1150 examples of grants of tithes to the new religious houses, and the subsequent monastic ownership of tithes among the Cistercian houses in England, became common. This situation became aggravated when many Savigniac houses joined the Cistercian order but did not abandon tithes ownership upon entering the order.[53]

Freedom from the payment of tithes from the goods produced by the monks and for their own use was granted by Pope Innocent II in 1132 to the Cistercian order. It was soon approved by the Council of Pisa in 1135.[54] While possession of tithes

---

[52] Giles Constable, *Monastic Tithes from their Origins to the Twelfth Century* (Cambridge: Cambridge University Press, 1964), pp. 198–200.

[53] Constable, *Monastic Tithes*, pp. 186–92.

[54] Constance H. Berman, 'Cistercian Development and the Order's Acquisition of Churches and Tithes in Southwestern France', *Revue Bénédictine*, 91 (1981), 193–203 (p. 200).

stopped being an issue, the refusal of the Cistercian order to pay them became a problem. The secular Church's attitude to the monks' payment of tithes changed significantly in the second half of the twelfth century. The firm refusal of the Cistercian order to pay tithes from their land against the wishes of the bishops became a political issue in the Church when the popes became heavily involved supporting Cistercian exemptions, particularly from the time of Innocent II (1130–43).[55] Papal involvement on the Cistercian side was directly related to inter-Church politics because many popes used the issue of tithes to win the support of the Cistercian order in other matters. Constable concludes that the policy of Innocent II towards the Cistercian order was most likely motivated by the need to acquire their support against the antipope Anacletus II (1130–38).

Not only did the secular Church oppose Cistercian exemption, but the exemptions from the payment of tithes also placed the Cistercian order in an advantageous position in comparison to the older orders, which also caused a great resentment from Benedictines towards the white monks. To curb these privileges, which came to be perceived as excessive, Pope Hadrian IV decreed in 1155 that the Cistercians were free from the payment only on *novalia*, that is the lands which were previously uncultivated.[56] His successor, Alexander III (1159–81), who was supported in his struggle against the antipope by the Cistercians, reversed this regulation, so that all the lands were exempted. The first abbey which received this privilege from the Pope was Rievaulx.[57] In the late twelfth century the monastic exemption from the payment of the tithes was increasingly condemned by the reformers of the secular Church, who wanted to establish better structures at ground level. This programme required money, which was often taken away from the parish churches by those who owned tithes, including monastic houses. One of these critical opinions was expressed by Archbishop Richard of Canterbury (1173–84), who wrote to the Cistercian Chapter General (*c.* 1180) complaining about the scale of the secular Church's losses due to the Cistercian exemption from tithe payment.[58]

A growing number of conflicts between Cistercian monasteries and the Church prompted the Chapter General to issue decrees in 1180 and 1190 banning any purchases of land, except those located in remote areas and free from tithe obligations.[59] This self-regulation was formalized in 1215 by the Fourth Lateran Council which limited exemption from tithes on any new acquisitions, even if the monks cultivated

---

[55] Constable, *Monastic Tithes*, pp. 220–42.

[56] Constable, *Monastic Tithes*, p. 286.

[57] *PL*, 200, cols 92–95.

[58] *PL*, 207, cols 252–55. On the criticisms of the Cistercian order at that time, see Jean Leclercq, 'Epitres d'Alexandre III sur les cisterciens', *Revue Bénédictine*, 64 (1954), 68–82.

[59] *Twelfth-Century Statutes from the Cistercian General Chapter*, ed. by Chrysogonus Waddell, Studia et Documenta, 12 (Brecht: Cîteaux-Commentarii Cistercienses, 2002), 1180: 1, p. 86.

it themselves, unless the land was classified as *novalia*, that is, previously uncultivated so that no tithes had been paid from it.[60] Although the Cistercian ban on land acquisitions which were liable for tithes payment was an ideological as much as practical statement, it was a very difficult rule to follow. Even in North Yorkshire there was little uncultivated land by the late twelfth century.

There is no simple explanation for how Rievaulx Abbey managed to develop and keep at least satisfactory, if not positive, contacts between itself and Archbishop Roger at a time when the secular Church became increasingly weary about the special position of the Cistercian houses. Firstly, it can be explained by the personal authority and charisma of Abbot Ailred, which clearly outshone that of his contemporary Cistercian abbots in the North. Secondly, the fact that Rievaulx Abbey did not possess any tithes removed an immediate cause for conflicts. The notable absence of tithes from the varied portfolio of Rievaulx's assets was not, I believe, a result of purely ideological choice, but rather motivated by practical reasoning. If Rievaulx was to adhere to the Cistercian 'ideal', if such a coherent ideology ever existed, the early donations of mills and even serfs could not have been accepted either. Although there is no direct evidence to claim that it was a conscious decision of the Abbots of Rievaulx not to accept any grants of tithes, there is a strong possibility that this was the case. The abbots of the Cistercian houses were in close contact with each other, thus the leaders of the Rievaulx community must have known how much of a problem these grants caused to their fellow Cistercian houses in the North. The meetings of the Chapter General were also an opportunity for the exchange of observations and experiences between the abbots. Among the Cistercian neighbours of Rievaulx, Fountains Abbey had several disputes over tithes payment with Archbishops Roger and William de Grey of York. The abbey also had to pay complicated compensation for the three churches which it held.[61] However, in numerical terms, Rievaulx was much less bothered on account of tithes payment, and it can only be linked to its strategy. If we compare the position of Rievaulx Abbey in terms of tithes and church ownership with the situation of Burgundian Cistercians, the contrast is even more striking. According to Bouchard, by the 1140s parish churches were a common gift to the Cistercian houses in this region. As late as 1177, Bishops Peter and Engelbert of Chalon gave to Cîteaux a total of thirty solidi from the income of various churches in their diocese.[62] At the same time the actions of the Archbishop of York were exactly opposite; instead of donating tithes to Cistercian houses he was actively revoking them. As I have argued in the introduction, the

---

[60] 'We therefore decree that on lands assigned to others and on future acquisitions, even if they cultivate them with their own hands or at their own expense, they shall pay tithes to the churches which previously received the tithes from the land, unless they decided to compound in another way with the churches': *Decrees of the Ecumenical Councils*, ed. by Tanner, I, 260.

[61] Wardrop, *Fountains Abbey*, pp. 95–99.

[62] Bouchard, *Holy Entrepreneurs*, p. 124.

comparison between the Cistercian monasteries in the northern peripheries of Europe and those in its Burgundian heartland is at best misleading since the social, political, and economic conditions were so different. The case of tithes ownership and payment is a good example of how different Cistercian practices were and how difficult it is to establish what should be seen as the Cistercian 'standard' or 'ideal'.

From the late twelfth century onwards we know much less about the contacts between Rievaulx and the see of York. After the death of Archbishop Roger in 1181, the subsequent Archbishops of York interacted with Rievaulx Abbey only on a very conventional level. These contacts consisted primarily of taking the customary acts of obedience of the newly elected abbots. Although the archbishops did not have formal visitation rights to Rievaulx Abbey, there are indications that they stayed as guests in this Cistercian house during their journeys within the diocese.[63] This evidence for the formal and stable contacts between the Archbishops of York and Rievaulx in the thirteenth century is further compounded by the involvement, discussed earlier, of the abbot of that house and the Abbot of Fountains in the canonization process of Archbishop William.

There were, however, new dangers facing the Cistercian order in England. Among thirteenth-century prelates, Archbishop Walter de Gray (1216–55) was an excellent administrator and experienced politician, having been the Chancellor of England.[64] His surviving register confirms the scale of his attempt to curb clerical marriage and non-residency of the secular clergy in his diocese, but his contacts with Yorkshire Cistercian houses were insubstantial and those with Rievaulx Abbey virtually non-existent.[65] Although Archbishop Walter's relationships with individual monastic houses are said to have been friendly, his actions towards the Cistercian order, as a whole, were not.[66] In 1242, in his role as a regent, during the military campaign of Henry III in France, the Archbishop attempted unsuccessfully to extract a year's crop of wool from the Cistercian houses in England.[67] This action is an

---

[63] *The Register of Walter Giffard Lord Archbishop of York 1266–1279*, ed. by W. Brown, Surtees Society, 109 (Durham: Andrews, 1904), p. 270; *The Register of John Le Romeyn Lord Archbishop of York 1286–1296*, part 1, ed. by W. Brown, Surtees Society, 123 (Durham: Andrews; London: B. Quaritch, 1913), pp. 42, 162; *The Register of Thomas of Corbridge Lord Archbishop of York 1300–1304*, vol. I, ed by W. Brown, Surtees Society, 138 (Durham: Andrews; London: B. Quaritch, 1925), p. 130; G. M. Hallas, 'Archiepiscopal Relations with Clergy of the Diocese of York 1279–99', *Yorkshire Archaeological Journal*, 60 (1988), 47–63 (p. 59).

[64] Robert Brentano, *York Metropolitan Jurisdiction and Papal Judges Delegate (1279–1296)*, University of California Publications in History, 58 (Berkeley: University of California Press, 1959), p. 29.

[65] A. Hamilton Thompson, 'The Registers of the Archbishops of York', *Yorkshire Archaeological Journal*, 32 (1936), 245–63 (p. 247).

[66] *VCH*, III, 26–27.

[67] *CPR 1232–1247*, pp. 330, 336; Matthew Paris, *Historia Anglorum*, vol. III, ed. by Frederic Madden, Rolls Series, 44 (London: Longman, 1869), p. 286.

indication of the growing importance of wool production for the economy of Cistercian houses and its subsequent influence on their relationships with the lay and ecclesiastical authorities. In the thirteenth and fourteenth centuries the Cistercian order in Britain was increasingly targeted financially by the kings who recognized that the white monks could be a rich source of money for the Crown.

The fast-changing relationships between Rievaulx Abbey and the Archbishops of York in the twelfth and thirteenth centuries are indicative as much of local considerations as of the more general trends in the Church. The support shown by Thurstan to the newly established abbey of Rievaulx was symptomatic for the first phase of Cistercian popularity and its programme of reform. The active role of the monk Ailred and Abbot William in the conflict over the election of Archbishop William to the see of York was the consequence of Cistercian adherence to Church reform. The determination with which the representatives of Rievaulx and Fountains Abbeys tried to prevent the election of what they considered to be a morally unacceptable candidate was strongly supported by St Bernard himself. The late twelfth-century contacts between Yorkshire Cistercians and the Archbishops of York were often strained as the Cistercian houses continued to redefine their position on such matters as tithes ownership. It can also be said that the later years of Rievaulx's history were marked by much more local interests, but the narrowing of Rievaulx Abbey's horizon was a factor in the abbey's success on a local scale in the accumulation of its estates. The effective coexistence or even cooperation with the anti-Cistercian Archbishop Roger indicates that Abbot Ailred and his successors were proficient negotiators and politicians on the local scale. Their choice of the direction in which Rievaulx Abbey developed was not only based on what was pertinent to Yorkshire in terms of the natural and social conditions, but also reflected broader concerns of the Cistercian order.

The Bishops of Durham and Rievaulx Abbey

Not only were the Archbishops of York important during the formative years of Rievaulx Abbey, but two Bishops of Durham were also early supporters of this house in the first half of the twelfth century. Newman asserts that the issue of personal friendships with the prelates was very important for the Cistercian order. It was central to the contacts between Durham and Rievaulx. The initial creation of the close links between Durham and Rievaulx was to a large extent a result of the personal connections of Abbot Ailred. His great-grandfather Alfred had been a member of the community of St Cuthbert in Durham, and his grandfather Eilaf I was a treasurer of the church of Durham. His father, Eilaf II, a hereditary priest at Hexham, was a tenant and benefactor of the community in Durham and in his later life he retired there as a monk. Another relative of Ailred, William Hovegrin, was an Archdeacon of Durham. Before Ailred left for King David's Scottish court, he was schooled in Durham under the direction of Prior Lawrence and developed devotion for St Cuthbert, the patron saint of Durham.[68] When Ailred became Abbot of Rievaulx his contacts with Durham acquired a new dimension. The high and respected position of the Abbot qualified him to act as a mediator and judge. Sometime between 1149 and 1152 Ailred was asked to resolve a conflict about seniority between Prior Roger and Archdeacon Wazo of Durham. Although other abbots and priors were also asked to intervene, Ailred's name opens the charter of notification about their findings and the decision reached.[69] The community of Durham knew his diplomatic skills and trusted him to resolve this sensitive matter. Even more so than in relations between the see of York and Rievaulx, Bishops of Durham and their officials knew and trusted the Abbots of Rievaulx.

The importance of the Durham bishopric in the early history of Rievaulx Abbey is attested not only by Ailred's personal contacts, but also by the grants given to the abbey by the Bishops of Durham. Twenty years after the foundation, towards the end of his life, in 1152, Bishop William of St Barbe (1143–52) gave an extensive grant in Crosby (in the parish of Leake) to Rievaulx Abbey. The compiler of the Rievaulx cartulary considered this donation to be very important and included it in the 'Iste sunt possessiones' list: 'In the year of our Lord 1152 William the Bishop of Durham gave us the grange of Crosby with all that belongs to it.'[70] The actual charter recording this grant has not survived, but the confirmation charters of William of St Barbe's successor, Hugh du Puiset (1153–95), have.[71] The chronological sequence of the donations by the Bishops of Durham was reconstructed by William Farrer. Firstly, soon after his succession to the Durham see, between 1153 and 1157, Bishop Hugh issued a charter of confirmation of his predecessor's grant in Crosby; therefore he used the term *concedimus* instead of *dedimus*.[72] This confirmation was on the

[68] Paul Dalton, 'Scottish Influence on Durham 1066–1214', in *Anglo-Norman Durham 1093–1193*, ed. by D. Rollason and others (Woodbridge: Boydell, 1994), pp. 339–52 (p. 343); Ailred's devotion for St Cuthbert is attested in the dedication of Durham monk Reginald to Ailred of his work on the subject of St Cuthbert. Reginald also included there a piece of rhythmical prose written by Ailred in honour of this saint during his journey to and from Cîteaux. *Reginaldi Monachi Dunelmensis Libellus de Admirandis Beati Cuthberti*, ed. by James Raine, Surtees Society, 1 (London: J. B. Nichols, 1835), pp. 1–3. The Scottish connections of Ailred also helped to establish Melrose, an important daughter house of Rievaulx in Scotland. In the grants of King William I the Lion of Scotland (1165–1214), monks of Melrose are described as 'de Rievalle'. London, British Library, Cotton Charters XVIII 13, 14.

[69] *Durham Episcopal Charters 1071–1152*, ed. by H. S. Offler, Surtees Society, 179 (Gateshead: Northumberland Press, 1968), pp. 147–48. The other judges were Abbot Robert of Newminster, Prior Cuthbert of Guisborough, Prior Richard of Hexham, and Prior German of Tynemouth.

[70] 'A.D. MCLII dedit nobis Willelmus Episcopus Dunelmensis grangiam de Crossebi cum pertinenciis suis': London, British Library, Cotton Julius D. i, fol. 15v [fol. 19v]; *Cartulary*, p. 260.

[71] *Durham Episcopal Charters*, ed. by Offler, p. 175.

[72] *EYC*, II, no. 952; *Cartulary*, no. 49.

condition that the monks should pay sixty shillings of annual rent for those three carucates of land. In addition, he added the marshland surrounding the houses of the peasants in Crosby, the meadow belonging to the same vill, and a mill there. This part of the grant, as Burton suggests, generated an additional income for the abbey, because the peasants had to pay the abbey to have their grain ground.[73] In return, Bishop Hugh was admitted into the fraternity of the abbey as a special advocate of the house. The monks' prayers during his lifetime and then after his death were promised to be as ardent as for their own abbot. In return Bishop Hugh was expected to act as a protector and defender of the abbey.

> Indeed the Abbot and the convent of this church accepted us in special fraternity as a father and as a special advocate, so that they should pray to God in life and in death, for us just as for their abbot, in all that concerns our salvation. We also receive them on the same occasion as special sons, so that in all their necessities and affairs they may come to us as to a father and to one who undertakes to defend them and maintain them, their house, and all things belonging to them in the protection of our hand.[74]

This charter is an important piece of evidence for Rievaulx's involvement in local politics and its ability to acquire powerful friends among prelates. Personal contacts were a key technique in the early development of the abbey and did not lose their importance in the later phases. Bishop Hugh was a supporter capable of protecting the abbey from the greed of both lay and ecclesiastical men and had the material resources to be its benefactor. The date of Hugh's charter coincides or pre-dates slightly the death of the abbey's founder and patron, Walter Espec, *c.* 1153. It was a time of uncertainty for the abbey, which had lost a founder and protector who was closely involved in the business of the abbey. The childless death of Walter posed a threat to a relatively young monastic community, as it broke a smooth succession of patronage. Espec was known to have a close relationship with the monastery and had shown a keen interest in its development. The distant nephews of the founder and patron had shown little attention to Rievaulx, so it is very likely that the monks actively looked for a replacement. Instances of monasteries undertaking initiatives to secure a protector in the place of hereditary patrons who did not adequately perform their role were not uncommon. The Benedictine house of Great Malvern secured the help of Walter de Beauchamp as its protector in the early years of King Henry III's

---

[73] Burton, 'Estates and Economy', p. 56.

[74] 'Abbas autem et conventus ejusdem ecclesie speciali familiaritate nos in patrem et specialem advocatum recipiunt ut et in vita et in morte pro nobis sicut pro abbate suo sint apud Deum devoti in omnibus que ad salutem nostram pertinent. Nos quoque vice eadem ipsos in filios speciales suscipimus ut in omnibus necessitatibus atque negotiis suis ad nos veniant sicut ad patrem et ad eum qui ipsos et domum ipsorum et omnia que ad ipsos pertinent sub manu protectionis nostre manutenenda et defendenda suscipimus': *Cartulary*, no. 49; *EYC*, II, no. 952.

reign, because its original patrons did not show any interest in the house.[75] A lay protector would bring with himself or herself a complex set of attachments and interests, which could put unwelcome demands on the abbey. Although a prelate was not free himself from the obligations of the networks of which he was a part, the fact that a bishop was also a member of the same organization — the Church — was a significant advantage. The declaration expressed by the Bishop of Durham in his charter must have been warmly welcomed by the convent. In return, the Bishop received prayers for his soul performed by the monks from a monastery which enjoyed a reputation for exceptional piety. It was a two-way process. The abbey was not a passive party receiving a favour from the Bishop; it was giving him in return a gift of fraternity. Possibly, it even initiated this exchange in the first place. Just as reciprocity was central to the contacts between Rievaulx and its lay benefactors, it was also fundamental to its relationship with the prelates.

The contract between the abbey and the Bishop drawn up in this charter appears to be personal. Although Hugh is identified as the Bishop of Durham, he became the special patron of the abbey as a powerful and important individual, not just because he was a bishop. This distinction was important for the Cistercian monks; they needed allies, but at the same time wanted to remain free from diocesan obligations and restrictions by keeping their contacts with the secular Church on the level of personal friendships rather than formal ties. Bishops, even if not enthusiastic towards Cistercian houses, had an obligation to support religious houses in their dioceses. In times of particular distress monks often had to turn for help to the prelates. If the bishops fulfilled these hopes, the monastic communities often commemorated them in prayers and in writing. One of the most striking examples comes from much further east than Yorkshire, from the Silesian house in Heinrichau. Bishop Thomas I of Breslau (d. 1268) was particularly commemorated and praised, more than any other bishop of this diocese, by the monastic *Liber Vitae* for his support in restoring monastic property after the Mongolian invasion in 1241.[76] The Bishop of Durham was commemorated at Rievaulx by the inclusion of his grant in the 'Iste sunt possessiones' list and a prominent location of his charters in the cartulary. More importantly, for him, the Bishop was also commemorated by the prayers of the monks.

Although Bishop Hugh of Durham became a special protector of the abbey, he does not appear to have been exceptionally generous, or rather his donations to Rievaulx Abbey seem carefully circumscribed. The type of document issued by

[75] Emma Mason, 'Timeo Barones et Dona Ferentes', in *Religious Motivation: Biographical and Sociological Problems for the Church Historian*, ed. by Derek Baker, Studies in Church History, 15 (Oxford: Blackwell, 1978), pp. 61–75 (p. 62).

[76] Rościsław Żerelik, 'Wspólnota zmarłych w świetle Nekrologu henrykowskiego' (The community of the dead in the light of the Henryków necrology), in *Klasztor w społeczeństwie średniowiecznym i nowożytnym* (The monastery in medieval and early modern society), ed. by Marek Derwich and Anna Pobóg-Lenartowicz (Opole-Wrocław: LARHCOR, 1996), pp. 199–210 (pp. 201–02).

Bishop Hugh is also very similar to those which Rievaulx Abbey received from the Archbishop of York. Between 1153 and 1167 the Bishop quitclaimed to Abbot Ailred an unspecified piece of land in Crosby, in the parish of Leake. In the same document, he confirmed the quitclaim by Geoffrey de Otrington and his brother Adam from the diocese of Durham, who surrendered their rights to this land in the presence of the Bishop and his court.[77] Bishop Hugh was also concerned about tithes payment in his diocese. Sometime between 1160 and 1164 he settled the dispute over the payment of the tithes of Crosby belonging to the church of Leake (in Allertonshire). The deal, which was confirmed in the charter issued by this bishop, stated that the monks of Rievaulx were obliged to pay two marks yearly as compensation to the church of Leake for the loss of tithes.[78] This agreement was then reconfirmed by Archbishop Roger of York, with the clause of ecclesiastical sanctions against anybody who would try to break the agreement.[79] Lovatt believes that the Archbishop's confirmation was an indication that the agreement between Rievaulx and Bishop Hugh was under threat by further conflicts, but apart from the existence of this confirmation, there is no other evidence of any conflicts between Rievaulx and the Bishops of Durham.[80] I suggest that these documents related to the tithes of Crosby show primarily that the Bishop of Durham had been concerned, just as the Archbishop of York, with financing parish churches. Although Bishop Hugh clearly had close and personal contacts with Rievaulx Abbey, he was not going to allow this house to diminish the income of his diocese. That was his role as a bishop, as much as it was his duty to be a protector of monasteries.

At this point, however, the similarity between the two prelates ends. The Archbishop of York never donated anything to Rievaulx Abbey, while the Bishop of Durham was among its benefactors. Hugh's support for the abbey was commemorated in the cartulary by the monastic community, which saw him as one of its most important early benefactors. The grant by Bishop Hugh du Puiset was recorded in the 'Iste sunt possessiones' list after the entry concerning the Crosby donation of his predecessor William: 'After that, Bishop Hugh of Durham gave us Cowton with all that belongs to it.'[81] This donation occurred between 1152 and 1160, although the land in Cowton had been in the monks' hands since Bishop William's time. Between 1144 and 1152 Bishop William had issued a charter confirming the agreement between Rievaulx Abbey and Asketill of Worcester and his son Ralph over the property in

---

[77] *Cartulary*, no. 51; *EYC*, II, no. 953. Atkinson's edition of that charter is missing a crucial *nos* before *terram de Crossby*, thus changing the meaning of the quitclaim.

[78] *Cartulary*, no. 50; *EYC*, II, no. 954.

[79] *Cartulary*, no. 221; *EYC*, II, no. 955.

[80] *EEA*, XX, no. 79.

[81] 'Postea dedit nobis Hugo Episcopus Dunelmensis Cotum cum omnibus pertinentiis suis': 'Iste sunt possessiones', BL, Cotton Julius D. i, fol. 15^{v} [fol. 19^{v}]; *Cartulary*, p. 260. The edition reads *preterea* instead of *postea*.

East Cowton.[82] Farrer suspected that this property was then re-leased to Rievaulx by Bishop William for the annual rent. However, it is possible that Cowton was originally granted to Rievaulx even earlier, during the abbacy of Maurice (1145–47), who had been sub-prior at Durham before becoming Abbot of Rievaulx.[83]

The actual form of Bishop Hugh's donation to Rievaulx is revealed in further charters. In 1153 Bishop Hugh converted the tenure of Cowton into a farm for rent, the boundaries of which were perambulated, but the document recording this act does not survive.[84] The proof that East Cowton was originally leased to the abbey is the charter of Bishop Hugh issued between 1154 and 1167. In this interesting document the Bishop of Durham declared his reasons for the grant and its conditions. Originally East Cowton was given to Rievaulx for a term only, but Hugh changed its status into perpetual free alms, kept on the condition that the abbey will pay sixty shillings yearly:

> May all men present and future know that we, by the tradition of charity and for the special esteem which we have towards our beloved son Abbot Ailred, grant to the church of Blessed Mary of Rievaulx and the brothers serving God there, the whole land in Cowton, that is three carucates of land, which they held from us for a term, to be possessed in free and perpetual alms, rendering to us and our successors each year sixty shillings at the terms appointed in Allertonshire, free and quit from all custom and service.[85]

The Bishop's declaration of his motivation for the grant, that is, his affection for Abbot Ailred, is another acknowledgment of the personal links between the abbey and the Bishop of Durham and the particular role of Ailred in creating these ties. Although the wording is conventional, the mention of his 'beloved son Abbot Ailred', and the esteem which the Bishop expressed for the Abbot of Rievaulx, was not an obligatory part of a charter; it was Hugh's choice to include it. Just as in the lay charters, the use of conventional phrases in the documents does not imply that the intentions behind it were insincere. The generic character of the legal language used in the charters hides more personal sentiments, but there is no reason to doubt their existence.

The contacts between Rievaulx Abbey and Bishop Hugh of Durham were friendly and personal, but the Bishop's role was not confined to protection of the monasteries. The Bishop wanted to ensure that his parish churches would not lose income

---

[82] *Cartulary*, no. 52, *EYC*, II, no. 957.

[83] Burton, 'Estates and Economy', p. 34.

[84] *Durham Episcopal Charters*, pp. 173–74; *EYC*, II, 292.

[85] 'Sciant tam presentes quam posteri quod nos, caritatis intuitu et pro speciali dilectione quam erga dilectum filium nostrorum Ælredum abbatem habemus, concedimus ecclesie Beate Marie Rievallis et fratribus ibidem Deo servientibus totam terram de Cotum, scilicet tres carrucatas terre, quas de nobis ad terminum tenebant, in liberam et perpetuam elemosinam possidendas, reddendo nobis et successoribus nostris per singulos annos sexaginta solidos ad terminos in Alvertonescire constitutos, liberas et quietas ab omni consuetudine et servitio': *Cartulary*, no. 53; *EYC*, II, no. 958.

because of the Cistercian tithes exemptions. His donations to Rievaulx Abbey were somewhat cautious, with various reservations protecting his rights. The offer to act as a patron to the abbey issued by the Bishop around the time of Walter Espec's death can also be seen a pragmatic act. Hugh gained prayers, and the monks gained a powerful protector. The monastic community was aware of the importance of the prelates, and Hugh's donation is mentioned in a very prominent location in the cartulary. The combination of personal connections and friendship combined with the pragmatic resolutions of the tithes disputes ensured a rather special connection between the Bishops of Durham and the abbey. In fact, Rievaulx was the only Yorkshire house which interacted with the Bishops of Durham to that degree. Yorkshire houses other than Rievaulx held lands in the diocese of Durham, namely Guisborough Priory, the abbey of St Mary's York, and Nun Monkton and Kirkham Priories, but only Rievaulx developed a long-lasting relationship with the Bishops of Durham.

Throughout the period when the see of York was occupied by archbishops with a negative attitude towards Cistercians, the support of other high ecclesiastics became very important for the monks. Moreover, the Abbots of Rievaulx appear to have been much better politicians than those of Fountains when it came to contacts with the prelates. Although Archbishop Roger, according to William of Newburgh, was a declared enemy of monks, his relationship with Rievaulx was at least, if not more than, satisfactory, whilst the Bishop of Durham offered substantial support to the abbey. Bishop Hugh's declaration of protection over the abbey and his admiration for Abbot Ailred indicate that their contact had a strong personal overtone. While discussing the complexity of the relationship between Rievaulx and Bishop Hugh of Durham we should remember that at the time of his election he was not a candidate preferred by the Cistercians. Archbishop Henry was also opposed to his candidature. According to A. Young the Archbishop of York may have preferred Master Laurence of Durham (a relative of Ailred of Rievaulx), who was also a preferred candidate of the Yorkshire Cistercians.[86] Once elected as the Bishop of Durham, Hugh became an active supporter of several monastic houses in his diocese. His role was also recognized by Pope Alexander III who sent several letters to this Bishop urging him to protect Rievaulx Abbey from his greedy diocesans encroaching on the

[86] In the older literature these struggles over the election to the bishopric of Durham were interpreted as conflicts between 'traditionalists' and 'reformers', the latter being represented mainly by the Cistercians and their supporters, but recently more complex explanations have been proposed. The political implication of Hugh's election can be interpreted in terms of balance between English and Scottish influences. The Bishop's election in Durham can also be viewed from the perspective of internal church affairs between the secular church, Benedictine and Cistercian monks, local politics, and forceful attempts by the Archbishop of York to control the internal affairs of Durham. A. Young, 'The Bishopric of Durham, 1093–1193', in *Anglo-Norman Durham*, ed. by Rollason, pp. 353–68 (pp. 364–65). See also Tom Licence, 'The Benedictines, the Cistercians and the Acquisition of a Hermitage in Twelfth-Century Durham', *Journal of Medieval History*, 29 (2003), 315–29 (p. 318).

abbey's land.[87] This evidence brings me to the conclusion that seeing the actions of churchmen and Cistercian monks as arising from high politics, from pro- or anti-Cistercian groups, does not provide a satisfactory interpretation of Rievaulx Abbey's contacts with either the Archbishops of York or the Bishops of Durham. Firstly, they were all a part of the larger network of personal connections and friendships, which appears to be centred upon Abbot Ailred. Secondly, all sides were also motivated by more immediate concerns and wanted to secure material advantages and protect their own interests, which may not reflect events in the realm of high Church politics.

Haseldine's statement on friendship as a key element of contacts between monastic orders, quoted at the beginning of the previous chapter, can be developed further to cover connections between religious communities and certain members of the secular Church. The relationship between Rievaulx Abbey and the Archbishops of York and Bishops of Durham evolved throughout the twelfth century. At the time of the abbey's foundation, Archbishop Thurstan of York was a supporter of the Cistercian movement and helped to establish houses of this new order in Yorkshire. This friendly line was continued by Henry Murdac, but after his death in the mid-twelfth century the Archbishops of York were much less keen to support Cistercian houses, which meanwhile came to be perceived as a threat to the economic interests of the archbishops in areas where both parties had a vested interest. The Bishops of Durham also assisted Rievaulx in its early formative years and beyond. The fact that William of St Barbe and Hugh de Puiset were personal friends of Ailred was the underlying factor of the contacts between Rievaulx and the prelates. The issue of tithes became in the second half of the twelfth century a particular reason for difficulties between Cistercian monks and the prelates. Rievaulx Abbey developed its own ways of resolving this issue. This theme will be further explored in the next section.

Archdeacons, Chapters, Deans, and Canons and their Connections with Rievaulx Abbey

As we move on to discuss the group of diocesan clergy consisting of chapters and their deans and canons as well as archdeacons, it is important to outline firstly the levels of interaction of these institutions and their individual members with Rievaulx Abbey. The administration of the York diocese was divided by the late 1120s into five archdeaconries: York (West Riding), East Riding, Cleveland, Richmond, and Nottingham.[88] The Archdeacons of York in the twelfth century did not have precisely circumscribed geographical areas of responsibility; the majority of them used

---

[87] *PU*, I, nos 83, 106, 107, 135.

[88] *Fasti Ecclesiae Anglicanae 1066–1300*, vol. VI, *York*, comp. by Diana E. Greenway (London: University of London, 1999), p. 30.

the title *archidiaconus Eboracensis* or *archidiaconus Eboracensis ecclesie*.[89] The chapter of Durham cathedral was an unsual case, having been turned into a Benedictine foundation by Bishop William de St Calais (1081–96).

In the York diocese, especially from the mid-twelfth century onwards, a good relationship with the secular hierarchy of the middle rank, particularly deans and cathedral chapters, was very important for Rievaulx, as for all religious houses, because of the absenteeism or even occasional hostility of the archbishops. Besides the formal influence of the cathedral chapters individual canons were often a part of the ecclesiastical networks of power, consisting of relatives of bishops, deans, or lay bureaucrats appointed to lucrative cathedral offices. Some Deans of York became bishops or archbishops later in their careers, so establishing good relationships with the monastic houses during their time in the chapters might help in their subsequent contact with these institutions.[90] The key role of chapters and their members for Rievaulx Abbey and many other religious houses lay in the services they provided. The dean and chapter were based locally and were therefore accessible and could issue valuable confirmation charters or act as witnesses more often than the itinerant bishops. Issuing confirmation charters for Rievaulx Abbey became particularly important in the second half of the twelfth century. In addition, the canons were particularly desirable witnesses. In their role of witnesses the canons could act as a collective group or on an individual basis, particularly if they had some personal or family connections with the abbey. This duality is also visible on the level of conflicts between Rievaulx and the chapters. When it comes to the arguments over the possession and payment of tithes, the disputes were firmly between two ecclesiastical institutions, one secular and one monastic. In other cases, however, individual canons had conflicts with Rievaulx over particular properties.

To make this complex situation clearer I will discuss first the contacts between the abbey and the archdeacons and chapters on an institutional level, and then I will analyze selected cases of contacts between Rievaulx Abbey and the individual canons to illustrate the range and scale of these interactions. Although the middle-ranking clergy had much less power and personal importance than bishops, their contacts with the abbey tell us much about the mechanism of interaction between the monastic community and the secular Church and the expectations of the Cistercian monks towards the prelates and their deputies. Since the examination of the contact between Rievaulx and the chapter and deans encompasses the twelfth and thirteenth

---

[89] C. T. Clay, 'Notes on the Early Archdeacons in the Church of York', *Yorkshire Archaeological Journal*, 36 (1944–49), 269–87, 409–34 (pp. 270–71).

[90] The following Deans of York became bishops: William of St Barbe (*c*. 1135–43) became Bishop of Durham, Hubert Walter (1186–89) became Bishop of Salisbury, Henry Marshal (1189–93/94) and Simon of Apulia (1194–1214) became Bishops of Exeter. C. T. Clay, 'Notes on the Chronology of the Early Deans of York', *Yorkshire Archaeological Journal*, 34 (1938–39), 361–78 (p. 378).

centuries, it also reveals a shift in the attitudes of the secular Church and the Cistercian order itself to such problems as tithes payment.

Our knowledge about the role of the York chapter and its individual members in the life of Rievaulx Abbey comes primarily from charters. Among the charters issued by the chapters of York and Durham and various archdeacons and deacons for Rievaulx Abbey there are two distinctive groups, which indicate two major reasons why the abbey interacted with the chapters. The first group consists of documents confirming legal actions of others or legal acts undertaken by others in the presence of the chapter. The second group contains records of conflicts and their resolutions between Rievaulx Abbey and the chapters. The majority of these were concerned with payment of tithes by the abbey.

The charters issued by the chapters outnumber those of the bishops, and this reflects a higher level of day-to-day interactions between Rievaulx Abbey and the chapters than with the bishops and archbishops, who were often absent from their dioceses. Canons also acted as witnesses to the charters issued for Rievaulx Abbey, individually or as a chapter, providing additional solemnity and security to the legal actions undertaken in their presence. As many as forty charters out of 245 (16 per cent) contained in the cartulary were witnessed by archdeacons, deans, chapters, and their members. Not only did the canons act as witnesses, but many of these legal actions were undertaken in York, as indicated in the charters. The Minster was a good setting to impress laypeople.

The largest group of documents issued by the deans and chapters are confirmations of actions undertaken by third parties. Similar type of documents, discussed in the earlier parts of this chapter, were often issued by bishops and reflected particular concerns of the abbey over the security of its properties. The cases referred to the authority of the chapters were also carefully selected. Two of the oldest attestations copied into the cartulary were issued by Dean Robert de Gant and the chapter of York, of the quitclaims of Ralph son of Serlo and Uctred son of Orm of their rights to Griff.[91] Both were Walter Espec's men, and the disputed property was part of the initial endowment. It was therefore crucial for the abbey to have undisputed possession of this land, and the quitclaim attested by the Dean of York provided an additional assurance. Among other confirmation documents issued by the chapter there is a cluster of charters related to the various grants in Hoveton, attestations of three of Roger de Mowbray's grants and one of Ralph Beler, and quitclaims by Peter de Hoveton, Sunnive wife of Lambert de Hoveton, Samson of Cornwall and his wife Hestilde, and Jocelin de Arecy and his wife Helewise de Clere.[92] Sometimes the confirmation or attestation of a charter by the chapter was only one layer in the more complex process of a property transfer involving the abbey and its lay neighbours.

---

[91] *Cartulary*, nos 227, 228. Robert de Gant, a former king's chancellor, was the dean between 1142/7 and 1157. *Fasti Ecclesiae*, comp. by Greenway, VI, 8–9.

[92] *Cartulary*, no. 229; *EYC*, IX, no. 153; *Cartulary*, no. 66; *EYC*, IX, no. 125; *Cartulary*, no. 230; *EYC*, IX, no. 128.

One of the charters from the group mentioned above, dated 1163–69, narrates several layers of legal actions. Originally Samson of Cornwall confirmed between 1163 and 1169 that he held the whole vill of Hoveton including four bovates of land as a gift from Roger de Mowbray's mother. Then Roger bought this property from Samson and his wife who made an oath in the hands of Mowbray's steward Ralph de Belvoir that neither Samson himself nor his heir would claim any rights to this property which was meanwhile given to Rievaulx by Roger de Mowbray; afterwards he gave the same statement in the presence of Sheriff Ranulf de Glanville. All these legal actions were confirmed by the charter issued by the York chapter.[93] It appears that Samson of Cornwall did not give up his rights to the four bovates and was persuaded or maybe forced to quitclaim them again between 1163 and 1169, and this act was also attested by Dean Robert Butevilain of York.[94] Although Samson was particularly persistent in his claims, the abbey required not only the help of its lay lord but also the authority of the Church, including the threat of ecclesiastical sanctions to force Samson into abandoning his claims.

Another example of use of the authority of the York chapter in addition to that of lay lords comes from 1161–67. Bernard de Balliol granted various pastures in Teesdale and Westerdale and made a pledge with twelve of his men in the hand of William de Mandeville. It was also attested by the chapter of York.[95] Bernard de Balliol's oath was given in the presence of the entire chapter of York, which added solemnity and increased the strength of the donation in the presence of many neighbours and Church officials. It was both the public character of this action and the existence of the written document as such which made this transaction secure for the abbey:

> And because I wish that this said gift of mine should be strong and unfailing, I have declared by my oath and pledge by my hand in the hand of William de Mandeville, and twelve free men of mine, who are witnesses of this charter, have pledged with me in the hand of the said William, in the presence of the whole chapter of York, that everything which is contained in this charter will be kept by me in good conscience. But also I have established the church of York as witness of all these things between me and the monks, so that if ever I or my heirs should attempt to deviate from this donation and the terms of this charter, this church will recall us by the Church's discipline to execute the terms of the donation.[96]

---

[93] *Cartulary*, no. 67; *EYC*, IX, no. 126.

[94] *Cartulary*, no. 232; *EYC*, IX, no. 129.

[95] *Cartulary*, no. 115; *EYC*, I, no. 562.

[96] 'Et quia volo ut hec predicta elemosina mea firma sit et stabilis, manu mea affidavi in manu Willelmi de Mandavilla, et xij liberi homines mei qui hujus carte testes sunt mecum affidaverunt in manu ejusdem Willelmi sub presentia totius capituli Eboracensis omnia que in hac carta continentur sine malo ingenio me servaturum. Sed et ecclesiam Eboracensem horum omnium testem inter me et monachos constitui, ita ut si aliquando ego vel heredes mei ab hac donatione et hujus carte tenore deviare temptaverimus, ipsa ecclesia ad hec exequenda nos ecclesiastica revocet disciplina': *Cartulary*, no. 115; *EYC*, I, no. 562.

By the terms of this charter, the lay donor and his heirs were bound to honour the grant to the abbey. Not only did several people witness this act and support the benefactor's oath, but also York chapter assumed the role of intercessory and executive in the case of any future dispute. Although the document is phrased in such a way that the York chapter appears to be appointed by Bernard de Balliol to its mediatory role, it is more likely that the inclusion of the chapter was initiated by Rievaulx Abbey.

Similarly to the confirmation grants issued by the bishops, the chapter was often asked to make more secure those grants which were particularly extensive or located in the key areas of the abbey estates. Dean Robert Butevilain and York chapter attested an extensive grant of pasture (between 1175 and 1186) of Ranulf son of Walter to Rievaulx Abbey in Folkton consisting of one tillage called Ravenesdale and a pasture for one thousand sheep.[97] When Torphin de Allerston granted a carucate, twenty-six perches of land for buildings, and a pasture for five hundred sheep in 1160, the chapter of York not only issued a confirmation charter, but also sealed the document, because Torphin did not have his own seal.[98] The choice of these pasture grants was not accidental; the abbey of Rievaulx had important reasons to ask the York chapter to confirm them. By the late twelfth century, Rievaulx Abbey had accumulated substantial stretches of pastures and built up large sheep flocks. The amount of vacant land was fast diminishing, and many lords, both lay and ecclesiastical, wanted to participate in profitable sheep farming. Wool production became an important part of Rievaulx's economy, thus the abbey wanted to protect its assets by means of secure confirmations.

Not all the contacts between the York chapters and Rievaulx were as exemplary as those described above. The second type of interaction, of a much more dramatic character, between the abbey and the chapters was concerned with the important issue of tithes. Although Rievaulx did not hold churches and refrained from tithe possession, the payment of these tithes by the house became a troublesome issue, particularly in the later part of the twelfth century. Despite the fact that the formal limitation of the freedom from tithes payment came only in 1215, the reputation of the wealth of the order had become widespread in the third quarter of the twelfth century.[99] In Yorkshire this perception of the somewhat excessive wealth of the Cistercian houses was compounded by the complexities of land possession. By the late twelfth century the region was covered by a network of religious institutions, and the increased competition between them was further aggravated by the growing reluctance of laypeople to alienate more land. The prelates and other Church officials became particularly concerned with assuring that the Church received full tithes payments. A growing tension over the recovery of tithes can be observed between

---

[97] *Cartulary*, no. 233; *EYC*, II, no. 1252. The original charter of grant issued by Ranulf was also copied in the *Cartulary*, no. 82; *EYC*, II, no. 1247; dated 1162–75.

[98] *Cartulary*, no. 86; Burton, 'Estates and Economy', p. 62.

[99] Berman, *Cistercian Evolution*, p. 109.

Rievaulx Abbey and the chapter of Durham. Rievaulx Abbey was not the only Cistercian house which experienced such difficulties, but it had shown a consistent approach to solving them. The multi-stage transfer of the properties in Crosby and Cowton to Rievaulx, discussed in the earlier part of this chapter, caused conflict with the chapter of Durham over the payment of the tithes from these vills. Between 1154 and 1170 monks of Durham and those of Rievaulx signed an agreement, which survives in two copies, one in the Rievaulx cartulary and one in the Durham Treasury, stating that Rievaulx Abbey should pay compensation for the loss of tithes of the thraves of East Cowton which were due to the church of Northallerton. The Cistercians were obliged to pay three marks yearly, in two instalments of twenty shillings at Pentecost and on St Martin's day. If Rievaulx Abbey failed to pay the compensation, the monks of Durham had a right to extract the tithes.[100] This clause is described by Lovatt as 'thinly-veiled threats' that if Rievaulx failed to pay it would lose the land.[101] This charter was then confirmed by Prior Germanus of Durham cathedral chapter between 1162 and 1189.[102] The form of the agreement was in many ways a compromise. The chapter of Durham received the money from Rievaulx Abbey, although the payment was called not tithes but compensation, thus preserving, at least nominally, the exemption of the Cistercian house. This type of compromise was characteristic of the strategy of Rievaulx Abbey and continued to be used in the thirteenth century.

The agreement did not last because Durham chapter still considered that it had lost too much in this deal. Eventually Rievaulx Abbey used the tried and tested method and applied to the highest Church authority for help. Between 1171 and 1181 Pope Alexander III informed Bishop Hugh of Durham and Prior Germanus of the chapter of Durham that they had no rights to extract any more money from Rievaulx Abbey for the tithes of East Cowton than was agreed and stipulated in their charter, and reminded them that the Cistercian order possessed immunity from the payment of tithes from the labour of its own hand. The Pope ordered Archbishop Roger and Bishop Hugh to see that any agreement with the monks concerning tithes was adhered to.[103] The Pope expected the prelates to be the executives of justice in their dioceses and to consider the rights of the Cistercian order just as they respected the rights of the chapters. A few years earlier, between 1174 and 1176, the same Pope Alexander III directed the Archbishop of York and Bishop of Durham to excommunicate those clerks who demanded tithes payment in Welburn from Rievaulx Abbey.[104]

These papal letters demonstrate that Rievaulx Abbey recognized that the authority of a distant, but Cistercian-friendly, pope could help in asserting its freedom from

---

[100] *Cartulary*, no. 236; *EYC*, II, no. 956.

[101] *Cartulary*, no. 54; commentary in the *EYC*, II, 293; *EEA*, XX, 91.

[102] *Cartulary*, no. 240.

[103] Cartulary, no. 258; *PU*, I, no. 194.

[104] Cartulary, no. 265; *PU*, I, no. 133.

tithe payment and was quick to ask for help in Rome. This trend continued, on a smaller scale, in the thirteenth century. One of Alexander III's successors, Pope Innocent IV, exempted Rievaulx Abbey in 1243 from the payment of tithes from properties acquired after Alexander III.[105] This was one of the infrequent situations when the high Church politics of the Cistercian order touched Rievaulx Abbey directly. One of the favourites of Pope Inncocent IV was a Cistercian monk, a former Abbot of L'Épau (Maine), who was behind many papal favours for the order.[106] I am not suggesting that he was involved in this case, but Rievaulx did benefit from the Pope's favours for the Cistercian order. Among the Yorkshire Cistercian houses Rievaulx Abbey was not alone in its application to papal protection against the claims of the secular churchmen; Fountains Abbey also received numerous bulls of protection.[107]

Despite the previous interventions of the Cistercian-friendly pope, the conflicts over tithes payments in the thirteenth century were markedly different for Rievaulx Abbey. Whilst in the twelfth century conflicts were concerned with the payment of the tithe from the land which was cultivated prior to its acquisition by Rievaulx, in the thirteenth century the chapter of York started to question the Cistercian right to the tithes exemption as such. The concept of Cistercian exemption from their payment was significantly eroded. This is best explained by the example of tithes of Pickering. It was a wasteland and had not been cultivated before it was granted to Rievaulx Abbey in 1158 and was subsequently cultivated by the lay brothers and employees of that house, but the chapter of York began to demand tithes from it. A series of charters documenting this conflict is preserved in the cartulary of the York chapter. In 1206 Dean Simon of Apulia (1194–1214) and the chapter of York reached the first agreement concerning this matter with Rievaulx Abbey. The abbey promised to pay Dean Simon and his successors twenty shillings of compensation for the alleged loss of tithes from the abbey's grange in Kekmarish (parish of Pickering).[108] Previously the monks paid only one mark yearly, but as Burton suggests, this increase was due to the growth of the value of this property.[109] Fourteen years later, in June 1220, Rievaulx Abbey made another agreement with Dean Roger de Insula (1220–33) and the chapter of York.[110] This time conflict was resolved with the help of the specially appointed papal judges — Priors Vivian or William of St Andrews (1220–24/26), William of Holy Trinity, York (1216–23), and Henry of

---

[105] *CPL*, p. 199.

[106] *The English Church and the Papacy in the Middle Ages*, ed. by C. H. Lawrence (Stroud: Sutton, 1999), p. 124.

[107] *PU*, III, nos 193–94, 208, 244, 270–71, 322.

[108] Liber Albus, London, British Library, Cotton MS Claudius B. iii, fol. 13; published incomplete, with an incorrect folio reference in *Cartulary*, p. 255. See also *Fasti Ecclesiae*, comp. by Greenway, VI, 9.

[109] Burton, 'Estates and Economy', p. 66.

[110] *Fasti Ecclesiae*, comp. by Greenway, VI, 10.

Marton (1199–1227) — and was corroborated by Archbishop Walter de Gray of York (1216–55). Rievaulx agreed to pay five marks yearly.[111] Among the witnesses were some of the prominent lay neighbours and benefactors of Rievaulx Abbey — William de Mowbray, John de Birkin, and Robert de Lasceles — as well as a member of the patron's family, Robert II de Ros. Nevertheless, this agreement was not the end of the conflict over the tithes of Pickering. On 13 February 1240 Abbot Adam of Rievaulx promised to pay tithes from all the new acquisitions in the parish of Pickering, even if they had the status of *novalia*, that is, land from which the abbey was legally free from the paying of tithes. The last known charter, which closed this four-decades-long conflict, was issued on 17 April 1241 by the papal judges delegate, the Dean and Subdean of Lincoln. Both parties, that is Fulk Basset, Dean of York (1239–43), and the Abbot of Rievaulx, Adam de Tilletai (1240–60), agreed after the hearing, which is related in the charter, that the abbey would pay two marks of compensation for the tithes of Kekmarish and Loftmarish in the parish of Pickering, and the conflict was pronounced closed for ever.[112]

This series of conflicts is a clear indication of the practical erosion of the Cistercian exemption from the payment of tithes and the flexibility which the monks had to adopt in dealing with this particular problem, even as far as paying tithes compensation from the *novalia* land. It was not only the growing demand of the secular Church for tithes payment from the exempted orders, but also Cistercian redefinition of their own attitude to the exempted status. This was compounded by the fact that by the early thirteenth century the popes were no longer supporters of the special position of the order, and Rievaulx Abbey, as many other houses, had to make financial compromises with the secular Church to accommodate their financial demands. During the conflicts over the tithes payment between Rievaulx Abbey and the chapter of Durham in the late twelfth century, Pope Alexander III issued bulls in favour of Rievaulx, protecting its exempted status, whilst in the first half of the thirteenth century when the same abbey clashed over the tithes payment with the chapter of York, the Pope appointed a judge delegate and the Cistercian exemption rights were completely ignored.

In the earlier sections of this chapter I have stressed the importance of the personal connections and friendships for the development of the contacts between Rievaulx Abbey and the bishops and archbishops. A similar process can be observed in relations between the abbey and the chapters. Besides the contacts on an institutional level, Rievaulx Abbey interacted with members of the cathedral chapters. Some canons also had personal or family interests in Rievaulx Abbey and acted as supporters of the house.

---

[111] Liber Albus, BL, Cotton MS Claudius B. iii, fol. 12^{v}; published incomplete, with an incorrect folio reference in *Cartulary*, pp. 255–56.

[112] Liber Albus, BL, Cotton MS Claudius B. iii, fols 11^{v}–12^{v}; published incomplete, with an incorrect folio reference in *Cartulary*, pp. 257–59; see also *Fasti Ecclesiae*, comp. by Greenway, VI, 10–11.

In some cases the economic interests of individual canons overlapped with those of Rievaulx Abbey, causing conflicts which left traces in the sources. Although the canons only held these lands because of their offices, these disputes should be considered rather as occurring between the abbey and a particular canon than between two institutions. These conflicts between Rievaulx and the canons shared many similarities with disputes between Rievaulx Abbey and its lay neighbours; indeed some neighbours were involved in resolving conflicts between the monastic house and the canons. The laypeople were often witnesses and provided information on the correct boundary divisions.

One of the recorded cases of such an individual dispute was a conflict between Rievaulx Abbey and Thomas son of Paulinus, Canon of York, who held the prebend of Stillington (comprising land in Stillington, Nawton, and Wombleton) between 1142/54 and 1191/94.[113] This dispute is known from Thomas's charter of quitclaim, issued between 1160 and 1165, which also narrates the earlier stages of this conflict. The canon tried to claim his rights to Nawton and Wombleton, which were given to the abbey by Roger and Nigel de Mowbray. The abbey firmly denied his right to these properties, and Canon Thomas discovered during his investigation of the possession rights that, contrary to what his people had told him, these boundaries were not correct.[114]

> For I brought the above said claims concerning the above said boundaries of Welburn, because my people told me, falsely, that they belonged to my land in Nawton and Wombleton. But since I did not wish to trouble the above said monks unjustly, I investigated painstakingly from faithful people and neighbours from this area and I learned most certainly and recognized the above said divisions to belong to Welburn, and that I have brought a claim unreasonably, concerning these boundaries. And for that reason I quitclaim the whole said claim against the said monks, and grant this land to them to enclose by a ditch freely along the said boundaries just as Robert de Daiville and my other neighbours from these vills for their part permitted them to do.[115]

It is possible that Canon Thomas simply tried forcefully to seize some of Rievaulx Abbey's property bordering with his prebend and, once unsuccessful, put all the

[113] *Fasti Ecclesiae*, comp. by Greenway, VI, 97–98

[114] *EYC*, I, no. 164.

[115] 'Nam predictam calumpniam movi super prefatas divisas de Wellebr[una] quia homines mei michi falso suggesserant quod pertinerent ad terram meam de Nagelt[ona] et de Wimbelt[ona]. Set quoniam nolui predictos monachos injuste vexare inquisivi diligenter a fidelibus hominibus et vicinis de eadem provincia et certissime didici atque cognovi prefatas divisas pertinere ad Wellebr[unam], meque super eas prefatam calumpniam contra rationem movisse. Et ideo totam predictam calumpniam omnino quietam clamavi sepedictis monachis et concessi eis terram suam fossato quiete claudere per supradictas divisas sicut Robertus de Daivilla et ceteri vicini mei de eisdem villis ex parte sua illos facere permiserunt': *Cartulary*, p. 247; *EYC*, I, no. 164.

blame on the others. But it is equally likely that his claims were motivated by a genuine mistake, and he simply did not know the direction of the borders, which were unmarked. His investigation among the neighbours revealed the true divisions between the properties, and the canon had no choice but to give up his claims. This case is another example of the importance of the neighbourhood and collective memory for preserving consensus among the community of landowners, no matter if they were religious or laymen. Although charters were increasingly used as proof of legal rights to properties, the boundaries were still primarily defined by the consensus of the local community of which religious houses and the clergy were a part.

A more positive aspect of Rievaulx's contacts with an individual canon can be seen in the example of Nicholas de Traili, a Canon of York, who was a nephew of Walter Espec, the founder of Rievaulx Abbey. Nicholas, a canon from 1135/43, held Strensall prebend in the North Riding between 1166 and *c.* 1185.[116] He witnessed six charters for Rievaulx Abbey as a member of the patron's family, but also, clearly, as a Canon of York who happened to have particular connections with the abbey.[117] His personal interest in Rievaulx Abbey has to be particularly stressed because he did not have any economic involvement in the area since the Yorkshire estates of Walter Espec were inherited by his cousin Robert de Ros. In contrast to other frequent witnesses from within the York chapter, Nicholas de Traili occurred also on documents lacking any other clerical witnesses. For example Canon Simon de Sigillo (1143/53–67/77) witnessed seven charters of Rievaulx, but he always appeared in the context of other members of the York chapter.[118] Since the patrons of the abbey from the Ros family were distant and rather unenthusiastic patrons, the nephew of the founder was potentially a useful ally, not only because he was a Canon of York, but also because he was a link to the memory of Walter Espec and appeared to show a personal attachment to Rievaulx.

Because of the low survival rate of documents it is difficult to assess how common and frequent were these personal contacts between Rievaulx Abbey and other canons, but it is very likely, on the basis of the known cases, that these contacts were related to the personal connections of the canons with either patrons and benefactors or individual monks from within the monastic convent. They could have been visitors to the abbey or stayed in the guest-house there. The informal character of such contacts did not leave traces in the sources, so the conflicts about borders and the witness lists remain as the most visible signs of connection between Rievaulx Abbey and the Canons of York.

---

[116] *Fasti Ecclesiae*, comp. by Greenway, VI, 99.

[117] *Cartulary*, nos 43, 60, 129, 184, 219, 229. For a discussion on Nicholas's family connections, see pp. 41–42 above.

[118] *Cartulary*, nos 57, 60, 82, 83, 148, 161, 229. Simon de Sigillo held the prebend in Langtoft (East Riding); he was succeeded by John, son of Letold: *Fasti Ecclesiae*, comp. by Greenway, VI, 84.

From the discussion in the earlier part of this chapter we can see that contacts between the chapters of York and Durham and Rievaulx Abbey were as important in their own ways as the connections between the abbey and their respective bishops. The deans and chapters were based locally and were more accessible than high prelates whose political activities often took them away from their dioceses. The deans and chapters often acted as mediators for the religious houses and issued numerous confirmation charters for the monasteries. In some cases it is possible to identify 'chains' of confirmation, that is, a particular property being confirmed and reconfirmed by various authorities, from deacons up to the highest authorities. The authority of the York chapter offered a unique combination of local knowledge and connections combined with the authority of the Church and the ability to enforce ecclesiastical punishments if necessary.

The issue of tithes was a particular problem, which continued to cause conflict between Rievaulx Abbey and the chapters of York and Durham throughout the twelfth and thirteenth centuries. It was not, however, unique to Rievaulx Abbey, but was an expression of a much wider trend in the Church. The erosion of the idea of the tithes exemption forced the Cistercian order to redefine their practice. The ability of the Abbots of Rievaulx to find a compromise for the issue of tithes payment helped to sustain positive contact with key figures in the diocese of York. The tool of tithes compensation was, in most cases, an effective method of achieving a compromise between views, which by the mid-thirteenth century had become rather divergent.

In the course of the first two hundred years of its existence, the abbey of Rievaulx developed important links with members of the secular Church. Although much had changed, in both a local and an international Church arena, from the time of the supportive Archbishop Thurstan to the time of the distant Archbishop Walter de Grey who saw the Cistercians primarily in terms of taxation opportunities, the abbey of Rievaulx managed to establish its place in the diocese and find support, if necessary, from the Bishops of Durham or from popes. The protection of a powerful individual could substantially help the abbey in a world of unstable alliances and greedy neighbours.

The relationship between Rievaulx and the canons was built primarily on personal contacts and connections. The prelates and deans often acted as protectors and mediators between Rievaulx Abbey and its disgruntled or potentially difficult benefactors. By issuing confirmation charters bishops and chapters helped to ensure the security of the abbey's estates. Nevertheless, the issue of tithes payment reveals the scale of tensions between the secular Church and the exempted orders. The case of Rievaulx Abbey does not confirm Berman's thesis concerning the reinforcement of the ideology of tithe exemption in the thirteenth century when new foundations and acquisitions were occurring on the marginal lands.[119] The example of Rievaulx Abbey shows that by the late twelfth century the Cistercian exemption was indeed increasingly questioned by the secular Church, and this trend became even more pronounced in the

[119] Berman, *Cistercian Evolution*, pp. 228–29.

thirteenth century. Initially Rievaulx Abbey used a combination of tactics to protect its exempted status, as the case of the conflict with the chapter of Durham shows. The Abbots of Rievaulx were prepared to make a compromise, but when that failed, they applied, successfully, to the authority of the pope. The thirteenth-century case of the dispute over the tithes of Pickering exemplifies the broader shift in the position of the exempted orders, which directly affected Rievaulx Abbey. The pope was no longer keen to protect the freedom of the Cistercian order, and a financial compromise, on terms increasingly difficult for the abbey, was the only available solution.

Considerable similarity can be seen between the ways in which the abbey resolved its conflicts with neighbours and the methods by which it settled its disputes with prelates. After all, they were also, in many ways, neighbours of the abbey and a part of the networks which encompassed the abbey. There was a contradiction in the Cistercian approach to the secular Church not only in the 'heroic' period of the order's history when the white monks wanted to improve the prelates by preaching, as Ailred did, or by direct intervention, as during the York controversy. This dualism continued beyond the twelfth century. While Cistercians wanted to disassociate themselves from the authority of the secular Church, they nonetheless needed to cooperate with bishops, deans, and chapters, who might no longer be close friends, but who remained as useful allies. If not for the sake of Christian unity and *caritas*, the monks of Rievaulx had to find consensus with them for the sake of the successful functioning of the abbey.

CHAPTER 6

Friendship and Commemoration

In the course of the discussion of the relationships of patrons, benefactors, and neighbours with Rievaulx Abbey, social or even political reasons appeared to be the important underpinnings of donations to this monastery. The family, kinship, and tenurial groups provided a context for these acts. However, this does not mean that the declarations of religious motivation expressed in the charters were only a cover-up for purely practical considerations. On the contrary, grants to the monasteries could only play their social role in an environment which believed in, and attached a high value to, the eschatological dimension of such grants. Unfortunately, due to the low level of document survival there are few direct indications of more complex religious connections between Rievaulx and its benefactors, but a careful analysis of the surviving fragments provides an indication of the range and type of these acts. However, it is impossible to make any quantitative assessment of their intensity and frequency.

Early medieval complexities of practices such as the commemorative rituals and types of document associated with them have been significantly better explored than the Cistercian practice in this respect. The achievement of Karl Schmid and Joachim Wollasch and their research groups in editing and analysing a broad variety of commemorative sources from Cluny, Corvey, Fulda, Lüneburg, Merseburg, Magdeburg, Reichenau, and St Gallen cannot be overestimated.[1] The Benedictine and Cluniac communities in these influential monasteries were engaged in a variety of commemorative practices focusing on the liturgy, but also creating written documents

[1] The impressive contribution of both scholars includes editions of sources and critical studies. For the full bibliography, see 'Verzeichnis der Schriften von Karl Schmid', in *Person und Gemeinschaft im Mittelalter: Karl Schmid zum fünfundsechzigsten Geburtstag*, ed. by Gerd Althoff (Sigmaringen: Thorbecke, 1988), pp. 617–35; 'Verzeichnis der Schriften von Joachim Wollasch', in *Vinculum societati: Joachim Wollasch zum 60. Geburtstag*, ed. by Franz Neiske, Dietrich Poeck, and Mechthild Sandmann (Sigmaringendorf: Glock und Lutz, 1991), pp. 326–45.

preserving names of their benefactors, friends, and associates. These pre-twelfth-century practices are, in many ways, better examined than the Cistercian commemorative tradition. This is partly due to the significantly higher volume of source material from the earlier period, but also to the obscurity and simplicity of Cistercian practice, which remained largely ignored by the historians. Again, the case of Rievaulx Abbey is well suited to test these assumptions and investigate the way in which commemorations formed a part of the carefully laid web of connection between the white monks and the laity.

As I have indicated earlier, benefactors, or prospective benefactors, had their own expectations towards the abbey, concentrating around the issue of commemoration and promises of spiritual reward for their donations, but also, as we have seen in a number of cases associated with the patron's family, mutual material help and a possible outlet for self-representation in the form of literary commemoration (as in the case of the founder) and burials in the fourteenth century (the Ros family). The white monks also had their own set of ideas about how their neighbours and benefactors should behave towards the abbey — continuing generosity and support beyond the first generation were the core concepts. A 'hands-off' attitude of powerful laymen was very much preferred by Rievaulx than the involved but rather overbearing approach discussed in the second chapter on the example of Gilbert de Gant and Rufford Abbey. These two sets of ideas held by the monastic community and its lay benefactors were often not dissimilar, as both parties shared the belief in the eschatological power of prayers. Even such fragmentary source material as that associated with Rievaulx shows that the benefactors and the monks were engaged in dialogue and negotiation about what they were prepared to give to each other and why.

The title of this chapter outlines two major areas of particular importance. As the discussion in earlier parts of the book has shown, friendship and continuing affinity to religious houses displayed by the benefactors played a major role in the abbey's continuing prosperity. Commemoration was at the core of laypeople's expectations from monastic communities and an important element of the monastic mission, although the Cistercian order introduced some important changes in that area. The tradition and practice of commemoration was already a complex set of ideas and rituals by the time of the emergence of this order.[2] The essence of the commemoration of the dead concentrated on a number of regularly repeated and complex rituals involving all or parts of a monastic community, such as daily Masses, recitations of the psalms, and yearly feasts for the dead *familiares*, that is associates, friends, and benefactors of the monastic community.[3] Karl Schmid and Joachim Wollasch argued

---

[2] There is a very extensive literature on the various forms of early medieval commemoration of the dead. For a good summary of the literature, see Megan McLaughlin, *Consorting with Saints: Prayers for the Dead in Early Medieval France* (Ithaca, NY: Cornell University Press, 1994), pp. 2–23.

[3] Arnold Angenendt, 'Theologie und Liturgie der mittelalterlichen Toten-Memoria', in *Memoria: Der geschichtliche Zeugniswert des liturgischen Gedenkens im Mittelalter*, ed. by

that there was, by the ninth century, a significant shift from the cumulative commemoration for the dead, in the form of the Mass, to the individualized commemorations of each person on the anniversary of his/her death.[4] In practice, this led to a huge burden on monastic communities. The frequency, length, and expense associated with these practices in the Benedictine and particularly Cluniac houses had almost reached crisis point by the twelfth century. It is therefore not surprising that the Cistercian order took a rather different approach to the rituals of commemoration. Besides this purely practical consideration, the return to the simpler, cumulative forms of commemoration and a reduction of the number of persons commemorated were linked, some scholars argue, to the Cistercian ideology of simplicity and emphasis on the collective rather than on the individual.[5] The commemorative practices of Rievaulx Abbey are a good test case for these interpretations.

Various forms of writing and recording information were central to the life of Rievaulx Abbey. It is shown in the scope and depth of Abbot Ailred's writing, in the form of the cartulary, and in the way in which charters were preserved and used as evidence in the court of law. As we have seen so far, a significant proportion of the written documents associated with the abbey are related in some way to contacts between laypeople and Rievaulx. The cartulary in particular provides a significant amount of information on how the abbey perceived them and how this information was structured and preserved. Holding lands acquired in the form of pious donations was intrinsically connected to the duty of prayer placed on the monastic communities — prayers for their living benefactors and for the departed ones. The creation of cartularies has been connected, as Jarosław Wenta asserts using the examples of Silesian and Pomeranian Cistercians, to this obligation, because these volumes record the information about the acquired properties together with the names of the donors.[6]

Other types of monastic writings were designed exclusively to serve commemorative purposes. Since the mid-ninth century many religious houses kept *necrologia*. In the Benedictine houses these lists were often a part of codices incorporating *martyrologium* and the Rule of St Benedict. The names of the dead individuals were entered under the day and month of their death and read daily in chapter. This structure

---

Karl Schmid and Joachim Wollasch, Münstersche Mittelalter-Schriften, 48 (Munich: Wilhelm Fink, 1984), pp. 79–199 (pp. 164–87); McLaughlin, *Consorting with Saints*, pp. 67–90.

[4] Karl Schmid and Joachim Wollasch, 'Die Gemeinschaft der Lebenden und Verstorbenen in Zeugnissen des Mittelalters', *Frühmittelalterliche Studien*, 1 (1967), 365–405 (p. 400).

[5] Stanisław Zakrzewski, 'Analecta Cisterciensia', *Rozprawy Akademii Umiejętności: Wydział Historyczno-Filozoficzny*, 2nd series, 24 (1900), 1–52 (pp. 23–44).

[6] Jarosław Wenta, 'Dziejopisarstwo cystersów a *Memoria* na przykładzie Henrykowa, Lubiąża i Oliwy' (The historical writing of the Cistercian order and *Memoria* on the examples of Henrykow, Lubiąż and Oliwa), in *Klasztor w społeczeństwie średniowiecznym i nowożytnym* (The monastery in medieval and early modern society), ed. by Marek Derwich and Anna Pobóg-Lenartowicz (Opole-Wrocław: LARHCOR, 1996), pp. 191–98 (p. 197).

was closely linked with the celebration of saints' days. This connection is further attested by the fact that the names of the dead from the *necrologium* and the names of the saints from the *martyrologium* were read one after the other.[7] These lists of the dead were an important means of commemorating departed monastic benefactors and were a way in which their connections with the religious houses were preserved. The individuals whose names were enrolled in these volumes were linked to the monastery, but not necessarily in a formalized way. The inclusion in a *necrologium* often indicated, although this was not necessarily spelled out, that a given person had been a valued benefactor, or a family member of one of the monks, or was buried in the monastery. The Cistercians modified the existing tradition of these practices, as they had done in other aspects of commemoration. In contrast to the Benedictine examples, Cistercian *necrologia* were much shorter, containing fewer names, showing a shift from individual to collective commemoration. Instead of countless prayers for individuals, the Cistercian order introduced a type of cumulative prayer across the order. Each year, on 20 November, the monastic communities which had been admitted to confraternity with the Cistercian order were commemorated in prayers, and on 11 January the same was done for individuals.[8] The Chapter General tried to control commemoration of the 'friends' of the order, by a selective admission of particular monastic communities, mainly Benedictine, and prominent individuals including the English King Henry II and French Kings Philip Augustus and Louis VIII.[9] There were strong attempts to prevent individual abbeys developing separate commemoration traditions as the Chapter General controlled the enrolment of monastic communities commemorated by the Cistercian confraternity prayers.[10] Joachim Wollasch explained the Cistercian departure from the earlier model of commemoration by economic pressure which Cluniac houses in particular had suffered, having been overburden by the obligation to commemorate thousands of individuals.[11] He compared a number of French Cistercian *necrologia* from the late twelfth and early thirteenth centuries with contemporary cases from Cluniac houses, such as a list from Marcigny-sur-Loire, which contains ten thousand names. Cistercian examples were not only significantly shorter, for example the *necrologium* of Cîteaux

---

[7] Otto Gerhard Oexle, 'Memoria und Memorialüberlieferung im frühen Mittelalter', *Frühmittelalterliche Studien*, 10 (1976), 70–95 (p. 74).

[8] Ph. Guignard, *Les Primitifs de la règle cistercienne: Publiés d'après les manuscrits de l'Abbaye de Cîteaux* (Dijon: Imprimerie Darantiere, 1878), pp. 308, 393–94.

[9] *Statuta*, 1238: 16.

[10] C. H. Talbot, 'Associations of Clairvaux, Clairmarais and Ter Doest', *Cîteaux in de Nederlanden*, 5 (1954), 233–45 (pp. 234, 243); *Twelfth-Century Statutes from the Cistercian General Chapter*, ed. by Chrysogonus Waddell, Studia et Documenta, 12 (Brecht: Cîteaux-Commentarii Cistercienses, 2002), 1196: 61, p. 375.

[11] Joachim Wollasch, 'Neue Quellen zur Geschichte der Cistercienser', *Zeitschrift für Kirchengeschichte*, 84 (1973), 188–232 (pp. 230–32).

compiled in the thirteenth century contained only two hundred entries, but also different in terms of who was included in the lists. There were primarily monastic communities listed in the Cistercian *necrologia*, which had been connected with each other by the bonds of mutual prayers, which contrasts sharply with the Cluniac list dominated by individuals, often lay.[12]

Whilst commemoration was aimed primarily at sustaining symbolic connections between the living and the dead, religious houses established a number of other forms which were intended for those still alive. The bond between a layperson and a religious house could also be formalized in a form of confraternity membership. Admittance into fraternity meant, in the most general sense, that an individual shared all the spiritual benefits of prayers and Masses performed for him or her in a given house in perpetuity.[13] The confraternities between two religious communities and between a religious community and individuals existed since the early Middle Ages, but the first type had its peak from the late eleventh to the thirteenth centuries; the second type continued to exist as a structured association between monasteries and laity in the late Middle Ages.[14] For Benedictines, the confraternity offered a tool for creating spiritual bonds between autonomous houses and, in the twelfth century, building connections with communities belonging to other orders.[15] The concept of fraternity was significantly developed by the Cluniacs and is often thought to be one of main reasons for the popularity of this order among laypeople, monks of other orders, and secular clergy who entered into confraternity with Cluniac houses. The bond within the confraternity was personal and vertical, with each member benefiting from the prayers of the monks.[16] The Cistercian order, which, in contrast, placed much less emphasis on the individualized intercessory prayers for benefactors, did not abolish the confraternity system. Prayers as an important way of maintaining bonds between religious houses themselves are exemplified by the promise of the mutual prayers exchanged between Rievaulx and Byland.[17] It was also a popular tool of asserting attachment between monasteries and particularly important supporters, as in the case of Rievaulx and Bishop Hugh of Durham.[18]

---

[12] Wollasch, 'Neue Quellen', p. 230.

[13] H. E. J. Cowdrey, 'Unions and Confraternity with Cluny', *Journal of Ecclesiastical History*, 16 (1965), 152–62 (p. 154).

[14] H. E. J. Cowdrey, 'Legal Problems Raised by Agreements of Confraternity', in 'Die mittelalterliche Lebensform der Verbrüderung', in *Memoria*, ed. by Schmid and Wollasch, pp. 233–54 (pp. 233–34).

[15] Janet E. Burton, 'A Confraternity List from St Mary's Abbey, York', *Revue Bénédictine*, 89 (1979), 325–33 (pp. 326–28).

[16] Cowdrey, 'Unions and Confraternity', p. 162.

[17] *Cartulary*, no. 243.

[18] *Cartulary*, no. 49; *EYC*, II, no. 952.

Among the 147 entries in the cartulary of Rievaulx Abbey, there are four cases of request for fraternity. Among the fifty-three charters of laypeople to Rievaulx Abbey, from the late twelfth and the first half of the thirteenth centuries, copied in the Dodsworth manuscripts there are two further fraternity requests. A more detailed look at these documents reveals that the admission of laypeople was an important tool in maintaining positive relationships with benefactors and neighbours. It helped to create ties with key individuals in the area, secure land in desirable locations, pacify quarrelsome neighbours, prevent future disagreements, and secure other practical arrangements, but not necessarily to reward the most generous donors. The fraternity of Rievaulx Abbey was offered to Bishop Hugh of Durham in return for his offer of acting as a special protector of the abbey and to a powerful aristocrat, William, Earl of Aumâle, for his quitclaim of a particular property and a promise of protection.[19] Besides these two leading individuals, the remaining part of the four groups was a mixed collection of laypeople whose relationships to Rievaulx Abbey had various forms and degrees of intensity.

The father of Geoffrey de Lasceles was admitted into the fraternity in return for just one tillage of land, but he was a member of a local family who supported the abbey from the early stages and continued to do so for a number of generations, by grants and by regular appearance in the witness lists. So this fraternity admission was not just a 'thank-you gesture' for a rather small grant, but an acknowledgement of a continuing relationship between the abbey and the Lasceles family. In the group of close neighbours of the abbey discussed in the second chapter, the Lasceles were generous donors for a number of generations, still adding further grants in the early thirteenth century.[20] Their donations allowed the abbey to build up East Harlsey grange. Why it was the father of Geoffrey de Lasceles who was admitted, not his son or some other member of this family, is less certain, but the admission of this individual should be considered in the context of the family, who held a special significance for the abbey.

One of the quarrelsome neighbours discussed in the third chapter, Jocelin de Arecy, was granted fraternity admission as part of a deal between him and the abbey intended to pacify and prevent any future actions against Rievaulx.[21] In this case, the monks were offering him, besides material compensation, a symbolic bond with the abbey, a promise of commemoration and prestige, and hope for eschatological reward. It should not be seen, however, as a sign of cynicism on the part of the Rievaulx community or Jocelin, but as an established way of building longer-term trust between monastic houses and laypeople. The two remaining family groups of recipients were Walter de Stainesby and his lords Stephen de Bulmer and Thomas Muscamp with all their wives and children, who were given that privilege for

---

[19] *Cartulary*, no. 185.

[20] For the analysis of the Lasceles relationship with the abbey, see pp. 107–09 above.

[21] *Cartulary*, no. 181; *EYC*, I, no. 611.

confirming Rievaulx rights to the fisheries on the river Tees, and Alan de Catherton with his wife, Eleanor, for their quitclaim of their right to a ditch near Baildon.[22] Hill asserts that these people also received free rights of hospitality, a privilege contained in the phrase 'all the benefits of the house'.[23]

These last two examples show that fraternity admissions were also intended as a reinforcement of ties between family and tenurial groups and the abbey, the most important types of units forming the social context of Rievaulx Abbey. Because a grant to the abbey was rarely an act of an individual, but one undertaken in the social context of the donor, the reciprocity was often directed to a whole group. The same holds true for the countergifts to which I will come back later in this chapter.

It is instructive to compare these instances of a grant of confraternity with cases from other Yorkshire houses. Four benefactors of Byland Abbey requested fraternity rights for themselves and their families in the same period, while several benefactors of Sallay Abbey made such requests. In the case of this last house, the fraternity and burial requests outnumbered by far any countergifts or monetary requests. There are also examples of such requests from Nostell, Guisborough, Pontefract, Easby, Watton, Kirkstall, and Fountains.[24] In light of this comparison, it seems that these low numbers from Rievaulx do not represent a true figure for the fraternity admittance at Rievaulx Abbey; one explanation might be that the admissions might have been done verbally in a public ceremony, without a written record. However, as I indicated earlier, the low survival level of Rievaulx documents makes quantitative statements, particularly any comparisons with other monasteries, rather problematic. The cartulary recorded comprehensively only grants made up to the 1180s, whilst only a small proportion of the later charters survived, which must have eliminated some evidence. The confraternity agreements between religious communities declined in the thirteenth century, but the confraternity admissions for individuals did not.[25] Moreover, some Cistercian houses developed separate confraternity lists and even *necrologia* commemorating key lay individuals only in the thirteenth and fourteenth centuries, and continued to add more names in the later centuries, so it is possible that Rievaulx Abbey followed the same route, although there is no trace of such documents originating from this abbey.[26]

---

[22] *Cartulary*, nos 49, 88, 181, 185; Bodl. Dodsw. vii, fol. 134^{v}; Dodsw. viii, fol. 89.

[23] Bennett D. Hill, *English Cistercian Monasteries and their Patrons in the Twelfth Century* (Urbana: University of Illinois Press, 1968), pp. 67–68: 'omnium beneficiorum domus sue'.

[24] Janet E. Burton, *The Monastic Order in Yorkshire, 1069–1215* (Cambridge: Cambridge University Press, 1999), p. 209.

[25] Cowdrey, 'Legal Problems', p. 233.

[26] The evidence for separate lists of commemorated individuals comes from Cistercian houses in Silesia, namely Henryków, Kamieniec Ząbkowicki, and Krzeszów. Michał Kaczmarek, 'Liturgia memoratywna u Cystersów' (Commemorative liturgy of the Cistercian order), *Nasza Przeszłość*, 83 (1994), 281–93 (pp. 284–92).

The donors could benefit spiritually from the close association with the abbey during their lifetime; in addition, being buried within the monastic grounds was highly desirable and symbolized a permanent attachment to a holy place. It was a commonly held belief that interment within the bounds of the holy space of the monastery could dramatically increase one's chances of salvation. Megan Cassidy-Welch elucidates that the Cistercian policy on burials was 'reflecting changing concerns of the living'.[27] Among these concerns was the issue of the terms and expressions of associations with the laity. The early regulations of the order from the late 1140s were against burials within the bounds of monasteries, with the exception of a very few selected individuals.

> For confession, Holy Communion, and burials, we receive no outsider other than guests and hired hands who die, namely, inside the monastery but neither do we receive offerings at the conventual Mass, except on the Purification of St Mary. For burials, however, two only whom we wish to receive from among our friends or familiars, along with their wives.[28]

Later on, between 1157 and 1179, the Chapter General also allowed for burials of the founders in the monastic church.[29] These statements are an important indication of the careful Cistercian policy of building links with the lay world rather than rejecting it. The restriction on the lay burials had an inbuilt mechanism for allowing particularly valued individuals to be buried at the discretion of the monastic community. In the thirteenth century, the order's regulations show that it was primarily the location of the lay graves, not the burials themselves, which was a controversial issue. A significant number of cases from German and French houses in the first half of the twelfth century, which were dealt with at the annual meetings of the Chapter General, demonstrate that laypeople, not only patrons but also benefactors, wanted to be buried in Cistercian houses and that local practice, in allowing them access, varied greatly.[30] The Chapter General was primarily concerned that laypeople should not be buried in the monastic churches and chapter houses, the holiest and also most prestigious spaces within the monastic precincts. Holiness was very much associated with prestige and, as such, desired by the laity. This controversy is also reflected in the rather late burials of members of the patrons' family at Rievaulx as discussed in

---

[27] Megan Cassidy-Welch, *Monastic Spaces and their Meanings: Thirteenth-Century English Cistercian Monasteries*, Medieval Church Studies, 1 (Turnhout: Brepols, 2001), p. 228.

[28] *Narrative and Legislative Texts from Early Cîteaux*, ed. and trans. by Chrysogonus Waddell, Studia et Documenta, 9 (Pontigny: Cîteaux-Commentarii Cistercienses, 1999), pp. 467–68.

[29] *Twelfth-Century Statutes*, ed. by Waddell, 1157/79: 63, p. 606; this is also discussed in detail in the forthcoming article by Jackie Hall, 'The Legislative Background to the Burial of Laity and other Patrons in Cistercian Abbeys', *Cîteaux: Commentarii Cistercienses*, special issue edited by Jacke Hall and Christine Kratzke. I would like to thank her for kindly sending me a copy of this article.

[30] Cassidy-Welch, *Monastic Spaces*, p. 232.

the first chapter. As Cassidy-Welch argues, the growing number of lay burials in Cistercian houses, in general, was not an indication of the increasing influence of the laypeople over these institutions, but rather of the changing ways of commemoration of the dead. The liturgical practices of commemoration were reduced in favour of burials in the sacred parts of the monastic church and its immediate surrounding.[31]

The only recorded case of a burial request at Rievaulx Abbey is certainly not a reflection of the real number. The archaeological material is also largely absent, thus cannot give an alternative indication of the existence of the lay burials within the monastic precinct. The only documented case is that of Jordan son of Matthew de Horbiry who gave to Rievaulx Abbey, between 1190 and 1204, his tillage of land in Flockton, and this was given 'with my body' (*cum corpore meo*). The charter is very brief and does not specify in which part of the monastery Jordan was going to be buried. This lack of precision was a common pattern; not many contemporary charters identified the location of the burial.[32] This was probably left to the discretion of the monastery, considering that Jordan did not come from a baronial family, and so probably could not command much influence over the abbey.

Due to the lack of information, Rievaulx Abbey's case cannot be used to test Cassidy-Welch's hypothesis, but in general, Yorkshire Cistercian houses do not appear to have had a uniform policy on lay burials, although there is evidence that the patrons were allowed to be buried in the monastic houses earlier then any other group of laypeople. Certain houses, for example Jervaulx and Sallay Abbeys, buried their patrons in the monastic church as early as the first half of the thirteenth century.[33] Fountains Abbey received ninety requests from a variety of laypeople up to 1300.[34] In the light of this information the only documented request of this sort directed to Rievaulx Abbey must be far from the real number of requests made to this house before the end of the thirteenth century. A very low survival rate of documents related to the early history of Rievaulx Abbey distorts statistics, but the existing information cannot be taken as a indication of an almost complete ban on lay burial there. It is fair to assume that Rievaulx probably attracted fewer applicants for burials than Fountains, but beyond that, it is impossible to make any quantitative statements. Fountains Abbey also attracted a number of aristocratic benefactors whose affinity stretched so far as requesting burials there, whilst Rievaulx did not.[35] As I have argued in the second chapter, this was a part of abbey's policy of restrained contacts with powerful laymen who, although generous and influential, could also exert unwanted pressure on the monastery.

---

[31] Cassidy-Welch, *Monastic Spaces*, p. 218.

[32] Bodl. Dodsw. viii, fol. 117^{v}; *EYC*, III, no. 1688.

[33] Cassidy-Welch, *Monastic Spaces*, pp. 235–36.

[34] Joan Wardrop, *Fountains Abbey and its Benefactors 1132–1300* (Kalamazoo: Cistercian Publications, 1987), p. 261.

[35] Burton, *Monastic Order in Yorkshire*, p. 209.

A symbolic but also practical way of commemorating benefactors was offered by pittances. These were extra servings of food or drink given to each monk to celebrate a festive occasion and to remember and pray for the benefactor who provided them. Cistercian houses, alongside other religious orders, commonly accepted this type of gift.[36] There are only two known cases of pittance granted to Rievaulx Abbey, and both of them occurred in the late twelfth century. In the 1190s the patron of Rievaulx Abbey, Robert II de Ros, gave an unspecified pittance to be distributed yearly in the abbey on All Saints Day.[37] Adam son of Peter de Birkin donated an annual pittance of bread and fish to be handed out to the monks on the anniversary of his death.[38] The first individual had strong formal reasons for providing such a gift, although the Ros family, as discussed in the first chapter, did not express much personal attachment to Rievaulx. The second donor, Adam son of Peter, examined in the second chapter, had strong ties to the abbey. He and his family showed a spectacular generosity to many houses whilst the wording of his charters expressed meaningful eschatological and personal motivation for the donations to Rievaulx. The pittance given by him was another expression of this bond and his desire to be commemorated at this particular monastery.[39]

It is likely that the low number of recorded pittances was again a result of losses sustained by the abbey's archive and the real number of pittances was much higher. This type of donation was a practice increasingly common in the thirteenth century and beyond, a period particularly badly documented at Rievaulx. The advantage of a pittance over other types of grants was its strongly commemorative dimension and explicit link with prayers. It is likely that the monks would have more incentive to pray for a particular individual who provided them with a meal, and that connection must also have been understood and appreciated by the donors themselves.

Fraternity admissions, prayers, and pittances were not the only means of creating and expressing bonds between the abbey and laypeople. The countergifts which the benefactors of Cistercian houses received from the monks should be considered as an element in building and sustaining long-lasting relationships between the religious houses and their benefactors. Their value was not based solely on the material gain, but also on the symbolic and public gestures which accompanied them. The existence of countergifts is known primarily from the donation charters, which recorded those acts of reciprocity given in return for the donations of laypeople. Texts of the charters emphasize this element of reciprocity very strongly and present

---

[36] David Postles, 'Lamps, Lights and Layfolk: "Popular" Devotion before the Black Death', *Journal of Medieval History*, 25 (1999), 97–114 (p. 110, n. 90).

[37] *Cartulary*, no. 47.

[38] London, British Library, Egerton Charter 2247; for an English summary of this charter, see *YD*, I, no. 211.

[39] For the analysis of Adam's generosity to several Yorkshire houses, see Burton, *Monastic Order in Yorkshire*, pp. 210–15.

them as directly connected to the original act of donation. Also, the positive feelings between a donor and recipient can be highlighted in the documents. When Hugh de Malebisse gave, between 1160 and 1165, a meadow in Scawton to Rievaulx Abbey, the countergift which he received from the monks was given to him, according to the phrase used in the charter, 'for love' (*pro caritate*).[40] However, the cartulary of Rievaulx Abbey and later charters use the language of reciprocity very sparingly, in contrast to many contemporary examples originating from other Cistercian houses in Yorkshire.[41] This difference cannot be attributed solely to variation in the styles of scribes; the absence of the rather standard phraseology of affection and reciprocity between monastic communities and laity reflects, to some degree, the situation of Rievaulx Abbey in relation to its benefactors. Smaller houses had often put more effort into attracting donors, while Fountains Abbey had learned during its early years that lay support was crucial and employed a range of gestures which were aimed at reciprocating their generosity. In that sense the cold style of many charters from Rievaulx might be a reflection of their attitude to donors. I would not go so far to assert that the Abbey disregarded its benefactors, but rather, that Rievaulx wanted and could afford to remain more distant from them.

The documented instances of countergifts given to laypeople by the monks of Rievaulx show rather pragmatic use of that tool. The majority of them are clearly specified in the charters as given in exchange for quitclaims to the abbey. Such countergifts served as compensation for the material loss incurred by the donor. Their presence was also a reflection of the situation and actions of such individuals. For example Alice, widow of William son of Richard de Aton, quitclaimed to Rievaulx Abbey in 1245 six bovates of land belonging to her dower but had sued the monks for the return of one third of that property. In order to prevent her taking any further legal action, the monks gave her five silver marks.[42] Sometimes the countergift was given to the key people who disputed or could dispute a donation, at that point in time or in the future. For example, between 1160 and 1170 Walter Ingram, with the consent of his wife, Holdierda, gave extensive meadows and pastures to Rievaulx Abbey in Arncliffe. In return, he received fifteen silver marks, his wife received a golden ring, and his sons, the heirs, were given two shillings.[43] Although this looks very much like a 'cover-up sale', I would be hesitant to use this term; rather, cases like this indicate that the difference between sale and grant was much less clear cut

[40] *Cartulary*, no. 74.

[41] Emilia Jamroziak, 'Making and Breaking the Bonds: Yorkshire Cistercians and their Neighbours', in *Beyond the Architecture of Solitude: Studies on Cistercians, Art and Architecture*, ed. by Terryl Kinder (Turnhout: Brepols, 2004), pp. 198–206 (pp. 200–01).

[42] 'Et pro ista remissione et quieta clamantia praefati monachi dederunt michi quinque marcas argenti': Bodl. Dodsw. vii, fol. 141^{v}; printed with omissions in *Cartulary*, pp. 230–31.

[43] 'Et monachi inde dant nobis xv marcas argenti et michi Holdeard unum an[n]ulum auri et duobus heredibus nostris duos solidos': *Cartulary*, no. 90.

for medieval people than it is for us. The sizeable countergift suggests that the monks were very keen to obtain this property and that Walter could not, for material or other reasons, give this land completely free. The reciprocity of the monks allowed him to display publicly his piety and generosity, and hope that the grant would aid his salvation, and in return the abbey secured a property which was particularly desirable. The fact that not only Walter, but also his wife and sons, received countergifts is an acknowledgement of their interests and claims to the property. It is also another indication that a grant to an abbey was not an individual act, but one always taken in the context of a family and tenurial group.

The acts of giving and receiving were done in public, with witnesses, usually members of the religious community receiving the grant and laypeople associated with the donor (family, neighbours, tenants, and associates of various kinds). The public character of those ceremonies was very important not only from the legal point of view, but also because, in that way, donor and recipient were giving a particular message about their status and their mutual relationship. This was one of the ways in which their public identity was created. The layperson was showing his or her piety and generosity by means of donating land to a religious house, but also indicating that he or she was in possession of wealth which allowed them to make such gestures. The countergift expressed, apart from the reciprocity, a special link between the benefactor and the donor. The monks, at least according to the formulae in the charters, had particularly positive feelings towards those individuals, which were expressed by means of the countergift. By giving something back to their benefactors, they were affirming this bond and telling the audience of neighbours and relatives about this. The countergift was therefore an important element in creating a lasting and durable relationship. The obligation created by a countergift was not connected to a particular moment in time, but to their social relationship as a continuing entity.[44]

The cases of countergifts associated with Rievaulx Abbey all had real material value. They were often expressed as money, but also as rings and animals. Countergifts in the form of animals were particularly common. When Sunnive, wife of Lambert de Hoveton, and her two daughters quitclaimed particular plots of land in Hoveton to Rievaulx Abbey, the monks gave them six silver marks and one cow. This was as much a symbolic as a real gift. In that way the abbey secured her quitclaim and compensated her for her loss at the same time. It was not some undercover dealing, for the attestation issued by Engelram, Dean of Ryedale, specified that the countergift was the direct result of their quitclaim.[45] Sunnive's neighbour Peter de Hoveton also quitclaimed five bovates of land in Hoveton to Rievaulx Abbey. The

[44] Arnoud-Jan A. Bijsterveld, 'The Medieval Gift as Agent of Social Bonding and Political Power: A Comparative Approach', in *Medieval Transformations: Text, Power, and Gifts in Context*, ed. by Esther Cohen and Mayke B. de Jong (Leiden: Brill, 2001), pp. 124–56 (p. 124).

[45] 'Monachi vero propter hoc dederunt eisdem mulieribus sex marchas argenti et unam vaccam': *Cartulary*, no. 239.

charter recording this act was issued by Dean Robert of York and the ceremony itself was conducted in York.

> And this [the quitclaim] he offered and he declared an oath in front of Saint Peter's altar, before us all, by his own hand, to hold to it lawfully and steadily. On account of that the monks gave the said Peter and his heirs twenty silver marks and one horse and his wife two cows and ten sheep with ten lambs.[46]

The countergift which Peter received from the monks had a substantial value. The fact that his wife also received part of it, clearly differentiated from that of her husband, indicates that the monks were concerned about her consent to the quitclaim. The different composition of the countergift which both of them received also represents a broader trend. Horses were given primarily, although not exclusively, to men, but cattle, cows, and sheep were often received by either men or women.[47] Since the original quitclaim of Peter to the abbey was concerned with rather insubstantial property, this countergift must have been a result of rather complex relations between the benefactors and the monks and was preceded by negotiations to obtain a property particularly desired by the abbey.

Countergifts to the benefactors of the Cistercian houses were neither straightforwardly symbolic nor purely contractual acts. Most of them played a rather complex role in securing undisputed possession of a given property, but also maintaining a positive relationship with people who might not otherwise become benefactors. Countergifts could make a donation affordable for an individual for whom the cost of a donation would be too high. Such a transaction was called a grant in free alms and was understood as such, but a benefactor was compensated for his/her material loss. The countergifts could also be described as a 'soft option' in their aim of preventing conflict. Giving some compensation was often an effective way of preventing future conflicts. This is particularly visible in the case of countergifts accompanying confirmations. The formulae used there make an explicit link between the confirmation and monastic reciprocity: 'on account of that alienation and confirmation the above said monks gave me two silver marks'.[48]

The public character of most of those ceremonies provided both parties with the security of witnesses. Moreover, the symbolic aspect of the countergifts can best be explored in this context. The benefactors who received something in return from the monks neither were denied, in this way, the spiritual privileges attached to this position, nor was their prestige diminished in any way. Since a gift to the monastery

---

[46] 'et hoc legitime et firmiter tenendum super altare beati Petri optulit et propria manu coram omnibus nobis affidavit. Monachi vero propter hec dederunt eidem Petro et heredibus suis xx. marcas argenti et unam equum et uxori sue duas vaccas et x. oves et decem agnos': *Cartulary*, no. 231.

[47] Jamroziak, 'Making and Breaking', pp. 203–04.

[48] Confirmation of Alice de Gant, 'Propter hanc concessionem et confirmationem dederunt mihi predicti monachi duas marcas argenti': *Cartulary*, no. 159.

was a good deed in itself, such benefactors could expect spiritual rewards regardless of the monks' prayers. The symbolic value of countergifts was also emphasized by the fact that the ceremonies were public, giving witnesses, usually the neighbours and relatives of the benefactor, a message about a close association between the donor and the monastic community.

While the charters discussed throughout this chapter indicate how the practical and legal side of grants to the abbey were intended to function, and how the symbolic gestures between the abbey and its benefactors helped to maintain relationships, there are not many sources which allow us to see how the abbey perceived land acquisition from its lay neighbours. To investigate this problem we have to look at the issue of gift-giving from the perspective of the religious community to see how the monks might think about their neighbours and benefactors. One of the early narrative sources created in the abbey, the *Vita* of Abbot Ailred by Walter Daniel, provides some information. It contains a passage which gives the perspective of the monastic community on the donations. It refers to the time when Ailred was the Abbot of Revesby (a daughter house of Rievaulx in Lincolnshire), but the ideas and sentiments expressed in this passage can also be applied to Rievaulx Abbey.

> The Bishop orders him [Ailred] to preach to the clergy in their local synods and he does so; to bring priests to a better way of life, as he does not fail to do so; to accept grants of land from knights in generous free-alms, and he obeys, since he had realized that in this unsettled time such gifts profited knights and monks alike, for in those days it was hard for any to lead the good life unless they were monks or members of some religious order, so disturbed and chaotic was the land, reduced almost to a desert by the malice, slaughter, and harrying of evil men. And so he desired that land, for which almost all men were fighting to the death, should pass into the hands of the monks for their good; and he knew that to give what they had helped the possessors of goods to their salvation, and that, if they did not give, they might well lose both life and goods without any payment in return.[49]

This extract contains several important ideas which shed some light on the ideology and practice of gift giving. Historically this passage refers to 1143–47, the early years of the reign of King Stephen, which were marked by the disintegration of royal control in Yorkshire and political struggles between prominent noblemen. There is something strongly pragmatic in Walter Daniel's explanation of grant giving. By donations of land to the abbey, people could improve their chances of salvation; moreover the property given to the Church would not fall so easily into the hands of enemies. Therefore, not becoming a benefactor of the abbey was unpractical behaviour — one might not only lose one's lands, but also waste possible spiritual reward. This almost commercial element of Ailred's thinking is stressed by the translator: 'he [Ailred] knew that to give what they had helped the possessors of goods to their salvation, and that, if they did not give, they might well lose both life and goods

[49] *Life of Ailred*, p. 28.

without any payment in return.'[50] The source of the commercial metaphor is biblical, rooted in the vocabulary of the Old Testament, but it does not necessarily mean that its usage, in the late 1160s when Walter Daniel wrote 'The Life', was purely stylistic. Biblical phrases and metaphors were commonly used to express contemporary concerns. Ailred and his biographer were more aware of the realities of the outside world than it might appear from his theological writing. In the older historiography Ailred has been seen mainly as a theologian, author of spiritual tracts, suffering from rather poor health, but more recently this picture has shifted towards seeing Ailred also as an abbot, politician, and active churchman. From a careful reading of the sources it appears that the literary tradition of the Abbot of Rievaulx as 'the gentle Aelred meek and mild, the sensitive soul with genius for friendship, otherworldly because clearly too good for this world' is in striking contrast with the evidence from the charters.[51] McGuire emphasizes that Ailred was aware of the importance of the lay visitors of the abbey, aristocrats, and representatives of the King, and he insisted that they should be received with care and attention, because the house needed their good will.[52] Ailred was a capable manager and administrator in a crucial period for the abbey when the core of its estates was formed. Above all, he understood the process of land accumulation by the abbey and the importance of lay benefactors in this.

Monks were pragmatic, which does not mean cynical. They had goods to offer, such as prayers and other spiritual benefits, which could be exchanged for other goods, in this case land, which was in the hands of laypeople. To the medieval mind, heaven, hell, damnation, or salvation were real, almost on the same level of reality as property. Transactions between laity and monks were not only a legitimate but also an appropriate cause of action to increase the chances of salvation. 'Concern for the salvation of one's soul and the souls of one's ancestors was of fundamental importance to all men and women. It underpinned the medieval psyche.'[53] This belief in salvation as the central goal of one's life and fear of retribution for a sinful life were shared by monks and laymen alike, and on this basis the ideology and practice of gift giving to religious institutions was built.

The names of the powerful barons and their much less significant men who gave grants to Rievaulx were preserved in the charters and eventually in the cartulary together with the locations of their donations. People and places were forever intertwined in this world of personal ties and obligations. According to Berman the

---

[50] 'Et sciebat possessoribus ad salutem proficere Deo dare quod habebant, qui nisi hoc darent eciam forsitan sine mercede cum uita et illud perdidissent': *Life of Ailred*, p. 28.

[51] Marsha L. Dutton, 'The Conversion and Vocation of Aelred of Rievaulx: A Historical Hypothesis', in *England in the Twelfth Century: Proceedings of the 1989 Harlaxton Symposium*, ed. by Daniel Williams (Woodbridge: Boydell, 1990), pp. 31–50 (pp. 48–49).

[52] Brian Patrick McGuire, *Friendship and Community: The Monastic Experience, 350–1250* (Kalamazoo: Cistercian Publications, 1988), p. 319.

[53] Emma Cownie, *Religious Patronage in Anglo-Norman England 1066–1135* (Woodbridge: Boydell, 1998), p. 151.

rhetoric of gift giving and reciprocity persisted in the Cistercian charters in the twelfth century, although by then the purely contractual exchanges between Cistercian monks and their benefactors eradicated any earlier notions.[54] This assessment of Cistercian practice is based on Burgundian sources, but while the monks of Rievaulx certainly did not practice the so-called gift economy, there was a significant amount of property movements back and forth between the abbey and its benefactors. As Stephen Moorhouse points out, 'monastic estates were never static in either size or content'.[55] These changing possessions were due to a variety of reasons: exchange, sale, quitclaim, or lawsuits, all of which occurred in the context of Rievaulx Abbey's estates. The interactions between Rievaulx Abbey and its neighbours and benefactors were occurring simultaneously at many levels: practical, economic, symbolic, and spiritual. The boundaries of these notions were much less clear-cut than our modern understanding. The intertwined motivations, aspirations, and hopes of both laypeople and the monastic community had been reflected in the sources in this tangled manner, which often makes it difficult to see that they were all significant at the same time. This, however, should not prompt us to dismiss them as a smoke screen of pragmatism and cold calculation. The symbolic and spiritual were elements of practices intended to built pragmatic and useful bonds between Rievaulx and its social context of laity, families, and tenurial groups.

---

[54] Constance H. Berman, 'The Debate on Cistercian Contracts: Regarding a Recent Book', *Cîteaux: Commentarii Cistercienses*, 43 (1992), 432–40 (pp. 435–36).

[55] Stephen Moorhouse, 'Monastic Estates: Their Composition and Development', in *The Archaeology of Rural Monasteries*, ed. by Roberta Gilchrist and Harold Mytum, British Archaeological Reports, 203 (Oxford: B.A.R., 1989), pp. 29–81 (p. 37).

Conclusion

The image of the world which is preserved in its cartulary gives the impression that Rievaulx Abbey was a point on which many social networks of North Yorkshire were converging. This remarkable source records the first sixty or seventy years of the existence of the monastic community and its views of its patrons, benefactors, and neighbours. The cartulary was a commemorative as much as a practical tool mapping the abbey's acquisitions in their social context. It is fundamental to our understanding of the early history of Rievaulx and central to this book.

Walter Espec, the founder, was also celebrated in the writing of Ailred of Rievaulx. He played an important role in the early years of the abbey and helped to establish a supportive circle of benefactors from among his followers and tenants. Many of these early links survived for a number of generations, attested by later grants and recurring appearances of family members in witness lists. But the close relationship of the founder and the abbey was broken after Espec's childless death. The distant and largely pragmatic relationship between the Ros family, the patrons, and Rievaulx deteriorated further in the thirteenth century when William de Ros decided to dispute the abbey's rights to Helmsley forest and other early donations from his ancestors. The relatively detailed court rolls give a glimpse of the abbey's strategy for dealing with lay aggressiveness and the growing importance of written documents as legal proof. In the twelfth century many disputes between the abbey and lay people were solved through a process of arbitration by neighbours using oral evidence, but in the following century, the authority of the court and the written word became more evident.

The relationship of Rievaulx Abbey with its lay neighbours was multilayered across various social strata, from barons to small tenants. The world around the abbey was not simply hierarchical, but was more like a three dimensional web. Because of the multitude of vertical connections in the neighbourhood, the abbey developed a great variety of contacts with lay people. The abbey received gifts of land and rents, exchanged properties, brought law-suits against those who encroached on its lands and negotiated mutually convenient agreements with others. Rievaulx was clearly seen by its neighbours as a landowner as much as a religious institution and as an active participant in the local land markets. All these different types of connections between the house and its neighbours often occurred simultaneously. Many families of benefactors of the abbey experienced all types of interactions across three or four generations.

The unsteady fortunes of barons and the rapid changes of possession among fee holders, such as the Mowbrays and Stutevilles, not only resulted in the disputed ownership of many properties, but also forced the abbey to look for benefactors among diverse families and tenurial groups, as well as to ask constantly for confirmations of grants acquired in the past. As I have argued in the second chapter, Rievaulx Abbey was careful and selective when making associations with powerful aristocrats. Whilst aristocratic donations were often larger than those offered by knights and their support carried more weight, they were also capable of exerting negative pressure on the monastery and damaging its interests. The strategy of Rievaulx shows a careful consideration of all these aspects and this approach was also an expression of Cistercian identity. The community of Rievaulx did not refuse to associate with the lay people, but it was a selective involvement in terms of who was allowed to be buried in the monastery and why, and who could be admitted into the fraternity or become its 'special' benefactor. The boundaries of the monastic space were protected literally and symbolically.

It is often asserted in the literature that the early growth of Cistercian foundations owed much to the interest in this order in the first decades of the twelfth century. A close study of Rievaulx and its social context reveals that from the very beginning fashion was only one of the factors. In addition, there was a growing spectrum of religious institutions in the locality to which the laity could give donations, including well-established Benedictine houses, new Augustinian priories, and a number of other Cistercian foundations. The ties of loyalty and family tradition helped Rievaulx Abbey to cultivate a circle of supportive benefactors and neighbours. Although from the early thirteenth century grants of land were smaller and less frequent, the contacts between Rievaulx and its lay neighbours were already well established and were often developed and formalized by the system of landholding. The abbey was a lord to many individuals and also rented other properties from its neighbours. The reappearance of names of people witnessing monastic charters gives an indication of the cycle of individuals who continued to display an attachment to the abbey. They might have been active benefactors, but also, especially from the end of the twelfth and throughout the thirteenth centuries, they might only have witnessed charters as a way of showing their support to the house. A great number of witnesses came from the families of early benefactors such as the Ingrams and Lasceles who lived close to the abbey and its estates. In the later generations these people usually did not give any new grants to the abbey, but their presence at donation ceremonies reinforced affinity between these families and the abbey. These gatherings were of mutual benefit to the abbey and to those who acted as witnesses. It was an opportunity for the abbey to strengthen its ties with the local communities, and the lay people could discuss issues of mutual interest among themselves and with abbey officials. The participation in the donation ceremony by the neighbours allowed them to display their attachment to the religious institution without incurring any material loss themselves.

From the perspective of the abbey, the vertical lord-tenant relations were often secondary in importance to lateral family and neighbourly connections. Cownie explains that '[t]he motivation behind religious patronage was always mixed; primarily governed by locality, lordship and tenurial status, it could also be influenced by ties of family or friendship, by shifts in fashion and by personal preferences and personalities'.[1] This is also true in the case of Rievaulx Abbey. Many of the Mowbrays' tenants and honorial officials granted land to Rievaulx Abbey following the example of, and encouraged by, their lords. The case of another Yorkshire family, the Lacys, shows that their tenants supported each new foundation — the chapel of St Clement's and St John's Abbey in Pontefract and then Nostell Priory.[2] Adam son of Peter de Birkin had strongly personal reasons for his extensive grants to the abbey. Often the precise personal, spiritual, and eschatological motivations of the patrons and benefactors of Rievaulx Abbey are difficult to uncover, but it does not mean that we should assume that they were absent. They were always implicit in the acts of donation and in the formulae of the donation charters. We will never know to what extent these declarations were a reflection of the personal considerations of the individual benefactors, but the people who gave land to Rievaulx Abbey lived in a society in which religion and its practice dominated the prevailing world view and it was hardly possible to perceive human existence in any other terms.

The lay people were the most numerous among the neighbours of the abbey, but were not the only type of neighbours which Rievaulx had to take into account. Other religious houses, Cistercian, Augustinian, or Gilbertine, could not ignore each other. On the contrary, the ideology of Cistercian monasticism encouraged friendships, mutual prayers, and commemorations between the monastic communities and their individual members. Personal contacts and even friendships between abbots helped to establish positive relations between various houses, but often the realities of being close neighbours, sharing the same pastures or forests, brought with them identical problems to those that occurred between the abbey and its lay neighbours. However, religious houses had their own ways of resolving conflict, favouring particularly arbitration by the abbots or priors of the neighbouring institutions, or for more difficult cases between the Cistercian houses, the arbitration by the delegation appointed by the Chapter General. This method of resolving disputes between religious houses was particularly popular in the twelfth century; later the courts of law often became the arena for solving conflicts and was paralleled by the increasing use of written documents instead of the sole reliance on the testimony of neighbours.

---

[1] Emma Cownie, *Religious Patronage in Anglo-Norman England 1066–1135* (Woodbridge: Boydell, 1998), p. 118.

[2] Cownie, *Religious Patronage*, p. 178.

Although the Archbishops of York and Bishops of Durham and their respective chapters were not neighbours of Rievaulx Abbey in a strict sense, they were an important part of its social context. The early history of Rievaulx, particularly during the abbacy of William, was marked by its active participation on the Church arena and the strong belief of the Cistercian monks that they should be actively involved in Church reform. Although the second half of the twelfth century and the subsequent history of the abbey was marked by more local considerations, the officials of the secular Church in the North played an important role in defending the rights of Rievaulx Abbey to its properties. The Archbishops of York and Bishops of Durham were not automatic supporters of the Cistercian monks, and Archbishop Roger of York was famously hostile towards Fountains Abbey. It is a tribute to the diplomatic skills of the Abbots of Rievaulx that the abbey's contacts with him were amicable.

The issue of tithes shaped much of the contacts between Rievaulx and the secular Church in the second half of the twelfth and first half of the thirteenth centuries. It was not simply a financial matter but, more importantly, one of defining Cistercian identity by upholding the order's exemption from the payment of tithes. The compensation payments, which Rievaulx usually negotiated as a settlement, helped to affirm the Cistercian principle whilst solving the financial grievance. Similarly, Rievaulx Abbey's refusal to hold churches and to derive income from the tithes belonging to them was not just an ideological statement, but a practical one as well, which spared this monastic community many of the bitter conflicts with the Archbishops of York which Fountains Abbey suffered on account of its appropriation of churches.

The rituals of reciprocity, commemoration, and friendship discussed in the last chapter had their own practical dimension, particularly in relation to settling disputes and maintaining long-term associations between the abbey and laity. The frequent pragmatic use of ritual was only possible and viable if both the religious community and its neighbours and benefactors believed in the spiritual value of the rituals. The patterns of admission of lay individuals into the confraternity of the abbey shows that fraternity was a useful tool in a whole range of situations which the monastic community could encounter in relation to its lay benefactors and neighbours. Importantly, the case of Rievaulx Abbey also exemplifies a change in the form and intensity of the commemorative practices between the Cistercian model and that of Benedictine and Cluniac houses. Although the Cistercian order significantly curtailed the individualized commemoration of the dead, for practical, economic, as well as ideological reasons, it did not abolish it; nor did it stop using the confraternity system. Moreover, the early tradition of mutual prayers for fellow monastic communities continued to develop in the spirit of Cistercian friendship and brotherly love as shown in the example of the agreement between Rievaulx and Byland.

Rievaulx Abbey, like other Yorkshire Cistercian houses used the tool of countergift to acquire particularly desirable properties. The presence of a countergift should also be seen as an indication of the situation of the donor. Particularly difficult or quarrelsome neighbours were often pacified in that way and disputes settled or averted. The countergifts were also used when a layperson wanted to donate land to the abbey but could not afford to do so without a financial compensation, or if such an individual was in difficulties and had to raise money, yet wanted to obtain some spiritual benefits at the same time. As I have argued in the last chapter, the countergifts were not an evidence of cover-up sales, but of complex negotiations between Rievaulx and its potential benefactors. As the works of Bouchard and Berman show, like many of their monastic predecessors Cistercian houses used countergifts, but this exchange was not an element of 'gift economy'. The example of Rievaulx Abbey shows again that countergifts were a clearly defined, practical tool for deliberately acquiring secure, permanent possession of land. The case of Rievaulx Abbey is also an important contribution to the debate on Cistercian identity and practice. The focus of this book lies in showing an example of variations in Cistercian practice within the crucial period of the order's development. The exploration of Rievaulx Abbey provides a strong argument that the conclusion drawn from the French evidence cannot be applied indiscriminately to the British Isles, and that Northern and Central European houses provide more useful parallels. The context of belonging to the international order not only gave Rievaulx ideological and practical support, but allowed it to operate according to the local needs and expectations whilst maintaining its Cistercian identity. The approach of the abbey to the issue of payment of tithes is a clear example of that.

Despite the existence of the cartulary of Rievaulx Abbey, which is a rich and unique source for the early history of the institution, in particular its contacts with neighbours, benefactors, other religious houses, and prelates, there is much that we do not know about Rievaulx because of the degree of destruction of other written sources produced there. Yet the existing evidence shows an intriguing case of a Cistercian house which, although careful in its association with the lay world, was cautiously navigating in the complex world of social ties to become a powerful and influential element of the religious, economic, and social landscape of medieval Yorkshire.

Bibliography

Primary Sources

Unpublished

London, British Library:
Additional MS 40008
Cotton Claudius B. iii
Cotton Claudius D. xi
Cotton Julius D. i
Additional Charters: 20564; 20578
Cotton Charters: V 13; XVIII 13, 14
Egerton Charters: 585; 2245; 2247–50; 2254
Harleian Charters: 43 B. 47; 43 G. 23–24; 83 E. 52; 83 G. 38
Stowe Charters: 372; 465; 573

Northallerton, North Yorkshire County Record Office:
Orde-Powlett papers, ZDO1/0208–0256

Oxford, Bodleian Library:
Dodsworth MSS: vii; viii; lxxxv; xciv; xcviii
MS Fairfax 7

Published

Abstract of the Charters and other Documents contained in the Chartulary of the Priory of Bridlington, ed. by W. T. Lancaster (Leeds: published privately, 1912)

Abstracts of the Charters and other Documents contained in the Chartulary of the Cistercian Abbey of Fountains, ed. by W. T. Lancaster, 2 vols (Leeds: J. Whitehead & Son, 1915)

Acta Sanctorum, ed. by G. Henschen and D. Papenbroch, vol. Julii 6 (Paris: Victor Palmé, 1867)

Ailred of Rievaulx, 'De sanctimoniali de Wattun', *Patrologiae Latina Cursus Completus*, ed. by J.-P. Migne, vol. CXCV (Paris, 1855), cols 789–96

———, 'Relatio de Standardo', in *Chronicles of the Reigns of Stephen, Henry II and Richard I*, vol. III, ed. by Richard Howlett, Rolls Series, 82 (London: Longman, 1886), pp. 181–99

——— [as Aelred of Rievaulx], 'Sermo in synodo de pastore et mercenario et fure et lupo', in *Sermones inediti B. Aelredi abbatis Rievallensis*, ed. by C. H. Talbot, Series scriptorum S. Ordinis Cisterciensis, 1 (Rome: Apud Curiam Generalem Sacri Ordinis Cisterciensis, 1952), pp. 150–56

Bernard of Clairvaux, *The Letters of St Bernard*, ed. and trans. by B. Scott James (London: Burns Oates, 1953)

Calendar of Charter Rolls, 6 vols (London: H.M.S.O., 1903–27)

Calendar of Close Rolls (London: H.M.S.O., 1892–)

Calendar of Entries in the Papal Registers Relating to Great Britain and Ireland, vol. I, *Papal Letters (1198–1304)*, ed. by W. H. Bliss (London, 1893)

Calendar of Patent Rolls (London: H.M.S.O., 1901–)

Canivez, Joseph, *Statuta Capitulorum Ordinis Cisterciensis ab anno 1116 ad annum 1786*, 8 vols (Louvain-la-Neuve: Revue d'histoire ecclèsiastique, 1933–41)

Cartularium de Abbatie de Rievalle, ed. by John C. Atkinson, Surtees Society, 83 (Durham: Andrews, 1889)

Cartularium Prioratus de Gyseburne Eboracensis Dioeceseos Ordinis S. Augustini, vol. I, ed. by W. Brown, Surtees Society, 86 (Durham: Andrews, 1889–94)

The Cartulary of Byland Abbey, ed. by Janet Burton (Woodbridge: Boydell and Brewer for the Surtees Society, forthcoming)

The Cartulary of the Cistercian Abbey of St Mary of Sallay in Craven, vols I–II, ed. by Joseph McNulty, Yorkshire Archaeological Society Record Series, 87 and 90 (Wakefield: Yorkshire Archaeological Society, 1933–34)

The Cartulary of St John of Pontefract, vol. II, ed. by Richard Holmes, Yorkshire Archaeological Society Record Series, 30 (Leeds: Yorkshire Archaeological Society, 1902)

Charters of the Honour of Mowbray 1107–1191, ed. by Diane E. Greenway, British Academy Records of Social and Economic History, n.s., 1 (London: Oxford University Press, 1972)

Charters of the Vicar Choral of York Minster: City of York and its Suburbs to 1546, ed. by Nigel J. Tringham, Yorkshire Archaeological Society Record Series, 148 (Leeds: Yorkshire Archaeological Society, 1993)

Chronica Monasterii de Melsa: A fundatione usque annum 1396 auctore Thoma de Burton, abbate, vols I–III, ed. by E. A. Bond, Rolls Series, 43 (London: Longman, 1866–68)

Collectanae Topographica et Genealogica, vol. V (London, 1838)

Curia Regis Rolls (London: H.M.S.O., 1922–)

Daniel, Walter, *The Life of Ailred of Rievaulx*, trans. and introd. by F. M. Powicke (London: Nelson, 1950)

Decrees of the Ecumenical Councils, vol. I, *Nicea I to Lateran V*, ed. by Norman P. Tanner (London: Sheed and Ward, 1990)

Dugdale, William, *Monasticon Anglicanum*, rev. by J. Caley, H. Ellis, and B. Bandinel, vol. V (London, 1846)

Durham Episcopal Charters 1071–1152, ed. by H. S. Offler, Surtees Society, 179 (Gateshead: Northumberland Press, 1968)

Early Yorkshire Charters, ed. by William Farrer, vols I–III (Edinburgh: Ballantyne, Hanson, 1914–16) and Charles Clay, vols IV–XII, Yorkshire Archaeological Society Record Series, extra series (Wakefield: Yorkshire Archaeological Society, 1935–65)

English Episcopal Acta, vol. V, *York 1070–1154*, ed. by Janet Burton (Oxford: British Academy, 1988)

English Episcopal Acta, vol. XX, *York 1154–1181*, ed. by Marie Lovatt (Oxford: British Academy, 2000)

Excerpta e rotulis finium in turri londonensi asservatis Henrico regis A.D. 1216–1272, vol. I, ed. by Charles Roberts, Record Commission (London: G. Eyre, 1835)

Feet of Fines for the County of York from 1218 to 1231, ed. by John Parker, Yorkshire Archaeological Society Record Series, 62 (Leeds: Yorkshire Archaeological Society, 1921)

Feet of Fines for the County of York from 1232 to 1246, ed. by John Parker, Yorkshire Archaeological Society Record Series, 67 (Leeds: Yorkshire Archaeological Society, 1925)

Feet of Fines for the County of York from 1246 to 1272, ed. by John Parker, Yorkshire Archaeological Society Record Series, 82 (Leeds: Yorkshire Archaeological Society, 1932)

'The Foundation of Kirkstall Abbey', trans. by E. K. Clark, in *Miscellanea*, Thoresby Society, 4 (Leeds: Thoresby, 1893)

The Great Roll of the Pipe, 7th year of John, Michaelmas 1205, ed. by Sidney Smith, Pipe Roll Society, n.s., 19 (London: Pipe Roll Society, 1941)

The Great Roll of the Pipe 11th year of John, ed. by Doris Stenton, Pipe Roll Society, n.s., 24 (London: Pipe Roll Society, 1949)

The Great Roll of the Pipe for the Thirty-First Year of the Reign of King Henry the Second, A.D. 1184–1185, Publications of the Pipe Roll Society, 34 (London: St Catherine Press, 1913)

Guignard, Ph., *Les Primitifs de la règle cistercienne: Publiés d'après les manuscrits de l'Abbaye de Cîteaux* (Dijon: Imprimerie Darantiere, 1878)

'Historia Ricardi Prioris Ecclesiae Haugustaldensis, de Gesti Regis Stephani', in *Chronicles of the Reigns of Stephen, Henry II and Richard I*, vol. III, ed. by Richard Howlett, Rolls Series, 82 (London: Longman, 1886), pp. 137–78

Historical Manuscripts Commission, *The Manuscripts of the Duke of Rutland at Belvoir Castle*, vol. IV (London: H.M.S.O., 1905)

The Honour and Forest of Pickering, ed. by Robert Bell Turton, North Riding Record Society, n.s., 4 (London: North Riding Record Society, 1897)

Magnum Rotulum Scaccarii de anno tricesimo-primo regni Henrici Primi, ed. by Joseph Hunter (London, 1833)

Narrative and Legislative Texts from Early Cîteaux, ed. and trans. by Chrysogonus Waddell, Studia et Documenta, 9 (Pontigny: Cîteaux-Commentarii Cistercienses, 1999)

Notes on the Religious and Secular Houses of Yorkshire, 2 vols, ed. by William P. Baildon, Yorkshire Archaeological Society Record Series, 17 and 81 (London: Yorkshire Archaeological Society, 1895 and 1931)

Original Papal Documents in England and Wales from the Accession of Pope Innocent III to the Death of Pope Benedict XI (1198–1304), ed. by Jane E. Sayers (Oxford: Oxford University Press, 1999)

Papal Decretals Relating to the Diocese of Lincoln in the Twelfth Century, ed. by W. Holzman and R. Kemp, Lincoln Record Society, 47 (Lincoln: Lincoln Record Society, 1954)

Papsturkunden in England, ed. by Walter Holtzmann, vols I and II (Berlin: Weidmann, 1931–36); vol. III (Göttingen: Vandenhoeck & Ruprecht, 1952)

Paris, Matthew, *Historia Anglorum*, 3 vols, ed. by Frederic Madden, Rolls Series, 44 (London: Longman, 1866–69)

Patent Rolls of the Reign of Henry III, 6 vols (London: H.M.S.O., 1901–13)

Pedes Finium Eboracensium Regente Johanne AD *MCXCIX–*AD *MCCXIV*, Surtees Society, 94 (Durham: Andrews, 1897)

Pleas before the King or his Justices 1198–1212, ed. by Doris M. Stenton, Selden Society, 83 (London: Bernard Quaritch, 1967)

Red Book of the Exchequer, vol. I, ed. by Hubert Hall, Rolls Series, 89 (London: Eyre & Spottiswoode, 1896)

Regesta regum Anglo-Normannorum 1066–1154, vol. III, ed. by H. A. Cronne and R. H. C. Davis (Oxford: Clarendon Press, 1968)

Reginaldi Monachi Dunelmensis Libellus de Admirandis Beati Cuthberti, ed. by James Raine, Surtees Society, 1 (London: J. B. Nichols, 1835)

The Register of John Le Romeyn Lord Archbishop of York 1286–1296, part 1, ed. by W. Brown, Surtees Society, 123 (Durham: Andrews; London: B. Quaritch, 1913)

The Register of Rolls of Walter Gray Lord Archbishop of York 1215–1255, ed. by J. Raine, Surtees Society, 56 (Durham: Andrews, 1872)

The Register of Thomas of Corbridge Lord Archbishop of York 1300–1304, vol. I, ed. by W. Brown, Surtees Society, 138 (Durham: Andrews; London: B. Quaritch, 1925)

The Register of Walter Giffard Lord Archbishop of York 1266–1279, ed. by W. Brown, Surtees Society, 109 (Durham: Andrews, 1904)

The Register of William Wickwane Lord Archbishop of York 1279–1285, ed. by W. Brown, Surtees Society, 114 (Durham: Andrews, 1907)

Rufford Charters, ed. by C. J. Holdsworth, 2 vols, Thoroton Society Record Series, 29 (Nottingham: Thoroton Society, 1972)

Sancti Bernardi Opera, ed. by Jean Leclerq, C. H. Talbot, and H. Rochais (Rome: Editiones Cistercienses, 1977)

Symonis Monachis Opera Omnia, vol. II, ed. by Thomas Arnold, Rolls Series, 75 (London: Longman, 1885)

The Taxatio Database, ed. by Jeff Denton, www.taxatio.man.ac.uk

Testamenta Eboracensia: A Selection of Wills from the Registry at York, vol. V, Surtees Society, 79 (London: J. B. Nichols, 1884)

Twelfth-Century Statutes from the Cistercian General Chapter, ed. by Chrysogonus Waddell, Studia et Documenta, 12 (Brecht: Cîteaux-Commentarii Cistercienses, 2002)

William of Newburgh, 'Historia Rerum Anglicarum', in *Chronicles of the Reigns of Stephen, Henry II and Richard I*, vol. I, ed. by Richard Howlett, Rolls Series, 82 (London: Longman, 1884), pp. 20–503

York Minster Fasti being notes on the dignitaries, archdeacons and prebendaries in the church of York prior to the year 1307, vol. II, ed. Charles Travis Clay, Yorkshire Archaeological Society Record Series, 124 (Wakefield: Yorkshire Archaeological Society, 1959)

Yorkshire Assize Rolls, for the Reign of King John and King Henry III, ed. by C. T. Clay, Yorkshire Archaeological Society Record Series, 44 (Leeds: Yorkshire Archaeological Society, 1911)

Yorkshire Deeds, vols I and II, ed. by W. Brown, Yorkshire Archaeological Society Record Series, 39 and 50 (Leeds: Yorkshire Archaeological Society, 1909 and 1914)

Yorkshire Inquisitions, vols II–III, ed. by William Brown, Yorkshire Archaeological Society Record Series, 23 and 31 (Leeds: Yorkshire Archaeological Society, 1898 and 1902)

Yorkshire Lay Subsidy being a Fifteenth Collected 30 Edward I (1301), ed. by William Brown, Yorkshire Archaeological Society Record Series, 21 (Leeds: Yorkshire Archaeological Society, 1897)

Secondary Literature

Alfonso, Isabel, 'Cistercians and Feudalism', *Past and Present*, no. 133 (1991), 3–30

Angenendt, Arnold, 'Theologie und Liturgie der mittelalterlichen Toten-Memoria', in *Memoria: Der geschichtliche Zeugniswert des liturgischen Gedenkens im Mittelalter*, ed. by Karl Schmid and Joachim Wollasch, Münstersche Mittelalter-Schriften, 48 (Munich: Wilhelm Fink, 1984), pp. 79–199

Baker, Derek, 'Ailred of Rievaulx and Walter Espec', *Haskins Society Journal: Studies in Medieval History*, 1 (1989), 91–98

———, 'Legend and Reality: The Case of Waldef of Melrose', in *Church, Society and Politics*, ed. by Derek Baker, Studies in Church History, 12 (Oxford: Blackwell, 1975), pp. 59–82

———, 'Patronage in the Early Twelfth-Century Church: Walter Espec, Kirkham and Rievaulx', in *Traditio – Krisis – Renovatio aus Theologischer Sicht: Festschrift Winfried Zeller um 65. Geburtstag*, ed. by Bernd Jaspers and Rudolf Mohr (Marburg: Elwert, 1976), pp. 92–100

———, 'The Surest Road to Heaven', in *Sanctity and Secularity: The Church and the World*, ed. by Derek Baker, Studies in Church History, 10 (Oxford: Blackwell, 1973), pp. 45–58

———, '*Viri religiosi* and the York Election Dispute', in *Councils and Assemblies*, ed. by G. J. Cuming and Derek Baker, Studies in Church History, 7 (Cambridge: Cambridge University Press, 1971), pp. 87–100

Bates, David, 'Normandy and England after 1066', *English Historical Review*, 104 (1989), 851–80

Bedos-Rezak, Brigitte, 'Diplomatic Sources and Medieval Documentary Practices', in *The Past and Future of Medieval Studies*, ed. by John Van Engen, Notre Dame Conference in Medieval Studies, 4 (Notre Dame: University of Notre Dame Press, 1994), pp. 313–43

Belisle, Augustin, 'Pastoral Spirituality of Aelred of Rievaulx', *Studia Monastica*, 25 (1983), 93–113

Bell, David N., review of Newman, *The Boundaries of Charity*, in *The Medieval Review*, at http://www.hti.umich.edu/t/tmr/ dated 1997.03.10.

Berman, Constance H., 'Cistercian Development and the Order's Acquisition of Churches and Tithes in Southwestern France', *Revue Bénédictine*, 91 (1981), 193–203

———, *The Cistercian Evolution: The Invention of a Religious Order in Twelfth-Century Europe* (Philadelphia: University of Pennsylvania Press, 2000)

———, 'The Cistercian Mystery: How Was the Order Formed and by Whom? Can the Anglo-Norman Sources Elucidate the Problem?', *Haskins Society Journal: Studies in Medieval History*, 13 (1999), 1–19

———, 'The Debate on Cistercian Contracts: Regarding a Recent Book', *Cîteaux: Commentarii Cistercienses*, 43 (1992), 432–40

———, 'The Development of Cistercian Economic Practice during the Lifetime of Bernard of Clairvaux: The Historical Perspective on Innocent II's 1132 Privilege', in *Bernardus Magister*, ed. by John R. Sommerfeldt, Cistercian Studies Series, 135 (Spencer, MA: Cistercian Publications, 1992), pp. 303–13

Bijsterveld, Arnoud-Jan A., 'The Medieval Gift as Agent of Social Bonding and Political Power: A Comparative Approach', in *Medieval Transformations: Text, Power, and Gifts in Context*, ed. by Esther Cohen and Mayke B. de Jong (Leiden: Brill, 2001), pp. 124–56

Bison, John, 'Gilling Castle', *Yorkshire Archaeological Journal*, 19 (1906–07), 105–92

Bond, C. J., 'Water Management in the Rural Monastery', in *The Archaeology of Rural Monasteries*, ed. by Roberta Gilchrist and Harold Mytum, British Archaeological Reports, 203 (Oxford: B.A.R, 1989), pp. 83–111

Bouchard, Constance B., 'Cistercian Ideals versus Reality: 1134 Reconsidered', *Cîteaux: Commentarii Cistercienses*, 39 (1988), 217–31

———, *Holy Entrepreneurs: Cistercians, Knights and Economic Exchange in Twelfth Century Burgundy* (Ithaca, NY: Cornell University Press, 1991)

———, 'Knights and the Foundation of the Cistercian Houses in Burgundy', in *Erudition at God's Service*, ed. by John R. Sommerfeldt, Studies in Medieval Cistercian History, 11 (Kalamazoo: Cistercian Publications, 1987), pp. 315–22

———, 'Monastic Cartularies: Organizing Eternity', in *Charters, Cartularies, and Archive: The Preservation and Transmission of Documents in the Medieval West*, ed. by Adam J. Kosto and Anders Winroth, Papers in Medieval Studies, 17 (Toronto: Pontifical Institute of Mediaeval Studies, 2002), pp. 22–32

Brentano, Robert, *York Metropolitan Jurisdiction and Papal Judges Delegate (1279–1296)*, University of California Publications in History, 58 (Berkeley: University of California Press, 1959)

Burton, Janet E., 'The Abbeys of Byland and Jervaulx and the Problem of the English Savigniacs, 1134–1156', in *Monastic Studies: Continuity and Tradition*, vol. II, ed. by Judith Loades (Bangor: Headstart History, 1991), pp. 119–31

———, 'A Confraternity List from St Mary's Abbey, York', *Revue Bénédictine*, 89 (1979), 325–33

———, 'The Estates and Economy of Rievaulx Abbey in Yorkshire', *Cîteaux: Commentarii Cistercienses*, 49 (1998), 29–94

———, 'The Foundation of the British Cistercian Houses', in *Cistercian Art and Architecture in the British Isles*, ed. by Christopher Norton and David Park (Cambridge: Cambridge University Press, 1986), pp. 24–39

———, *Kirkham Priory from Foundation to Dissolution*, Borthwick Paper, no. 86 (York: Borthwick Institute of Historical Research, 1995)

———, 'Monasteries and Parish Churches in Eleventh- and Twelfth-Century Yorkshire', *Northern History*, 23 (1987), 39–50

———, *Monastic and Religious Orders in Britain 1000–1300* (Cambridge: Cambridge University Press, 1994)

———, *The Monastic Order in Yorkshire, 1069–1215* (Cambridge: Cambridge University Press, 1999)

———, 'The Origins and Development of the Religious Orders in Yorkshire c. 1069–1200' (unpublished doctoral thesis, University of York, 1977)

———, 'The Settlement of Disputes between Byland Abbey and Newburgh Priory', *Yorkshire Archaeological Journal*, 55 (1983), 67–72

Butler, Lawrence, 'The Archaeology of Rural Monasteries in England and Wales', in *The Archaeology of Rural Monasteries*, ed. by Roberta Gilchrist and Harold Mytum, British Archaeological Reports, 203 (Oxford: B.A.R., 1989), pp. 1– 28

Cassidy-Welch, Megan, *Monastic Spaces and their Meanings: Thirteenth-Century English Cistercian Monasteries*, Medieval Church Studies, 1 (Turnhout: Brepols, 2001)

Chandler, Victoria, 'Politics and Piety: Influence on Charitable Donations during the Anglo-Norman Period', *Revue Bénédictine*, 90 (1980), 63–71

Chłopocka, Helena, and Winfried Schich, 'Die Ausbreitung des Zisterzienserordens östlich von Elbe und Saale', in *Die Zisterzienser: Ordensleben zwischen Ideal und Wirklichkeit* (Cologne: Rheinland-Verlag, 1981), pp. 93–104

Clanchy, M. T., *From Memory to Written Record: England 1066–1307*, 2nd edn (Oxford: Blackwell, 1993)

Clay, C. T., 'Notes on the Chronology of the Early Deans of York', *Yorkshire Archaeological Journal*, 34 (1938–39), 361–78

———, 'Notes on the Early Archdeacons in the Church of York', *Yorkshire Archaeological Journal*, 36 (1944–49), 269–87, 409–34

C[okayne], G. E., *Complete Peerage, or a History of the Houses of Lords and all its Members from the Earliest Times*, rev. by V. Gibbs, H. A. Doubleday, and G. H. White, 13 vols (London: St Catherine Press, 1910–59)

Constable, Giles, 'Aelred of Rievaulx and the Nun of Watton: An Episode in the Early History of the Gilbertine Order', in *Medieval Women: Studies in Church History, Subsidia I*, ed. by Derek Baker (Oxford: Blackwell, 1978), pp. 205–26

———, *Monastic Tithes from their Origins to the Twelfth Century* (Cambridge: Cambridge University Press, 1964)

———, *The Reformation of the Twelfth Century* (Cambridge: Cambridge University Press, 1996)

Coppack, Glyn, *Book of Abbeys and Priories* (London: English Heritage, 1990)

———, 'Some Descriptions of Rievaulx Abbey in 1538–39: The Disposition of a Major Cistercian Precinct in the Early Sixteenth Century', *Journal of the British Archaeological Association*, 139 (1986), 100–33

Coppack, Glyn, and Peter Fergusson, *Rievaulx Abbey* (London: English Heritage, 1994)

Coss, Peter, *Lordship, Knighthood and Locality: A Study in English Society, c. 1180–1280* (Cambridge: Cambridge University Press, 1991)

Cowdrey, H. E. J., 'Legal Problems Raised by Agreements of Confraternity', in 'Die mittelalterliche Lebensform der Verbrüderung', in *Memoria: Der geschichtliche Zeugniswert des liturgischen Gedenkens im Mittelalter*, ed. by Karl Schmid and Joachim Wollasch, Münstersche Mittelalter-Schriften, 48 (Munich: Wilhelm Fink, 1984), pp. 233–54

———, 'Unions and Confraternity with Cluny', *Journal of Ecclesiastical History*, 16 (1965), 152–62

Cownie, Emma, *Religious Patronage in Anglo-Norman England 1066–1135* (Woodbridge: Boydell, 1998)

Crouch, David, *The Beaumont Twins: The Roots and Branches of Power in the Twelfth Century* (Cambridge: Cambridge University Press, 1986)

———, 'From Stenton to McFarlane: Models of Society of the Twelfth and Thirteenth Centuries', *Transactions of the Royal Historical Society*, 6th series, 5 (1995), 179–200

———, *The Image of Aristocracy in Britain, 1000–1300* (London: Routledge, 1992)

———, *The Reign of King Stepen, 1135–1154* (London: Harlow, 2000)

Dalton, Paul, *Conquest, Anarchy and Lordship: Yorkshire, 1066–1154* (Cambridge: Cambridge University Press, 1994)

———, 'Eustace Fitz John and the Politics of Anglo-Norman England: The Rise and Survival of a Twelfth-Century Royal Servant', *Speculum*, 71 (1996), 358–83

———, 'Scottish Influence on Durham 1066–1214', in *Anglo-Norman Durham 1093–1193*, ed. by D. Rollason and others (Woodbridge: Boydell, 1994), pp. 339–52

Davis, G. R. C., *Medieval Cartularies of Great Britain: A Short Catalogue* (London: Longman, 1958)

Delamotte, P. H., and J. Cundall, *A Photographic Tour among the Abbeys of Yorkshire* (London, 1856)

Dictionary of National Biography, ed. by L. Stephen and S. Lee, 63 vols (London, 1885–1900)

Dobson, R. B, *The Jews of Medieval York and the Massacre of March 1190*, Borthwick Paper, no. 45 (York: St Anthony's Press, 1974)

Donkin, R. A., 'The Cistercian Grange in England in the Twelfth and Thirteenth Centuries with Special Reference to Yorkshire', *Studia Monastica*, 6 (1964), 94–144

Duby, George, *The Early Growth of the European Economy: Warriors and Peasants from the Seventh to the Twelfth Century*, trans. by Howard B. Clarke (Ithaca, NY: Cornell University Press, 1974)

———, *Rural Economy and Country Life in the Medieval West*, trans. by Cynthia Postan (Columbia: University of South Carolina Press, 1990)

Dutton, Marsha L., 'Aelred, Historian: Two Portraits in Plantagenet Myth', *Cistercian Studies Quarterly*, 28 (1993), 113–43

———, 'The Conversion and Vocation of Aelred of Rievaulx: A Historical Hypothesis', in *England in the Twelfth Century: Proceedings of the 1989 Harlaxton Symposium*, ed. by Daniel Williams (Woodbridge: Boydell, 1990), pp. 31–50

———, 'Introduction' to Walter Daniel, *The Life of Ailred of Rievaulx*, trans. by F. M. Powicke (Kalamazoo: Cistercian Publications, 1994), pp. 7–88

Early Yorkshire Families, ed. by Charles Clay and Diane E. Greenway, Yorkshire Archaeological Society Record Series, 85 (Leeds: Yorkshire Archaeological Society, 1973)

English, Barbara, *The Lords of Holderness 1086–1260: A Study in Feudal Society* (Oxford: Oxford University Press, 1979)

The English Church and the Papacy in the Middle Ages, ed. by C. H. Lawrence (Stroud: Sutton, 1999)

Epperlein, Siegfried, 'Gründungsmythos deutscher Zisterzienserklöster westlich und östlich der Elbe im hohen Mittelalter und der Bericht des Leubuser Mönches im 14. Jahrhundert', *Jahrbuch für Wirtschaftsgeschichte*, 3 (1967), 303–35

Evans-Pritchard, Edward, *Anthropology and History: A Lecture Delivered in the University of Manchester* (Manchester: Manchester University Press, 1961)

Fasti Ecclesiae Anglicanae 1066–1300, vol. VI, *York*, comp. by Diana E. Greenway (London: University of London, 1999)

Fergusson, Peter, '"Porta Patens Esto": Notes on Early Cistercian Gatehouses in the North of England', in *Medieval Architecture and its Intellectual Context: Studies in Honour of Peter Kidson*, ed. by Eric Fernie and Paul Crossley (London: Hambledon Press, 1990), pp. 47–59

Fergusson, Peter, Stuart Harrison, and Glyn Coppack, *Rievaulx Abbey: Community, Architecture, Memory* (New Haven: Yale University Press, 2000)

Foulds, Trevor, 'Medieval Cartularies', *Archives*, 18 (1988), 3–35

France, James, *The Cistercians in Scandinavia* (Kalamazoo: Cistercian Publications, 1992)

Freeman, Elizabeth, *Narratives of a New Order: Cistercian Historical Writing in England, 1150–1220*, Medieval Church Studies, 2 (Turnhout: Brepols, 2002)

———, 'Nuns in the Public Sphere: Ailred of Rievaulx's *De Sanctimoniali de Wattun* and the Gendering of Authority', *Comitatus*, 27 (1996), 55–80

Galbraith, W. H., 'The Death of a Champion', in *Studies in Medieval History Presented to Frederick Maurice Powicke*, ed. by R. W. Hunt, W. A. Pantin, and R. W. Southern (Oxford: Clarendon Press, 1948), pp. 283–95

Gallagher, Philip F., 'Conditions of Land Tenure and their Religious Implications', in *Studies in Medieval Cistercian History*, vol. II, ed. by John R. Sommerfeldt (Kalamazoo: Cistercian Publications, 1976), pp. 106–22

Geary, Patrick, 'Entre Gestion et Gesta', in *Les Cartularies: Actes de la Table ronde organisée par l'École nationale des chartes et le G.D.R. 121 du C.N.R.S. (Paris, 5–7 décembre 1991)*, ed. by Olivier Guyotjeannin, Laurent Morelle, and Michel Parisse, Mémoires et Documents de L'école des Chartes, 39 (Paris: École des Chartes, 1993), pp. 13–26

———, *Phantoms of Remembrance: Memory and Oblivion at the End of the First Millennium* (Princeton: Princeton University Press, 1994)

Genet, Jean-Philippe, 'Cartulaires, registres et histoire: L'example anglais', in *Le Métier d'historien au moyen âge: Études sur l'historiographie médiévale*, ed. by Bernard Guenée (Paris: Université de Paris I Panthéon-Sorbonne, Centre de recherches sur l'histoire de l'Occident médiéval, 1977), pp. 95–138

Glidden, Aelred, 'Aelred the Historian: The Account of the Battle of Standard', in *Erudition at God's Service*, ed. by John R. Sommerfeldt, Studies in Medieval Cistercian History, 11 (Kalamazoo: Cistercian Publications, 1987), pp. 175–84

Golding, Brian, 'Burials and Benefactors: An Aspect of Monastic Patronage in Thirteenth-Century England', in *Symposium on England in the Thirteenth Century: Harlaxton Conference Proceedings*, ed. by Mark Ormrod (Harlaxton: Harlaxton College, 1985), pp. 64–75

———, *Gilbert of Sempringham and the Gilbertine Order c. 1130–c. 1300* (Oxford: Clarendon Press, 1995)

———, 'St Bernard and St Gilbert', in *The Influence of Saint Bernard: Anglican Essays*, ed. by Benedicta Ward, Fairacres Publications, 60 (Oxford: S.L.G. Press, 1976), pp. 42–52

Goody, Jack, *The European Family: An Historico-Anthropological Essay* (Oxford: Blackwell, 2000)

Gransden, Antonia, *Historical Writing in England c. 550 to c. 1307* (London: Routledge, 1974)

Graves, Coburn V., 'The Economic Activities of the Cistercians in Medieval England (1128–1307)', *Analecta Sacri Ordinis Cisterciensis*, 13 (1957), 3–60

Green, Judith, *The Aristocracy of Norman England* (Cambridge: Cambridge University Press, 1997)

———, 'Aristocratic Loyalty on the Northern Frontiers of England c. 1100–1174', in *England in the Twelfth Century: Proceedings of the 1988 Harlaxton Symposium*, ed. by Daniel Williams (Woodbridge: Boydell, 1990), pp. 83–100

———, *The Government of England under Henry I* (Cambridge: Cambridge University Press, 1986)

Hall, Jackie, 'The Legislative Background to the Burial of Laity and other Patrons in Cistercian Abbeys', *Cîteaux: Commentarii Cistercienses*, special issue edited by Jacke Hall and Christine Kratzke, forthcoming

Hallas, G. M., 'Archiepiscopal Relations with Clergy of the Diocese of York 1279–99', *Yorkshire Archaeological Journal*, 60 (1988), 47–63

Harper-Bill, C., 'The Piety of the Anglo-Norman Knightly Class', in *Proceedings of the Battle Conference on Anglo-Norman Studies II 1979*, ed. by Allen R. Brown (Woodbridge: Boydell, 1980), pp. 62–77

Haseldine, Julian, 'Friendship and Rivalry: The Role of *Amicitia* in Twelfth-Century Monastic Relations', *Journal of Ecclesiastical History*, 44 (1993), 390–414

Hill, Bennett D., *English Cistercian Monasteries and their Patrons in the Twelfth Century* (Urbana: University of Illinois Press, 1968)

A History of Helmsley, Rievaulx and District, ed. by John McDonnell (York: Stonegate Press, 1963)

Hodgson, R. I., 'Medieval Colonisation in Northern Ryedale', *Ryedale Historian*, 10 (1980), 47–62

Holdsworth, Christopher, *The Piper and the Tune: Medieval Patrons and Monks*, The Stenton Lecture 1990 (Reading: University of Reading, 1991)

Hollister, C. Warren, *Henry I*, ed. by Amanda Clark Frost (Yale: Yale University Press, 2001)

———, 'Henry I and the Anglo-Norman Magnates', in his *Monarchy, Magnates and Institutions in the Anglo-Norman World* (London: Hambledon Press, 1986), part 10, pp. 93–107

———, 'The Origins of English Treasury', in his *Monarchy, Magnates, and Institutions in the Anglo-Norman World* (London: Hambeldon Press, 1986), pp. 209–22

Hollister, C. Warren, and John W. Baldwin, 'The Rise of Administrative Kingship: Henry I and Philip August', *American Historical Review*, 83 (1978), 867–905

Hudson, John, *Land, Law, and Lordship in Anglo-Norman England* (Oxford: Clarendon Press, 1994)

Jamroziak, Emilia, 'Considerate Brothers or Predatory Neighbours? Rievaulx Abbey and Other Monastic Houses in the Twelfth and Thirteenth Century', *Yorkshire Archaeological Journal*, 73 (2001), 29–40

———, 'Making and Breaking the Bonds: Yorkshire Cistercians and their Neighbours', in *Beyond the Architecture of Solitude: Studies on Cistercians, Art and Architecture*, ed. by Terryl Kinder (Turnhout: Brepols, 2004), pp. 198–206

———, 'Rievaulx Abbey and its Patrons: Between Cooperation and Conflict', *Cîteaux: Commentarii Cistercienses*, 53 (2002), 51–71

———, 'Rievaulx Abbey as a Wool Producer in the Late Thirteenth Century: Cistercians, Sheep and Big Debts', *Northern History*, 40 (2003), 197–218

Janauschek, Leopoldus, *Originum Cisterciensium*, vol. I (Vienna, 1877)

Johnson, Penelope D., *Prayer, Patronage and Power: The Abbey of la Trinité, Vendôme, 1032–1187* (New York: New York University Press, 1981)

Kaczmarek, Michał, 'Liturgia memoratywna u Cystersów' (Commemorative liturgy of the Cistercian order), *Nasza Przeszłość*, 83 (1994), 281–93

Karras, R. M., 'Friendship and Love in the Lives of Two Twelfth-Century English Saints', *Journal of Medieval History*, 14 (1988), 305–20

Knowles, David, 'The Case of St William of York', in his *The Historian and Character and other Essays* (Cambridge: Cambridge University Press, 1963), pp. 76–97

———, *The Monastic Order in England: A History of its Development from the Times of St Dunstan to the Fourth Lateran Council 940–1216* (Cambridge: Cambridge University Press, 1963)

Knowles, David, and R. Neville Hadcock, *Medieval Religious Houses, England and Wales* (London: Longman, 1971)

Lavoie, Raymond V., Jr, 'English Monasteries' Techniques for Avoiding Property Disputes, 1250–1380', *Comitatus*, 23 (1992), 46–63

Leclercq, Jean, 'Epitres d'Alexandre III sur les cisterciens', *Revue Bénédictine*, 64 (1954), 68–82

Lekai, Louis J., *The Cistercians: Ideal and Reality* (Kent, OH: Kent State University, 1977)

———, 'Ideals and Reality in Early Cistercian Life and Legislation', in *Cistercian Ideals and Reality*, ed. by John R. Sommerfeldt, Cistercian Studies Series, 60 (Kalamazoo: Cistercian Publications, 1978), pp. 4–29

Licence, Tom, 'The Benedictines, the Cistercians and the Acquisition of a Hermitage in Twelfth-Century Durham', *Journal of Medieval History*, 29 (2003), 315–29

Little, Lester K., *Religious Poverty and the Profit Economy in Medieval Europe* (London: Paul Elek, 1978)

Madden, James E., 'Business, Monks, Banker Monks, Bankrupt Monks: The English Cistercians in the Thirteenth Century', *Catholic Historical Review*, 49 (1963), 341–64

Masoliver, A., '"De spirituali amicitia" by Saint Aelred of Rievaulx: From "Particular Friendship" to Holy "Philia" and "Agape"', *Studia Monastica*, 44 (2002), 373–90

Mason, Emma, 'Timeo Barones et Dona Ferentes', in *Religious Motivation: Biographical and Sociological Problems for the Church Historian*, ed. by Derek Baker, Studies in Church History, 15 (Oxford: Blackwell, 1978), pp. 61–75

Mauss, Marcel, *The Gift: Forms and Functions of Exchange in Archaic Societies*, trans. by Ian Cunnison (London: Cohen and West, 1954)

McDonnell, John, 'The Evolution of the Monastic Grange', *Journal of the North Yorkshire County Record Office*, 2 (1975), 78–95

———, 'Medieval Assarting Hamlets in Bilsdale, North-East Yorkshire', *Northern History*, 22 (1986), 269–79

McGuire, Brian Patrick, 'The Cistercians and the Transformation of Monastic Friendships', in his *Friendship and Faith: Cistercian Men, Women, and their Stories, 1100–1250*, Variorum Collected Studies Series (Aldershot: Ashgate, 2002), pp. 1–63 (III)

———, *Friendship and Community: The Monastic Experience, 350–1250* (Kalamazoo: Cistercian Publications, 1988)

McLaughlin, Megan, *Consorting with Saints: Prayers for the Dead in Early Medieval France* (Ithaca, NY: Cornell University Press, 1994)

Milis, Ludo J. R., *Angelic Monks and Earthly Men: Monasticism and its Meaning to Medieval Society* (Woodbridge: Boydell, 1992)

Miller, Edward, 'Farming in Northern England during the Twelfth and Thirteenth Centuries', *Northern History*, 11 (1976), 1–16

Miller, Edward, and John Hatcher, *Medieval England: Rural Society and Economic Change 1086–1348* (London: Longman, 1978; repr. 1990)

Monasticon Cisterciense Poloniae, vols I–II, ed. by Andrzej Wyrwa, Jerzy Strzelczyk, and Krzysztof Kaczmarek (Poznań: Wydawnictwo Poznańskie, 1999)

Monkhouse, W., *Brief Historical and Descriptive Account of Rievaulx Abbey with Lithographic Views and Ground-plan of the Abbey* (York, 1845)

Moorhouse, Stephen, 'Monastic Estates: Their Composition and Development', in *The Archaeology of Rural Monasteries*, ed. by Roberta Gilchrist and Harold Mytum, British Archaeological Reports, 203 (Oxford: B.A.R., 1989), pp. 29–81

Morant, R. W., *The Monastic Gatehouse and Other Types of Portal of Medieval Religious Houses* (Lewes: Book Guild, 1995)

Newman, Martha G., *The Boundaries of Charity: Cistercian Culture and Ecclesiastical Reform 1099–1150* (Stanford: Stanford University Press, 1996)

Nicholl, Donald, *Thurstan Archbishop of York: 1114–1140* (York: Stonegate Press, 1964)

Nouzille, Philippe, *Expérience de Dieu et théologie monastique au* XII*e* *siècle: Étude sur les sermons d'Aelred de Rievaulx* (Paris: Editions du Cerf, 1999)

Oexle, Otto Gerhard, 'Memoria und Memorialüberlieferung im frühen Mittelalter', *Frühmittelalterliche Studien*, 10 (1976), 70–95

Partner, Nancy F., *Serious Entertainments: The Writing of History in Twelfth-Century England* (Chicago: University of Chicago Press, 1977)

Poole, Reginald L., 'The Appointment and Deprivation of St William, Archbishop of York', *English Historical Review*, 45 (1930), 273–81

Postan, M. M, *The Medieval Economy and Society* (1972; repr. Harmondsworth: Penguin, 1976)

Postles, David, 'Choosing Witnesses in Twelfth Century England', *Irish Jurist*, 23 (1988), 330–46

———, 'Country *Clerici* and the Composition of English Twelfth- and Thirteenth-Century Charters', in *Charters and the Use of the Written Word in Medieval Society*, ed. by Karl Heidecker, Utrecht Studies in Medieval Literacy, 5 (Turnhout: Brepols, 2000), pp. 27–42

———, 'The Garenden Cartularies in BL, Lansdowne 415', *British Library Journal*, 22 (1996), 161–71

———, 'Heads of Religious Houses as Administrators', in *England in the Thirteenth Century: Proceedings of the 1989 Harlaxton Symposium*, ed. by W. M. Ormrod (Stamford: Watkins, 1991), pp. 37–50

———, 'Lamps, Lights and Layfolk: "Popular" Devotion before the Black Death', *Journal of Medieval History*, 25 (1999), 97–114

———, 'Pledge of Faith in Transactions in Land', *Journal of the Society of Archivists*, 7 (1982–85), 295–98

Potter, Julie, 'Monastic Freedom vs. Episcopal and Aristocratic Power in the Twelfth Century: Context and Analysis of the *De libertate Beccensis*', in *Negotiating Secular and Ecclesiastical Power: Western Europe in the Central Middle Ages*, ed. by Arnoud-Jan A. Bijsterveld, Henk Teunis, and Andrew Wareham (Turnhout: Brepols, 1999), pp. 73–85

Resl, Brigitte, 'Von Nutzen des Abschreibens: Überlegungen zu mittelalterlichen Chartularen', in *Vom Nutzen des Schreibens: Soziales Gedächtnis, Herrschaft und Besitz im*

Mittelalters, ed. by Walter Pohl and Paul Herold (Vienna: Österreichische Akademie der Wissenschaften, 2002), pp. 205–22

Richardson, W., *The Monastic Ruins of Yorkshire*, 2 vols (York, 1844)

Ritchie, Graeme R., *Normans in Scotland* (Edinburgh: Edinburgh University Press, 1966)

Roby, Douglass, 'Chimera of the North: The Active Life of Ailred of Rievaulx', in *Cistercian Ideals and Reality*, ed. by John R. Sommerfeldt, Cistercian Studies Series, 60 (Kalamazoo: Cistercian Publications, 1978), pp. 152–69

Roehl, Richard, 'Plan and Reality in a Medieval Monastic Economy: The Cistercians', *Studies in Medieval and Renaissance History*, 9 (1972), 83–113

Rosenwein, Barbara H., *Negotiating Space: Power, Restraint and Privileges of Immunity in Early Medieval Europe* (Manchester: Manchester University Press, 1999)

———, *To Be the Neighbor of Saint Peter: The Social Meaning of Cluny's Property, 903–1049* (Ithaca, NY: Cornell University Press, 1989)

Sacred Trust: The Medieval Church as an Economic Firm, ed. by Robert B. Ekelund and others (New York: Oxford University Press, 1996)

Sanders, I. J., *English Baronies: A Study of their Origin and Descent 1086–1327* (Oxford: Clarendon Press, 1960)

Sayers, Jane, 'English Cistercian Cases and their Delegations in the First Half of the Thirteenth Century', *Analecta Sacri Ordinis Cisterciensis*, 20 (1964), 85–102

———, *Papal Government and England during the Pontificate of Honorius III (1216–1227)* (Cambridge: Cambridge University Press, 1984)

Schmid, Karl, and Joachim Wollasch, 'Die Gemeinschaft der Lebenden und Verstorbenen in Zeugnissen des Mittelalters', *Frühmittelalterliche Studien*, 1 (1967), 365–405

Senior, John S., 'The Selection of Dimensional and Ornamental Stone Types Used in Some Northern Monasteries – the Exploitation and Distribution of a Natural Resource', in *The Archaeology of Rural Monasteries*, ed. by Roberta Gilchrist and Harold Mytum, British Archaeological Reports, 203 (Oxford: B.A.R, 1989), pp. 223–50

Silber, Illana F., *Virtuosity, Charisma and Social Order: A Comparative Sociological Study of Monasticism in Theravada Buddhism and Medieval Catholicism* (Cambridge: Cambridge University Press, 1995)

Squire, Aelred 'The Literary Evidence for the Preaching of Aelred of Rievaulx', *Cîteaux: Commentarii Cistercienses*, 11 (1960), 245–51

Stringer, Keith, 'A Cistercian Archive: The Earliest Charters of Sawtry Abbey', *Journal of the Society of Archivists*, 6 (1980), 325–34

Talbot, C. H., 'Associations of Clairvaux, Clairmarais and Ter Doest', *Cîteaux in de Nederlanden*, 5 (1954), 233–45

———, 'New Documents in the Case of Saint William of York', *Cambridge Historical Journal*, 10 (1950–2), 1–15

Thomas, Hugh M., *Vassals, Heiresses, Crusaders and Thugs: The Gentry of Angevin Yorkshire, 1154–1216* (Philadelphia: University of Pennsylvania Press, 1993)

Thompson, A. Hamilton, 'The Registers of the Archbishops of York', *Yorkshire Archaeological Journal*, 32 (1936), 245–63

Thompson, Benjamin, 'From "Alms" to "Spiritual Services": The Function and Status of Monastic Property in Medieval England', in *Monastic Studies: The Continuity of Tradition*, vol. II, ed. by Judith Loades (Bangor: Headstart History, 1991), pp. 227–61

'Verzeichnis der Schriften von Joachim Wollasch', in *Vinculum societati: Joachim Wollasch zum 60. Geburtstag*, ed. by Franz Neiske, Dietrich Poeck, and Mechthild Sandmann (Sigmaringendorf: Glock und Lutz, 1991), pp. 326–45

'Verzeichnis der Schriften von Karl Schmid', in *Person und Gemeinschaft im Mittelalter: Karl Schmid zum fünfundsechzigsten Geburtstag*, ed. by Gerd Althoff (Sigmaringen: Thorbecke, 1988), pp. 617–35

Victoria County History: Yorkshire, 3 vols (London: Constable, 1907–13)

Waddell, Chrysogonus, 'The Myth of Cistercian Origins: C. H. Berman and the Manuscript Sources', *Cîteaux: Commentarii Cistercienses*, 51 (2000), 299–386

Waites, Brian, 'The Monastic Settlement of North-East Yorkshire', *Yorkshire Archaeological Journal*, 40 (1959–60), 478–95

Walker, David, 'The Organization of Material in Medieval Cartularies', in *The Study of Medieval Records: Essays in Honour of Kathleen Major*, ed. by D. A. Bullough and R. L. Storey (Oxford: Clarendon Press, 1971), pp. 132–50

Wardrop, Joan, *Fountains Abbey and its Benefactors 1132–1300* (Kalamazoo: Cistercian Publications, 1987)

Weeks, John, 'Fundamental Economic Concepts and their Application to Social Phenomena', in *The New Economic Anthropology*, ed. by John Clammer (New York: St Martins Press, 1978), pp. 21–30

Wehrmann, Paul, *Kloster Kolbatz und die Germanisierung Pommerns*, Königliches Bismarck-Gymnasium zu Pyritz (Pyritz: [n. pub.], 1905)

Wellstein, G. D., 'Die grauen Mönche als Träger deutscher Kultur im Osten', *Ostdeutsche Monatshefte*, 6 (1926), 117–31

Wenta, Jarosław, 'Dziejopisarstwo cystersów a *Memoria* na przykładzie Henrykowa, Lubiąża i Oliwy' (The historical writing of the Cistercian order and *Memoria* on the examples of Henrykow, Lubiąż and Oliwa), in *Klasztor w społeczeństwie średniowiecznym i nowożytnym* (The monastery in medieval and early modern society), ed. by Marek Derwich and Anna Pobóg-Lenartowicz (Opole-Wrocław: LARHCOR, 1996), pp. 191–98

West Yorkshire: An Archaeological Survey to A.D. 1500, vol. II, *The Administrative and Tenurial Framework*, and vol. III, *The Rural Medieval Landscape*, ed. by M. L. Faull and S. A. Moorhouse (Wakefield: West Yorkshire Metropolitan County Council, 1981)

Whitaker, T. D., *A Series of Views of the Abbeys and Castles in Yorkshire* (London, 1820)

Wightman, W. E., *The Lacy Family in England and Normandy 1066–1194* (Oxford: Oxford University Press, 1966)

Wilmart, André, 'Les Mélanges de Mathieu Préchantre de Rievaulx au Début du XIIIe Siècle', *Revue Bénédictine*, 52 (1940), 15–84

Wollasch, Joachim, 'Neue Quellen zur Geschichte der Cistercienser', *Zeitschrift für Kirchengeschichte*, 84 (1973), 188–232

Wollenberg, Klaus, 'The Cistercian Monastery of Kaisheim: Aspects of its Economic and Social History', paper presented at the 36th International Congress on Medieval Studies, Kalamazoo, 3 May 2001

Wood, Susan, *English Monasteries and their Patrons in the Thirteenth Century* (London: Oxford University Press, 1955)

Young, A., 'The Bishopric of Durham, 1093–1193', in *Anglo-Norman Durham*, ed. by David Rollason and others (Woodbridge: Boydell, 1994), pp. 353–68

Zakrzewski, Stanisław, 'Analecta Cisterciensia', *Rozprawy Akademii Umiejętności: Wydział Historyczno-Filozoficzny*, 2nd series, 24 (1900), 1–52

Żerelik, Rościsław, 'Wspólnota zmarłych w świetle Nekrologu henrykowskiego' (The community of the dead in the light of the Henryków necrology), in *Klasztor w społeczeństwie średniowiecznym i nowożytnym* (The monastery in medieval and early modern society), ed. by Marek Derwich and Anna Pobóg-Lenartowicz (Opole-Wrocław: LARHCOR, 1996), pp. 199–210

Index